An Introduction to Urban Historical Geography

An Introduction to
Urban Historical Geography

Harold Carter

Gregynog Professor of Human Geography, University College of Wales, Aberystwyth

Edward Arnold

© Harold Carter 1983

First published 1983 by
Edward Arnold (Publishers) Ltd
41 Bedford Square, London WC1B 3DQ

Edward Arnold (Australia) Pty Ltd
80 Waverley Road
Caulfield East
Victoria 3145

First published in the United States of America 1983
by Edward Arnold
300 North Charles Street
Baltimore
Maryland 21201

British Library Cataloguing in Publication Data

Carter, Harold
    An introduction to urban historical geography.
    1. Cities and towns—History
    1. Title

    ISBN 0-7131-6386-0

Text set in 9/10 pt Times Compugraphic by Colset
Private Limited, Singapore
Printed and bound in Great Britain by Butler & Tanner
Ltd
Frome, Somerset.

Contents

Preface

It is now a decade since I wrote a book which was conceived as a general introduction to the study of urban geography. That volume is now in the second printing of its third edition. It was produced at a time when urban studies were at the 'take off' stage and had not reached the 'high mass consumpion' condition of contemporary times, but even so I was fully aware of the high degree of selectivity which was involved. As part of the process of conscious choice I decided to include only a minimum of historical material and also to devote limited attention to what can be called political geography within which the whole planning process is contained. It was a decision which did not go without comment from reviewers, but at the time I had concluded that two other separate volumes remained to be written to supplement the basic introduction. They were tentatively called '*Urban Geography: An Historical Approach*' and '*Urban Geography: A Political Approach*'. Unfortunately other demands on time, including progressive revisions of *The Study of Urban Geography* and the immense developments in urban studies, have meant that the envisaged programme went forward very slowly. Indeed, so much has now been produced in the area of political influences, and in all interpretations of them, that the idea of a book on the political approach has been largely pre-empted. However, no general work has appeared on the lines of the other proposed volume and so it is here presented, albeit under a modified title.

It is also true that a considerable amount of work has appeared in urban historical geography and even more in the closely related field of urban history over the last 10 years. So much so that writing the book and making some attempt at a general synthesis has involved a perpetual process of modification as new work has been published. But no attempt has been made to set clear limits in time or space, though the Western world predominates, and like the earlier book this one is highly selective. As its central purpose, however, it retains firmly the intent of providing the student with a general introduction to urban historical geography whilst at the same time indicating how much is unconsidered but also noting sources where development can be found.

The book has been written with the firm conviction that any understanding of present towns must be derived in good measure from an awareness of those processes which were operative in the past and those conditions which obtained. It is also presented in the strong belief that contemporary decision making is likely to be that much more realistic and profitable if it is set against knowledge of the urban past.

Although there is no specific relationship, I would like to acknowledge a Social Science Research Council grant to a project on the social and residential areas of a Welsh town in the mid-nineteenth century. When a broad synthesis is attempted of what must be mainly the work of other scholars it is essential that at some point it touches primary personal research, however circumscribed the point of impact may be.

I owe a great deal to my colleagues at University College of Wales, Aberystwyth not only for specific discussions but for the general background against which this book has been written. In particular I must mention my colleagues, Dr C.R. Lewis, with whom I share the teaching of urban historical geography and Dr R.A. Dodgshon who have read the manuscript and made many criticisms and suggestions which I have adopted.

I am greatly indebted to Miss Linda James, who typed varied versions of the initial manuscript as well as the final draft. I have greatly appreciated her tolerant and efficient help. I am also grateful to Mr M.G. Jones who drew some of the maps and Mr David Griffiths who produced photographic versions of them all.

Finally, I must publicly pay tribute to the support of my wife, Mari, who provided the conviction that at least one of the proposed volumes was worth attempting and whose support has been constant and unfailing.

Harold Carter
University College of
Wales,
Aberystwyth. Summer 1982

Acknowledgements

The publishers would like to thank the following for permission to reproduce copyright material:
Academic Press Inc (London) Ltd for figs 2.19, 2.20, 3.10, 8.8, 10.3 and 10.7; George Allen & Unwin for fig 7.2; American Geographical Society for figs 2.39 b and c and 6.7; Annals of the Association of American Geographers for figs 2.3, 2.16, 47 a and b; 5.6, 5.7, 7.10 and 9.2; Edward Arnold (Publishers) Ltd for fig 9.3; Arts et Metiers Graphiques for figs 2.23, 2.25 and 2.30; B T Batsford Ltd for figs 3.5, 3.6 and 3.7; Professor M W Beresford for 2.24 and 2.26; M Biddle and R Shoesmith for fig 3.11; G C Boon for fig 2.15; G Calza *et al* for fig 2.9; Cambridge University Press for figs 1.3, 3.14, 5.5, 8.15 and 9.4; E Chapin for fig 7.5; Grady Clay for fig 6.6; The Colonial Society of Massachusetts for fig 2.35 a and b; Croom Helm Ltd Publishers for 5.3 a, b, c and 5.4; B Cunliffe for fig 3.1; Economic Geography for fig 5.1; Peter G Goheen for figs 10.5 a and b and 10.6 a and b; Wm Dawson & Sons Ltd and Dr Patten for fig 4.1a; Edinburgh University for fig 1.1; K C Edwards for fig 7.8; The Herbert Press Limited for fig 1.2; Hutchinson Publishing Group Ltd for figs 5.9 and 5.10; The Institute of British Geographers for figs 8.1, 8.6, 8.16, 9.1, 9.5 a and b, 10.2 a and b, 10.10; The Johns Hopkins University Press for fig 2.5, Dr D J Keene for fig 7.1, J Langton for fig 4.5; Editions Jacques Lanore Henri Laurens for figs 2.8, 2.14 and 3.7 a and b; Leicester University Press for fig 4.4; Longman Group Limited for figs 2.28 and 2.29; Macmillan Accounts and Administration Ltd, London and Basingstoke for fig 2.1, Macmillan Publishing Co Inc for figs 1.5 and 2.31; Methuen and Co for fig 5.11; Oxford University Press Inc New York for 8.3 and 8.4 copyright © 1971 reprinted by permission; Oxford University Press, Oxford for figs 3.9, 8.5, 8.13 and 8.14; Oxford University Press, Hong Kong for 1.4 a and b; Praeger Publishers Inc for fig 2.24a and 2.26; Presses Universitaires de France figs 2.17, 2.21 and 2.22; Princeton University Press for fig 5.2; Professor Steen Eiler Rasmussen for 6.3; J Robb for fig 10.8; Professor H B Rodgers for fig 4.3; R T Rowley for fig 3.8; Sidgwick & Jackson Publishers and The British School at Rome for fig 2.11; Society of Antiquaries of London for fig 3.12; Thames and Hudson Ltd for fig 2.2; A von Gerkan for figs 2.4 and 2.6; University of Wales Press and L Caroe for fig 4.2 and John Wiley & Sons Ltd for 7.11.
The lines from John Betjeman's 'The Metropolitan Railway' are reproduced by permission of John Murray Ltd.

List of Figures

Foreword: An Historical Approach to Urban Geography

It is as well to recognize at the outset that a book which claims to present an historical approach to urban geography necessarily precipitates critical problems of definition, and consequently of approach. Over the last 20 years increasing numbers of books, journals, papers and courses in higher education have appeared which prefix a standard academic field with the adjective urban – geography, economics, sociology, anthropology, politics and history are but the major examples in the social sciences. These problems of definition are common to all and, peripheral sophistries set aside, the core issue is quite simple. Are these specialisms discrete and distinctive in that the urban context creates unique conditions demanding intrinsic interpretations, that is the generation of urban theory, or are they simply indicative of an area of interest, a source from which exemplification is drawn, and little more? Polarized in such a bare manner, and in the form of a rhetorical question, the alternatives are too stark, but both demonstration and clarification can be attempted using an example from the field of urban sociology.

Manuel Castells's book *The Urban Question* (1977) includes a chapter called significantly, 'The myth of urban culture'. In it he sets out to examine the notion of 'urbanism as a way of life' as set out by Louis Wirth in a paper with that title first published in 1938. The basis of Wirth's case was that the size, density and heterogeneity of the populations of contemporary cities generated a unique way of living, or culture. Put in another way, the city constituted an independent variable. Amongst other characteristics of such a way of life Wirth noted what he called the fragmentation of roles. 'Characteristically, urbanites meet one another in highly segmented roles. They are, to be sure, dependent upon more people for the satisfaction of their life-needs than are rural people and thus are associated with a greater number of groups, but they are less dependent upon particular persons, and their dependence upon others is confined to a highly fractionalized aspect of the other's round of activity. This is essentially what is meant by saying that the city is characterized by secondary rather than primary contacts. The contacts of the city may indeed be face to face, but they are nevertheless impersonal, superficial, transitory and segmental' (Wirth, 1964, 71). Castells's critique of this passage is that Wirth is providing an interpretation not of

what is necessarily and exclusively characteristic of urban dwellers but rather a condition engendered by the nature of the Western capitalist mode of resource exploitation.

> The celebrated 'fragmentation of roles', which is the foundation of 'urban' social complexity is directly determined by the status of the 'free worker', which Marx showed to be necessary to assuring maximum profitability in the use of the labour force. The predominance of 'secondary' relations over 'primary' and the accelerated individualization of relations also express this economic and political need of the new mode of production to constitute as 'free and equal citizens' the respective supports of the means of production and of the labour force. (Castells, 1977, 81)

In summary, the urban environment of itself does not produce a specific culture; rather the nature of the socioeconomic system both begets urbanization and the specific class and personal relations to be found in the city, but not only in the city. Again, put in another way, the city is a dependent variable. This being so, while the urban context is as acceptable as any other for examining certain relationships and the culture of industrial capitalism, it does not of itself generate situations demanding novel theoretical interpretations.

A second and parallel example can be derived from contemporary debate on the so-called inner city problem. Many social scientists greatly deprecate the use of the term inner city since it employs a locational characteristic and implies an environmental determinant, just like Wirth's urbanism as a way of life. Moreover, such an implication suggests that the problems can be met by manipulation of the environment, that is by managerial measures, whereas it is contended that only the radical, or revolutionary, restructuring of the whole socioeconomic system offers any permanent solution. The locational characteristic is in this interpretation largely irrelevant, other than at a superficial descriptive level, and, therefore, the work of the geographer as locational or spatial analyst, identifying the parameters of deprivation and mapping their extent, is merely definitional and of a low order of importance. It will be apparent that this attack on what has come to be called 'spatial fetishism' is mainly, though certainly not exclusively, a product of radical geography which seeks to ascribe all explanation in the contemporary non-communist world to a first cause in the operation of the capitalist system.

Similar problems of necessity characterize urban history. A most appropriate source to start a discussion is the inaugural lecture given by the late H.J. Dyos on his becoming the first Professor of Urban History at a British university. 'Urban history', he maintained, 'it must now be clear, is a field of knowledge, not a single discipline in the accepted sense. . . . It can have, therefore, no absolute test of admissibility, unless and until we can be quite clear what we mean by "urban" and are confident that we can define it in exclusive terms' (Dyos, 1973, 20). As the author added, 'there's the rub', for that exclusive definition is according to the arguments presented above, not possible. In his inaugural lecture Dyos moved away from this critical issue to advance an eclecticism in approach, calling it a 'catholicity, positively healthy', and to show how the subject matter of urban history could be separated from that of other urban studies. In this he made little progress other than by the identification of urban history in a circular fashion as a field in which some historians chose to work.

Dyos returned more cogently to the same theme in 1977. 'When is the history of urban society not urban history? The question of the identity and coherence of urban history is worth putting in this way because it implies not only a larger historical whole which it cannot subsume but a relationship with other branches of history to which it must in the last analysis relate. . . . The pursuit of urban history dissolves into larger historical issues and emerges from them . . . in ways that sometimes make exclusive formal definitions of it look decidedly chimerical' (Dyos, 1977, 3). Here is replication and acceptance of the basic case set out above in the example derived from Castells and that in relation to the inner city. Urban history can only be pursued as part of the analysis of those broad socioeconomic changes with which history is concerned so that the distinctiveness and exclusiveness of the specialism is greatly attenuated for, to repeat, the city is a dependent variable.

If what has been presented so far suggests not only considerable difficulty in the definition of urban geography, urban sociology and urban history but also, more critically, casts doubts on the justifiability of such discrete fields of enquiry, then it would seem foolish to compound both difficulty and doubt by attempting to combine two of them in the development of an urban historical geography. At this point, therefore, a more direct consideration of the nature of an historical approach to urban geography is demanded. This can be divided into two parts. The first is the more superficial, links back to the point made in Dyos's inaugural lecture, and concerns the distinction between urban history and urban historical geography. The second is more fundamental and concerns the relationship to the central problems with which this Introduction began.

The contrast between an approach specifically historical and one specifically geographical resurrects the Kantian discussion on the study of time and space. However, all urban history must be place-specific; it is related to locations and becomes geographical, just as geographical studies must have a time dimension and are historical. What might be termed spatial urban history and urban historical geography overlap and merge. Dyos notes that urban history differed 'from its first cousins in this country, economic history and geography, in being more interested than they can afford to be, in their different ways, in the humanistic and functional elements composing the urban scene' (Dyos, 1973, 25). Perhaps one can apply the traditional apophthegm that 'history is about chaps, geography is about maps', thus repeating Dyos's contention that urban history is more concerned with urban life and townspeople and their formal and informal institutions whilst urban geography is more concerned with patterning and distribution. That is not an easy distinction to make but it is neither possible nor desirable to draw a firm line of demarcation.

The second problem is not as easily resolved. The current fashion in geography undoubtedly favours the logic of the arguments which have already been set out. These are usually called 'structural' in the sense that emphasis is placed upon the deep underlying structuring of polity, economy and society which are the ultimate controls of the superstructural patterns and distributions on the earth's surface. It is worthwhile considering two sources in which this view is developed.

The first is an article, or progress report as it is termed, by A.R.H. Baker significantly called, 'Historical geography: a new beginning?'. Baker comments,

Much historical geography has been focused upon *landscapes* transformed by *man* rather than upon man as an agent of landscape change, upon artefacts rather than upon ideas, upon actions rather than upon attitudes, upon external forms rather than internal processes. In short, much historical geography is open to many of the criticisms which have become levelled against the geographical fraternity of spatial analysis. Consideration of man as a passive object rather than an active subject is, perhaps, the most serious criticism which might be made of such work both in traditional geography and in modern spatial analysis. (Baker, 1979, 561)

Such a view, if accepted, would lead to the rejection of an approach to historical urban geography based upon the city as artefact and with spatial patterning as the central theme. But Baker's argument contains a non-sequitur. If the focus is upon the artefact, if the starting point is the pattern, there is not the slightest reason why in consequence man should be seen as passive and why narratives of his actions should take precedence over interpretation of his attitudes and ideologies. Indeed, the geographical stance is surely that the evidence for attitude and ideology lies in the artefact. In the urban context, the artefact is the social and physical fabric of the town which reflects attitudes and ideologies. Perhaps that smacks too much of inductive approach for modern fashion but even deductive theory derived its being from apprehensions of the real world.

Baker continues, 'ideologies structure time and space: studies in historical geography therefore embrace ideologies as well as being themselves explicitly ideological' (Baker, 1979, 562). Even so: but those structures in time and space constitute the prime subject matter, even if ideologies are essential for interpretation.

The second source is the book by R.J. Johnston, *City and Society. An outline for urban geography*. This attempts to deploy a structuralist approach and, indeed, the second chapter, which follows on a discussion of the concerns of urban geography, is called, 'The changing structure of society'. It is described by its author as 'a sketchy outline of the general trends that have resulted in contemporary world societies'. It takes some 22 pages and is, to use the author's words, 'a framework only, with complete absence of detail . . . and is little more than a cartoon of what is, in effect, the entire span of human, economic and social history' (Johnston, 1980, 50). In this brief sentence the whole problem is made manifest for to follow the lines proposed by structuralists would involve an outline (but surely better still a deep and penetrating study) of the whole of human history from which all the characteristics of the city would be derived. Castells writes, 'Urbanism is not a concept. It is a myth in the strictest sense since it recounts, ideologically, the history of mankind' (Castells, 1976, 70). Such an approach has its logic, perhaps it had an exponent in Lewis Mumford, but it also has its gross unrealities. Moreover, in abrogating the central geographical concern with spatial structure and viewing it as an appendage to socioeconomic history, it debases the central theme of the subject.

At this point the discussion of generality needs to be replaced by a special illustration. One of the standard concerns of the urban geographer is the way in which the residential areas of the Western city have become segregated by what is usually called social class. This the structuralist would maintain is quite simply the class system becoming spatially manifest. It follows that the first task is to consider the nature of the class system. Castells, as one would expect, is quite clear on this issue. 'Urban stratification refers to the spatial dimension of the theory of social stratification, and this does not require new intellectual tools' (Castells, 1976, 71). Presumably the only issue worthy of discussion is social stratification, anything else is of a marginal and minor order. But it is a vast question, especially if an historical perspective is added, one in its own right and the notion that it can be regarded as some prefatory gloss to the study of social areas in cities by geographers is hardly tenable.

It is, however, possible to regard the issue in a different way. The geographer's basic concern is with spatial patterning and it is a legitimate question to ask whether a population is segregated by virtue of any attribute – sex, age, creed, colour or wealth. If any of these can be established one can then ask what light does that segregation,

its extent and nature, throw on the structuring of society. It follows that the geographer needs to be as well informed of the nature of social stratification as if his approach was structural. But the beginning is the observed facts (ideologically gathered, it is true, but that can not be avoided by any approach), the basis perhaps unfashionably inductive and the prime method geographical.

The relevance of the discussion to which the Introduction has been so far devoted lies in the critical decision as to the approach which this book adopts. Essentially that approach is geographical and hence concerned with the identification, interpretation and explanation of spatial patterns. In this it contrasts with urban history where such patterns are of peripheral and consequential rather than of fundamental interest. The book does not accept an explicit structural methodology, not because it is rejected as invalid but rather because such a methodology is fundamentally aspatial and also because at this stage it is impractical since it calls for a prefatory history of mankind.

At this point three premises can be advanced which have been dominant in the organization of the volume:

1 The geographer in his interpretation of the city and systems of cities needs to know and comprehend the antecedents of present spatial patterns.
2 The geographical interpretation of either the past or the present is greatly enriched if they are seen as part of developmental sequences, even if there are no relict elements visible.
3 Geographical or spatial analysis should contribute to those explanations of the urban past and urban change which are the concern of the urban historian.

Out of those three premises, four issues are derived which in consequence form the structuring elements of the book.

1 The origin and diffusion of cities

There are two problems contained in this one heading. The first concerns the origin of the city insofar as it is conceived as a distinctive settlement form emergent from earlier, rural beginnings. The second relates to the spread of cities, or how the world became urbanized. Here some difficulty arises for there is contrast conceptually between the concrete notion of the physical emplacement of cities, or of the city as artefact, and the abstraction of urbanization which refers to the proportion of a population in a given territory living in cities. In this first part the emphasis must be on the concrete and tangible so that after a review of how the city began as a settlement form there must follow a consideration of the spread of that form over the earth's surface. This necessarily demands explanation of how cities came into being, that is originated, in particular areas, a somewhat different issue than the origin of the city *per se*. As is inevitable in a book of restricted length selection is imperative and one area has to be used as representative.

The structure derived from the discussion under this

heading can be set out thus:

The origin of the city
i.e. of the settlement ⟶ The spread of the city
form 　　　　　　　　(i) Relocational diffusion
　　　　　　　　　　　　which includes
　　　　　　　　　　(ii) City beginnings in
　　　　　　　　　　　　specific areas

2 The process and structuring of urbanization

Having considered the origin and spread of the city as a physical artefact it is appropriate to turn to the abstract concept of urbanization. Immediately four related topics are generated. The first of these is the actual measurement of the urban population which, although a purely technical one, is even so of critical importance. Before the coming of the first national censuses in the late eighteenth and early nineteenth century it is extremely hazardous to assess the proportion of the population living in cities so that problems of definition and assessment have to be met. Against that background it is appropriate to review the process of urbanization, the nature of the way in which populations of territories became progressively urban in character. This is intimately linked to a third topic which is concerned with the relationships between the sizes of the cities both at single points in time and as an evolutionary sequence. It is necessary to review whether any systematic relationships between the sizes of cities can be established and, if so, what they imply in terms of the political and economic development of nations and territories. Finally the relationship between cities subsumes the relationship which each city has with its own surrounding territory, its hinterland, so that, too, becomes a matter to be investigated.

The structure of this second part can be set out under the four main themes thus:

The process of urbanization
　(i) Measurement
　(ii) The process of urbanization
　(iii) Inter-city relations
　　　The city system
　(iv) City-region relations

3 The internal structure of cities: Form or layout

This has long been the most familiar and most widely considered aspect in urban historical studies. It takes the form of narrative histories of town plan evolution. Since such histories are, in consequence, widely available there is little purpose in replicating them here, neither is there the space available. The most recent example to appear in English is a translation of Leonardo Benevolo's book, *Storia della città*, as *The History of the City* (Benevolo, 1980). This runs to 1011 pages. Lavedan's earlier classic *L'histoire de l'urbanisme*, was made up of four volumes.

It is only possible here to discuss a selected and limited range of material with the emphasis on the basic principle that the physical form reflects and comments on the politico-social structure of the creators.

Studies in this genre have been mainly concerned with the layout of what can be called the initial settlement and many tend to deal solely with that, giving the impression of a set of exemplifying cities which have remained unchanged from their times of origin. In many cases the impression is justified since the best examples are precisely those which have not been subject to alteration or modification and preserve the features originally established. Growth, however, brings change in two ways. First there is extension and the creation of suburbs, while second there is infilling by which open sections of the original town are built upon. Both of these can vary greatly in extent. Suburban growth can leave the initial settlement a small node in an extensive built-up area; infill, together with redevelopment, can greatly modify and even obliterate the first nucleus. These two aspects of change need to be considered so that the structure of this part becomes:

Town plan ⟶ (i) Initial layout
　　　　　　　(ii) Modification by extension:
　　　　　　　　　suburbs
　　　　　　　(iii) Modification by infill and
　　　　　　　　　redevelopment.

4 The internal structure of cities: Land use and the segregation of population

The fourth topic, constituting the concluding part of the book, deals with the uses of city territory. Again, there are two aspects. The first is the direct nature of the use to which the land is put. There is a naive notion that uses in the earlier as in the smaller cities were undifferentiated and that with time and growth specialization took place so that city space became divided into discrete areas dominated by single or associated uses in characteristic locales. This view needs to be pursued and examined. The second aspect is related to the disposition of population across urban space, or more mundanely of residential areas, particularly in relation to the various ways in which the total population can be divided. The dominant and familiar bases are ethnic or cultural identity, social class or socioeconomic status and life-cycle stage. The last is perhaps the one to become apparent most recently and emphasis is placed on the first two so that the nature of the occurrence and the evolution of ethnic and class-based residential areas need to be reviewed. This gives a content which can be set out thus:

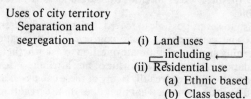

Uses of city territory
Separation and
　segregation ⟶ (i) Land uses
　　　　　　　　　　including
　　　　　　　　(ii) Residential use
　　　　　　　　　(a) Ethnic based
　　　　　　　　　(b) Class based.

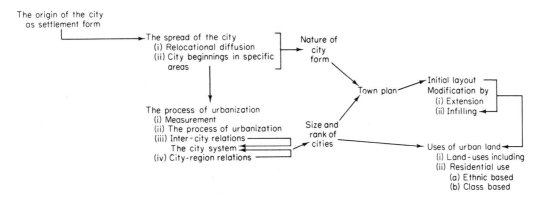

0.1.   The organization of an historical urban geography.

The four major topics which have been discussed are not discrete aspects of urbanism for they are clearly linked. The spread of the city as artefact can be directly translated into the process of urbanization while that process resolves itself into a system of cities. That system is constituted by members of contrasted form and layout while the growth implied as part of differential development creates suburbs and fills in the lacunae in the built area. Finally that same growth leads to segregation of both land uses and populations itself occurring in close relation to the nature of urban infill and suburban extension. The whole structuring of an urban historical geography as it has been presented can be displayed by indicating the links between the four topics (Figure 0.1).

These topics are repeated in the four parts into which the book is divided. As is evident from the discussion in this Introduction, the organization of the book is based on the internal spatial characteristics of towns and the external relations between them. It is neither historical in the sense that separate periods, however defined, are dealt with in sequence, nor 'structural' in the sense that it is based on critical phases of socioeconomic organization. The basis is spatial as it should be in a book which purports to contribute to urban geography.

Further reading

Two books which greatly contributed to the development of urban history in the USA and Britain respectively are:
HANDLIN, O. and BURCHARD, J. (eds.) 1963: *The Historian and the City*. Cambridge, Mass.
DYOS, H.J. (ed.) 1968: *The Study of Urban History* London.
The first chapters of these books are devoted to the general discussion of urban history. Dyos further developed ideas in his inaugural lecture:
DYOS, H.J. 1973: *Urbanity and Suburbanity*. Leicester
and in his editorial prefaces to:
The Urban History Yearbook (1974 *et seq.*).
The critique of urban studies developed by Castells is best considered in:

CASTELLS, M; 1977: *The Urban Question: A Marxist Approach*, trans. A. Sheridan. London.
A general review of geographical methodology which covers points raised in the chapter is:
JOHNSTON, R.J. 1979: *Geography and Geographers. Anglo-American Human Geography since 1945.* London,
while the same author's book
JOHNSTON, R.J. 1980: *City and Society. An Outline for Urban Geography*. London,
relates problems arising from methodology to urban geography.
A useful 'progress report' on historical geography is:
BAKER, A.R.H. 1979: Historical Geography: A New Beginning. *Progress in Human Geography* 3(4), 560-570,
a paper which includes a bibliography as a guide to recent comment.
A vigorous defence of urban history is made by:
HERSHBERG, T. 1981: The New Urban History: Toward an Interdisciplinary history of the city, being Chapter 1 in HERSHBERG, T. (ed.), *Philadelphia. Work, Space Family and Group Experience in the 19th Century* (New York), 3-35.

Part I Urbanism: its origins and diffusion

1

Urban Origins: The General Case

1 Introduction: Geography and urban origins

The consideration of urban origins was an integral part of geographical writing long before a systematic field called urban geography came into being. The explanation of that paradox is related to three fundamental tenets of early geographical methodology as it emerged in the latter part of the nineteenth century and beginning of the twentieth.

The first of these tenets was geographical determinism, firmly established by Friedrich Ratzel as the core of anthropogeography and, even in its less strident interpretation as a man–land relationship, still a definition of purpose accepted by some geographers today. At a time, therefore, when the physical environment was seen to act with a blind brutality it seemed self-evident that the most civilized form of human settlement must itself have been the product of distinctive environmental factors. Moreover, the evidence was to hand, for it was easy to argue that the riverine lowlands of the Near East constituted a special milieu where the surpluses accruing from the cultivation of crops and the domestication of animals provided the foundations for urban life.

Alongside this tenet of geographical belief went a second intellectual concept, mainly drawn from early anthropology and the place of archaeology within it. This was diffusionism, closely related to environmentalism. By this it was argued that traits which were established by the control of a particular physical milieu were spread first to contiguous areas and thence to distant places with different physical conditions. Cultural similarities under contrasted environments could in this way be explained by the diffusion process. The city was seen as an independent creation in the distinctive environment of the riverine lowlands of the Middle East but the notion of the city was subsequently spread east to the Indus and west to Crete and, continuing in this line, to Greece and Rome. The foundation of Greek colonies and the extension of the Roman Empire brought city life into Europe.

There was a third conviction implicit in nineteenth-century geographical ideas, the simple belief in evolution, whereby complex forms were thought of as developments from simple beginnings in a neat sequen-tial fashion. Contemporary anthropologists proposed well defined periods which translated mankind from Savagery through Barbarism to Civilization. These periods was paralleled by settlement types, rather as in a spatial fashion Geddes's 'valley section' indicated a change from quarrying and lumbering in the remotest reaches where there were only temporary camps, through the hamlet and the village lower down the valley where lowland was more extensive, finally reaching a climax in the town (Geddes, 1949; Applebaum, 1970). Time and space both demonstrated a pattern of convergence on the city where in temporal terms civilization began and where in spatial terms it was manifested.

In this way the study of urban origins formed a convincing centrepiece demonstrating the effectiveness of the geographical method. Creation, evolution and diffusion came together like the well fitting pieces of a jigsaw puzzle.

There is little need to add that all these three views have been challenged, although it is equally necessary to point out that they all have also been reiterated. But the modern urban geographer looks at the origin of cities as one of a number of social scientists concerned with a common problem. Lucien Febvre in his *Geographical Introduction to History* stressed that one of the major problems which faced the geographer in his study of towns was the radical difference between factors of origin and factors of growth (Febvre, 1932). What is true of individual towns is also true of urbanism in general, for the nature of origin may have little to do with subsequent world-wide development. Nevertheless, in seeking an understanding of the geography of towns through their history it is at least appropriate to begin at the beginning. Presumably that beginning is definition.

2 The definition of a city

It is not easy to present any acceptable definition of a town or city relative to the contemporary world; it is much more difficult to set out one applicable to all ages. Moreover, definitions can themselves become involved with origins. Thus Max Weber approached the problem by excluding all the cities of the Orient; 'Neither the "city", in the economic sense, nor the garrison, the inhabitants of which are accoutred with special political-administrative structures, necessarily constitute a "community". An urban "community", in the full meaning of the word, appears as a general phenomenon only in the Occident. Exceptions occasionally were . . . found . . . but only occasionally and in rudiments' (Weber, 1958). This view necessarily shifts the emphasis onto the equally intractable notion of a 'community' for which Weber supplies his well known definition. In that definition a predominance of trade-commercial relations is specified with: '(1) a fortification; (2) a market; (3) a court of its own and at least partially autonomous law; (4) a related form of association; and (5) at least partial autonomy and autocephaly . . .' (Weber, 1958, 80–1). But already definition and ideas on origin are intertwined for it would be nonsense to propose a fortification as a universal attribute of urbanism. Even so Weber's definition points in the direction followed by most other scholars. If one turns to Paul Wheatley, one of the most fascinating of writers on urbanism, a further attempt at definition can be introduced. The beginning is neatly circular, 'city' is used generically to denote any urban form, and carries none of the ancillary connotations of age, status or origin implicit in contemporary, everyday American or English usage (Wheatley, 1971, xviii). Wheatley's definition of urbanism, however, provides more substance – 'that particular set of functionally integrated institutions which were first devised some 5000 years ago to mediate the transformation of relatively egalitarian, ascriptive, kin-structured groups into socially stratified politically organized, territorially based societies . . .' (Wheatley, 1971, xviii). This provides a more effective definition of 'community' than Weber's recourse to specific institutions and echoes much of the writing in sociology on the nature of the urban process. It picks up the old contrast between 'gemeinschaft' and 'gesellschaft' as expounded by Tönnies in 1887 and reinterpreted as 'mechanical' as against 'organic' solidarity by Durkheim. This contrast circled back into anthropology in the 1940s in the form of Robert Redfield's folk–urban dichotomy, the vaguely evolutionistic contrast between preliterate, homogeneous, religious, familial, personalized primitive and peasant communities and the literate, heterogeneous, secular, individualized, depersonalized urban society. Again the same theme is at the basis of Louis Wirth's well known theme of 'Urbanization as a Way of Life' (Wirth, 1938). As formal, legal, institutional factors are emphasized this urbanization process is viewed in the words of Maine as a 'movement from Status to Contract' (Maine, 1894, 170). Martindale and Neuwirth comment, 'Maine felt the critical problem lay in the substitution of a principle of territoriality for kinship and a transformation of the legal order isolating the individual from his status in the family, freeing him for the plastic entry into "contracted" relations' (Martindale and Neuwirth, 1958, 47). This is close to the 'special political-administrative structures' of Weber and, indeed, leads directly to the definitions usually proposed by historians looking at urbanism in western Europe. Maitland urged simply that 'the borough community is corporate; the village community is not' (Maitland, 1898, 18). This corporate status was seen, however, as a later stage of development from an agglomeration originally brought about by defensive needs, so that for Maitland the garrison was the point of urban origin.

The contrast to these sociopolitical definitions of the town are those which rely mainly on physical characteristics, mainly size and degree of agglomeration. The evidence for the first cities is archaeological evidence and it follows that the visible features of excavated sites should become the criteria of urban existence. James Mellaart writes, 'Already, after a mere three seasons' work (1961–3) the results may fairly be described as a spectacular addition to our knowledge of the earlier phases of the human achievement in terms of urban settlement. For already Catal Huyuk ranks, with Jericho in Jordan, as one of man's first known essays in the development of town-life. Before 6000 BC Catal Huyuk was a town, or even a city, of a remarkable and developed kind' (Mellaart, 1967, 15). So abruptly does this archaeological evidence appear in the record that the term 'The Urban Revolution' used by Childe has become widespread and his paper bearing that name one of the best known (Childe, 1950). Childe outlined a list of ten features which distinguished the new cities from the old Neolithic villages. They can be summarized under five headings.

1 *Size.* The urban settlements were of a completely different order of size from anything which had previously existed. Estimates of the Sumerian cities range from seven to twelve thousand. It is suggested that Ur had 30,000 inhabitants. The early cities of Mesoamerica are now given populations of over 100,000. It is because of this complete change in scale that Childe proposed the idea of an urban revolution.

2 *Structure of the population.* A key feature was occupational specialization, for the change from the old agricultural order meant that the employment of full-time administrators and craftsmen was possible. In this way residence not kin-ship became the qualification of citizenship. Moreover, the rule of the priest-kings, who guaranteed peace and order to the lower classes, inevitably involved social stratification. Here again one is close to the sort of definition as represented by that of Wheatley.

3 *Public capital.* The creation of a 'community' also meant the emergence of public capital which could be devoted to erection of monumental buildings and the sustaining of full-time artists.

4 *Records and the exact sciences.* The need to keep records promoted the beginnings of a written script and mathematics, both of which become intimately bound up with 'civilization'.

5 *Trade.* This is by no means an innovation of the city but the establishment and maintenance of a network of trade routes is, and it becomes a hallmark of urbanization.

If this list be examined then it will be seen to be made

up of two elements. The first is the outward and manifest signs of new settlement forms, signs which Wheatley called 'explicitly delineatory rather than explanatory' (Wheatley, 1971, 373), and the second the structural changes in society which brought them about and which have already been discussed. If Childe's conclusion that the urban revolution marked the 'first approximation to an organic solidarity based upon functional complementarity and interdependence between all its members', is put alongside a modern definition of urbanization by Lampard, 'the concentration of differentiated but functionally integrated specialisms in rational locales' (Lampard, 1955, 192), then the similarity is obvious. The city is essentially a form of social organization based on the occupational specialization and social stratification of a territorially based population which has acquired a formal corporate identity. How much this search after elusive definition will help in the equally difficult problem of identifying origins remains to be seen.

3 Urban origins: A review of theories

Social scientists, including historians and archaeologists, have proposed four explanations for the emergence of towns:
1. Hydraulic theories or environmental bases to urbanism
2. Economic theories or the growth of markets
3. Military theories or growth about defensive strongpoints
4. Religious theories or growth about shrines.
Each of these can be reviewed in turn.

(i) Hydraulic theories: The concept of a surplus

The basis of these theories rests on a fairly simple assertion which is well represented by Sir Leonard Woolley's opening to his discussion of 'The Urbanization of Society' in the UNESCO 'History of Mankind'. He writes:

> It is an axiom of economic history that real civilization can begin only in regions where the character of soil and climate makes surplus production possible and easy; only so is man relieved from the necessity of devoting all his energies and all his thought to the problem of mere survival, and only so is he able to procure from others by means of barter those things which minister to well-being and promote advance but are not naturally available in his own land; moreover, such conditions must prevail over an area large enough to maintain not merely a small group of individuals but a population sufficiently numerous to encourage occupational specialization and social development. So does civilization begin. (Woolley, 1963, 414)

Here all the elements of the environmental theme are set out with the implication that specialization is a consequence of the ability to pay an income from surplus production and that from this not only social stratifi-

cation follows, but the detachment of the specialist from tribe and kin makes residence the urban qualification. The surplus is the catalyst for that transformation which defines urbanism. To that conclusion can be added the view that the progress of agriculture, and the creation of a surplus, was largely a consequence of irrigation and that irrigation itself necessarily established a pattern of complex bureaucratic controls which brought into being an administrative system of an urban character; social change is in part the consequence of administrative necessity. From this two key concepts arise for discussion, for specialization and social stratification are but consequences. These are (i) the idea of a 'surplus' and (ii) the notion of a hydraulic society.

(a) The idea of a surplus can be interpreted in two ways. The first is the simple one of a product over and above that necessary to sustain life, often called a biological surplus, whilst the second is the more sophisticated Marxist concept of 'surplus value'. Since Marxist commentators such as Childe have been attracted to this basic economic interpretation of city origins they have tended to adopt the 'surplus' view, but also to align it more with standard Marxist theory.

The notion that due to progress in agriculture, possibly related to irrigation, a surplus accrued which was the foundation of all the changes which are subsumed in the concept 'urbanization', has come in for considerable criticism. This has been, essentially, because it is too simple an interpretation. This biological surplus is presumably an excess product over the minimum which is needed to sustain life or, as H.W. Pearson puts it in an extended critique, 'there is a level of significance which once reached provides a measure – so to speak the dam over which the surplus flows. This surplus which is beyond needs, however these happen to be defined, is then in some sense available . . .' (Pearson, 1957, 323). This straightforward idea of the biological surplus carries little conviction for it is manifestly impossible to define in absolute terms a level below which life cannot be sustained and above which a disposable surplus is generated. There can be no absolute surplus and it follows that the idea can only be contemplated in relation to particular cultural contexts or as Lampard writes, 'natural endowment was less the "gift" of nature than a function of human resourcefulness and adaptive behaviour. In short Childe's celebrated "surplus" like the definitive city itself, was a societal product' (Lampard, 1965, 533). This is also the view of Robert Adams who, considering 'The Evolution of Urban Society', argues that 'the transformation at the core of the Urban Revolution lay in the realm of social organization' and that in that so-called Revolution it was 'changes in social institutions that precipitated changes in technology, subsistence and other aspects of the wider cultural realm, such as religion, rather than vice versa' (Adams, 1966, 12). This immediately robs the surplus of its primacy as a progenitor of those changes which are called 'urbanization'. 'Because the surplus is conceived of as individual and special to each and every society it is difficult or impossible to say anything of any great import about its specific role in either the emergence of urban forms or the functioning of urbanism in general' (Harvey, 1973, 220).

This apparent rejection of an economic-based argument is anathema to a Marxist interpretation, for it implies that super-structural features of society, religion for example, can generate fundamental change, rather than the basic organization of the means of production. This leads to the introduction of 'surplus value' and 'surplus labour' and their alienation (Harvey, 1973). 'The economic surplus is a derivative of Marx's concept of surplus value. Surplus value is the difference between the value produced by a worker in a given period and the share of that value necessary for the maintenance of the worker and the capital stock. Since, in a competitive situation, a commodity exchanges at its cost of production, the worker is paid only his cost of subsistence no matter that he produced in excess thereof' (Stanfield, 1973, 2). Marx, however, explicitly accepted that the surplus is culturally determined; 'there enters into the determination of the value of labour power a historical and moral element' (Marx, 1967). In primitive and egalitarian societies surpluses arise but are used to support the weak and to provide a hedge against environmental uncertainties, but in redistributive societies they are alienated as surplus products. That is, some sort of surplus exists in all social groups but it is the 'cornering' of this surplus by one element and its subsequent use to exploit other elements that is the trigger which sets off the urbanization sequence. This 'cornering' takes place initially by what is called 'primitive accumulation'. Primitive accumulation is first established either by the collection of fixed assets or the appropriation of labour power. This then becomes the basis of the surplus value which one group expropriates and so alienates social increment as private property. This is the key to urbanization for there is now a surplus to be invested and this, as Rosa Luxembourg argued (1913, 77), sets in train a series of transformations. Investment of the expropriated surplus in permanent forms creates the built city, while expansion to create demand leads to conspicuous consumption and the monumental city. The need for expansion also generates economic imperialism and creates war and the need for defence. All those 'explicitly delineatory' aspects of urbanism, therefore, follow in the train of economic change, from the emergence of a class structure to the establishment of garrisons and strongpoints, and even to the use of religion to legitimize expropriation as 'a moral thing'.

A number of points remain which tend to suggest that the whole argument is circular. It can be contended that a growing size of population is more likely to create the conditions in which 'accumulation' can take place, so that agricultural intensification is admitted as an element in urbanization. Again, while the economic explanation can be applied to the essential socioeconomic transformations it does not altogether convince in relation to the actual ecological process of agglomeration. Why should an exploited group remain attached to the expropriators and exploiters and not simply move away? It could be that the economic impetus provided by the city resulted in more favourable conditions for the so-called exploited, and that they benefited from the initiative, enterprise and development brought about by the alienating group. This sort of explanation, however, seems to become a justification of competitive 'capitalism', so that even a Marxist interpreter has to admit that the binding of the population to the city may be by religious belief and commitment, or any other factor which keeps the population immobile. Slavery apart, it can be argued that all those conditions which eventually defined feudalism were designed to tie down the population, but these bonds were loosened in the city and they are in consequence associated with a rural rather than with an urban situation. These reservations tend to shift interest to the other explanations of the origins of towns, even if no more than as ancillary rather than as fundamental causes. Before considering these it is necessary to review briefly the second key concept under the 'surplus' heading, irrigation, and its relation to the agricultural intensification noted earlier in this section.

(b) The idea of the hydraulic society is closely related to an ecological interpretation of urbanization, that is, that it was a consequence of increasing size and density of population and that this was brought about by irrigation. C.J. Gadd in considering the cities of Babylonia writes:

> The military power was sustained in the Sumerian cities by a wealth which manifested itself also in many splendid products of material civilization. The foundation of this wealth was the fertility of the land and that fertility depended in its turn upon irrigation. The control of the regular spring floods by an elaborate system of dams and canals must have been a slow achievement, but it was clearly recognized by the Sumerians as a supreme necessity and the resulting prosperity was so marvellous in their eyes that they were constrained to regard the complete irrigation system as the work of none less than a god. (Gadd, 1962, 34)

The working out of the consequences of irrigation in greatest detail is to be found in Karl A. Wittfogel's book *Oriental Despotism*. Wittfogel, as the subtitle of his book – *A comparative study of total power* – implies, was more concerned with the state and political power than the city as such. In the index to his book the word 'urban', or its equivalents, such as 'town' and 'city', do not appear. Nevertheless, there are clear associations. Wittfogel's thesis proceeds from the basis that 'the characteristics of hydraulic economy are many but three are paramount. Hydraulic agriculture involves a specific type of division of labour. It intensifies cultivation. And it necessitates cooperation on a large scale' (Wittfogel, 1957, 22). Intensification induces the appropriate population concentration, whilst cooperation leads to the need for a managerial and bureaucratic society. Power ultimately will reside in the managers and out of this despotic control results. 'The effective management of these works involves an organizational web which covers either the whole, or at least the dynamic cores, of the country's population. In consequence, those who control this network are uniquely prepared to wield supreme political power' (Wittfogel, 1957, 27). The division of labour, the centralization of power and the administrative structure engender concentrated settlement so that the town emerges. So do all the associated characteristics. Thus Wittfogel maintains that the need for comprehensive works of defence arises as soon as irrigated agriculture is practised, for the whole system is fixed and unmovable and must be defended *in situ*. Again, 'a government apparatus capable of executing all these hydraulic and non-hydraulic works could easily be used in building palaces . . . monuments and tombs. It could be used wherever equalitarian conditions of a primitive tribal society yielded to . . . no longer tribal forms of autocracy' (Wittfogel, 1957, 45). Social transformation and monumental buildings are thus consequences of hydraulic agriculture. In short, urbanization itself can be viewed as following upon the development of irrigation. There is no point here in following Wittfogel into his establishment of Asiatic society and oriental despotism. To a large extent irrigation can be looked upon as creating the surpluses already discussed and the manipulating managers can be identified as the alienators of the surplus value.

These ideas have received added support from investigations in other areas of nuclear urbanism. Rene Millon's excavations at Teotihuacan (Millon, 1972) in Mexico have shown it as the site of a city of some 70,000 to 125,000 people while studies carried out by William Sanders 'show that the change from rainfall farming to irrigation was correlated with rapid population growth, nucleation, monument construction, intense social stratification and expansionist warfare' (Harris, 1968, 686). In turn, Sanders and Price (1968) have interpreted the differences between Maya civilizations and the highland Mexican hydraulic empire and conclude that the former were based on slash-and-burn farming. 'These were true civilizations, but they lacked the nucleated settlements of urban civilizations' (Harris, 1968, 686). The implication from this is that only in relation to hydraulic agriculture did urban settlements appear.

It is evident that dependability of production, as well as diversity of resources, are conditions which favour urban settlement. To those conditions irrigated agriculture must have made a clear contribution. There is, however, no agreement on the extent to which the irrigation schemes demanded an extensive bureaucracy. Moreover, there are critical areas such as Mesopotamia and Egypt where there is no evidence of the major irrigation schemes demanded to produce urbanization, as distinct from minor, small-scale, adaptive projects. Adams argues, 'there is nothing to suggest that the rise of dynastic authority in southern Mesopotamia was linked to the administrative requirements of a major canal system' (Adams, 1966, 68) and, again, that where Egypt

is concerned there are no records of the construction of irrigation other than at a local level or reference to administrative posts connected with irrigation (Butzer, 1976). But even if all such evidence is discounted the whole argument may well be circular for possibly only the nucleated and organized forces of the city could have initiated and carried out the great irrigation schemes which are a consequence, not the creator, of urbanization. Nevertheless, in any argument for urbanization based on surplus production the impact of irrigation is an essential factor to be considered.

(ii) Economic theories: The city as market place

Two closely interrelated interpretations can be given to economic theories of urban origins. The first can be called 'mercantile' for it views the city as the product of long-distance trade, whilst the second can be called 'market' for it interprets the city as the centre created by a region to focus its internal processes of exchange. In this consideration no attempt will be made to treat these separately.

The Egyptian hieroglyph for a town was a cross within a circle and this is often seen as symbolizing two dominant functions of the earliest towns (Lopez, 1966). The cross represents the meeting of routes at the market place, while the circle stands for the defensive walls, so that the city as a protected market place is overtly set down. But the modern view of the city as the translation of the demand for a permanent focus by trade has been largely derived from a retrospective application of traditional ideas about the origin and development of European towns in the post-Roman period. These ideas were widely disseminated in the writings of Henri Pirenne who strongly advocated commerce as the creator of the medieval town (Pirenne, 1925). If it were established that the towns of western Europe had emerged because of their commercial activity then it would seem self-evident that a similar stimulus had generated towns at all periods. These views were reinforced, as Polanyi points out, by the discovery of the Code of Hammurabi since it was ostensibly a commercial code of law. 'Civilization, so much seemed evident, had been born from man's commercial instincts; and the cradle of our own world, that of a businessman's culture, had been uncovered in Babylonia . . .' (Polanyi, 1957, 15).

A main exponent of the economic origins of cities is Jane Jacobs who forcibly argues the case which she epitomizes as, 'cities first – rural development later' (Jacobs, 1969, 3–48). By this interpretation agricultural intensification is taken as being a consequence of city growth and not the other way round. 'Both in the past and today, then, the separation commonly made, dividing city commerce and industry from rural agriculture, is artificial and imaginary. The two do not come down different lines of descent. Rural work – whether that work is manufacturing . . . or growing food – is city work transplanted' (Jacobs, 1969, 18). In order to illustrate the process of urban origins Jacobs sets up an imaginary city called New Obsidian which deals at first in that stone. 'Since at least 9000 BC', she asserts, 'and possibly earlier the trading of the local obsidian had taken place by custom in the territory of a neighbouring hunting group who had become regular customers for the obsidian and, subsequently, go-betweens in the trade with more distant hunting peoples. It is the settlement of this group that has become the little city of New Obsidian' (Jacobs, 1969, 19). This trading post once established generates specialization and once more all the changes associated with urbanization are underway. Critical amongst the items traded is food and this must be non-perishable. It therefore comes in the form of live animals and seed and those responsible for looking after these supplies eventually turn to domesticating the animals and obtaining their own crops from the sown seed; agriculture is created by urban demand. The market place becomes a key feature in the urban layout; 'in the barter space, the two worlds (that of the townsfolk and the alien traders) meet. The square is thus the only "open space" in the city itself, left open originally because what has since become a busy meeting and trading spot was at first a space of separation, deliberately kept empty' (Jacobs, 1969, 23).

Jane Jacobs tries to provide a real-world parallel to her New Obsidian by quoting Catal Huyuk, a Neolithic town in Anatolia whose origins date to 7560 BC. This was excavated by James Mellaart (Mellaart, 1967) and one of the conclusions which Jacobs draws from his evidence is that 'Civilization came directly – without a break – from the hunting life'. That evidence is mainly in the art forms which are strongly related to the Upper Palaeolithic tradition of naturalistic painting carrying the implication that part of the population of Catal Huyuk was of Upper Palaeolithic stock, that is, the old hunting, food-gathering stock preserving the remains of an Upper Palaeolithic heritage. 'Catal Huyuk had a valuable resource and a trade in that resource to be sure, but it had something else valuable and more wondrous. It had a creative local economy. It is this that sets the city apart from a mere trading post with access to a mine. The people of Catal Huyuk had added one kind of work after another into their own local city economy' (Jacobs, 1969, 35). It was this which produced the almost explosive development in the arts and crafts which Mellaart records. Mellaart is not drawn into the speculative conclusions which Jane Jacobs derives however and concludes 'it would be premature to speculate further about the ancestry of Catal Huyuk' (Mellaart, 1967, 226).

There are at least three reasons why the market origins of towns must be regarded with some scepticism. The first is that in contrast to modern free trading principles, economic relations and trading in the early towns seem to have been controlled by treaty arrangements carried out by 'traders by status' who formed part of the urban bureaucracy. ' "Prices" took the form of equivalencies established by authority of custom, statute or proclamation.' Given these conditions then no market place is necessary and there is evidence that this was the case. 'Babylonia, as a matter of fact, possessed neither market

places nor a functioning market system of any description' (Polanyi, 1957, 116). Jacobs's scenario of the emergence of towns of the New Obsidian variety, therefore, seems to have no basis in fact and, indeed, the large open spaces which she describes as the locations of markets never existed. They are features of much later times set back by her into the remote past.

The second reason for disbelief in the market as the creator of towns is the simple fact that in more recent times both the centre of long-distance trade, the fair, and that of local exchange, the market, have been carried on without bringing permanent settlement into being. Fairs in Britain were often held on open sites remote from actual villages or towns. The North African suq is a good example of a market held without reference to settlement (Fogg, 1939a and b), while the whole growing literature on periodic markets confirms the same point. There is certainly no necessary relation between market and fixed, large settlement.

The third reason is, to some extent, a reiteration of the second. As Wheatley writes, 'it has not yet been demonstrated clearly and unequivocally that . . . a generalized desire for exchange is capable of concentrating political or social power to the extent attested by the archaeological record, or . . . that it can bring about the institutionalization of such power' (Wheatley, 1971, 282). If the market need not generate permanent settlement, still less is it likely to precipitate all those complex changes in social and economic structure which are the concomitants of urbanization. Although trade was an important element in the early city its intensification must be seen as an offshoot of urbanism rather than a creator of it.

(iii) Military theories: The city as strong-point

It has been noted that the circular element in the Egyptian hieroglyph for a town symbolized a wall or a set of external defences. Accordingly it can be contended that the origin of cities lay in the need for people to gather together in search of protection. Once that agglomeration had been brought about under the oversight of a military caste, then the other changes characterizing urbanization took place. In support it is adduced that defences appear at the same time as towns. Thus Mellaart notes that 'the need for defence may be the original reason for the peculiar way in which the people of Catal Huyuk constructed dwellings without doorways, and with the sole entry through the roof'. Those who were responsible for the layout of the city did not build a solid wall but fringed the settlement with an unbroken line of houses and store-rooms where access was only through the roofs. 'The efficiency of the defence system is obvious and, whatever discomfort it involved for the inhabitants of the city, there is no evidence for any sack or massacre during the 800 years of the existence of Catal Huyuk' (Mellaart, 1967, 69). Again, Kathleen Kenyon writing of 'the first Jericho', the pre-pottery Neolithic settlement, records, 'The first settlement is quite clearly on the scale, not of a village, but of a town. Its claim to a true civic status is established by the discovery . . . that it possessed a massive defensive wall' (Kenyon, 1957, 65–6). The equating of a defensive wall with civic status need not necessarily have implications for origin, but the discovery of a town wall with 'its foundations resting on bedrock' certainly does. The wall is associated with a great rock-cut ditch and a massive tower. 'We have, therefore, indications that the elaborate system of defences has a very long history. The earlier stages have not yet been fully traced. But the earliest . . . with the nucleus of the tower and a free-standing stone wall must in itself have been sufficiently magnificent. . . . It belongs to the earliest phase in the history of the town. . . . We have now reached bedrock in several places without finding any suggestion of a yet earlier phase' (Kenyon, 1957, 72).

The evidence quoted above suggests that from the earliest identifiable times in the oldest known towns there were elaborate and strong defences, providing grounds for the belief that military necessity might have been a cause for the origin of towns. Even Wheatley from his strongly committed viewpoint is forced to admit that, 'Warfare may often have made a significant contribution to the *intensification* of urban development by inducing a concentration of settlement for purposes of defence and by stimulating craft specialization' (Wheatley, 1971, 298–9). The critical difficulty is that much of the evidence is capable of a completely circular form of interpretation. From the viewpoint of the believer in the economic surplus, formal and institutionalized warfare is itself the creation of the so-called urban revolution. Tribal raiding and intergroup fighting obviously go back to pre-urban times, but as occasional and sporadic affairs; organized war of the sort which characterized Babylonia, for example, only developed with a city based civilization. 'The inscriptions of the third Early Dynastic period and the King-list which is the main authority for its history are all greatly preoccupied with war, and when it is added that the outstanding pictorial monuments are devoted to the same subject there can be no surprise that the age has gained an ill repute for militarism' (Gadd, 1962, 30). This militarism follows as a result of those classes who had alienated the economic surplus in the cities, initiating policies of external aggrandizement. War in this sense is not a cause of socioeconomic change but rather is generated by it. If 'protection' is needed, then protection from whom? And if the conflicts were not of a different order why were not towns generated at an earlier date? If the answer is that a certain size and agglomeration of population were needed, then the catalytic role of warfare and defence is lost over against the forces which led to demographic growth and ecological organization. Moreover, although defences appear in the earliest of towns, not all early towns have defences. But there is a great danger of this becoming a 'chicken and the egg' type of dispute to which no answer of any certainty can be provided.

It must be accepted that some settlements were from the beginning defensive strong-points and, accordingly,

the close agglomeration and the institutional organization which are a necessary part of elaborate communal defences possibly played a role in the emergence of towns.

(iv) Religious theories: The city as temple

Riaz Hassan in writing on the origins of Muslim cities adopts the view presented by that great medieval geographer and historian, Ibn Khaldun, who distinguished between two types of cultural systems. The first of these was the Nomadic Culture (Umran Badawi) characteristic of pre-Islamic Arab societies, and the second was urban or Civilized Culture (Umran Hadari) characteristic of post-Islamic societies. If the distinguishing features of these two 'cultures' are examined then they appear as essentially those of the 'Folk' and 'Urban' conditions. Hassan continues, 'The Urban Culture could not exist without respect for authority, attachment to a certain locality and deference to the rights of others. The transition from the "Nomadic Culture" to the "Civilized Urban Culture" required that the limitations of the "Nomadic Culture" be overcome. In order to overcome these limitations a new rationale for social organization was required.' This new rationale was provided by religion (Islam). Religion in this manner became the highly effective force which created new loyalties and provided 'a social solidarity superior to and more lasting than that based on natural kinship . . . so that Islam provided the most effective instrument for the use and development of urbanization' (Hassan, 1972, 108–9).

This interpretation of the primary role of religious belief in the origin of Islamic cities is essentially parallel to that which can be put forward in relation to the origin of cities in general. It is also closely akin to the case for nationalism put forward by Reissman in relation to modern urbanization. 'Nationalism', he maintains, 'is a pivoted element in the social transition which is being analysed. Its social function, briefly, is to provide a social rationale that makes the transition possible. For nationalism supplies the ideology that can command loyalties, motivate action and legitimate the changes to be effected' (Reissman, 1964, 188). In these words, and in developing this theme, Reissman uses the terms, 'ideology', 'a rationale', 'a body of plausible beliefs', which reiterate those used by Hassan and might well be religious in connotation. He concludes, 'Born in the city, nationalism assumes control of a Society's destiny and in time spreads out to the countryside where it can weld together the disparate social elements and social groups into a unified community' (Reissman, 1964, 194). This view of post-industrial urbanism can, *mutatis mutandis*, be reinterpreted in terms of the ancient city where the equivalent and critical forces were not those derived from political nationalism but from belief in a need to propitiate the gods and to align this material microcosm with the immaterial macrocosm of the other world. But whatever the interpretation, one is close to Sjoberg's basic view that the power structure is critical. 'We must, if we are to explain the growth, spread and decline of cities, comment upon the city as a mechanism by which a society's rulers can consolidate and maintain their power and, more important, the essentiality of a well developed power structure for the formation and perpetuation of urban centres' (Sjoberg, 1960, 67). This is a view closely parallel to that of Wittfogel (see p. 4) but within the context of the argument of a sacred basis to the town it is fundamental that the power structure developed and became ecologically effective in the hands of the priesthood.

In a more objective sense the process of agglomeration is related to the designation by tribal groups of sacred territories administered by the priesthood. The priests, therefore, in their role of ensuring the safety and security of the people – not by walls against physical enemies, but by rites against the menaces of nature – became the first group to be detached, the first specialized sector of the population. The sacerdotal elite in this way operated as disposers of 'surplus' produce brought as offerings. Change was instigated, not as Jane Jacobs would have it through a free market, but through the concentration of the surplus in priestly hands. Moreover, the dominance of the sacred territory not only brought people to it and bound them to it so that actual physical agglomeration took place, but the same process meant that citizenship, the crux of belonging, was defined by a specific religious territorial allegiance. C.J. Gadd records of the cities of Babylonia, 'It has already been observed as peculiar to this period that it had developed a form of human government which seemed to reproduce upon earth exactly the hierarchy of heaven, so that it was sometimes hardly clear whether gods or men were the acting parties' (Gadd, 1962, 46). It is little wonder that cities were so often thought of as being the creations of the gods themselves.

One further line of evidence can be put forward. There is a clear association of shrines and temples with excavated cities. Inevitably no inductive evidence of this order can ever be complete but the predominant role of religious buildings in city layouts cannot be easily put aside. Again, Catal Huyuk as one of the earliest cities can be cited and there, of the 139 living rooms excavated in levels 2 to 10, as many as 40 probably served Neolithic religion.

There can be little doubt that religion played a significant part in that process of transformation which brought cities into being. What is less convincing is why the particular metamorphosis should have taken place at a point or period in time, since belief in some other world and cult practices do not seem to begin with urbanism. Moreover, if markets do not produce permanent settlement neither do shrines – 'the tribal market functioned as the capital of the tribe, especially when the nearby shrine was that of the patron saint of the tribe. Neither market nor shrine, however, was surrounded by either an agglomeration of dwellings, or by civic, religious or commercial buildings' (Fogg, 1939a, 322–3). Wheatley, however, argues that the period of urban beginnings was marked by a 'growing distinction, in contrast with tribal religion, between gods and men, a distinction which necessitated the elaboration of a communication system mediated through worship and sacrifice' (Wheatley, 1971, 319). The mediators in this way became the alienators, alienating people not from any material surplus but from direct relations with the other-world forces and, in political terms, from each other. Nevertheless, for this to take place, a progression is postulated from terminal food collecting, through primary village farming efficiency to developed village farming efficiency, from which condition the dispersed ceremonial centre emerges and by a process akin to synoecism the compact city develops. That is, ecological and technological progression becomes an essential basis. Again the argument can become circular, for it can be proposed that any one group alienating and expropriating a surplus would exploit the irrationality of the expropriated in order to legitimize the process. The masses accept social transformation because belief is exploited and the early citizen is reconciled to the situation in the same way as the immanence of the next world was used in the nineteenth century to persuade people to accept the inequalities and the miseries of this. Perhaps such a view suggests the relationship postulated between the protestant ethic and the rise of capitalism. But such a notion is a very long way from the proposal of a linear and direct relationship between religion and industrial urbanism. It is equally inappropriate to suggest a relationship of such a character in the context of urban origins.

4 A summary of theories of urban origins

It is possible to initiate a discussion of the various theories on urban origins by considering, very briefly, the Industrial Revolution and the cities it brought into being. If it does nothing more it will indicate how complex these major socioeconomic transformations are. In school textbooks it was traditional to present the Industrial Revolution through an account of technical innovations, discoveries which 'revolutionized' the modes of production. This has long since been abandoned for it is a narration of the correlates of change rather than its initiator. Again, towns were built quite simply and directly about mine, mill and factory and yet to call these the 'causes' of towns and cities is true only in an elementary way. In order to trace those forces which transformed industry and created towns it would be necessary to review the whole pattern of economic and social change in the preceding centuries. Yet this, too, depends on what is meant by 'origin'. In a direct sense the factory was the town's origin. So it is with the beginnings of urbanism, and much of the debate seems simplistic in the extreme as single, direct causes are sought. Certainly monumental buildings, even defensive walls and temples, are somewhat akin to mines and factories. They are critical indicators of the changes taking place, and of the agglomeration seed, yet in themselves were no more than evidence of large-scale, deeper-lying processes.

Undoubtedly the critical factor in the beginning of towns was the gradual progression of technology and a growing density of settled or village population, perhaps lifted to a critical take-off point by the intensity of cultivation made possible by irrigation. Even so in that progression, even without Childe's notion of an urban revolution, a catalyst metamorphosed the old kin-structured, tribal organization into a class-based territorial one. That catalyst was probably the intricately related role of temple, fortress and market place. Perhaps the best summary is Wheatley's:

> It is doubtful if a single autonomous, causative factor will ever be identified in the nexus of social, economic and political transformations which resulted in the emergence of urban forms . . . whatever structural changes in social organization were induced by commerce, warfare or technology, they needed to be validated by some instrument of authority if they were to achieve institutionalized permanence. (Wheatley, 1971, 318)

At this point it is tempting to suggest that the notion of an 'urban revolution' might well be the root cause of much of the difficulty and obscurantism which has characterized the debate on urban origins. The whole topic still rests under the shadow of Childe's proposition for the concept of a single cause is inexorably linked with the idea of a revolution. The analogy with the so-called Industrial Revolution, which has already been made, might well be appropriate for there, too, the view of a revolution simply caused by technological change has long been abandoned. Industrial settlement there certainly was but one wonders whether the causes of its origin, in those simple terms, is a sensible question to ask. Perhaps the time has come to look critically at the concept of an urban revolution and to consider the city as emergent from a longer period of social and economic change and cultural adaptation in which an elaborate complex of factors was mingled.

5 Areas of nuclear urbanism

The title of this section begs the question to be raised. It assumes that there was more than one area or region where towns emerged and by the use of the qualification 'nuclear' implies that a different form of urban development characterized some other areas. The most complete consideration of the 'courses towards urban life' is that by Braidwood and Willey (1962) and they conclude,

> In all regions considered, societies that were either wholly or predominantly native ones passed from a status of food-collecting to one of a more or less effective food production, at least by the time Columbus had discovered America. In two New World areas (Mesoamerica and Peru) and in three Old World areas (Southwestern Asia, India and China), the threshold of civilization and urbanization was also attained at least by the beginning of the Christian era if not signifi-

cantly earlier. In other native areas, civilization and urbanization came later, largely as a result of some more effective form of expansion or diffusion . . .'. (Braidwood and Willey, 1962, 330)

In an attempt to make a distinction between the five areas named above and those where 'urbanization came later', the terms primary urbanization and secondary urbanization have been used, but these bring problems of definition. Wheatley excludes altogether as elements of secondary urbanization, city development as a result of imperial conquest or colonial extension and he proposes only the indirect inducement of urban growth, presumably by a form of stimulus diffusion (Clarke, 1968, 418–19). This is probably justified in that completely alien imposition, the planting of towns, is in contrast to the triggering-off by contact of changes already latent. But to exclude a clear means by which the city was translated from one area to another and through which the urbanized world was effectively extended in areal coverage, seems an arbitrary mode of denying a process at least analogous to diffusion. In many ways it is simpler to adopt Fried's distinction between 'pristine' and 'secondary' states, with the latter referring to the 'superimposition of a conqueror stratum while the former developed *sui generis* out of purely local conditions' (Fried, 1960, 729). Whatever the term used, the implications are the same, that only in limited areas did towns emerge from settled village agriculture and that elsewhere they were the products either of the direct physical impact of already urbanized societies or of some form of influence emanating from urbanized areas which precipitated change in a society already having predisposing conditions. It follows that there are two problems. The first is to consider the significance of diffused influences and the second to undertake a brief survey of the so-called nuclear areas.

(i) Diffusion and independent origin

The opposition between these two views of how cultural features develop has been one of the long-standing disputes within both archaeology and anthropology and like many such issues can at times be semantic rather than substantive. Harris, for example, dismisses diffusionist notions with scant respect writing of 'the fundamental sterility of the attempt to explain cultural differences and similarities by appealing to the non-principle of diffusion' (Harris, 1968, 377). Again, he argues 'as soon as we admit, as the archaeology of the New World now compels, that independent invention had occurred on a massive scale, diffusion is not only superfluous but the very incarnation of antiscience' (Harris, 1968, 378). The same sort of attack is made by Wheatley on Mortimer Wheeler's conclusions in relation to the Indus civilization,

> I am at a loss to understand what Sir Mortimer Wheeler had in mind when he declared, 'So also, we may suppose, in the third millennium BC India

(Pakistan) received from Mesopotamia the already established idea of city-life civilization, but transmuted that idea into a mode substantially new and congenial to her'. Apart from the imposition by an already established political authority of urban foundations . . . cities formerly could come into being only where an appropriate conjunction of internal forces induced spontaneous readjustments of social, political and economic relationships. (Wheatley, 1971, 7)

Reduced to simplicity this proposes that cities could be created only where cities could be created, or rather less naively, that apart from colonial imposition, urbanism could only be generated where the conditions were apposite, where the courses towards urban life had reached a critical take-off point. There is little point in prolonging this discussion for there is now little in favour of the old view that the city had emerged in Mesopotamia and Egypt and had subsequently been diffused both eastward to the Indus and thence to southeast Asia, and westward to Crete and Greece and thence via Greek colonies and Roman foundations, through Europe; and then spread from southern and western Europe across the Atlantic into the Americas. It is unreal to think of anything so elusive as a 'city idea' or 'the city' in abstract being diffused, and presumably the mechanism of transfer in this physical sense must have been imperial and colonial in context. This was certainly true at the 'end' of the Old World line in Britain. It is equally important to recognize that a transplanted town could create those conditions which would ensure its survival, that is that all those 'spontaneous readjustments' could be caused by, as well as be the cause of, urbanism and it is in that sense that diffusion must be accepted. At a time when models of innovation and diffusion play such a prominent role both in archaeology and human geography it is interesting to see the basis being dismissed as a 'non-principle' and unscientific. But Clarke considering this problem notes that the 'process of diffusion operates upon entities of attribute, attribute complex, artefact type, type complex and assemblage levels. Archaeological entities of higher status cannot be said to 'diffuse' although they migrate in other ways and by other processes in which diffusion will often play an integral part' (Clarke, 1968, 414). The town is clearly an entity of a higher status and presumably the migration must be part of the imperial and colonial extensions already discussed.

In relation to urban origins the critical objection to a unified model of diffusion or migration is the appearance of urbanism in middle and south America. In spite of investigations into the external links of prehistoric America it has never been suggested that the cities of Mesoamerica are the products of cultural stimuli derived from the Old World. Willey writes, 'Insofar as we can tell, urban life, and other qualities of civilization, arose indigenously in southern and central Mesoamerica from antecedent patterns of village agriculture. Certain elements of urbanization and civilization then spread

northwards and westward in Mesoamerica in late Classic and Postclassic times' (Willey, 1962, 101). Although the latter part of this statement has diffusionalist implications, once the theme of a single beginning in the Near East is abandoned then the whole interpretation by diffusion alone breaks down and it is necessary to look not for one but several nuclear areas of urbanism.

(ii) Areas of nuclear urbanism

Braidwood and Willey, after a wide-ranging consideration of seven New World and eleven Old World areas, considered that the threshold of civilization and urbanization had been reached in five areas by the beginning of the Christian period. These were southwest Asia, Mesoamerica, Peru, India and China (Braidwood and Willey, 1968, 330). Other areas certainly approached but apparently did not overstep the threshold of urbanism. The Zimbabwe-Monomatapa culture was probably 'never a truly urbanized society in the strict sense of the term, since there is no indication that classes of professionals or a religious hierarchy, a centralized exchequer or public building programmes ever existed, but it must have come nearer to this form than any other southern African culture' (Clarke, 1968, 26). Wheatley, however, adds the Yoruba territories of Nigeria, but the problem of definition, as well as the chronological qualification, tends to cast doubts over many areas. Figure 1.1 is reproduced from Wheatley and summarizes the relative chronology of urban genesis in the areas usually included.

6 The layout of the first cities

All the evidence as to the internal structure of the first cities is excavated evidence and is, therefore, of physical form and it is from physical form that inferences have to be made.

It is virtually standard practice to identify two groupings of the internal physical form of cities. The first consists of those which can be called 'planned' in which there is a discernible and formal organization of space and by implication control by a central authority, and, second, those which are called unplanned where no such organization can be identified and where development was presumably a fragmented and individual process. It is not possible to give any rigour to this rather simple division. It is, as yet, subjective and based on no measurements or quantified basis. Moreover, cities are built over a period of time and may combine both formal planning and uncontrolled development. Again, and even more relevantly, within a broad geometric framework established by a central authority there can be haphazard small-scale building derived from individual actions. Even so it is a useful, if crude, distinction to maintain, since it is a reflection of the degree of centralized control brought to bear upon urban layout. To a degree, of course, it reflects parallel contrasts in

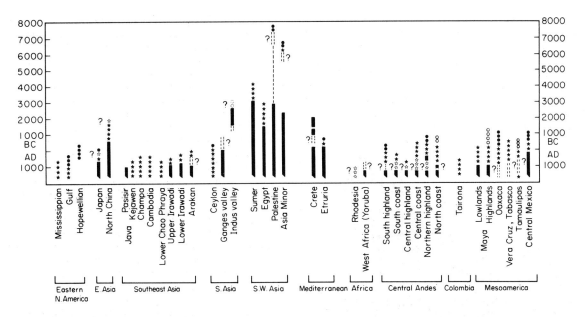

1.1. The relative chronology of urban genesis (after
Wheatley).

architectural and artistic fashion, for a disciplined and classical formalism on the one hand can be contrasted with an exuberant and Gothic spirit on the other. But artistic movements in various ways reflect social mores. It is possible for Romantic movements, even under strong authority, to seek out and display informal and unregimented shapes, but it is more likely for authoritarian regimes to disapprove of that individuality which inspires irregularity. A reasonable accordance of socio-political conditions and artistic movements can be proposed and the problem of their working in different directions set aside.

It might appear that town plans would throw some light on town origins since the driving force, military, economic or religious, would impress itself upon the internal structure. But, in the first instance, the process of agglomeration about the castle, market place or shrine would be progressive and gradual and only at a later, even if a critical stage, would complete central control be exerted by the appropriation of all developed space and its reformation. Apparently both planned and unplanned towns can be identified from the archaeological record and the two polar extremes of formally organized planning and uncontrolled, individual building appear from the beginnings of urbanism.

This standard contrast between planned and unplanned is most often illustrated by the contrast between Ur in Mesopotamia and Mohenjo-daro in the Indus valley. They have one characteristic in common, that of size, since estimates of the populations of both are usually set about 35,000. Ur is perhaps most frequently quoted because of its early excavation by Sir Leonard Woolley (Woolley, 1942) and its popular association with the biblical account of the Flood. Some few significant features can be set out. The city reached the height of its power, what Woolley called 'The great days of the Third Dynasty', during the reign of Ur-Nammu (2112–2095 BC). The inner city was bounded by a defensive wall which rose '26 feet or more above the plain and acted as a retaining-wall to the platform on which the town buildings were raised' (Woolley, 1942, 63). This rampart was some 77 feet thick and encircled a space three-quarters of a mile in length and nearly half a mile in width, a fitting testimony to the need for protection which the city demanded. But within the city was the great 'tenemos' or sacred precinct. Woolley notes that 'two fragmentary inscriptions on stone found in the temple of the Moon-goddess . . . record the founding by Ur-Nammu of a temple or shrine . . .' (Woolley, 1942, 62), so that at the outset there was a religious element. This religious area of the moon god, with its four corners orientated towards the four cardinal points of the compass underwent major reconstruction under Nebuchadnezzar (404–561 BC) when it seems that an overall rectilinearity was superimposed on the haphazardly grown city. 'The old Sacred Area had consisted of religious foundations of all sorts grouped together . . . the unity was ill-defined . . . and it would seem that in fact the Sacred Area in many places merged imperceptibly into the lay quarters of the town. Nebuchadnezzar reformed all this' (Woolley, 1942, 88). Here then is order, at least at the critical centre being created out of haphazard growth for it would seem incontrovertible that the residential areas had grown without any control. Woolley concluded that apart from the processional way there was no formal planning identifiable at Ur – 'the streets were narrow, winding and unpaved' – and the whole town showed the lack of

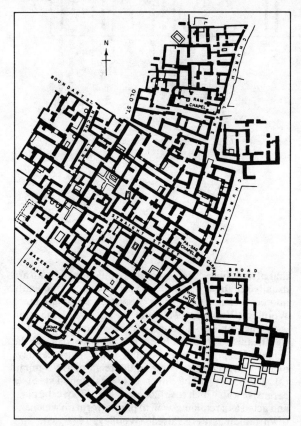

1.2.   The excavated area at Ur (after Woolley). The plan is of the Larsa period and is dated to the eighteenth century BC.

form of a primitive village with the accidents of land ownership and building determining the orientation of the narrow lanes. Figure 1.2 shows part of the excavated residential areas and demonstrates the lack of any formal organization.

At this point another element in the determination of forms comes into play. This is house type, for to a degree a complete plan will be a response to the form which the individual house takes. Woolley was greatly impressed by the sophistication of the two-storey houses he excavated. 'In Abraham's time men lived in houses built with walls of burnt brick below, rising in mud brick above, plaster and whitewash hiding the change in

materials, two storeys high, and containing as many as 13 or 14 rooms around a central paved court which supplied light and air to the house. The streets . . . [had] . . . on either side blank walls unbroken by windows . . .' (Woolley, 1942, 89). Given the narrow streets and the crowded, claustrophobic environment the house with a central court was the only way of providing tolerable living conditions. At the same time it was culturally adapted to the seclusion of women and the keeping of slaves. This type of house meant that a traditional way of life could be preserved in a densely built-up and unplanned urban agglomeration.

Apart from the residential areas there were the symbols of two of the proposed bases of urban origins and of central control. The great defensive rampart denotes the necessity of a military function. The city was itself dominated by the tenemos, always being redeveloped as an area apart. These were the indications of planning, even if the residential areas were the consequence of individual decisions and the complex pattern of land holding.

In contrast to Ur can be set out the great centres of the Indus or Harappan culture, especially Mohenjo-daro described by Mortimer Wheeler in his book *The Indus Civilization* (Wheeler, 1968). The period of the ascendency of the culture was from 2500 to 1500 BC when the Indus valley was controlled by what are sometimes regarded as the twin centres of Mohenjo-daro and

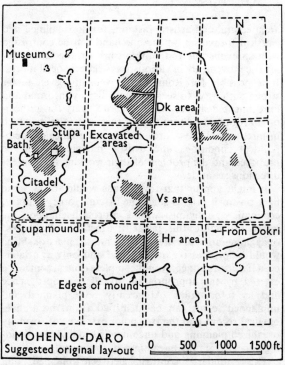

MOHENJO-DARO
Suggested original lay-out

1.3.   Mohenjo-daro (after Wheeler). The general street plan. The shaded and labelled areas refer to those parts which had been excavated.

Harappa, some 400 miles apart. The dominating feature of Mohenjo-daro is what Wheeler called, 'a carefully engineered civic layout from as early a period as had been reached by excavation'. The city was laid out in a grid pattern made up of 16 large blocks (Figure 1.3). The central block of the western row contained what is described as a citadel or 'monumental architectural complex raised on a natural or artificial mound and constituting something in the nature of an acropolis' (Wheatley, 1971, 232). Although individual residences were not set out in geometrical form there was an overlying and dominating grid which characterized not only Mohenjo-daro but the series of cities within the complex so that 'the carefully engineered civic layout' was the prime feature. The uniformity of culture which extended over such a large area has obviously suggested an overriding political or theocratic control, what Wheeler called 'a social discipline which originally dictated and so long sustained the geometric precision of the city's ground plan' (Wheeler, 1968). Indeed, Fairservis has suggested that the major cities were primarily cult centres without resident populations (Fairservis, 1961), but given the evidence of granaries and the extensive built area, this seems unlikely.

In contrast to Ur, therefore, Mohenjo-daro displays an overall geometric layout. Unplanned and planned, organic and inorganic growth seem to be present from the beginnings of urbanism. In a way this is not surprising. However rapid the transformation from non-urban to urban in the terms already considered it is still possible to envisage the initial stage of formless agglomeration about a central and controlling point, be it shrine, castle or market place, although at a very early date the appropriators of the surplus value would begin to exercise authority and consciously develop a design of the urban form. Hardoy's interpretation of the growth of Teotihuacan in central Mexico epitomizes the physical process by which the city emerged.

The valley of Teotihuacan was occupied during the formative period by a rural population living in small settlements located along the slopes of the valley. The process of densification and nucleation was slow through the formative period and was characterized by a gradual migration of the settlements toward the alluvial plain. Between 100 BC and AD 100 an urban centre nucleated half or more of the population of the valley in one permanent settlement possibly as a consequence of increased social differentiation and changes in the use of land' (Hardoy, 1967, 23).

This is the process of synoecism by which out of the rural settlements the urban form was born, a physical manifestation of the process of urban origins which was earlier considered.

Hardoy has no doubt that the nucleating centre was a ceremonial complex and this would seem to give some logic to the process of the formal geometrical organization of space. As geometry appears the question is raised as to why it did so when it would have seemed easier merely to let agglomeration take its own course. The answer could be a military one in that defence is easier with clearly defined paths of movement, yet at Catal Huyuk this was achieved in a very different fashion. 'The planners did not build a solid wall, but surrounded the site with an unbroken row of houses and store-rooms accessible only from the roof. . . . To take the settlement would involve close fighting from house to house in a maze of dwellings . . .' (Mellaart, 1967, 68-9). Thus even if there were regularity in materials and houses the military success of defence depended on irregularity. It is also possible that the need of access to markets would impose some order but it is doubtful if this needed to take a rigid form. A consideration of the motivation for order, therefore, reduces the basic need to one religious or magical: the city was organized in earthly space to replicate or symbolize the order which pertained to other world structures and this ensured survival and prosperity.

The most immediate way of exemplifying this concept is to consider the instructions of the prophet Ezekiel as to how Jerusalem was to be constructed by the Israelites on their return from the Babylonian captivity.

The oblation that ye shall offer the Lord shall be of five and twenty thousand in length, and of ten thousand in breadth . . . and the sanctuary of the Lord shall be in the midst thereof. . . . And these are the goings out of the city on the north side, four thousand and five hundred measures. And the gates of the city shall be after the names of the tribes of Israel: three gates northward; one gate of Reuben, one gate of Judah, one gate of Levi.

The passage continues to detail each of the sides and gates and concludes, 'and the name of the city from that day shall be, The Lord, is there' (Ezekiel, 48, 30-4). It is perhaps also significant that in the 21st chapter of The Revelation the new, the holy Jerusalem, derived from Old Testament traditions, is envisaged in the same way, 'And had a wall great and high, and had twelve gates, and at the gates twelve angels, and names written thereon which are the names of the twelve tribes of the children of Israel. On the east three gates; on the north three gates; on the south three gates and on the west three gates' (Revelation, 21, 12-13). Here sacred and profane space mirror each other, while the orientation to the points of the compass of each of the walls also carries with it the implication of an assimilation of an earthly city into a heavenly order.

Wheatley (1971, 418) adapts the basic modes of symbolism used in the process just outlined, from the work of Mircea Eliade (1949). These are:

1 'Reality is a function of the Imitation of a Celestial Archetype. This is the view that there exists another world order which must be reproduced in this.' The various cosmologies which have been produced, and which most will be familiar with as explanatory illustrations to works like *Paradise Lost* or the *Divine Comedy*, all attempt to identify the celestial

archetype. To build it in this world was the surest way to security.

2   'The Parallelism between the Macrocosmos and the Microcosmos necessitates the practice of ritual ceremonies to maintain harmony between the world of the gods and the world of men.' If the most effective means are used of propitiating the gods and ensuring that peace and prosperity are maintained then an appropriate ceremonial is essential and in this the conjunction of this finite and material world with an infinite and spiritual world is critical.

3   'Reality is achieved through participation in the Symbolism of the Centre, as expressed by some form of Axis Mundi.' The most effective symbol, and the most sacred place, is that where earth and sky meet, the axial point where sacred and profane come together. But it was inappropriate, it was impossible indeed, for this to happen on the flat, so at that point great towers, ziggurats or pyramids were built, to mark the most sacred place and raise it above the common plain.

4   'The technique of orientation necessary to define sacred territory within the continuum of profane space involves an emphasis on the cardinal compass directions.' This relation to the cardinal points has already been noted in the biblical passages quoted. The other-world orientation is derived from the skies to which this world orientation is most securely bound by faithful representation.

By all these means the city becomes more than a symbol of a religious system, it is organized and structured as the world beyond and in this way harmony is ensured. Lampl writes, 'The city appeared as such a wondrously complex and complete organism that only a god could have created it' (Lampl, n.d., 7); but a god *had* created it, for it was built in the image of his domain.

A most effective illustration of the above principles and processes is the great ceremonial complex of Angkor in Cambodia (Coedes, 1963). The present ruins of Angkor Thom are those of the last city built on the site by Jayavarman VII in the late thirteenth century so that the central gnomon was a Buddhist sanctuary.

The city was surrounded with a wall and moat forming a square almost two miles in each side, its sides being directed towards the four cardinal points. There are gates in the middle of each side and a fifth one on the east leading to the entrance of the royal palace. The towers above the gates are crowned with the same fourfold faces of Lokesvara as those of the central temple. Thus, that smaller world, the city of Angkor, and through its means the whole Khmer empire were both put under the protection of the 'Lord of the Universe'. The cosmic meaning of the city was further emphasized by a curious device. The balustrades of the causeways leading over the moat to the city gates were formed by rows of giant stone figures, partly gods, partly demons, holding an enormous seven-headed serpent. The whole city thus became a representation of the churning of the primeval milk ocean by gods and demons, when they used the serpent king Vasuki as a rope and Mount Meru as churning stick. This implies that the moat was meant to symbolize the ocean, and the Bayon, the temple in the centre of the city, on which all the lines of churning gods and demons converged, Mount Meru itself. (Heine-Geldern, 1963, 4)

This was the last city, the last of a series of structures for each of the Khmer Kings had to identify that specific location, that *axis mundi*, which was particular to him and favoured his reign. The result was that each king had to create a new centre and build a new palace (Bayon) so that the configuration changed with each ruler (Figure 1.4) as the necessity for ensuring the parallelism of macrocosmos and microcosmos was met. It follows that 'the enclosure at Angkor Thom was simply a religious, administrative and aristocratic centre, where lived – clustered around the capital and principal temple (Bayon) – the civil and military functionaries, the priesthood, the rich families and the army . . .' (Briggs, 1951, 219). This constituted an enormous superstructure for a list for the temple of Ta Prohm at Angkor built by Jayavarman VII included 18 high priests, 2740 officials, 2202 servers and 625 dancing girls (Milnes, 1972). To support these, tens of thousands of peasants were needed especially to produce food and craft articles. This is the specialization of occupation which is inherent in urbanism. But the markets and homes of the masses were in the suburbs along the Barays, or large artificial lakes to the east and west of the walled city, and along the banks of the Siemreap River even to the mouth (Briggs, 1951, 219). At this period the main markets were outside the southern and eastern gates for the central city square was used for festivals and parades. The markets were characterized by no permanent structures for Chou Ta-Kuan, a Chinese traveller who visited Angkor in 1296–7 records, 'most of the commerce was carried on by women. . . . They had no permanent shops in the ground. For a desirable place rent was paid to the authorities' (Pelliot, 1951, 12–13).

A familiar picture of a so-called pre-industrial city emerges from the above description. There was a completely dominant central ceremonial complex carefully engineered to align the city with cosmic structures and forces. The rich and the powerful lived at the centre while the poor lived at the margins. The markets were neither central nor dominant but a product of the demands arising from nucleation by the ceremonial centre.

The great city of Teotihuacan, with a population which might have been as high as 200,000 (Millon, 1972), provides a similar situation, though with even more organized planning of the residential areas. Figure 1.5 is a reproduction of the plan of the central part. The city is essentially cruciform and dominated by the great north–south axis of the so-called Calle de los Muertes (the Street of the Dead). This is crossed by an east–west axis simply referred to as the Eastern and Western Avenues. Rene Millon, who has produced a complete

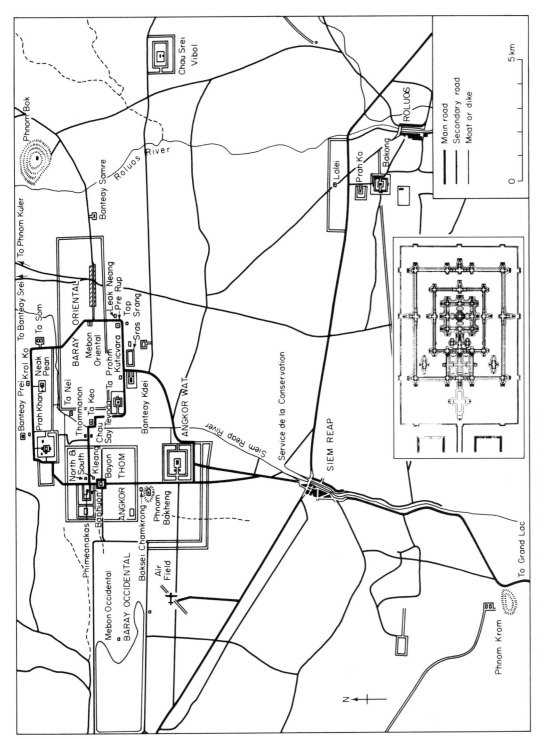

Phnom Bok

Chau Srei Vibol

To Phnom Kuler

Roluos River

Banteay Samre

Phnom Krom

ROLUOS

Bakong

Prah Ko

Lolei

Banteay Prei Krol Ko   To Bantoay Srei

Ta Som

Neak Pean

Prah Khan

BARAY ORIENTAL

Mebon Oriental

Leak Neang

Pre Rup

Top

Sras Srang

Ta Nei

Ta Prohm

Kuticvara

Thommanon

Ta Keo

Ta Say Tevoda

Chau

Banteay Kdei

ANGKOR WAT

Service de la Conservation

Siem Reap River

SIEM REAP

To Grand Lac

Bophon

North & South Kleang

Bayon

ANGKOR THOM

Phimeanokas

Phnom Bakheng

Baksei Chamkrong

Air Field

Mebon Occidental

BARAY OCCIDENTAL

N

Main road
Secondary road
Moat or dike

0   5 km

1.4.   Angkor: The general layout and ground plan (after Coedes). The inset, bottom centre, shows the ground plan of Angkor Wat.

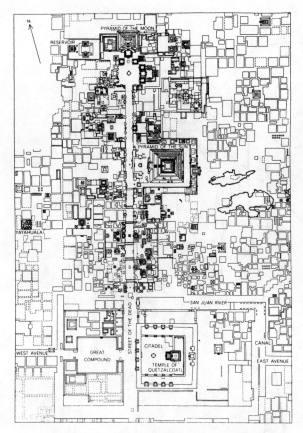

1.5.   Teotihuacan: the central area of the city (after Hardoy). The formalism of its plan, the orientation of its axes and the monumentalism of its principal streets. There is no scale on the original from which this was derived but the north-south extent is some 3,000 metres. The city's population is estimated to have been between 50,000 and 100,000.

map of the city from air photographs, comments that 'with some exceptions, buildings in Teotihuacan are oriented to the north–south axis which gives the plan of the city on orderly appearance even in areas of great crowding' (Millon, 1972, 137–8). The main axis, the Street of the Dead, was the main processional way; it extended from the Pyramid of the Moon at the far north beyond the citadel at the main intersection with a length of over 6000 metres. It connected the principal religious monuments. Millon concludes that Teotihuacan stands for the present as the most highly urbanized centre of its time in the New World. Far removed from Ur and Mohenjo-daro and from Angkor in both time and space, the formalism of its plan, the orientation of its axes and the monumentalism of its principal street are still in accord with those forces which imperatively gave shape to the earliest towns.

7   Conclusion

This chapter has reviewed notions on the origins of urbanism, on the regions involved and on the forms developed. Although it would be too simple to ascribe the whole process of the emergence of cities as directly related to the process of synoecism activated in relation to a shrine or temple, nevertheless magic or religion was clearly a major element in the transformation of kin-related small-scale communities into place-related populations in occupationally specialized cities. Other agglomerative processes, be they brought about by the consequence of an intensively irrigated agriculture, the need for defence or the requirements of central places of commerce and trade, most certainly played a part. It is perhaps paradoxical that the forces of agglomeration brought into play by the magnetic attraction of religion and creating on earth the patterns of reality beyond the apparent realness of the present, should have brought into play also those forces, which, deriving from the break-up of those egalitarian, kin-based, ascriptive, small-scale communities, were eventually to be so destructive of traditional and inherited beliefs. It may be significant that in the Old Testament the city was seen not as the work of God, who had created a garden, but the work of man, and a marked man at that – 'Cain went out from the presence of the Lord and dwelt in the land of Nod on the East of Eden . . . and he built a city (Genesis, 4, 16–17).

Further reading

By far the most erudite discussion of the problem of urban origins by a geographer is:
WHEATLEY, P. 1971: *The Pivot of the Four Quarters*. Edinburgh. It is not, however, an easy book from which to obtain a rapid outline and the same author's short essay:
WHEATLEY, P. 1967: Proleptic observations on the origins of urbanism. In STEEL, R.W. and LAWTON, R. (eds): *Liverpool Essays in Geography*. Liverpool,
is also useful. Wheatley is a protagonist of the religious basis to urban origins and writes in a style which can be called either scholarly or pretentious.
Standard works by non-geographers are:
ADAMS, R.M. 1966: *The Evolution of Urban Society*. Chicago.
BRAIDWOOD, R.J. and WILLEY, G.R. (eds.) 1962: *Courses Towards Urban Life. Archaeological Considerations of some Cultural Alternates*. Edinburgh.
KRAELING, C.H. and ADAMS, R.M. 1960: *City Invincible: Urbanization and Cultural Development in the Ancient Near East*. Chicago.
WHITEHOUSE, R. 1977: *The First Cities*. Oxford.
WOOLLEY, L. 1963: The urbanization of society. Part Two, Chap. 11 in HAWKES, J. and WOOLLEY, L. (eds.): *History of Mankind Vol. 1, Prehistory and the Beginnings of Civilization*. London.

A useful compendium of material, although it is somewhat unsorted and very variable in quality, is contained in:

UCKO, P.J., TRINGHAM, R. and DIMBLEBY, G.W. (eds.) 1972: *Man, Settlement and Urbanism*. London.

Briefer considerations are given in:

LAMPARD, E.E. 1965: Historical aspects of urbanization. In HAUSER, P.M. and SCHNORE, L.R. (eds.): *The Study of Urbanization*. New York, 519–44.

SJOBERG, G. 1960: *The Pre-industrial City*. New York, 25–79.

SJOBERG, G. 1966: The origin and evolution of cities. In FLANAGAN, D. *et al* (eds.): *Cities*. New York.

The best source for a Marxist interpretation is:

HARVEY, D. 1973: *Social Justice and the City*. London, especially 216–40.

The significance of markets and trade is dealt with in:

POLANYI, K. *et al.* (eds.) 1957: *Trade and Market in the Early Empires*. New York,
and
JACOBS, J. 1969: *Economy of Cities*. New York.

The various nuclear areas can be considered in relation to the specific sources cited in the references, the extensive bibliography in Wheatley's *Pivot of the Four Quarters* and in the appropriate volumes of the *Cambridge Ancient History*.

2
The Diffusion of Urbanism

1 Introduction: The meaning of diffusion

In the general consideration of urban origins in chapter 1 the view that there was a single point of innovation, of the creation of the city, from which subsequent diffusion took place was considered and rejected. It was argued that 'the city', bringing major changes in social organization and economic structure as an integral part of its appearance, could not be spread as an abstract idea to be recreated in physical terms in new lands. It is possible that the 'idea' could make an impact, and there are examples of non-urban peoples building towns under the direct influence of urbanized intruders. But this invokes two conditions. The first is that those basic metamorphoses essential to the successful establishment of urbanism were already in train. The second is that diffusion can be accepted, but only where the operative process was that of actual physical transfer through conquest or colonization. That is, any form of what some geographers have called contagious diffusion is rejected; urbanism does not spread amongst peoples in the same way as diseases or abstract ideas. But a form of relocational diffusion is acceptable. Indeed, by its very nature the city could be of critical significance in the effective occupation of new territories by already urbanized populations. 'Occupation' in this sense can include both conquest and colonization, since although there are differences the two can easily be associated without any great distortion.

The effectiveness of the building of towns in new territories lay in the fact that the town's defensive nature could be easily transformed into an offensive one; from being a walled retreat into which a threatened people could retire it could become an advanced outpost from which an attacking group could push forward. It has already been suggested that organized warfare, involving the permanent acquisition of new territory as opposed to tribal raiding or folk migration, might well have started with the city and the need for the expropriating group to continue a process of aggrandizement and acquisition. A systematization of the flow of wealth (surplus value) from the new territories became essential in these circumstances and it was most effectively accomplished through the market place. Trade could be focused compulsorily upon the town which in this way exerted economic control over the whole life of the territory. Finally the introduction of a new religion and the enforcement of a new faith not only provided a means for making conquest and colonization legitimate but induced culture change, so that invaded territories were transformed from being alien acquisitions to being extensions of the homeland. It is not surprising that the European conqueror and colonist of so many lands is caricatured as having a sword in one hand and a bible in the other, for these were the means of making occupation effective and permanent. Following the army and the church came the trader and the merchant. The physical manifestations of these three elements found their common and often adjacent locations in the city, for castle, church and market place were universal urban features. There is much that is common to all times and in all places in the process that has been outlined, whether one considers the extension of the Greek city state, the spread of the Roman town, the occupation of New Spain by the conquistadores or the spread of settlement in North America. The Greek acropolis, agora and temple are functionally the same as the fort, trading post and church of the typical Hollywood set of settlement on the American frontier.

The next sections analyse three of these episodes of the physical extension of the urban realm as the city is spread from the areas of nuclear urbanism to become a world-wide phenomenon. The first of these is the extension of the city in Classical times within and beyond the Mediterranean basin, the second considers the role of the city in the assimilation of the medieval marchlands of Europe and the third reviews the moving frontier of urbanization in North America as the lands of that new world were settled. In this study some attempt will be made to examine the changes, and especially the consistencies, in physical form which were associated with, and indeed formed a part of, the process of diffusion.

2 The Greek polis and the Mediterranean

(i) Origins and character of the Greek city

The emergence of the Greek city is in many ways parallel to the appearance of the first cities in the areas of nuclear urbanism. The word already introduced to epitomize the process – synoecism (p. 8) – is the Greek word precisely used to describe the process by which a central organizing location grew out of the needs of a dispersed rural population. Before going further it is as well to clarify the meaning of the word 'polis', for it did not in any sense refer to a nucleated urban settlement. After the post-Mycenaean Dark Ages the characteristic organization of settlement in the classical Greek world was that of a mosaic of small, rural communities. A number of these constituted the larger territorial community which was the polis, it was neither city nor state in the modern meaning of these words, although city-state is the conventional translation. 'Sometimes, the territory and the town have different names. Thus, Attica is the territory occupied by the Athenian people; it comprised Athens – the "polis" in the narrower sense – the Piraeus, and many villages; but the people collectively were Athenians, not Attics, and a citizen was an Athenian in whatever part of Attica he might live' (Kitto, 1962, 71). Within the polis, therefore, a central city might arise, but this was not a universal process. Finley presents three types of arrangement. The first was the walled nucleated settlement, but the second was almost exclusively rural – 'the Spartans always resided in villages (or in barracks . . .), and then there was the third "type" in which the population was divided between an urban sector and the countryside' (Finley, 1963, 22). N.J.G. Pounds summarizes this whole situation in writing,

> The transition from village to polis did not turn the villagers into townsfolk; they remained farmers, and the polis probably was as agricultural in function as the aggregate of the villages had been. Although the polis may in time have acquired conspicuous public buildings, they must have remained, in terms of economic function, merely large villages, whose inhabitants had . . . a longer journey to their fields than they would have had from their earlier and more scattered settlements. (Pounds, 1969, 143)

For the purpose of the present study the exact nature of the polis, although relevant, is of secondary interest. What matters is the nature of the central settlement. Most explanations are fairly standard. Kitto can be quoted. 'In a period so unsettled the inhabitants of any valley or island might at a moment's notice be compelled to fight for their fields. Therefore a local strong-point was necessary, normally a defensive hill-top somewhere in the plain. This, the "acropolis" ("high-town"), would be fortified, and here would be the residence of the king. It would also be the natural place of assembly, and the religious centre. This is the beginning of the town' (Kitto, 1962, 68). Continued growth and extension is then introduced by Kitto with reference to economic development and specialization. 'We saw that the economic system implied by Hesiod and Homer was a closed household economy . . . as things became more stable a rather more specialized economy became

possible: more goods were produced for sale. Hence the growth of a market' (Kitto, 1962, 68). This is again the process of synoecism. It is worth noting, however, that the section quoted from Kitto above includes the phrase 'the religious centre', and at a later point in his discussion of the polis he writes more explicitly –

> Religion too was bound up with the polis. . . . So that in spite of the panhellenic Olympian system, and in spite of the philosophic spirit which made merely tribal gods impossible for the Greek, there is a sense in which it is true to say that the polis is an independent religious, as well as a political unit. The tragic poets at least could make use of the old belief that the gods desert a city which is about to be captured. The gods are the unseen partners in the city's welfare. (Kitto, 1962, 75-6).

Here, again, is the basic religious theme in the process which brings about the development of a common central point, the temple or shrine, which is the precipitator of agglomeration. Two further points can be noted. The proposal by Fustel de Coulanges, as early as 1864, that cities arose out of the designation of territory as sanctuaries and that citizenship was based on the sharing of adherence to a common god, was made in relation to the cities of Greece and Rome (Fustel de Coulanges, 1864). The second point is that the union of the various 'communities' of Attica, from which the city of Athens was derived, was celebrated by a religious feast to the goddess Synoecia. Even if the goddess were invented for this special occasion that invention symbolizes the solemn and religious nature of the process of unification.

The city of ancient Greece was, as in the nuclear areas, based upon religion, defence and commerce and administration acting as agglomerating forces. These were in turn clearly represented as the dominant physical features in the city. The temple appropriately represents the peak of Greek architectural achievement. It was, certainly at first, located on the acropolis, which was the defensive strong-point, so that religious aura and military control were synthesized into one. Below them was the third element, the agora, the market place but much more than that the place of assembly, the centre for the conduct of public affairs. This was at first a simple piece of open ground but eventually was transformed by the collection of buildings related to the transactions of commerce and the operation of civil government. Eventually, too, altars and temples were attracted to the agora although they did not there equal in venerability those of the acropolis. The city grew about these generative elements, so that the residential areas accumulated slowly about the central buildings. In contrast to the effort and investment which went into the monumental and public structures the residential areas were cramped, unplanned, ill-drained and unhealthy. 'The houses in which the growing population lived were mostly huddled together in irregular groups, between which the narrow streets insinuated themselves. The main streets, leading in from the gates, converged erratically upon the agora. Insofar as the plan of the city had any recognizable structure, this was provided by the agora and the streets radiating from it. . . . On this loose framework the city arranged itself informally; there was little deliberate or far-sighted planning in the old cities' (Wycherley, 1962, 9).

Lastly, there was the completion of the defensive system by circuit walls. Initially the acropolis was the sole strong-point and walls did not become common until the sixth and fifth centuries BC. They were then constructed around the existing settlements and had no formal shape, being adapted to the physical geography of the site on the one hand and the shape of the settlement on the other.

All these conditions of the older Greek cities are admirably illustrated by Athens itself (Figure 2.1). The city grew on a plateau surface, some 60 metres above sea level, but with a series of rocky hills arising from it. Of these the acropolis became the predominant. 'Ils ont préféré l'Acropole plus centrale et parce qu'un prestige religieux, attesté par le culte de tres anciennes divinités, renforçait la sécurité promise par l'isolement et la roideur des pentes' (Lavedan and Hugueney, 1966, 129). The acropolis gathered its distinctive collection of buildings, which have become part of the general human heritage, over a long period of time, the main period of reconstruction being in the second half of the fifth century after the Persian destruction of the city. The agora developed at the northern foot of the acropolis and was linked to it by the winding Panathenaic Way. Again, the agora attracted a series of buildings erected over a long period, until its destruction at the end of the third century AD. As far as it can be reconstructed the general plan of growth about this monumental and ceremonial centre was radial concentric, but only in the loosest and least precise interpretation of that term. Roads tended either

to follow the contours and hence become roughly concentric, or to link the centre with the gates in the circuit wall, and become radial. A succession of defensive enceintes was built, but the one usually represented is that of Themistocles included on Figure 2.1. It is an irregular enclosure with unevenly spaced gates, in keeping with the general pattern of early Greek cities already noted. Finally, all the evidence indicates that the nature of the residential areas was in marked contrast to the public buildings. 'Demosthenes said of the Athenians that "in private life they were severe and simple". The evidence abundantly confirms this. The Pseudo-Dicaearchus described Athens itself as . . . "ill supplied with water. The streets are nothing but miserable old lanes, the houses mean". Excavations in the industrial quarter of classical Athens, to the west of the acropolis, revealed the basic simplicity, even the primitive quality of life even in Athens' (Pounds, 1969, 139).

This section has so far described the origins and character of the city in the poleis of the Greek 'homeland'. It was these which were 'diffused' through Greek colonization in the Aegean, the Black Sea and the Mediterranean. In this process the nature of the city plan itself was changed, for within relocational diffusion there is no necessity for the diffused item to remain absolutely constant in character, indeed change and adaptation are themselves critical parts of the process.

(ii) The areas of Greek colonization

The words 'colony' and 'colonization' are conventionally used to describe the poleis or settlements established during the extension of the Greek world from its Aegean homeland both to east and west. But the words demand qualification. Finley writes, 'The Greek word we . . . translate as "colony" is *apoika*, which connoted "emigration" ' (Finley, 1963, 26–7), while Kitto presents a slightly different version, 'The Greek *apoika* means, literally "an away-home" ' (Kitto, 1962, 47). Both authors are making the same point, that these new foundations were not dependent colonies, in the later European use of the word, founded primarily to provide raw materials for processing and consumption in the homeland, and maintained in a subject condition. They were not only new but independent foundations having no tributary relation to the mother city.

The basic reasons for the colonizing movement, or migratory drive, are not easy to identify, nor are they especially relevant in the context of this analysis. It is appropriate to adopt the simplest of explanations; that population growth in agricultural communities established in a terrain where cultivable land was necessarily limited in extent, brought about a pressure of people upon land which was most easily solved by emigration. Although the new cities were not dependencies of the mother city, nevertheless the emigration movement was not haphazard. The Oracles were consulted for propitious locations, indeed the Delphic Oracle can be

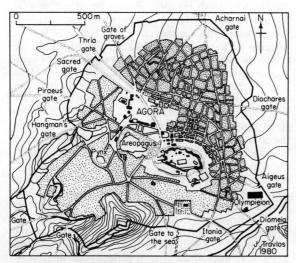

2.1.   Athens in the fifth century (after Wycherley). Although some streets are on known lines, most are restored on probable lines.

regarded as an assembler of information, a generator of awareness space through indirect contact! Individual poleis organized and equipped expeditions to establish the new settlements and also, poleis combined with each other in these projects. But arising as it did from a demand on limited land the movement was primarily directed to providing such cultivable land. In consequence, essentially agricultural settlements were set up, not trading posts or markets. Inevitably, as it was found that new crops could be grown and that novel materials were available, and also that the surrounding barbarians could supply exotic products, so trade grew and the market function developed. It would be wrong to imply, therefore, that commercial activity played no part, but it was a later and secondary aspect of emigration.

This colonizing or migratory movement seems to have taken place in two waves (Finley, 1963, 26–7). The first of these began about 750 BC and was widely shared by the poleis. In general it was a westward-directed movement which resulted in the establishment of settlements on the coasts of the Ionian Sea and in Magna Graecia (Sicily and southern Italy). Towards the end of the seventh century this extended to southern France and Libya and to Spain. Emporium, in modern Catalonia, is an example of a settlement founded in the mid sixth century, primarily as a trading post. The second wave was largely derived from the two cities of Megara and Miletus. It spread east to southern Thrace and the Sea of Marmora and by 650 BC reached the Black Sea and encircled it with Greek colonies. Two maps (Figures 2.2 and 2.3) are reproduced which demonstrate the areas involved. From the viewpoint of the issues being considered in this chapter this migratory or colonizing process is critical because it transfers the city from its Greek source in the Aegean to the coastal areas of the Mediterranean and the Black Sea. The areas marked on Figure 2.3 are the areas of a newly urbanized world whose subsequent extension is depicted in Figure 2.2. But before this further diffusion is

considered the nature of the element being diffused needs some further consideration.

(iii) The physical character of the colonial cities

It is useful to develop a review of the physical characteristics of the Greek colonial cities by a consideration of the plan of Miletus. It was not in a strict sense a 'colony', but it is the plan which is most frequently reproduced in texts on town planning (von Gerkan, 1924). Miletus was sacked and destroyed by the Persians in 494 BC and rebuilt during the period following on liberation, usually given as sometime after 479 BC. The reconstruction of the plan by von Gerkan (1924) is reproduced as Figure 2.4. From an analysis of this map a number of features can be derived which to some extent were general to all the cities.

1   It is evident that the whole city was constructed in relation to a coherent and controlling plan. It was not the result of gradual and unorganized extension but was conceived as one complete whole. This can be maintained in spite of the differences that exist between the northern and southern parts.

2   The dominant feature of this coherent plan was the rigid grid system according to which the city was laid out. The word 'rigid' in this sense means the complete dominance of rectangularity. In detail it was certainly not a true grid.

    (a) The perpendicular or longitudinal axes were dominant forming a series of strips, which were then cut into elongated blocks by the laterals.

    (b) There were two separate grid systems, one to the north and one to the south, and these differed from each other in detail.

3   Although in the south two of the streets crossing at right-angles seem to be a little wider and were thus given some greater emphasis, nevertheless there was no dominant central intersection. The grid was an even one without internal emphasis on particular streets; no orthogonal axes can be identified.

4   The public buildings and the main squares were set within this grid system occupying distinct blocks, so that the streets ran at tangents to them rather than focused upon them or radiated from them. Public buildings occupied a distinctive area at the conjunction of the northern and southern components.

5   The equal division of the residential areas meant that all the houses were alike, at least in their external dimensions. The gridding gave little opportunity for the development of any great variation in size or physical character of individual houses.

6   The city was orientated generally, though not precisely, along a north–south axis. Most interpretations of this alignment tend to dismiss any religious significance and argue that it was much more relevantly a product of the physical environment. Classical writers, such as Hippocrates, discussed the preferred orientation of cities and argued for a scheme which shut out the cold north winds and gained maximum benefit from facing the sun,

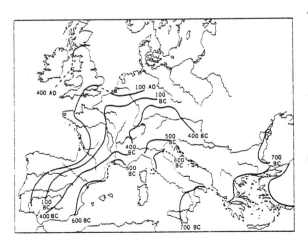

2.2.   The urbanization of the Classical World: the diffusion of the polis (after Pounds).

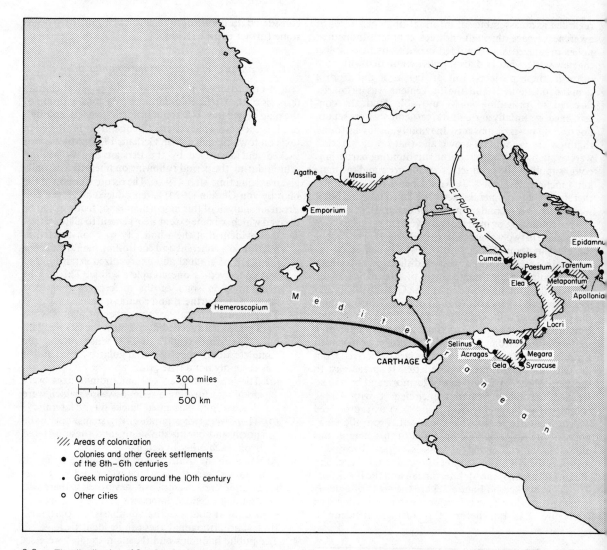

2.3.   The distribution of Greek colonization (after Cook).

especially the low-angled winter sun.

7   The grid was laid out regardless of site conditions. The site of Miletus is a very irregular promontory which culminates in two hills separated by the deeply penetrating inlet which forms the Gate of Lions. But although of necessity the total layout made concessions to the shape of the peninsula, the actual grid was superimposed without any regard for the uneven relief. To an extent this was only possible because of the dominance of pack animals as a means of transport rather than wheeled vehicles, so that the grading of the slope of streets was of little matter.

8   There was no acropolis. The defensive, elevated strong-point was left out of these planned schemes and protection ensured by site and circuit walls. The consequence was to put further emphasis on the agora, where the temples were now located.

9   The later defensive wall which was constructed around the city was irregular in shape. Rectangularity of the total city area, as against that of internal structure, was neither sought nor achieved.

Two other examples can be briefly considered, largely to reinforce the generalizations which have been presented, but also to develop two of them.

Olynthos (Figure 2.5a and b), located in Macedonia, was another city which was reconstructed after Persian destruction in the year 479 BC. It was eventually destroyed by Philip of Macedon in 348. After the Persian sack, the old city on a southern hill was abandoned and a new town was built on a more extensive plateau surface to the north (Figure 2.5a). Most of the features derived from the consideration of Miletus can be identified, including a much more direct north–south orientation. But Olynthos is usually quoted because of the careful

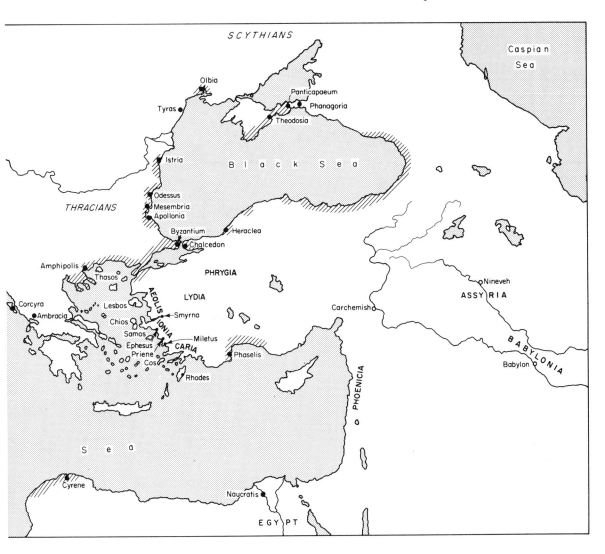

excavation of the residential areas for within them the uniformity that is characteristic has been taken to indicate 'an apparently well established house-type' (Wycherley, 1962, 187) (Figure 2.5b). Each block was subdivided into ten houses. These were all very similar, with the main entrance into a courtyard which faced south and the north side being a blank wall presumably presented to the cold winds from that direction. But there was variation in the disposition of internal space within the house, allowing for some individual and personal manipulation.

The second example, Priene (Figure 2.6), had been first built in the valley of the River Meander but about the middle of the fourth century its inhabitants decided to move it to a more protected site on the southern slopes overlooking the valley (Figure 2.6). Again the same features can be identified as were present in Miletus and

Olynthos. But the slope was extremely steep, falling from a maximum altitude of 380 metres down to 25 metres within the walled area. The actual town was built on the gentler slopes but even there the total altitudinal range was some 100 metres. In this case the only solution to such a gradient involved in the construction of a grid was to convert the streets lying across the slopes into flights of steps. Perhaps it is also useful to add that whereas the population of Priene is estimated to have been some 4000, that of Miletus was nearer 100,000. Regardless of size, the basic planning principles remained the same.

At this point in the consideration of the diffusion of town plan it is not the transference from the Greek homeland to the colonial territories that is at issue. That is self-evident, and by it the city itself, and the grid plan, is shifted along the southern shores of Europe and becomes part of the settlement pattern of the continent. What is at

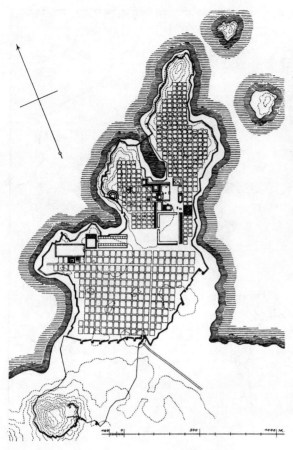

2.4.   Miletus (after von Gerkan).

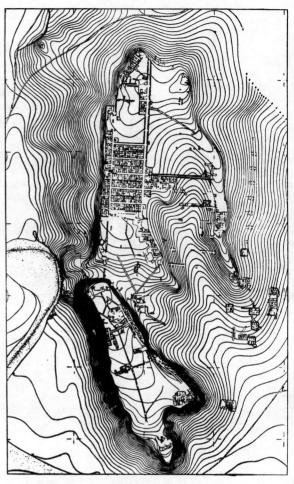

2.5.   Olynthos (a) A general plan of the city
(b) Detail of a small section of the city.

issue is how did the grid plan arise. Three answers have
been suggested (Castagnoli, 1971).

1   It was derived from the Near East, thus having a
    direct link with the areas of nuclear urbanism and
    establishing a diffusion chain which reaches from
    Mesopotamia and Egypt, through the Greek world to
    southern Europe. Thence by the Romans the grid was
    to be taken to the western and northern fringes of
    that continent.
2   The grid layout was the invention of Hippodamus of
    Miletus who is, in consequence, regarded as the
    father of town planning. Miletus was a model for the
    other cities and his great attested work is the building
    of the Piraeus.
3   It is such a basic and simple way of ordering space
    that it was independently and spontaneously
    generated within the Greek world and then ascribed
    to Hippodamus, in the characteristic way in which
    myths arise through the linking of features or events
    needing 'explanation' with distinctive characters.

These are not independent interpretations. It can be suggested that (1) and (2) should be combined, so that the
role of Hippodamus was to synthesize and reinterpret

the tradition of city building from the orient in which the
Greeks had a clear interest and with which they were in
direct contact. But perhaps the critical evidence in
relation to (2) is whether it is possible to identify regularly
gridded Greek cities before the fifth century, that is
before the time of Hippodamus. Thus Olbia, a colony of
Miletus on the Black Sea, and Selinus in Sicily are quoted
as sixth century BC grid-plan towns, although the
evidence in the case of Selinus is complex and controversial. Perhaps the conclusion of Castagnoli, first
written in 1956, is the most pertinent,

The orthogonal grid layout is characteristic of the plan
invented by Hippodamus. However, many cities which
followed this scheme were laid out prior to his time,
and it is not uncommon to speak of 'Hippodamean'
cities that antedate Hippodamus. According to Nissen
and von Gerkan, this type of plan gained widespread
use during the diffusion of the colonies in the seventh

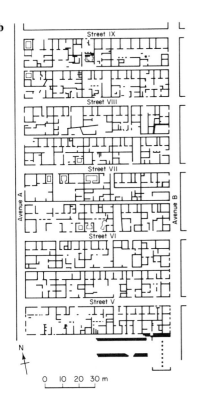

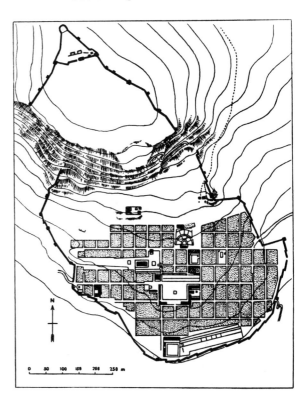

2.6. Priene (after von Gerkan)

and sixth centuries BC. Hippodamus then might be considered a symbol or at best an urbanist who based his fame on theorizing a pre-existing system . . . speaking with caution, because the evidence is certainly incomplete, we could say that Hippodamus – who perhaps was born at the beginning of the fifth century and perhaps worked on the plan for Miletus, but who certainly was an established urban designer by the middle of the fifth century – should not be associated with the simple orthogonal system of ancient origins but with that which has developed into the uniform and regular grid pattern known to exist in the fifth century. (Castagnoli, 1971, 71)

Commenting again in 1970 Castagnoli added, 'Examples of Hippodamean cities like Metaponto, that certainly preceded Hippodamus, lead us to conclude with even more assurance that Hippodamus was not the creator of this type of city planning; his name is linked with it only through his studies of the political organization and the social system, and especially through his planning of Piraeus' (Castagnoli, 1971, 129).

If now the origins of this grid scheme are sought prior to the time of Hippodamus then one is taken back further towards the areas of nuclear urbanism. Indeed Castagnoli writes of the acropolis of Zernaki Tepe in Urartu

as having 'many elements of Hippodamean planning'. This extends the line back in time to the eighth century BC and in space to Anatolia. In terms of diffusion, therefore, the line becomes tenuously established by which a distinctive form of settlement was derived from the eastern margins of Europe and diffused throughout its length by the extension of the Greek world and particularly by its Hellenistic successor. During the Hellenistic period the process of extension was continued and the conquests of Alexander spread the city in its Greek form back towards the areas of origin. Alexandria (Figure 2.7a) was established in 331 BC on a strip of land between the sea and Lake Maroeotis. It was dominated by a major longitudinal axis running approximately east–west. Most of the detail has been lost but certainly it was built on a regular grid plan, but dominated by a series of public buildings, parks and gardens which gave it distinction in the Greek world. Roland Martin sees in Alexandria the confluence of the restrained geometric tradition of the Greek legacy with the monumentalism of the orient and, indeed, of Egypt (Martin, 1956, 118).

The more restrained tradition can be seen in the Seleucid foundation of Dura-Europos, built at the end of the fourth century BC to defend the upper Euphrates (Figure 2.7b). The site was a level plateau on which the regular grid of twelve north–south and nine east–west

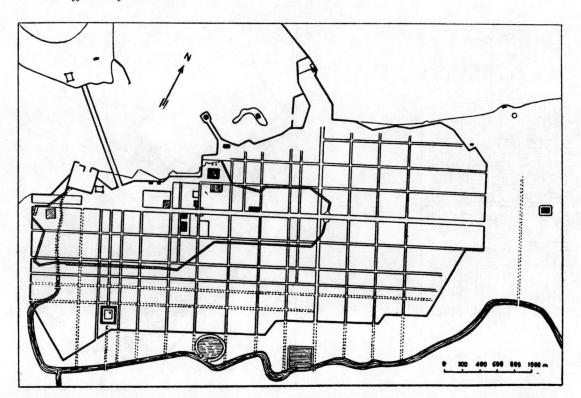

2.7.   (a) Alexandria (after Mahmoud Bey). Alexander
decided on the city's establishment in 331, the
architect employed being Deinocrates of Rhodes. It
was not until later under Ptolemy II (285–246 BC) that it
became a major city. The ancient plan is completely
covered by the modern city and the plan indicated here
is a nineteenth-century reconstruction which has by no
means obtained general acceptance. Lake Mareoetis
lies to the south. (b) Dura Europos. The river Euphrates
lies to the north. There was only one gate, that on the
western side. There is no modern city so that an
accurate reconstruction has been possible. See F.E.
Brown, *The excavations at Dura Europos, Ninth
Season*. New Haven, 1944.

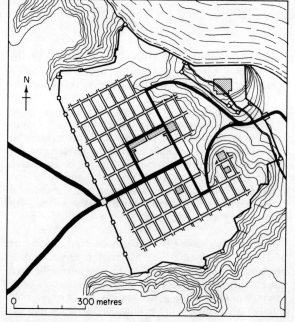

streets was developed. A large central area was reserved for the agora. The southern side of the agora coincided with the major axial line and the main buildings were developed along the north side. Kriesis writes of this period,

> To support their policy, Alexander the Great and his successors founded on geopolitically important sites and built up as strategic strongholds, a whole network of towns and cities, which evolved into centres spreading Greek culture and civilization, over the greatest part of the then known world. It was one of the greatest 'colonial' town planning and building actions which was ever accomplished in history;

and he quotes F.E. Brown writing on the excavations at Dura,

> The Dura plan on this evidence falls into place as an exemplar of a uniform and standardized Seleucid planning system which employed the same unit and the same proportions in varying simple multiples as the circumstances required. The development of such a system was the natural outcome of what was in the early Hellenistic period very literally a mass production of cities. (Kriesis, 1965, 126)

But if the Hellenistic period saw the retransmission of the city to the Near East and the East on a mass-production basis, it was the power of the Roman Empire which carried it to the western fringes of the Old World and it is to a brief consideration of this later movement that attention must now be directed.

(iv) The Roman inheritances

Rome itself arose out of the same process of synoecism that has been already analysed and demonstrated. The unification of the peoples occupying the seven traditional hills was celebrated in the Feast of the Septimontum (Bloch, 1960). More germane to the present discussion is the spread within the Roman empire of a distinctive group of urban forms. The word 'inheritance' has been consciously used to introduce this section since there is little doubt that the greater part of the inspiration behind Roman town planning was derived from Greek sources. But it is not an area without controversy and in that controversy the critical element is the role played by the Etruscans (Bloch, 1958). Contrary to the view that has so far been put forward it is possible to argue that the Etruscans, rather than deriving their culture from the indigenous Iron Age Villanovan base, were an immigrant population from Asia Minor who brought with them the grid plan from that source, as exemplified by Marzobotto (Castagnoli, 1971, 51–4) (near Bologna) and Capua (Castagnoli, 1971, 46–51), and that it was from Etruscan sources that the Greek gridded city is to be derived. These views have, however, comparatively little support and it is more logical to look upon the two examples quoted as representing inspiration from Greek sources, and indicating that Etruscan cities are Greek

derivations, and not the other way about. But from whatever source the Romans derived the grid, they made many modifications to the Hippodamean pattern and it is the context of these changes that Etruscan contributions can be possibly identified.

(a) Orthogonality. The plans derived from Hippodamean principles were characterized by a regular division of city space by a series of streets following a north–south line creating strips, subdivided by a series of streets lying east to west. This was changed in many of the Roman city plans to a dominance of a central orthogonal axis consisting of one major north to south line (cardo) crossed by one major east to west line (decumanus). The Roman layout was then derived from a block pattern about this axis, rather than from the elongated strips of the Greek city. The explanation of this change can be found in Etruscan influences. At this point, perhaps, it is necessary to note that the central axis had a much more ancient lineage for the cross within the circle was the Egyptian hieroglyph for a city. Nevertheless, Castagnoli, who reacts strongly against any notion of religious influences in the layout of classical cities and interprets Etruscan planned towns as derived from Greek sources, is prepared to accept that 'the only characteristic of Etruscan city planning that can be documented now given our present inadequate knowledge, is the axial system' (Castagnoli, 1971, 74). Etruscan ritual is well known from Roman authors and Roman cities are written of as founded '*etrusco ritu*'. 'Etruscan urbanism', writes Lavedan and Hugueney, 'as all ancient urbanism, rests on religion' (Lavedan and Hugueney, 1966, 288). They proceed to present the argument already considered (p. 13–14), that for success and prosperity the city must be set in line with the will of the gods by ceremonies of inauguration and consecration. This is done in the sacred area, the Templum, which is sometimes mistakenly interpreted as including the whole city. The sacred rites included establishing the outer limits of the city, which most commentators accept, and then defining the internal divisions, which all commentators do not accept. But the interpretation of the internal structure would proceed, it is postulated by those who take the latter view, by the basic division set by the sun, first into northern and southern sections and then into eastern and western by its rising and setting. The key instrument may have been the 'groma' by which the east–west line was established by sunrise on the day of inauguration. The heavens were seen as divided into four by the two axes which, transferred onto the earth's surface, became the cardo and decumanus. 'La ville est ainsi tracé a l' image du monde'. There, then, it is contested is the stress laid in Roman plans upon the orthogonal axis. Lavedan and Hugueney proceed to maintain that it was probably derived from the Near East as a result of Etruscan contacts (Lavedan and Hugueney, 1966, 297).

(b) Rectangularity. By no means all outlines of Roman cities were regular but, even so, a further major contrast with Greek cities was the substitution of a clearly planned rectangular defensive system for the irregular walls

adapted to site and settlement which Greek cities displayed. Lavedan and Hugueney again seem to derive this from the Etruscans. The Near Eastern source of urbanism could suggest a circular basis – the cross within a circle – but there is no evidence at all for radial concentric schemes. Lavedan and Hugueney further suggest that the setting down of the basic axis might well have led to the adoption of the rectangle as the simplest surrounding definition. It is possible, however, to avoid invoking such an explanation by associating rectangularity with the standard Roman process of centuriation, of the regular division of rural land. Castagnoli writes, 'it was in the Roman colonies from the fourth century on that axial symmetry found its most rigorous application, extending even to the perimeter of the quadrangular or square city, and it was here that it was most extensively used. Such a rich production of cities and widespread use of agrarian surveying was quite naturally the object of much theorizing by scholars of the late Republic. Yet the Roman urban planner was little moved by celestial speculation and adopted the principles of axial symmetry because they corresponded to Roman taste' (Castagnoli, 1971, 121). And again in 1971 he argued, 'The conception of the Italic and Etruscan city as being of sacred origin still enjoys widespread respect; Marzobotto, Roma quadrata and centuriation, are considered examples' (Castagnoli, 1971, 136). Roma quadrata refers to the disputed view that an axial plan characterized the early layout of the Palatine Hill. Castagnoli writes, 'I maintain that Roma quadrata is a relatively late invention of the Romans, for they imagined primitive Rome to be similar to the quadripartite cities which they founded from the fourth century on' (Castagnoli, 1971, 136).

But the references to such a vague notion as 'Roman taste' must be suspect, for it seems a poor explicand and one which must itself be derived from an underlying source in the culture. Although, therefore, it must be recorded that there is strong opposition to the derivation of the rectangular Roman city with a dominant axis from an Etruscan source, that appears at least to offer some basis to explain the significant change from the city layout of Hippodamus.

(c) Focality. The orthogonal or axial plan by stressing the central intersection gives particular significance to one point. Although hardly a creative influence it can be argued that this was a symbol of military discipline and imperial power that was crucial in the Roman empire. This can be contrasted with the more even distribution, a democratic situation, implied by the regular unstressed division of the Greek city.

(d) Militarism. The city was an element in the spread and maintenance of Roman power so that town and encampment became closely allied. The result was that the traditional layout of the military fortress (Figure 2.8) had an impact upon the civil settlement. This is seen in the adoption of twin north–south axes, rather than one. The military camp had two main street lines, the *Via principalis* and *Via quintana*, and many cities were built on the same principle.

(e) Variation. It is proper to emphasize the similarity that characterized town plans throughout the Roman empire. Nevertheless, within a general uniformity considerable variety existed, mainly brought about either by increasing the axes, as just noted, or setting the main intersection somewhat off centre.

Most studies of Roman urbanism reproduce lengthy series of plans from most parts of the Roman empire. The following illustrations are intended only as brief exemplification of the general features identified in the preceding paragraphs. A standard example of the perfect axial plan is the castrum of Ostia (Figure 2.9), which has the added advantage of being a very early foundation dated to the last years of the fourth century BC (Calza *et al.*, 1953). Two major axes, cardo and decumanus, dominated the layout and crossed at the geometrical centre of the town dividing it into four equal quadrants. It is assumed that these were subdivided into blocks. There are four gates marking the intersection of the axes with the walls, and both streets and defences are perfectly aligned in relation to the cardinal compass points. The original settlement was small, measuring only some 195 × 125 metres, and it was subsequently destroyed and rebuilt and then recreated as the seaport for Rome by Claudius, so that much of the original castrum has been destroyed by later building.

A further example of this basic orthogonal plan is the city of Florence where the Roman grid can still be traced (Figure 2.10). The date of its foundation as a colony is not known but it is usually ascribed to a period before the end of the first century BC. The plan was again based on a central axis orientated north–south and with four gates, one in each of the walls where cardo and decumanus met

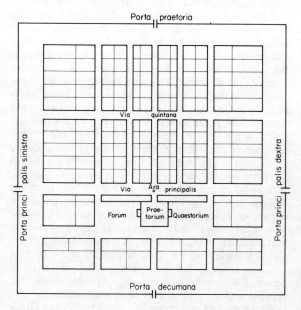

2.8.   The plan of a Roman military camp (after Marquardt).

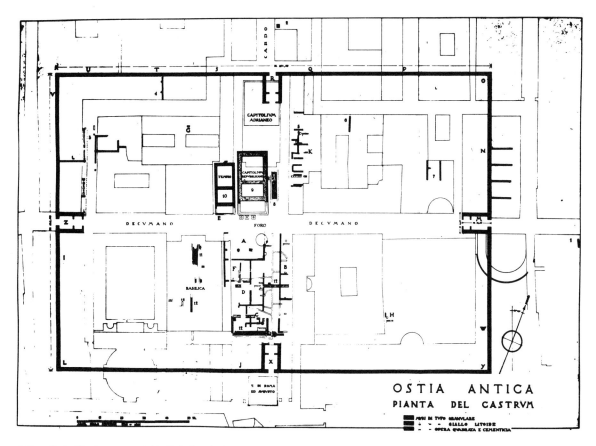

2.9. Ostia. The town was divided into four by two orthogonal axes.

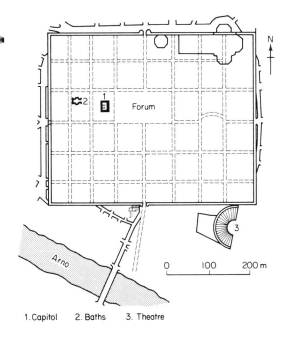

1. Capitol   2. Baths   3. Theatre

2.10. Florence (a) The Roman city: 1 Capitol, 2 Baths, 3 Theatre

(b) The layout of the central area of the city about 1795. The streets which seem to have preserved the Roman street lines are thickened.

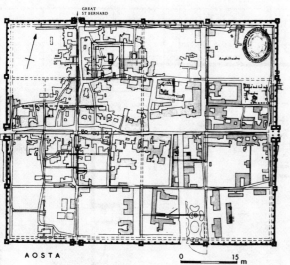

AOSTA

2.11.   Aosta. The Roman street plan can be clearly identified below the modern built-up area.

2.12.   Caerwent. The layout of the Roman town. Forum, town hall and temple at centre; baths opposite; narrow-fronted shops along main street.

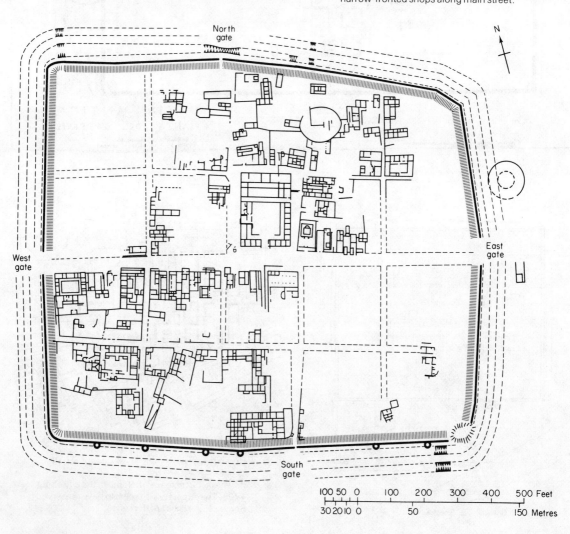

them. The city was subdivided into blocks which were almost, though not perfectly, square, with 60-metre sides.

Two examples of towns can be included which were fashioned after the military encampments and hence have modified forms of the simple orthogonal plan. Aosta (Augusta Praetoria) was a characteristic 'colonia' of the Emperor Augustus founded in 25 BC for veterans leaving the army (Figure 2.11). It had considerable strategic significance controlling the valley of the Dora Baltea. The city is a perfect rectangle measuring 724 × 572 metres. Its alignment is just off a complete accordance with the compass points. The east–west streets are dominated by the decumanus which occupies its typical location at the central point and has the two gates at either end. It is in the north–south direction that variation occurs. There are not one but two dominant street lines, each leading to two gates in the defences. This is a direct resemblance to the *Via principalis* and the *Via quintana* of the military camp and there is evidence that the latter name, *Via quintana*, was in fact used for one of these streets in medieval times. A close parallel can be seen in the only civil settlement established by the Romans on their western military frontier in Wales. This was Caerwent (Venta Silures), the Roman foundation of the central settlement of the Silures tribe, which replaced a hill-fort which lay a mile to the northwest. Again, the main east–west street was dominant and seems to have contained the main shops (Figure 2.12). It led to the major gates. There are two other east–west streets, but four running north to south and these divide the town

into 20 blocks. There is no single dominant north–south street, however, and the north and south gates are at the extremities of different streets, again suggesting the dual emphasis noted in Aosta.

The offsetting of the central axis is particularly well marked in Turin (Augusta Turinorum) founded in 28 BC (Figure 2.13). It is rectangular in shape measuring 669 × 720 metres. Again, it is not orientated directly to the compass points though it can be suggested that its outline was related to the sunrise position at the mid-winter solstice. Seven streets from east to west and eight from north to south divide it up into a regular pattern of blocks. Within this pattern the main axis is emphasized with the streets leading to the principal gates, but the north–south line is clearly offset to the east, again suggesting a parallel with a *Via principalis*.

Finally many of these features can be identified in a settlement on the Rhine frontier, for Cologne derives its name from its Roman function as a colonia - Colonia Agrippinensis (Figure 2.14). The earliest settlement dates back to 50 BC but the planned colonia was laid out in 12 BC. The regular grid of blocks is created by some eleven north–south street lines intersected by seven from east to west, for orientation to the cardinal points is precise. Again, here, the main north–south axis to the gate is offset, although it seems that the forum was located at the geometric centre. The surrounding walls were not rectangular and appear to be adapted either to the site, especially the lines of minor streams, or to the settlement which pre-existed the planned colony. It is significant that one of the major centres of lowland England,

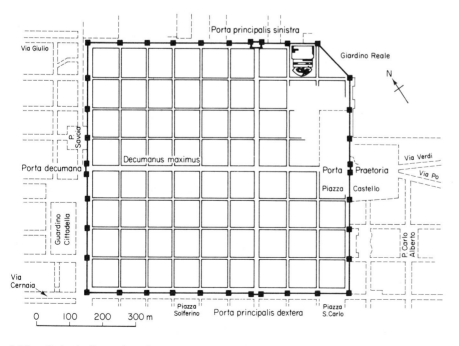

2.13. Turin: the Roman layout.

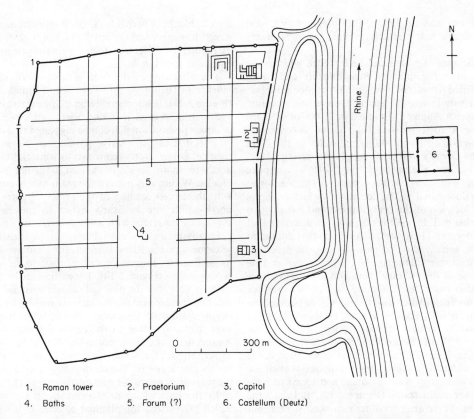

1. Roman tower
2. Praetorium
3. Capitol
4. Baths
5. Forum (?)
6. Castellum (Deutz)

2.14.   Cologne: The Roman 'colonia': 1 Roman tower, 2 Praetorium, 3 Capitol, 4 Baths, 5 Forum, 6 Castellum (Deutz).

Calleva Atrebatum (Silchester), the central settlement of the Atrebates, was walled at a late date when there was already the threat of destruction with the collapse of the imperial system (Boon, 1957). As a result the walls were adapted both to the threat at that time and the settled area and so lack the regularity and rectangularity which were otherwise so ubiquitous (Figure 2.15).

(v)   The Roman city and the Roman empire

Three points can be derived from the material presented in section *(iv)*.

1   The Roman city was inherited from the Greek world.
2   The inheritance, namely the Hippodamean plan, was modified and adapted and in that process it is possible that Etruscan influences played a significant role.
3   Although variations do occur, they were always variations on a basic theme, the grid plan.

Within the Roman Empire, which was itself the creation of a city, the town as a unit of settlement was spread to the frontiers, whether they were western as at Caerwent, northern as at Cologne, or southern into North Africa, as at Timgad or Carthage. Three types of Roman settlement were developed in the occupation of these territories.

1   *The city with full privileges.* This category included the *colonia* where the population was usually of Roman citizenship and the town was chartered. The *colonia* were settlements of discharged veterans, each soldier being given an allotment of land, its size dependent on rank. Still chartered, although of a lower order, was the *municipium* which could either have full Roman rights or the limited Latin rights. The *municipium* can be regarded as an intermediate status before upgrading to *colonia* was achieved (Reynolds, 1966, 70).
2   *Towns of peregrine status.* These were more often than not a 'take over' of the strong-points, the 'oppida' of the native population.
3   *The military forts* or encampments which often generated surrounding settlement.

The process of conquest, based on these elements, relied on the town as the centre of tribal organization, as a military strong-point and as the nodal centre in the imperial system. If reference is again made to Figure 2.3, and if the evidence of Figure 2.16 is added, then it will be seen that by AD 400 only Ireland in the west lay outside the direct impact of an invading urban civilization. By this date the foundations, in some cases in a literal sense, of urban Europe had been laid. London was already a

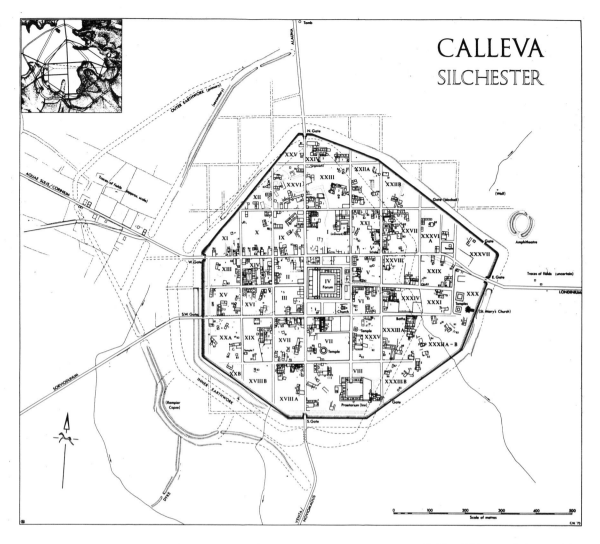

2.15. Silchester: the layout of the Roman town of Calleva (after Boon).

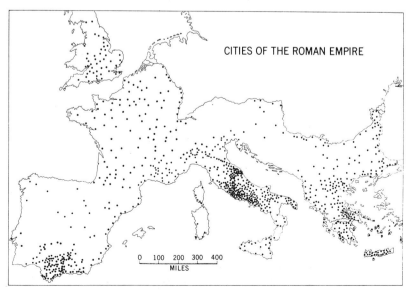

CITIES OF THE ROMAN EMPIRE

2.16. The cities of the Roman Empire circa AD 200 (after Pounds).

great centre of trade, even if Lutetia (Paris) was only an insignificant centre for the unimportant tribe of the Parisii.

3   The medieval marchlands of Europe

(i) Introduction

Van Werveke, writing of the rise of towns in the Middle Ages, sets out an essential theme relative to the extension of the urbanized territories; 'as for that part of Germany beyond the Rhine which had not formed part of the Roman Empire, the town was completely unknown in ancient times' (Van Werveke, 1963, 3). During the Middle Ages the growth of the urban world, which had been halted during the period of folk migrations which created what is usually referred to as the Dark Ages, was once more resumed and carried 'the town' to those parts where the town was previously completely unknown'. But it was a twofold process. The Roman occupation, especially in the border regions, had only been weakly established and was primarily military in character. There were large areas which remained open for what can be called internal colonization, which if it had been started with the break-up of the empire was completed at a much later date as the web of towns and communications was thickened and economic development generally advanced. Both within and without the old imperial bounds there was a process of occupation and colonization within which the town played a dominant role. Ennen has suggested a threefold division of Europe in relation to this process, 'In regard to the continuity of civilization, three different regions of town life can be distinguished in Europe: (1) the north German area, to the east of the Rhine and in Scandinavia, which was not directly influenced by the urban culture of the Mediterranean, (2) the zone which corresponds to northern France and the valleys of the Rhine and Danube, where the remains of the towns of antiquity disappeared to a large degree, but not without leaving some evident traces . . . and (3) the southern regions where Roman urban traditions continued with respect to the possession of land, housing and manner of life' (Ennen, 1956, 397). In relation to the spread of urbanism Ennen's regions (1) and (2) are critical, for the argument runs that the urban concept was reawakened and given a new physical form in the second region and then diffused into the first. This introduces two problems. The first is that of general urban origins in Europe, of how the town arose out of the ruins of the classical world, and the second the way in which it subsequently spread by both internal and external colonization.

(ii) Origins and character

The problem of urban origin in Europe is among the most widely debated of historical problems. This section is intended as a review of the literature, for it will certainly make no original contribution.

The clearest introduction to the whole issue has been offered by J.F. Benton who, with an appropriate warning that a great deal of complexity is concealed in a simple list, set out eigth major theories which have been put forward in relation to European urban origins (Benton, 1968). These are:

(a) Mercantile settlement theory.   Towns grew when merchants involved in long-distance trade began to settle at locations which were of particular significance in relation to major lines of movement. This is perhaps the most influential of all the views, largely because of its association with the name of Henri Pirenne. Writing of the defensive castles of the feudal princes Pirenne asserts,

> But the revival of commerce soon completely altered their character. The first signs of its action are observable in the course of the second half of the tenth century. The wandering life of the merchants, the risks of every sort to which they were exposed, in an age when pillage formed one of the means of existence of the smaller nobility, caused them, from the very beginning to seek the protection of the walled towns and burgs, which stood at intervals along the rivers or natural routes by which they travelled. During the summer these served as halting-places, during the bad season as wintering-places. (Pirenne, 1937, 40–1)

Perhaps the only element of controversy is the source of these merchants, for by implication from the above statement they were foreigners. Ganshof has denied this interpretation, 'Pirenne did not believe that the incoming element in the "portus" (one of the names of the merchant quarter) was necessarily foreign, for example Saxon or Frisian . . . what he says, rightly or wrongly, is that the elements who peopled the "portus" and who based their activities there, were external to the population of the "Castrum" . . . and to the hinterland of the Castrum. They were not necessarily foreigners' (Ganshof, 1959, 202–3).

(b) Market theory.   Here the emphasis is on the local trade generated from the immediate area rather than on long-distance commerce. This is epitomized in the right to hold a market. As the quotation from Ganshof above indicates, the complete contrast between local and long-distance trade is not easy to sustain, but Pirenne's emphasis was on the merchant moving constantly but settling his family and business in the town and that means stressing the longer-distance trade.

(c) Artisanal theory.   The division of labour which occurred between agriculture and handicrafts created a specialist group, the members of which associated together to create the town; the emphasis here is on production not trade. In general this explanation becomes more popular outside the Romanized areas and is usually put forward in relation to the development of small towns in the east German and the Slav lands. It also tends to have support from Marxist interpreters of medieval town growth.

(d) Association or guild theory.   This is based on the

power of associations for social or religious reasons who, through a community of interest, acquired special privileges and liberties. This is a tenable legal theory but it is not easy to translate it into the ecological terms of an influence creating agglomerated populations.

(e) Military theory. This is the view which has already been discussed in relation to the nuclear areas of urbanism, that agglomeration comes about from the need to establish protected strong-points. Another name is 'the garrison' theory which has been discussed at an earlier stage of the enquiry into urban origins (pp. 6–7).

(f) Ecclesiastic theory. This is not to be compared with the religious explanation of urban origins which was developed earlier, although there are common elements. It compares directly with military theory, but the protection in this case is provided by the rights, privileges and immunities of the church. The result was the agglomeration of settlement about major ecclesiastical foundations.

(g) Free village theory. This assumes that the liberties of the town developed directly from those of the village. It must imply that the villages had developed a good deal of autonomy for this transition to take place. That in turn involves major transformations in socioeconomic conditions.

(h) Romanist theory. In this view towns are taken to be direct successors of Roman cities, without any major break in the continuity.

It is evident that these do not form eight mutually exclusive modes of explanation, for one or more could have operated together. It is also true that one or more could have acted independently at the same time and, again, acted in different areas or at different times. Thus the Romanist theory might well be right in relation to the towns of southern Gaul, while of little relevance to those of the Roman frontier areas. Ennen emphasizes that there is no one overriding explanation – 'Medieval towns present no uniformity' (Ennen, 1956, 411). The problem is made no easier by the influence of chauvinistic and other influences which impinge upon it and pressurize scholars to bolster national identity by demonstrating that towns were not 'foreign' introductions. Tikhomirov in his study *The Towns of Ancient Rus* concludes that 'it was not foreign trade but the separation of the handicrafts from agriculture, the intensification of exchange between industrial and agricultural production, the development of agriculture and feudal relationships that was the prime cause of the growth of Rus towns in the tenth to thirteenth centuries' (Tikhomirov, 1959, 481). This is a clear invocation of what has been called the 'artisanal theory', but the accompanying reiteration of national independence casts a natural doubt on its validity; 'It follows, therefore, that the earliest Russian towns were founded by the eastern Slavs rather than by some other people. The eastern Slavs were, consequently, the first and principal founders of towns and urban life in Kiev Rus. Since towns are wellsprings of culture, it is the Slavs who are mainly to be credited with the development of Russian cities. The history of Russian

cities deals a decisive blow to miscellaneous concepts which present the Normans, the Khazars and Goths and other peoples as the architects of Russia's state system and culture' (Tikhomirov, 1959, 14). Again Tikhomirov writes, 'It should be remembered that Russian towns were new settlements, which emerged independently of Roman or other ancient towns. . . . Their peculiar economic and social structure took shape independently and was entirely the result of efforts on the part of the ancient Russians' (Tikhomirov, 1959, 54). It may well be that Tikhomirov's interpretation is correct and the work of other well known east European historians, such as Alexander Gieysztor for example, would seem to support it (Gieysztor, 1959). But the evident motivation which lies behind the conclusion does little to promote confidence in it.

This brief diversion into the many difficulties which are inherent in the simplification of a complex problem can be used as a jumping-off point for a review of the physical form of these towns. For this one must start not at the areas far beyond the fringes of the Roman Empire but at those areas where the Roman imprint, at least in an attenuated form, remained. This must necessarily be that area between the Loire and the Rhine which was not only in the middle critical area identified by Ennen (p. 34) but which formed the basis of a major study by François Ganshof (1943), himself a student of Pirenne. Ganshof based his analysis on the theme set out by Pirenne that it was commerce and trade which were the fashioners of the medieval town. Indeed, Ganshof stressed the significance of the urban renaissance of the high Middle Ages by introducing Schmoller's view, passed on by Pirenne, that the two most vital features in the whole history of post-Roman Europe had been the urban renaissance and the invention of the railway. This broad phase of urban growth involved two elements in terms of physical make-up. The first was an element of localization which played an essentially static role. This was the strong-point, castrum, castellum or castle which acted as the fixation feature. Alongside this grew the second element, the merchant quarter called portus (poort or port) or vicus (vik) or burgus (burgh or bourg), the dynamic part of the town, initiating and sustaining growth. This is the critical interpretation in Ganshof's own work where he calls the static, localizing part the pre-urban nucleus.

The pre-urban nucleus could be one of three types. It could be the Roman Castrum, preserving through the vicissitudes of the Barbarian invasions a tradition of settlement, of military control and of central administration which could be reused or revitalized. It could be the fortified residence or castle of the emerging royal families or the newly created nobility, for in the shadows of such establishments security was to be found. Finally, the nucleus could be an ecclesiastical foundation. These three, incorporating three of the theories of origin (*(e)*, *(f)* and *(g)* on pages 34–5), are viewed as playing a passive role and remaining as little more than isolated fortresses or monasteries unless they were translated into towns by the active influence of trade and commerce which created

2.17.   Rheims: the plan of the early town (after Ganshof).

Key

———   Gallo-Roman enceinte

----   Enceinte of the Bourg St Remi, 923–925

-·-·-   Medieval wall of the 13th–14th centuries

M   Place des Marchés

ND   Notre Dame

Vesle River

Rue Barbâtre

St Remi Cathedral

the second element which was grafted onto the pre-existing nuclear strong-point. Whether it was primarily a local or a long-distance trade is perhaps of less importance, although the more wide-ranging the commercial activity, the greater the stimulus to growth and the greater the contrast between the local and the incoming populations. Above all else the merchant needed security, security for his place of exchange or sale, security for his goods in transit and security for his family. All these were achieved beneath the protection of the three types of pre-urban nuclei which have been outlined. Moreover, there was a great gain to be made by secular and ecclessiastical rulers from the encouragement of trade for it provided income from tolls and dues and extended controlling influence along the trade routes. The zone of military and administrative control could be effectively transformed into a region of economic penetration linked structurally to the market centre of exchange. Castle and market grew symbiotically, control and peace encouraging trade and trade extending control, and ultimately this was recognized physically, as well as symbolically, by the walling around of both constituent elements of the town; the medieval city had emerged in a distinctive form.

(iii) Physical character of the medieval city

The general pattern in which the medieval town grew has been examined in the previous section. At this stage it is necessary to consider that general manner in a little more detail in order to isolate the critical elements and show how considerable variety indicates again a range of wide departures from the basic theme. This is best accomplished by the examination of a number of examples.

The first of these is Rheims (Figure 2.17) which is appropriately situated in the second area identified by Ennen, and within the critical area between the Loire and the Rhine. The town is located on the River Vesle, a left-bank tributary of the Aisne at a point where that river breaks through the scarp-line usually called the Falaise de l'Ile de France. It therefore occupied a significant position in relation to access to and from the central core of the Paris Basin. The settlement dates back to pre-Roman times when it was the 'oppidum' or central settlement of the Remi. With the Roman occupation the tribal territory became a 'civitas', with the old centre translated into the Gallo-Roman city of Durocortorum. As such, the significance of its location meant that it became the capital of the Roman province of Belgica Secunda.

Hubert (1959) has identified four key phases in the early (that is from the fifth to tenth centuries) topographical development of towns in Roman Gaul and these add some detail to the outline presented in the previous section. These key phases he cites as
1 The attenuated or diminished city of the late empire.
2 The religious town ('ville sainte') of the Merovingian period.

3 The urban revival of the early ninth century, associated with the relative calm of the Carolingian peace.
4 The return to fortification of the 'cité' (civitas) and also the fortification of the 'bourg' as a result of the Norman invasions.
It is possible to add a fifth and later succeeding phase to these four from the general review in section (ii)
5 The walled protection of both cité and bourg and their unification into one complex settlement.

These phases can be identified in the development of Rheims. The Gallo-Roman civitas was presumably laid out in a grid but underwent a period of decline after the Frankish invasions of the latter part of the third century. Even so, much was retained and Rheims is an example of a city where the first merchant quarter and the oldest market place were developed, the latter on, and the former about, the Roman forum (Ganshof, 1943). The Place de Marchés occupies the site of the forum in a direct line of continuity. Ganshof makes the point that the majority of the fortified civitates were very small in area and that much of the available space was occupied by religious buildings. This lack of space within the pre-urban nuclei was one reason why in most instances the newer merchant sector or quarter had to develop away from the existing core. Rheims, with an area of between 20 and 30 hectares, was one of the larger of the civitates and this is possibly one reason why the internal market and merchant quarter developed without any locational shift. Here then is the diminished city identified as the first phase by Hubert. The second phase was marked by the development of religious institutions, and this was of prime importance in the growth of Rheims. At the basis of this feature were Roman legal constraints which forbade burial within city walls. The earliest Christian martyrs were, therefore, buried outside the defences of the civitates. Their tombs became objects of veneration and accordingly the foundations of complexes of chapels, lodging houses and eventually, perhaps, an abbey (Hubert, 1959, 545). In this way, a 'suburbium' or 'bourg' developed quite separate and apart from the pre-urban nucleus. This was certainly the case at Rheims where the first Christian community grew about the tomb of St Remi, who was buried about one kilometre outside the Roman civitas in 553 (Lavedan and Hugueney, 1974). An abbey was established on the spot and by 924–5 this was surrounded by its own defensive wall presumably in response to the Norman threat as indicated by Hubert. 'In France', writes François Ganshof, 'we know of several instances where a "burgus" developed some distance from the pre-urban nucleus, especially about or alongside an abbey which was usually fortified; this "bourg" has, therefore, played the part of the generating cell of the town, sometimes together with another commercial agglomeration' (Ganshof, 1943, 31). This, Ganshof argues, was the case at Rheims. There was already the merchant quarter within the civitas, and by the eleventh century a 'burgus' had developed about the Abbey of St Remi which seems to have had a market by 991. The abbey seems to have taken special measures to guarantee the rights both of the market and the 'bourg' (Figure 2.17).

The abbey was not the only religious foundation in the environs of the pre-urban nucleus, nor was physical attack the only menace to its well-being. Plague and pestilence were dominant features of the age and the towns sought protection from them through the guardianship of the saints and the guarantees of the church. Hubert quotes a homily of St Avit of the early sixth century in relation to Lyon, 'This city is more effectively defended by its basilicas than its ramparts' (Hubert, 1959, 544). Rheims was protected by basilicas related to each of the four main gates (Figure 2.18) and a series of churches, dating to the fourth, fifth or sixth centuries, existed about the settlement to provide both the proper rites for the dead, who were buried without the walls, as well as succour for the living. By the eleventh century the two parts existed side by side, both of them separately fortified as a consequence of the threat presented by the Norman invasions (Figure 2.17).

The subsequent feature which bound these parts together was the first 'enceinte urbaine', that is the first defensive wall which included both parts. At Rheims this occurred at a comparatively late date, in the latter half of the thirteenth century. This was possibly due to the fact that the early precocious development of the city had slackened, for it had witnessed the baptism of Clovis and the coronation of the Frankish kings. The wall when it was eventually built included not only 'civitas' and 'bourg' but a number of the other minor nodes gathered about the other churches which have been mentioned. Initially, therefore, it included a good deal of open, essentially rural, land within its 6500 metre perimeter.

Three other points need to be made. The need to develop new buildings, especially those related to the cathedrals, meant that much of the underlying Roman grid plan was overstepped and this resulted, as in Britain (chapter 3), in a gradual loss of the complete rigidity of the chequer-board scheme. In some cases, as at Rheims, it remained identifiable but considerably modified. The second point is that the link between cité and bourg, a new line of significant movement, became a new axis of development often athwart the other grid scheme. At Rheims the Rue de Barbatre was the new axis of the medieval town. The third point is that in many towns not one but a succession of urban enceintes was established, further structuring the form of continuing extension. At Rheims because such a large area was included within the first enceinte no others became necessary.

This brief analysis of the early development of Rheims has highlighted the major features which developed as Gallo-Roman city was transmuted into medieval town. It must be emphasized, however, that the special relationships of the composing elements were not in any way constant and that cité, bourg and surrounding walls occurred in an immense variety of different articulations. It was this feature that gives the complexity which characterizes the internal structure of medieval towns,

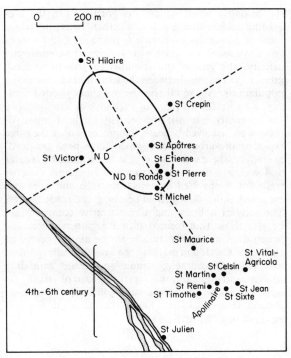

2.18.   The early religious foundations at Rheims (after Hubert).

even if dominating themes can be isolated.

Alzey, Bad Kreuznach, Bonn and Xanten are examples of the case where the Roman castrum remained isolated and the succeeding merchant town grew up alongside it. At Bonn there are, however, parallels with Rheims. The Roman 'Castrum Bonna' became part of the royal domain at the time of the Frankish conquest and possessed both a mint and a market. 'Even though only the southwestern part of the original area of the legionary fortress, around the church of St Peter, seems to have been occupied by the Latin population in Frankish times, the Bonnburg was still very important under the Frankish kings and their successors' (Gutkind, 1964, 265–7) (Figure 2.19). As at Rheims a parallel settlement grew about the martyr's chapel which was built in the cemetery of the civilian settlement and from which the cathedral of St Cassius Florentius developed. Ennen called this a 'much visited place of pilgrimage' and under the control of the Bishops of Cologne it grew to rival the Bonnburg, as the Villa Basilicata. It was probably fortified by the eighth century and about the middle of the tenth the large market place outside the defended settlement was established. Around this, the merchant quarter collected – partly related to the tracks which linked it with the Bonnburg. But when in 1244 walled defences were erected it was the religious and merchant elements only which were included and the Roman castrum was left outside as an isolated remnant which had no surviving function.

Trèves (Trier) is probably the most widely quoted

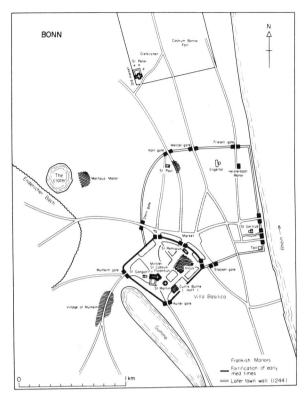

2.19.   The historical topography of Bonn (after Böhner).

example where the medieval town not only lay within the pre-existing Roman settlement rather than alongside it, but where the succeeding town of the Middle Ages was itself much smaller. The Roman settlement of Augusta Trevinorum became a colonia about AD 50. It was one of the largest cities of Gaul with a perimeter of 6500 metres and an area of some 258 hectares. (These can be compared with the late medieval wall at Rheims and the 20 to 39 hectares of Durocortorum.) Augusta Trevinorum was established on the characteristic gridded plan of the Roman colonial settlement, with thirteen streets from east to west crossed by eight running north to south (Figure 2.20). It was the capital of the province of Belgica Prima and that role, together with the fact that for a short while in the fourth century AD it was the imperial capital, accounted for its very large extent. Such a large city could not be sustained under the very different conditions which followed the Frankish incursions when it was repeatedly attacked and a considerable amount of physical destruction took place. The result was a very clear diminution of the settled area. It was characterized by what Kurt Böhner has termed 'the disintegration of the late Roman town into private domestic units' (Böhner, 1977, 193). Elsewhere churches established in or beside late Roman cemeteries developed into abbeys and became fortified having their own markets and jurisdictions, but Trier (Figure 2.20) became the centre of a bishopric and the cathedral became the node about which

growth took place. Even so, private manors were founded outside the fortified enceinte which seems to have been constructed about 956-64. Such were Böheim and Oren. But the generative cell was the cathedral nucleus. The oldest market appears to have been about the Moselle bridge, but in 958 Bishop Henry established a new market place immediately outside the cathedral precinct and this attracted most of the trade. The first urban enceinte of 1102-24 and the later medieval walls took in the cathedral precinct and the main market but only part of the much larger Roman settlement, the town of the Middle Ages was but a small area within the defences of the former Gallo-Roman city. It is further evident (Figure 2.20) that if the layout of the medieval town be superimposed upon the Roman grid there is no relationship discernible, an indication of the extent to which the lineaments of August Trevinorum had been lost. The new street lines were those which linked the curtes, the private manors, with the cathedral core. Even the regenerated part owed little to its predecessor in terms of morphology.

Examples of towns have been examined where the roles of abbey and cathedral were critical – 'la priorité chronologique du facteur religieux est indiscutable'. But away from the heartland and margins of Roman Gaul it was the secular nuclei which held the key in the form of the fortified residences of the nobility, particularly the counts who became the deputed controllers of the territories and ruled them from these defended strong-points. 'In Flanders and Brabant almost all the towns were formed in the immediate environs of the castle of a count. This castrum or castellum usually dates to the tenth century.' It was made up of a fortified area within which were located the seigneural residence, usually a church and some other associated buildings. This area was very limited in extent. The castrum established by the Counts of Louvain covered only some five hectares. It is usually accepted that this castrum was the successor of an earlier Chateau de Cesar founded after a defeat of the Normans by the German Emperor in the ninth century. The castrum as it was relocated occupied a strongly defensive site since it was in a marshy lowland protected by arms of the River Dijle which made it into an island (Figure 2.21). It was immediately adjacent to this nucleus that population collected and the merchant and market quarter emerged. Here there is an immediate adjacence of pre-urban nucleus and the trading element, of castrum and bourg. Louvain was granted 'the privilege to hold markets in the twelfth century. The first was the fish market. Other markets soon followed' (Gutkind, 1970, 61). In the eleventh century a cloth hall had been erected and so the suburbium developed, but in an unordered and ill-controlled fashion. By 1149 both the castellum, the pre-urban nucleus, and the merchant or trading suburb had been surrounded by a circular defensive wall, thus uniting them in the one town. 'By the thirteenth century the whole of the inner town was traversed by many tortuous, narrow and winding streets, some of which led to the gates in the fortifications. The

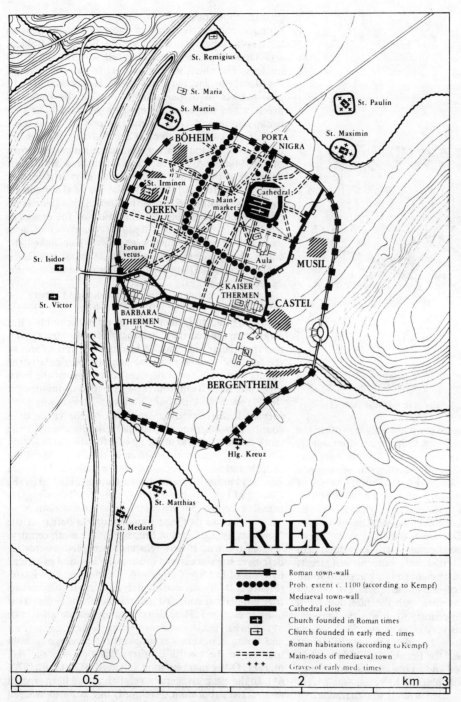

2.20.   The historical topography of Trier (after Böhner).

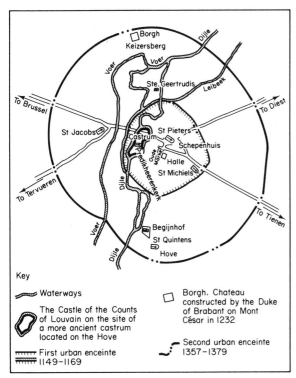

2.21.   Louvain: the medieval city (after Ganshof).

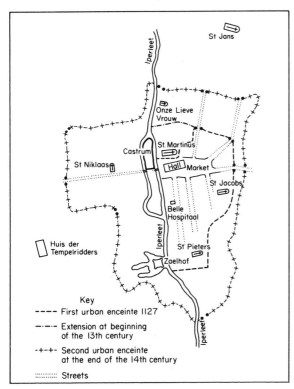

2.22.   Ypres: the medieval city (after Ganshof).

reconstruction of the Chateau de Cesar, about 1230, was the turning point in the history of Louvain' (Gutkind, 1970, 61).

By this change the ducal centre was moved from the cramped island site to a location outside the walls. Medieval rulers often hesitated over the construction of a second enceinte about the suburbs which had grown, for often these were composed of turbulent populations best kept outside. But at Louvain, with the move of the chateau, it became necessary to protect it and the surrounding areas and these were eventually enclosed by the second enceinte of 1357–63. Seven major gates gave access via seven main street lines which converged on the central market or Grande Place (Figure 2.21).

Ypres can be cited as an example parallel to that of Louvain with the market and merchant area developing immediately adjacent to the castrum, in this case the castle of the Counts of Flanders located on an island in the River Iperleer (Figure 2.22). The first enceinte dates to the beginning of the twelfth century (1127) so that the two structural elements were set alongside each other, the castrum remaining outside this walled area. A minor extension took place at the beginning of the thirteenth century to include the suburb developed about the abbey of St Martin. Eventually a further enceinte was built at the end of the fourteenth century after the suburban extension had been greatly damaged by siege in 1383. Again Ennen's account of the development of Ghent brings out the same general process of development.

This review of some examples of medieval city development, limited in scope as it has been leads to two major conclusions.

1   The process of growth involved the continuation of civitas or castrum as a pivotal strong-point and the development, in relation to it, of bourg or suburbium. In consequence it was a very uneven process and was often slow and haphazard in nature. From this there followed a lack of formal planning, for it is a process of break-up and re-formation, or if the term is preferred, of organic evolution. The street layout, even of the most regular of Roman plans, was overstepped in many cases by new building so that it in part disappeared, though in some examples it was preserved and is still identifiable. In other cases, however, simple physical destruction obliterated all traces. Out of this emerges the irregularity and complexity of medieval city plans.

2   From the process of 'natural' evolution those elements which could be used in both internal and external colonization were selected and preserved. Prime amongst these was the castle, rapidly developing its own complex morphology. Closely associated was the market, and the town, which as earlier reviews have pointed out (p. 37), gave economic control and the means for cultural change. From the heartland of the old empire the stage was set for the expansion of urbanism and the extension of the urbanized world.

(iv) The extension of urbanism in Europe: the west

It is a matter of dispute whether the extension of
urbanism in Western Europe was primarily related to the
colonization of new agricultural land or to the military
occupation of territory; whether the market was the
primary instrument or the castle. To a large extent the
debate lacks real meaning, especially stated in such bare
terms. Both economic development and successful
control were part of the same process and the role each
one played depended upon the regional circumstances.
But it is possible to accept Lavedan's division of this
period of urban growth into two (Lavedan and
Hugueney, 1974, 61). The first of these is the eleventh
and twelfth centuries when the occupation of new lands
through agricultural reclamation was predominant, and
the second is the thirteenth and fourteenth centuries
when a series of conflicts is at least germane to the
generation of new towns.

The character of the first period is epitomized by
Lavedan's phrase, 'L'âge des sauvetés a précédé l'âge des
bastides' (Lavedan and Hugueney, 1974, 61). This was
the view expounded by R. Latouche in his study of Maine
in the eleventh and twelfth centuries, and which by
implication can be applied to other areas in France
(Latouche, 1937). Latouche argued that one of the
primary features of the period reviewed was the reclamation of land and the settlement of population in order to
bring new areas into effective use. The local rulers, both
lay and ecclesiastical, could promote this movement into
new land by encouraging the growth of settlement about
castles or monasteries, or about newly founded churches,
by the granting of freedoms and liberties in return for

taxes and tolls levied on both land and trade. Critical to
the success of any venture was the grant of the market to
the new settlement. In this way what had been forest or
marshland was brought under effective and productive
use, not only guaranteeing successful holding of the
region but, at the same time, securing an income.

It is not easy to detach this period simply from the one
which went before when pre-existing points, already
identified as pre-urban nuclei, especially castles and
churches, were the pivots about which settlement
collected. Nor is it easy to make a sharp distinction
between these elements and the succeeding bastide
towns. Thus Beresford clearly regards Mogron (Landes)
and Nogaro (Gers) as bastides; 'Was Richard an
innovator, bringing to Gascony an urban lesson learned
further north? It would not seem so. Before the English
connection began in 1174 . . . the abbot of St Sever . . .
had founded Mogron in 1074. Some historians place the
foundation of Nogaro as early as 1060 . . .' (Beresford,
1967, 352). Lavedan, however, treats these as *sauvetés*
. . . 'A l'Abbaye de Saint-Sever on doit Mugron en
1074', and, 'Dans le midi de la France, vers 1060, Saint-
Austinde, archevêque d'Auch, avait fondé Nogaro'
(Lavedan and Hugueney, 1974, 62–3). Both of these
occur in his discussion of 'L'époque des sauvetés'. It is
inappropriate, therefore, to look upon this 'époque des
sauvetés' as a clear break between the post-Dark Ages
revival of urbanism and the peak of bastide founding in
the west which came in the middle and latter part of the
thirteenth century. Nevertheless, it is an intermediate
period when very small towns were founded and began
that movement which was to increase greatly the density
of urban settlement. The critical feature in contrast to the

2.23.   Beaumont en Argonne (after
Lavedan).

earlier period, though again it is not always quite so simple to identify, is the notion of the founding of *new* towns or at least a conscious and deliberate reorganization of existing settlement based on a market and administrative centre.

The problem of identification arises in the case of the *sauveté* which Lavedan introduces as one of the best known examples, Beaumont-en-Argonne. It was certainly not a settlement founded *de novo* in the twelfth century for one had been established on the site between 970 and 989, a settlement which had not succeeded in developing. Accordingly in 1176 the Archbishop of Rheims provided the settlement with a new and liberal charter and so initiated a period of comparatively rapid growth. Significantly the settlement was located in the clay lands of the Argonne and, although coming under the heading of the reorganization of existing settlement, is characteristically related to the exploitation of new agricultural land. The basic principle was to provide liberties for the inhabitants who had to pay for the right to become burgesses and were assigned a portion of land. Rights of sanctuary were also given to all within the town, apart from thieves and murderers. The form of the town (Figure 2.23) was largely determined by its hill-top location; it was essentially radial-concentric about the church and a large main square. It suggests a rather loose control of the actual physical layout. Most of the *sauvetés*, and many were established by the religious orders such as the Benedictines, were of this order having either a predominantly agglomerated, quasi radial-concentric form or a linear or axial form. They lacked that tightly planned layout which was to be once more reintroduced into urban development in the form of the bastide.

The bastide town's main inspiration was undoubtedly military, although that was far from its exclusive function and not all bastides were dominated by, or even possessed, great defensive works. Nevertheless, the emergence of the form in southwestern France must be associated with warfare. Its main exploitation must be related to the conflict between the French crown and the Counts of Toulouse, who supported the Albigenses during the crusading wars against their heresy between 1208 and 1228; to the conflict between the French and English Kings after the marriage of Henry II to Eleanor of Aquitaine in 1154 laid the basis for the English claims in Gascony and their extension beyond; to the conflict derived from feudal rivalries. Even in this setting it would be wrong to associate the bastides in southwest France with great military strategies or even the organized defence of frontier territories. The classic paper is that by J.-P. Trabut-Cussac (1954) which asks the direct question, 'Bastide ou Forteresses?' His study of the Agenais comes to the conclusion that bastides were mainly undefended and that often defences were constructed later, on the demand of the inhabitants who feared local disorder and not at the time of establishment by the town founder. This leads Beresford to conclude that such evidence, together with the late peak in town

plantation, suggests 'a retarded colonization that took new vigour in the mid-thirteenth century' derived from the reaction to the 'devastation within the most fertile parts of the southwest during the civil war of the Albigensian Crusade between 1209 and 1244; and the increase in the area of vineyards in many parts of the Garonne basin after the English had lost Poitou' (Beresford, 1967, 363–4). Equally it can be argued that Edward I's commitment to the bastides of Gascony was mainly related to the reinforcement of political power and the enhancement of revenues.

This is not the place for a detailed historical discussion of the progress of bastide founding, the evidence has been provided by Beresford (1967) (Figure 2.24a and b)

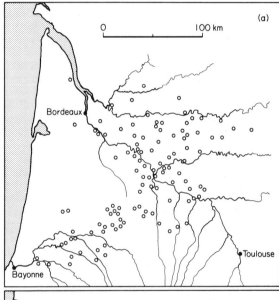

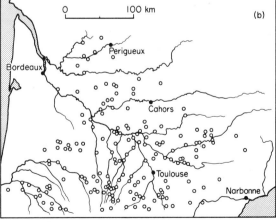

2.24. (a) English and Anglo-French bastides in Gascony. The map includes those acquired from the French in and after 1279. (b) French bastides in southwestern France (after Beresford). This map should be taken with Fig. 2.24(a) in order to assess the full intensity of plantation in this area, largely after 1240.

and he has also developed an incisive discussion of 'The Chronology of Town Plantation in Gascony'. The point here is that evidence from distribution maps indicates the spread of urbanization, especially as the economic argument underlines, into those areas where the effective colonization and occupation of rural areas had been delayed and where the means of communication were limited.

The bastide was above all else the foundation of one person and laid out at one time. It is true that there are cases of examples based on existing settlement, but essentially these are new foundations. Although the profession of 'lotisseur' was recorded in Paris in 1292, in general it seems that the towns were laid out on the spot, in an *ad hoc* manner and without plans drawn up in advance, and by a variety of persons with differing experience, including administrators and engineers. It is significant that when in 1296 Edward I wished to consider how best to lay out a town advice was sought from an *ad hoc* colloquium, when 24 English towns were ordered 'to elect men from among your wisest and ablest who know best how to devise, order and array a new town to the greatest profit of ourselves and the merchants' (Beresford, 1967, 3). There was obviously no standard authority or professional body of expertise to put to work. It would be mistaken to overstress the uniform grid-pattern rectangularity of all the bastides for there were considerable variations from it, especially where site conditions were uneven. Again, street widths varied depending on whether they were to carry vehicles or not. The result was a great deal of variety, not covered by the simple term 'grid plan' which is frequently employed. Even so, the conditions set out by Stanislawski which occur where grid layouts are pre-dominant are clearly met (Stanislawski, 1946). These were new towns found in colonizing circumstances and where a measured disposition of intra-urban land was required.

Three examples have been chosen to indicate at once both the common features of the bastides and the variety in foundation and layout which characterized them.

The first example, Montauban, was also one of the earliest and hence one of the most widely cited (Figure 2.25). It was founded in 1144 by the then Count of Toulouse as part of the reaction to the threat from the French crown. It was peopled largely by the inhabitants of nearby Montauriol which lacked the liberties the new town offered. In relation to the French threat it occupied both a strategic location and a defensive site. It was established where the main route from Paris across the Massif Central debouches from the limestone uplands of Quercy on to the plain of the Garonne and its tributaries. Toulouse itself is some 45 kilometres to the southeast. It was built on what can be called a peninsular site formed by the confluence of three rivers incised into a plateau surface. These are the Tarn, the Tescou and a smaller stream, the Garrigue. This confluence creates a trapezoid-shaped area and the town was very closely related to that site control in its own shape (Figure 2.25). Moreover, the Place Nationale, the market square, again

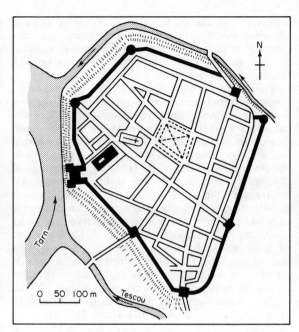

2.25. Montauban: the general layout of the planned town (after Devals).

echoed the same form, its sides being parallel to the walls and the breaks of slope of the site. The central square was the basic plan element in relation to which the rest of the town was adjusted, for the major streets again were developed in parallel with two streets meeting at each corner (Figure 2.25). Lavedan calls this type a bastide based on two axes, since there is equal stress on the streets which cross at right-angles rather than on one single long axis. But the geometry of this scheme is far from being rigid and the internal blocks are not consistent either in size or shape. The church makes a diagonal with the general layout, being located off the western corner of the trapezoid 'Place'. Lavedan argues that many of these features make Montauban a prototype for later bastides, while Gutkind emphasizes the departures from rectangularity by concluding that it combines 'a certain measure of regularity with a spontaneous diversity' (Gutkind, 1970, 48).

The second example is again widely used to demonstrate bastide features, largely because it was the subject of a minutely detailed, two-volume study by L. Testut (1920). This is Beaumont du Perigord which was founded for Edward I in 1272. As in many other cases the royal authority combined with local notables in its building in the arrangement called 'pareage'. It was one of a number of bastides near the political frontier in north Gascony. As the name suggests, this is another example of a clearly defensive site. This took the form of an elongated hill which was virtually rectangular in shape, measuring some 340 by 140 metres. Again the site controlled the form which the town took for it was also rectangular and the walls, which were added later after

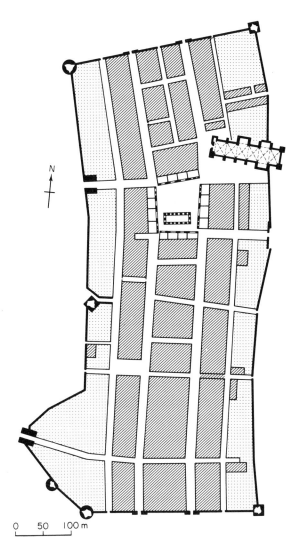

2.26. Beaumont du Perigord (after Beresford). Plan of streets, chequers, walls, market place and church.

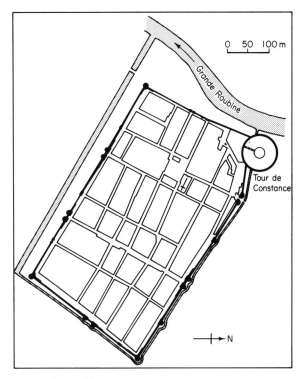

2.27. Aigues Mortes.

1320, follow the breaks of slope (Figure 2.26). The plan was based on two principle and parallel streets which followed the crest of the hill. Since the crest is not a straight line, however, the two streets were themselves not straight but diverted slightly off a true line to the north of the market place, which occupies a position between the two streets. As at Montauban, laterals broke across at either end of the square so that two streets met at each corner (Figure 2.26). The square itself seems to have had arcaded shops around it, and the church is set off on a diagonal. The two major streets were some six to seven metres wide and the laterals which cross them were narrow and irregularly placed so that they divide the town into unequal blocks. There were six gates, one at each end of the principal streets and two in the side away

from the steepest break of slope where access was difficult.

The third example is removed in location and in concept, but is quoted as an example of classic rectangularity. This is Aigues Mortes (Morize, 1914; Fliche, 1925) in the Rhone delta (Figure 2.27). It was created by Louis IX (St Louis) as a harbour and base from which to mount the crusades. It was built on flat, marshy land where site constraints were very different from those of the hill-top conditions of Montauban and Beaumont. The land was acquired from the Abbey of Psalmodi in 1240 and the town was given its charter in 1246. It quickly attracted a wide variety of merchants concerned with sea traffic in the Mediterranean. Since the site was level the shape was a precise rectangle measuring 550 by 300 metres. The internal structure was made up of five east-to-west streets bisected by five north-to-south. Both these series run parallel to the defending ramparts, although there were slight shifts especially brought about by the main square, which was itself offset from centre. The blocks were neither symmetrical nor uniform in size or shape. The church was located on the northeast diagonal off the main square. The defences of Aigues Mortes were again set up at a later date and the famous Tour de Constance, which stands outside the town and its walls, may have been intended as the sole defence. Perhaps the main point to stress is that even here there is very considerable departure from the true grid of the

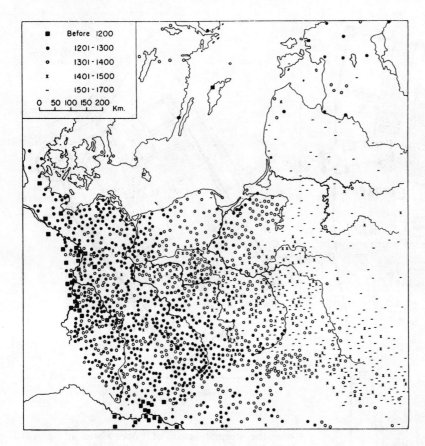

■	Before 1200
●	1201 – 1300
○	1301 – 1400
x	1401 – 1500
–	1501 – 1700

0   50 100 150 200 Km.

2.28.   Urban foundation in east central Europe (after C.T. Smith)

complete chequer-board plan.

This brief consideration of the south and west of France, with three examples of urban foundation there, must stand as a general representation of wider processes by which the urbanized area was extended and the urban occupancy of territory was intensified. It is not possible to present a comprehensive review in terms both of chronology and geographical area, so that, for the moment, the Moslem urban creations in Spain and those of the Reconquest must be left, and instead one turns here to consider the great eastward extension that carried the founded city far beyond the old 'limites' of the Roman Empire.

(v) The extension of urbanism in Europe: the east

It is an oversimplification but nevertheless a tenable generalization to argue that the Carolingian-initiated *'Drang nach Osten'*, the push to the east, included the foundation of towns both as a means of controlling territory and of exploiting the economic potential of new lands and different products. The town was thus carried eastward, as indicated in Figure 2.28, by translated diffusion from those civitates established along the Rhine –Danube frontier of the Roman Empire. Within this

there is a twofold process. The first is the emergence of the small-scale 'fora', the market towns, while the second is the founding of major strong-points and long-distance trading centres which became the linchpins of the growing urban system.

The first of these, the emergence of the smaller, local centres, can be partly related to the market theory of urban origins and partly to the artisanal theory. Van Werveke introduced these as 'towns, with a dual role as producers and consumers, whose radius of action did not extend beyond the immediately neighbouring country-side. There was neither merchant class engaged in distant trade nor an artisan class occupied . . . with products intended for a foreign clientele. The population was composed . . . of artisans working for the local and regional market, exchanging their products for the raw material and foodstuffs provided for them by the agricul-tural population' (Van Werveke, 1963, 22). Such towns developed within the German lands, actively encouraged by local magnates. The word 'forum' is often used to designate these centres since they were not so much weekly markets as permanent sites designated for the purpose of transaction. The tolls collected in these markets went to the granter of the privileges and, at first, these were largely the religious houses. 'In the course of

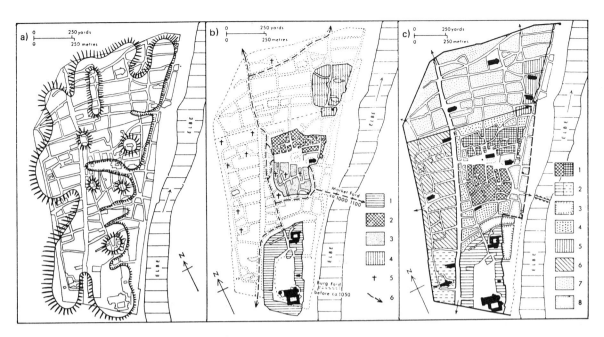

2.29.　Magdeburg: the urban plan (after C.T. Smith).
　　(a)　Magdeburg. The fortifications which constituted
　　　　separate early nuclei took clear advantage of the
　　　　spurs and heights overlooking the Elbe (after
　　　　Mrusek).
　　(b)　Magdeburg circa AD 1000:
　　　　1.　The Carolingian castle-site (805) on the
　　　　probable site of a Saxon lord's house; the Saxon
　　　　royal palace: the monastery of St Moritz (937)
　　　　2.　Cathedral (968) and the earlier and irregularly
　　　　laid out part of the Ottonian town.
　　　　3.　The later and regular Ottonian town with
　　　　market place of circa 1200.
　　　　4.　The Count's burg.
　　　　5.　Towered houses of urban merchants and
　　　　officials.
　　　　6.　Long-distance routes (after Mrusek).
　　(c)　Magdeburg circa 1250:
　　　　1.　The Ottonian town.
　　　　2.　The Immunity of the Cathedral.
　　　　3.　Monastic land.
　　　　4.　Gradual spread of settlement in the eleventh
　　　　and twelfth centuries.
　　　　5.　Area of the former Count's burg, subsequently
　　　　used for ecclesiastical building in the thirteenth
　　　　century.
　　　　6.　Expansion of the town 1152–1192.
　　　　7.　Planned urban expansion 1213 1236.
　　　　8.　Spread of settlement along the river bank in the
　　　　twelfth and thirteenth centuries (after Mrusek).

the following centuries the process of founding markets
shifted more and more towards the east and at the same
time the proportion of laymen among the lords of
markets gradually increased (Van Werveke, 1963, 23).
Moreover, with the disintegration of the German
kingdom the role of the petty nobility became more

significant and the need for defence greater so that castle
founding became more closely linked to town building.
　The second element in the growth of towns in these
German and Slav lands is perhaps the more significant.
The great towns of the Roman frontier, especially
Cologne and Mainz, were the bases from which major
lines of expansion were pushed deep into Slav territory.
The first of these lines was based on the Hellweg, the
great Carolingian routeway which ran along the northern
edge of Hercynian Europe from Duisburg to Paderborn
and thence to the Weser-crossing and on to the Elbe at
Magdeburg, with a branch to the south to Halle. To the
north it is possible to identify a line to the Baltic coast to
Bardowick, the settlement of which Lubeck was the
successor. The third line is that which from the Bavarian
base ran along the Danube valley to the old Roman settlement of Vindobona (Vienna). As Dickinson comments,
'All these early medieval routes ran from east to west,
and, with their western termini in the two great early
medieval emporia of Mainz and Cologne, they had their
eastern termini in the outposts of Christianity and trade
at Bardowick, Magdeburg, Erfurt and Halle' (Dickinson, 1953, 162). The relative stability of the German
kingdom meant these were largely the foundation of the
Emperor and the Church. 'Of about 120 towns identified
in Germany in the eleventh century about 40 were on the
sites of bishops' seats, 20 were near monasteries and no
less than 60 grew around royal foundations, including
some 12 near the sites of royal palaces. Cologne, Mainz
and Magdeburg were the most important of the last'
(Smith, 1967, 323). At this period beyond the limits of the
German lands lay the marcher territories; it was into
these lands that settlement was to spread. There were two

basic means. The first was military. For example, the conquests of the Teutonic Knights in Prussia and beyond were accompanied by town founding. The first two cities were Chelmno and Torun founded in 1233 and granted Magdeburg Law (see below). The second was commercial as the traders and merchants pushed further east seeking new supplies of staple commodities as well as exotic products. They attached themselves to existing settlements and formed merchant quarters added to Slav defensive nucleations. They built new settlements in occupation of the land. Dickinson estimates that over 1500 towns were established between 1200 and 1400 (Dickinson, 1953, 167). Experienced planners, called locatores, were employed to lay out and recruit settlers to these new towns. They allocated the lots, provided assistance in the early years and even arranged water supplies and built defences. The result, writes Lavedan, 'was extraordinary. It is in these territories, where German met Slav, that some of the finest urban creations of Europe are found: Berlin and Dresden remain German; Breslau-Wroclau, Posen-Poznan are no longer so; there are also Frankfurt-on-Oder, Rostock, Stettin, Danzig' (Lavedan and Hugueney, 1974, 121). This intensely complex spread of urban settlement has only been treated in briefest outline but the major features are clearly apparent in Figure 2.28. If the Romans had brought urbanism to those parts of the continent of Europe which lay within their empire, the period following the accession of Charlemagne and petering out in the late fourteenth and fifteenth centuries, saw the extensive diffusion of urbanism both within and without the old limits of civilization.

Three examples can be used to epitomize the characteristic features of these towns. The first is Magdeburg on the Elbe, at the early frontier of German occupation (Smith, 1967). Its early morphology (Figure 2.29) presents a characteristic assemblage of the varied elements which went into the make-up of a town on this settlement frontier, even if the destruction by Tilly in 1631 and bombing in World War II have meant that nothing remains in the present city layout. Both situation and site combined to emphasize the significance of the city. A series of islands in the river Elbe provided a relatively easy crossing while an elevated bluff on the left bank gave defensive strength. These local qualities of site occurred in a position where routes along the northern edge of the middle mountains of Europe converged on the river crossing. The result was that the site seems to have been used since prehistoric times and was probably the site of a Saxon lord's house. This by the early ninth century had been converted to a Carolingian castle, for there are references to such a feature by the year 806. The castle seems to have been associated with a church, dedicated to St Etienne, founded by Bishop Hildegrim. Finally there is again evidence that it was a place where merchants, who wished to trade with the Slavs, were obliged to base themselves.

Military defence, religious administration and commercial activity even by that early period seem to have been grouped as the basic urban functions. Their location was the southern area of the riverside bluff (Figure 2.29). The major boost to Madgeburg's fortunes came in the early tenth century when Otto I made his residence there from 929 to 937. To the north of the Carolingian castle he built a cathedral and endowed this new part of the city with a large market place. The initial part of this addition was quite irregular in form but the later developments were more regular and ordered. Again further to the north, for the riverside site controlled the direction of growth, there appears to have been a burg of a local count, but this was replaced in the early thirteenth century by a 'new town', set out with greater regularity. The economic success of Magdeburg was ensured by its bridgehead role between the German lands to the west and the Slav lands to the east. The extent of its influence can be gathered by the area covered by the Law of Magdeburg, that is the areas where towns adopted the legal uses of Magdeburg for their own functioning. ' "Magdeburg Law" spread east of the Elbe to include northeastern Bohemia, and the northern lowlands as far as a line from Königsberg to the Carpathians. The wide distribution of Magdeburg law was facilitated by the fact that the great stream of emigration came from central Germany, and by the existence of a single great political entity, Poland, which gave to all its towns Magdeburg law or its derivatives' (Dickinson, 1953, 168). The result of this economic success, which made Magdeburg a world city of its day, was to lead to the integration of the many elements into one walled town. The internal structure of the city effectively represents the various morphological forces at work; the Carolingian castle; the imperial residence and its transformation of the early small Carolingian 'Königshof' into a city endowed with those basic elements which were to control territory and exploit it, cathedral and market; the later integration of the separate adjacent elements of urbanism on the site into a unified city.

The second example to be considered became the base for a much larger area, for the Law of Lubeck characterized the northern coastlands of Germany and the Baltic, a distribution which can be associated with the activities of the Hanseatic League. Lubeck effectively illustrates the use, as a pre-urban nucleus, of a pre-existing Slav strong-point, essentially a 'grod'. The 'grody' were small fortified settlements with primarily military and local control or administrative functions. The Wends seem to have established such a settlement after 1040 on what was virtually an island site, formed by the confluence of the Trave and Wakenitz rivers (Figure 2.30). This attracted a small colony of German merchants. But the nascent settlement was destroyed by the Slavs in 1138 and in its place Adolf of Schauenburg established a new settlement in the south of the island. It was eventually ceded to Henry the Lion who constructed a new central part consisting of market place and town hall with the cathedral located to the south. The town was given a generous charter of liberties and its success

2.30. Lubeck (after Lavedan). The dotted lines to the north identify the earliest Wend fortress, those to the south the settlement established by Adolf of Schauenburg which became the main religious centre with the Cathedral. The broken line indicates the central area where Henry the Lion established the commercial settlement with the town hall, market, and Church of St Michael.

ensured. It was walled around in 1163.

The third example is Breslau-Wroclau which provides a useful illustration of the different interpretations of urban growth which can be put forward (Kalinowski, 1972). Like Magdeburg, Wroclau developed in relation to an island-aided river crossing, but in this case a crossing of the Oder. There is no dispute about the origins of the city for a grod was established on the island of Tumski by the Slavs and about it a suburbium of German merchants grew occupying the islands within the Oder. In relation to this nucleus, on the same islands as the 'grod', the cathedral was located (Figure 2.31), so that the city shows that characteristic move towards the integration of the various contributors to the fully fledged urban entity. But in 1241 the town was destroyed in the Tartar invasions. In the early 1260s it was completely rebuilt in a clear and fairly rigid geometrical form on the left bank of the Oder. Although the blocks are not uniform in shape, the rectangularity has been

interpreted in German sources to indicate that it was German merchants returning to the site who laid out the new town which was characterized by a new great market square. Polish historians point to the fact that the parish churches were established before the German return in 1263 and that the basic reconstruction was Polish. Certainly the carefully engineered layout suggests that it was established by people well acquainted with town planning. Again, the settlement was walled about in 1260 with an extension giving a second enceinte about 1291 (Morelowski, 1960).

This brief survey of three cities provides a basis for the abstraction of the major elements which played a part in the morphological structure of cities founded or developed in the areas beyond the former Roman frontiers and eventually in the eastern marches which bordered that first Europe which came into being under Charlemagne.

1 *The defensive strong-point*: (i) In Germany this is often the count's castle, the 'Königshof'. (ii) In the Slav territories it is the 'Grod' or 'Gorod', a fortified settlement with a primarily military and administrative function. At this point it is necessary briefly to qualify the universality of the strong-point and to reintroduce the views of Tikhomirov (1959) which were considered earlier. In the Slav lands it is possible to identify what Hensel has termed 'incipient towns' and what Herrmann has called 'embryonic towns'. All these refer to an artisanal interpretation of urban

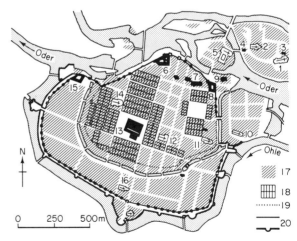

2.31. Wroclaw (after Kalinowski):
1. St John's Cathedral.
2–5, 7, 9–12, 14, 16. Churches.
6. The Ducal Castle (Castrum 11)
The Grod (Castrum 1) was located on the island of Tumski where the Cathedral (1) is located.
13. Market established 1260–3.
8–15. Arsenals.
17. The built-up area in 1562.
18. The original pattern of plots.
19. Line of inner defences constructed 1260–1263.
20. Outer defences of 1350, rebuilt in 1562.

origins and introduce a standard Marxist view. These settlements were organized in order to appropriate the surplus and hence were non-agricultural and characterized mainly by craftsmen. Even so, defence rapidly became an important feature. If Novgorod can be intrepreted in its earliest growth as a process of synoecism related to three agricultural settlements, its name indicates what became predominant, for it was after all Novgorod or Newcastle.

2 *The suburbium*: This is a closely associated agglomeration mainly made up of artisans attracted to a secure base. The specialization of occupations as against agricultural pursuits created the suburbium.

3 *The church*: The crusading and missionary zeal of the church meant that the various orders established houses and created offshoots amongst the heathen. These became the centres of religious administration and pushed urban influence into remote territories.

4 *The market*: The German merchants in particular grafted themselves on to strong-point and suburbium, creating new quarters and generating growth.

5 *New towns*: Not only were existing points of settlements developed, but completely new towns were established. The 'bastide' of the west is best represented in the east by those carefully, geometrically laid out towns of the Teutonic Knights (Kalinowski, 1972).

In this way, and by extension of the argument, in Russia (Gutkind, 1972) also, the whole of what is conventionally known as Europe became urbanized.

4 The city crosses the Atlantic: The urbanization of North America

In chapter 1 it was accepted that the city had independent origins in a number of regions which were called the areas of nuclear urbanism. Amongst these regions were parts of what are now Mexico and Peru, so that the heading of this section, The city crosses the Atlantic, is not strictly accurate. Nevertheless, contemporary American urbanism must be considered as having been re-introduced by those Europeans who at the end of the fifteenth and during the sixteenth and succeeding centuries 'discovered' and colonized the Americas. It would be absurd to attempt a review of the origins and progress of urbanization on the American continent within the limited space which is available, but it is worthwhile considering the mode and form of town development within the limited area of what is now the United States, with two purposes in mind. The first is to continue the presentation of the process of the diffusion by which during the historical past the whole of the earth's surface became characterized by cities as the basic settlement feature. The second is to show that in spite of the great differences in environment, and also in time period, the fundamental process was the same. However vastly different Cologne or Bonn and San Francisco or Pittsburgh might be, underlying their historical origin and growth are surprisingly similar factors.

Urban origins in what was to become the United States are clearly and unequivocally the consequence of a colonizing process. In that the native peoples were all but eliminated so that exploitative colonization became effective settlement and occupation, this does no more than align it with Australia, and perhaps New Zealand, as being the most successful. It is no great distortion to regard it as a continuation of that process of expansion of the European core lands which had reached its limits in the east as it filtered and attenuated into the vast lands of Asia, and in the west when it reached the Atlantic shores. But venture and discovery bridged the great ocean and brought the cultures of the nations of the ocean margin, such as those of England, Holland, France and Spain, as well as of Portugal in the south, to the New World; and their cultures were by then essentially urban.

An examination of the beginnings of American cities will reveal that the same threefold bases which characterized towns in Europe underlay their foundation across the Atlantic. Forts and churches were the earliest nuclei on which administration, primarily secular, was based and around which markets or trading posts developed. At first some were unplanned agglomerations but soon the formal, organized grid became the basis of town planning. Indeed, due to the later incidence of this diffused urbanism, forms evolved earlier in Europe were transplanted from the outset as part of the initial settlement phase. Thus descendants of the bastide appear as part of the occupation process in these new lands and, in consequence, the separation of a period of uncontrolled, 'natural' agglomeration from a succeeding one of more formal, organized control is not tenable, even though it is partly discernible.

The nature of urban foundation can be effectively demonstrated in a consideration of the Spanish occupation of the south and west in what are now the States of Texas, New Mexico, Arizona and California. This occupation also extended north from the Caribbean to Florida and it is worth quoting Reps's comment on the role of St Augustine, founded in 1565, although the actual site was moved in 1566. Appropriately it can be considered the first American city. 'St Augustine combined three distinct functions in one community. The city was, first of all, a military post with its fort and military garrison. Secondly, it was designed as a civil settlement for trade, farming and handicraft industry. And, finally it was intended as a centre from which religious orders would begin the work of converting the Indians to Christianity. Toward the end of the sixteenth century it became the policy of Spain to establish separate settlements for these three types of activity: missions for religious orders . . .; presidios for military establishments . . .; and pueblos or villas as civil settlements for farming, trade and town life' (Reps, 1965, 33–6). But these three elements did not easily remain so distinct and often became blurred both in function and location. The critical issue, however, is to make the parallel with the European experience:

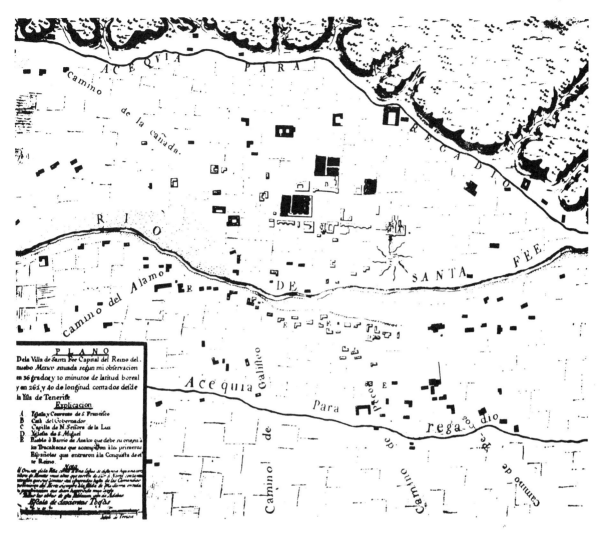

2.32.   Santa Fe, New Mexico, in 1766.

Castrum = Fort/presidio
Cathedral or monastery = Mission
Burg = Pueblo

It is possible to add the fact that the new towns became the administrative centres and provincial capitals, thus:

Civitas = Provincial capital

Spanish settlement is worthy of greater note, however, in that the direct relocational diffusion of the city is not attested solely by the evidence in the form of settlements but also by extensive documentation. This is found in those ordinances on town founding which occur in the Laws of the Indies which were promulgated in 1573 by Philip II. These give detailed instructions not only as to location, site, organization and government, but also as to layout: 'The main plaza is to be the starting point for the town. . . . The plaza should be square or rectangular, in which case it should have at least one and a half its width for length. . . . From the plaza shall begin four principal streets: one from the middle of each side and two streets from each corner of the plaza . . .'. Mundigo and Crouch have provided a translation of those ordinances relating to town founding and an interpretation of their sources and of their consequences for urban development in the Americas – 'a formidable physical imprint and social heritage in all the areas of Spanish influence'. They have also presented studies of the inheritance from Spain on the plan forms of Santa Fe, St Louis and Los Angeles. Even so, they have to conclude that 'the fact that all three of these cities were peripheral to the Spanish (later Mexican) territory allowed them even in their beginnings more freedom than other more centrally located sites' (Mundigo and Crouch, 1977, 254). The result is that it is probably more realistic to consider the early forms as the pre-urban nuclei rather than as the determinants of present-day layout. Two examples can be considered which indicate respectively earlier loosely agglomerated settlement and the role of the pre-urban nucleus.

La Villa Real de la Santa Fe de San Francisco (Santa Fe), the very name of which significantly combines elements of the civitas and of the ecclesiastical, was founded in 1609 on the site of an Indian pueblo and can claim to be the next oldest US town to St Augustine. It became the capital of the Spanish province and eventually of the State of New Mexico. It was founded by Don Pedro de Peralta whose first act was to erect the Governor's palace which was located on the north side of the central plaza, the plaza mayor, according to the ordinances. But the formal plan was soon lost. A visitor in the eighteenth century, Father Dominguez recorded his views of Santa Fe, 'The Villa of Santa Fe (for the most part) consists of many small ranchos at various distances from one another, with no plan as to their location, for each owner built as he was able, wished to, or found convenient' (Adams and Chavez, 1956, 39–40). The critical phrases are the last, for in spite of the attempt to exercise control and generate order, on the frontiers of settlement, where central power was most attenuated, the natural tendency for each owner to build as he wished reasserted itself, to produce a settlement which was more the product of gradual evolution rather than the regularity of the planning process or the Laws of the Indies (Figure 2.32). But even within this situation the major public buildings were the dominant features. Dominguez identified the 'semblance of a street' and at one end was the Governor's palace, and at the other end the church, 'the power and the glory' were in positions which throw back many thousands of years and to towns established in the south of the Americans. Even today, however attenuated, the impact of the Law of the Indies is tangibly visible in Santa Fe.

The role of the mission as the pre-urban nucleus of American towns is most clearly displayed in California (Wright, 1967). The exploration of Alta California was carried out from the Mexican bases with the major Spanish purpose of finding havens for the ships which had crossed the Pacific from the Philippines. It was supported by Franciscan priests intent on gaining these new lands for Christianity. Under Charles III who became king in 1759, military concerns became rather more significant and hence the initiation of the mission system by Franciscans rather than Jesuits. But the religious arm, under Father Junipero Serra, and the military, under Governor Gaspar de Portola, began the extension of control into Upper California with the founding of the missions and presidios which were to be the pre-urban nuclei of so many of the great Californian cities (Figure 2.33) from San Diego to San Francisco de Solano (Sonoma). An examination of the most well known of these will clearly demonstrate the role of the early core.

By 1775 the decision had been taken to found a settlement on the great bay of San Francisco. This was carried

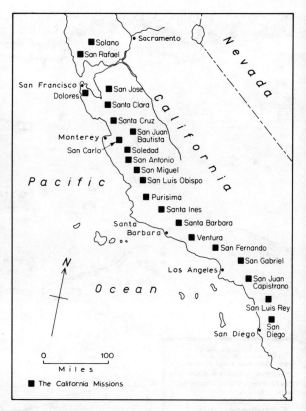

2.33.   The Californian missions.

b

a

2.34. San Francisco (a) in 1848; (b) in 1852.

out not by sea but overland from Monterey, through an expedition led by Juan Bautista de Anza and accompanied by Father Pedro Font. Sites were duly selected on the peninsula for the Presidio, on the mesa dominating the harbour, and also for the mission which was reached on the 'Friday of Sorrows' and hence called the Arroyo de los Dolores, so that what was to be San Francisco de Asi became initially widely known as Mission Dolores. It was some three miles from the Presidio. By 1776 the new settlers had arrived and Presidio and Mission were built. According to Scott an Englishman, a William A. Richardson who had jumped ship and lived at the Presidio, became the first settler at the small port village which grew under the name of Yerba Buena and occupied what is now the area of Portsmouth Square (Scott, 1959, 19). He established a small retail business and built his own house on the one street in the town – Calle de la Fundacion. By 1839 the problem of orderly extension had become evident and in that year a Swiss named Jean Vioget was given the task of devising a plan so that additional lots could be added. He established a grid of 12 blocks with present Kearny Street and Grant Avenue as the north–south streets and Jackson, Washington, Clay and Sacramento as the east–west lines, although the lines were out of true (Figure 2.34). In 1846 San Francisco was taken over by the United States and the discovery of gold three years later was to initiate its spectacular growth. Before then, in 1847, an Irishman, Jasper O'Farrell, had been employed to extend Vioget's grid, regardless of terrain, in order to retain convenience of lot subdivision. His one departure was to align Market Street on the diagonal direction of the old track to Mission Dolores, so that the city became based on two grids 'spliced together' (Scott, 1959, 24). By 1849, when that great extension was to take place which was to make San Francisco the archetypal 'instant city' (Barth, 1975), the city was based on the three traditional elements. Mission Dolores was the religious foundation of the settlement, the Presidio, the defensive and military, and Yerba Buena, the merchant quarter grafted onto them. San Francisco was to grow in a unique American fashion, though a grid superimposed on a most uneven terrain was certainly not new, but, even so, the line of Market Street and the large area still reserved to the American Government for defence purposes on the site of the Presidio, still reflect the control of pre-urban nuclei (Figure 2.34b).

The rapid urban extension of the second half of the nineteenth century represents a late phase in American urbanization and in order to trace that process it is necessary to move east to consider English and French colonization, the French exploiting in particular the great waterways of the St Lawrence and the Mississippi–Ohio system. It is possible to generalize this extension of urbanization – interpreted here as urban foundation rather than urban growth – over the United States by identifying a number of phases (Borchert, 1967). Like all generalizations this tends to distort many facts and ignore others, but it presents the critical issues in a concise way.

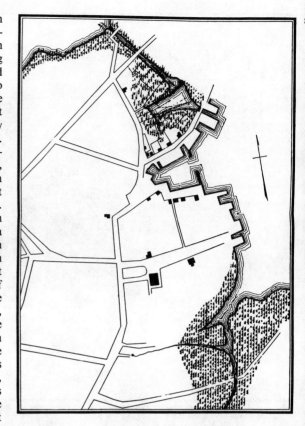

2.35.   Boston (a) about 1650; (b) in 1778

(i) The first urban frontier

This was the area of the 13 coastal colonies which were established from the European bases. Reps divides the territories involved into four areas (Reps, 1965). The first and the earliest were the Tidewater Colonies of Virginia and Maryland of which Jamestown was the first and Baltimore became the largest; the New Towns of New England which were led in size and repute by Boston; the Towns of the Middle Colonies which were dominated by New York and Philadelphia; the Colonial Towns of Carolina and Georgia of which Charleston was the chief, followed by Savannah. All these towns had been established by 1750 when the largest in population terms were Boston, Newport, Middletown, Norwich, New York and Philadelphia. The examples which have been cited make it evident that there were some which were the consequence of natural growth and others were planned and planted as ready-made towns.

Perhaps the supreme example of natural growth in the whole United States is Boston. This is the city where most Americans get confused because it is not set out on the ubiquitous grid, and where the meandering streets were supposedly the result of straying cows since intelligent

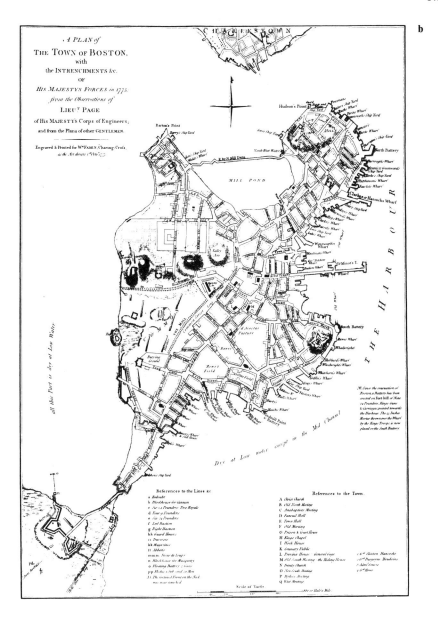

b

mankind presumably always built to a regular plan. The city was established in 1630 as the principal settlement of the Massachusetts Bay Colony (Whitehill, 1959) and the main control of its form was probably the irregularity of the peninsular site, as well as the lack of any pre-emptive demand for equal lot divisions. The result was that the plan was probably developed about the spine of the main line of movement which ran from the point at which the town site was joined to the mainland by a very narrow isthmus, northeastwards to the point at which the town dock was located and where Dock Square had grown to provide space for the handling of cargo (Figure 2.35a). The 'Old Wharf' had enclosed the harbour but it had

fallen into disuse soon after its completion in 1673 and the dominant feature was the Long Wharf, started in 1710. The line of Long Wharf was continued in King Street and Queen Street (now State Street) and the intersection of this line with the spinal street marked the central point where the Town Hall, the market and the Governor's House were located. Figure 2.35b which depicts Boston in 1778 indicates these features, as well as the proliferation of wharfs which had taken place. The beginnings of the grid of Back Bay is apparent, although Beacon Hill is only partly developed and the Common provided open space for military development.

In contrast to Boston, Charleston in South Carolina

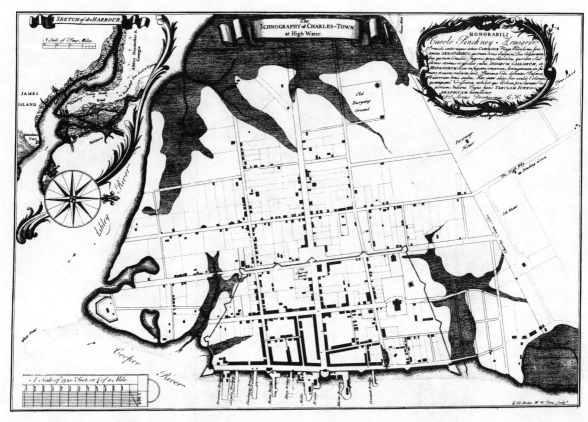

2.36.   Charleston in 1739.

(ii) The second urban frontier

was fairly carefully laid out in 1672 on the instructions of the London Government. The Governor arranged 'an irregular grid of eight blocks surrounded by a line of fortification . . . fronting on the Cooper River' (Reps, 1965, 175). This was apparently but part of a large scheme which had been brought into being by the mid eighteenth century. This consisted of a grid scheme with two principal streets intersecting at right angles and the intersection being made in the form of an open square. Reps's summary admirably illustrates the plantation of a planned town derived from distant sources 'They might well have copied the plan of Londonderry, doubled the scale, added an extra tier of blocks all round, and laid it on their delta site in the Carolinas' (Reps, 1965, 177) (Figure 2.36).

The strengths of the centres of this first urban frontier fluctuated in relation to their hinterlands, 'There was no primate city or national metropolis . . . Lukermann has observed that the entire family of Atlantic ports was characterized by small hinterlands and a primary orientation toward the sea and Europe and could in fact be considered part of the West European urban system' (Borchert, 1967, 314). In both form and function, therefore, these towns of the first urban frontier were clearly related to the homelands of their founders.

By the end of the eighteenth century, and especially after the War of Independence had cut the ties with England, the coastal cities began to develop, not as parts of a European system, but as independent American cities. This led to a relative stagnation in the cities of the north, but rapid development in those which could push communications westwards into new lands. But the lengthening communication lines needed depots or entrepôts at their western limits and so along the line of the great river system of the Mississippi–Ohio the second urban frontier arose, mainly in the period 1790–1820. This story has been most effectively narrated by Richard C. Wade in his book, *The Urban Frontier*. 'The towns', he asserts, 'were the spearheads of the frontier. Planted far in advance of the line of settlement, they held the West for the approaching population. . . . In a single generation this whole transmontane region was opened to settlement. In the process towns grew up along the waterways and in the heart of fertile farm areas. The names of many of these – such as Rising Sun . . . – were soon forgotten but others – like Pittsburgh, St Louis, and Cincinnati – became familiar words' (Wade, 1965, 1–2). The earliest, established a thousand miles into the wilderness in 1763–64, was St Louis. Others in addition to the above were Lexington and Louisville, Detroit,

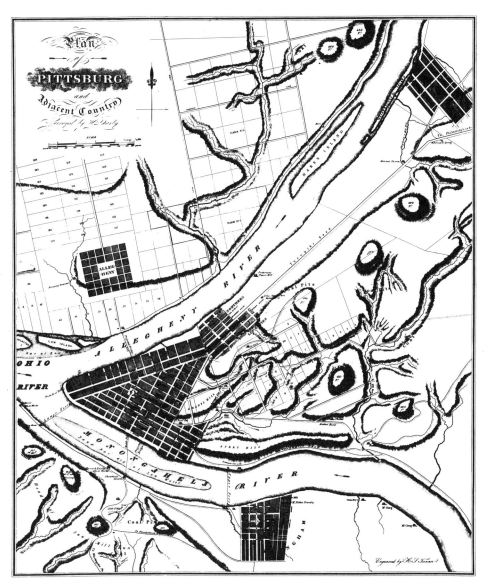

2.37. Pittsburgh in 1815.

Buffalo and Cleveland. In terms of urban form, however, a critical point was reached with the Land Ordinance of 1785 which effectively predicated a grid system for all the new towns.

One example must suffice here. Pittsburgh occupied a site which had long been contested by the English and French, for its location at the confluence of the Allegheny and the Monogahela gave it an immensely rich accessible hinterland. The military history of the site indicates its value. In 1753 the English established a log fort – Fort King George which was almost immediately taken over by the French and renamed Fort Duquesne. Even at this fairly late stage of the mid eighteenth century, the castrum as pre-urban nucleus is clearly

identifiable. In 1758 the strong-point had become Fort Pitt but war with the Indians meant that it failed to develop a market quarter. In 1764, however, 'Colonel John Campbell laid out four squares on the Monogahela River, bringing Pittsburgh its first and basic town plan. Though modest in scope, it determined the orientation of the town's future development' (Wade, 1965, 10). In 1768 a large area of western Pennsylvania was acquired by Penn's heirs and this included Pittsburgh. It was reserved and surveyed as the Manor of Pittsburgh and in 1784 George Wood and Thomas Viceroy were hired to plat the site. Usage prevented a complete alteration of Campbell's work, so that two new major lines were established fronting the Allegheny, Penn and Liberty streets, and the theme established by Campbell was

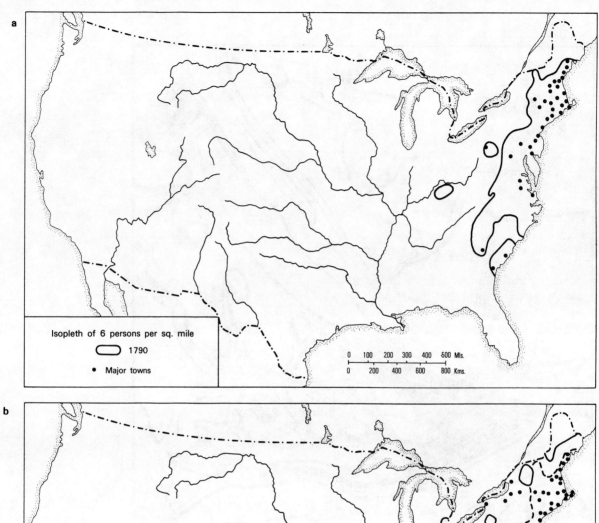

a

Isopleth of 6 persons per sq. mile

1790

• Major towns

| 0 | 100 | 200 | 300 | 400 | 500 Mls. |
| 0 | 200 | 400 | 600 | 800 | Kms. |

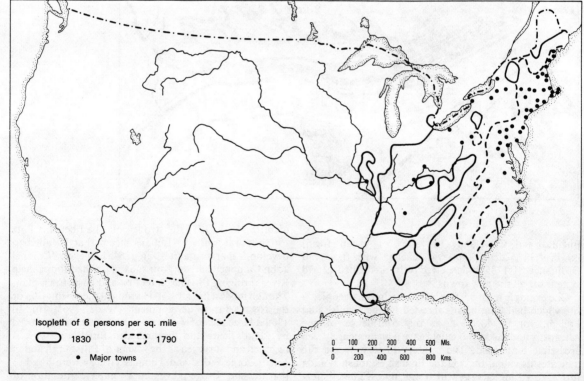

b

Isopleth of 6 persons per sq. mile

1830   1790

• Major towns

| 0 | 100 | 200 | 300 | 400 | 500 Mls. |
| 0 | 200 | 400 | 600 | 800 | Kms. |

2.39.   Metropolitan growth in the United States (after
         Borchert) (a) 1790; (b) 1830; (c) 1870; (d) 1920.

c

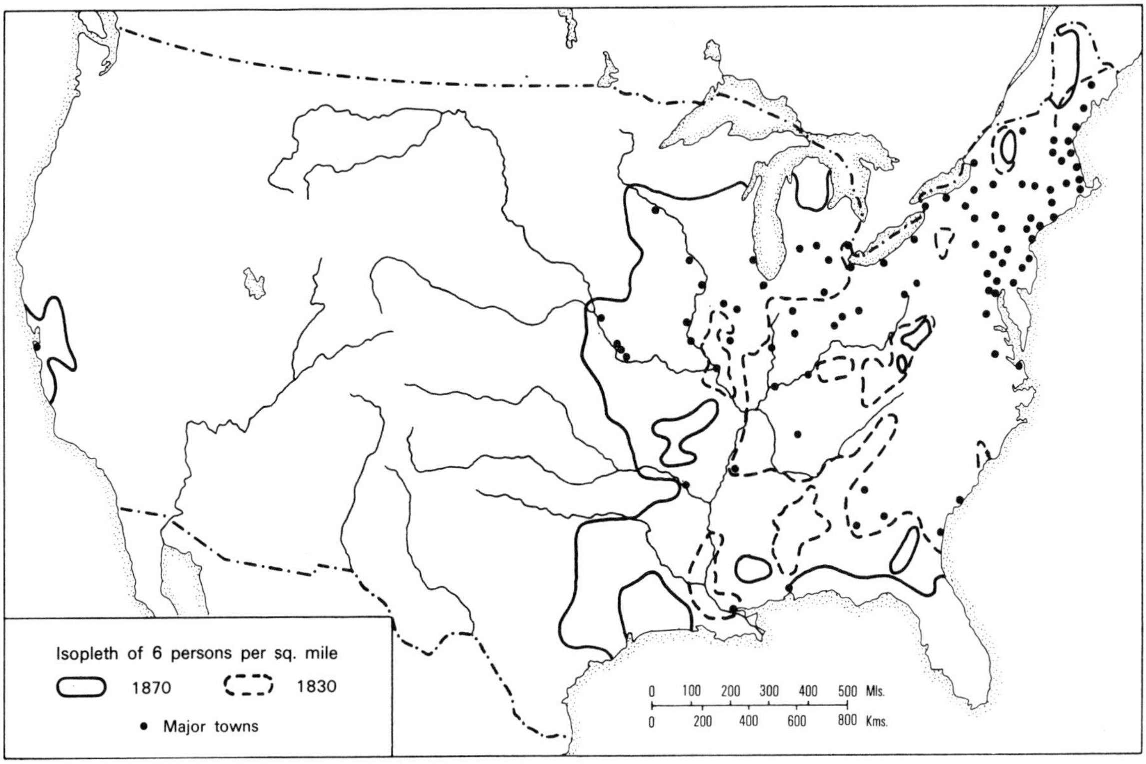

Isopleth of 6 persons per sq. mile

◻ 1870   ⊏⊐ 1830

● Major towns

0   100   200   300   400   500 Mls.
0   200   400   600   800 Kms.

d

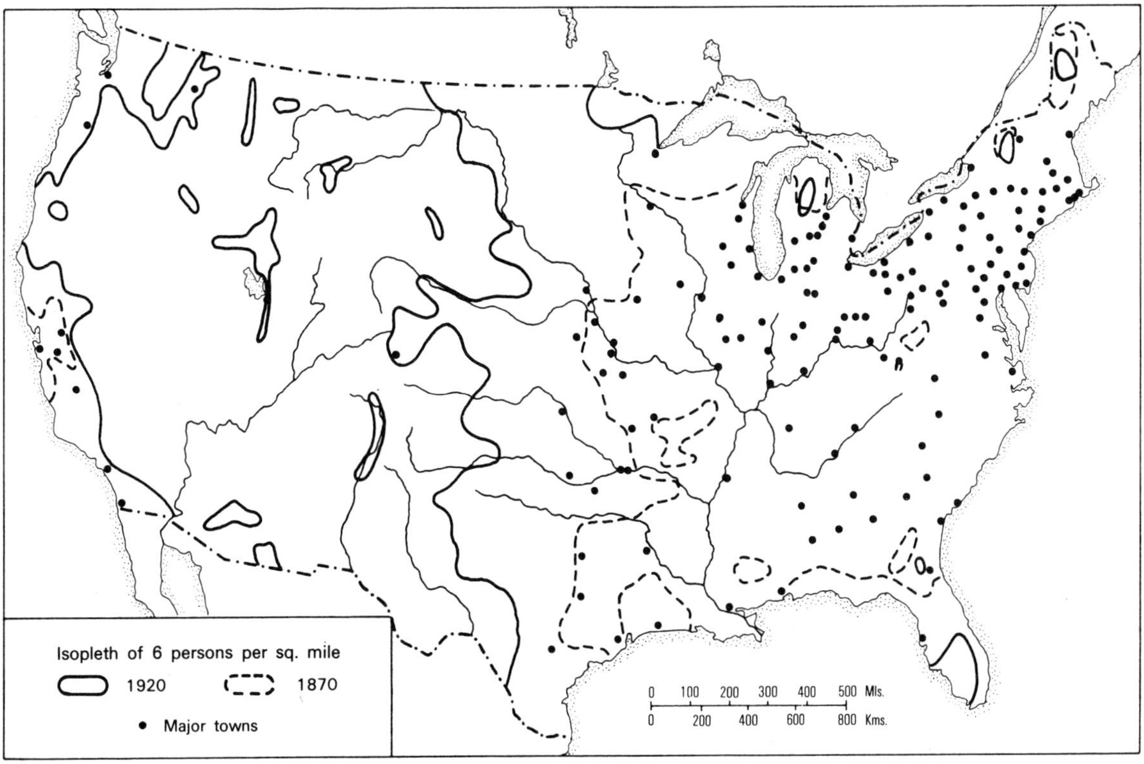

Isopleth of 6 persons per sq. mile

◻ 1920   ⊏⊐ 1870

● Major towns

0   100   200   300   400   500 Mls.
0   200   400   600   800 Kms.

continued so that two plan elements met along the line of Liberty street. A public square, the site for a Court House, was reserved between Fourth and Fifth street, south of Liberty (Figure 2.37). This type of development characterized most of these new gridded towns of the second urban frontier.

(iii) Western diffusion

This third phase in the urbanizing of America characterizes the middle portion of the nineteenth century. Two distinctive events epitomize the force at work; the Erie Canal was opened in 1825 and the transcontinental railway had been completed by 1869. It was this revolution in transport which brought into being a whole new series of settlements. Chicago is the archetype of these cities created by the railway (Green, 1965). The urban frontier was extended to the Rockies and, with the gold finds of 1849, to the west coast, where the foundation of pre-urban nuclei has already been noted. Two features characterized these towns. The first is that they were of immense variety and included a range of Utopian cities, amongst which was Salt Lake City. The second is that they were indigenous American cities. Much of the urban founding on the second frontier still preserved the east-coast traditions, many towns looked to Philadelphia as the mother city. But the towns of this phase were what can be called prefabricated towns, boom towns, the towns of boosterism, often ephemeral, like those founded along the railroads, and without even the limited civic spirit and control of those back east. Many are the towns which created the mythology of the West.

Two examples can be briefly introduced. The first was the creation of the search for gold, for in 1857–58 it was reported that gold had been discovered by Green Russell whose camp was located at the confluence of the South Platte river and the small Cherry Creek, although the name Pike's Peak Gold Rush referred to the mountain 70 miles to the south. By 1859 some 46,000 people had reached the area and a series of settlements sprang up (Barth, 1975, 101). 'Some of these settlements were scarcely more than mining camps and were doomed to disappear altogether. Others, such as Black Hawk, Central City, Golden, Pueblo, and, most important of all, the towns on Cherry Creek, profiting by the demise of the weaker, endured' (Green, 1965, 134). So the cluster of huts built by Russell became a town and by 1858 the newcomers had formed a town company to sell lots and develop a community. 'The community at Cherry Creek remained not as a mining camp, but as a supply centre. For hard on the heels of the gold seekers had come the real-estate speculators and the shopkeepers' (Green, 1965, 134). One of these speculators was General William H. Latimer who, arriving in 1858, found that all the land has been taken so he formed a company, built a log cabin on the opposite bank of the creek and gave a name to his settlement – Denver City after the former governor of the Territory of Kansas. In 1860 the competing companies, both of which were on land which was by treaty Indian territory, merged to become Denver. But the appropriation of Indian land brought the consequences of retaliation and Barth notes that, 'From the fall of 1863 to the fall of 1864, Denver resembled an army camp more than the peaceful city of white people that its residents yearned for' (Barth, 1975, 123). The military fort role, though not basic, was inevitably involved when the occupation of territory was part of the process of urban extension. But Denver's growth was immediate and rapid. The changes are epitomized by changes in street names as outlined by Barth. The early city, the first town company, had taken as partners two mountain men who had been employed as mediators with the Indians. One was William McGaa after whom a street was named. But in the 1860s the city was anxious to have an overland stage brought through the settlement and so the street was renamed Holladay Street after Ben Holladay's Overland Stage. But as the city grew the street became well known especially for prostitution and eventually was renamed Market Street.

If gold created Denver, then Laramie was made by the railway (Pence, 1968). As in so many cases there was a pre-urban nucleus, Fort Sanders, the guardian of the Ben Holladay Overland Trail and the Creighton to Denver to Salt Lake City Telegraph line. By 1868 the Union Pacific railway was being pushed through the area and the depots towns were built at regular intervals. In April 1868 the railway land agent opened his office for disposal of the town lots and by early May the railway reached the site platted within the military reservation, although Fort Sanders was some three miles away. The name itself was derived from that of Jacque La Ramie, a French Canadian trapper who had been killed by Indians in 1817 and his name given to two rivers. The original plat of Laramie is shown in Figure 2.38 and as to be expected it is the traditional grid. Again the basic conditions were present – new city, colonizing conditions, equal disposition of land. The subsequent history of Laramie is at once the account of lawlessness on the frontier and of people trying to build a civilized community; it is the story told over and over again by the Western film. But by the last quarter of the nineteenth century the account of urban *origins* in the United States comes to an end and the story of urban *growth* takes over.

The four maps in Figure 2.39a – d are produced from a series by Borchert concerned with metropolitan evolution (Borchert, 1967). The size element has been eliminated since that is not the concern at this stage. These effectively summarize the general pattern of urban advance from the east, the skip to the west coast in the mid nineteenth century and the gradual squeezing out of the western mountains and deserts. Like the maps of Roman cities (Figure 2.16) or the bastides in southern France (Figures 2.24a and b) or of the advance of the town into eastern Europe in the Middle Ages (Figure 2.28), these depict the inexorable advance of the urban frontier, the diffusion of urbanism.

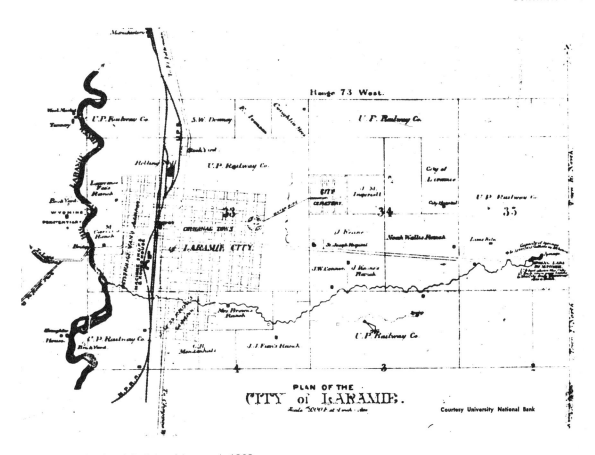

2.38. Laramie: the original plat of the town in 1868.

5 Conclusion

This chapter has not attempted a complete analysis of the way in which the world became urbanized. It has rather been illustrative, and has used the Western world as the area of exemplification. The universal process which has been identified is one of occupation and colonization. In colonialist movements the city is the linchpin. Whether it be the Roman occupation of Gaul, the Anglo-Norman occupation of western Britain and Ireland, the Germanic penetration east into the Slav lands or the American expropriation of Indian territory, everywhere the diffusion of urbanism showed recurrent characteristics. Accordingly it displayed the same elements. The first was the defensive strong-point to hold and secure the new territory. The second was the church which by its conversions, forced or otherwise, translated the indigenous culture into that of the occupier and secured the adherence of the conquered people. The third element was the market, by which the territory was exploited through an established and controlling central place which became the focus of communication and of organization.

Colonialism in this sense is not used in a pejorative way, for it involves the bringing of the wilderness into effective human occupation, though that wilderness was seldom uninhabited. It may seem that this conclusion is far too simple, as indeed it is, but it is also widely applicable. Thus urbanism was further spread in the nineteenth century by industrialization into areas where human occupance was thin. It can be argued that the three basic elements went along. If the coal mine was the new basis of wealth, rather than precious metals, the coal-owners had to ensure security for their investments by effective policing. The church had a role and, at least in one interpretation, can be looked upon as supplying an opiate for the people, reconciling them to the misery of this world in the expectation of reward in the next, as long as they conducted themselves in a proper way, humbly and reverently before their betters! The truck system was forced on mine and factory owners because of the lack of shops and markets, but it too gave the essential economic control into the hands of the powerful. To a large extent, the history of urbanism in a political sense has been that of the struggle of the inhabitants of cities to gain democratic control of their own destinies, whether it be from feudal baron, lawless frontiersmen or industrial magnates. The historical geographer of towns should, perhaps, concentrate his attention on the universality of the process of urban diffusion by which the ecumene was extended.

To a degree also the process which has been revealed explains some of the ambivalence towards urbanism for to so many peoples it represented a force at once alien and destructive of the folk culture. Even to the early rural Americans the city became the centre of the new immigrants changing an established way of life. There is much in the view of Sinclair (1962, 431) that the final struggle between the old and the new was symbolized in prohibition, which he called the last victory of the corn belt over the conveyor belt, of the old white Anglo-Saxon, protestant ruralism over the new metropolitan urbanism. It is also, perhaps, relevant that European urban communities came to maturity out of a victory of the residents over the vested interest of local magnates; in the United States the vested interest lay in the exploiting private concerns over which the supremacy of the community has yet to be achieved (Warner, 1968). The process of urban origins and diffusion has, therefore, much that is both common and vital, but the multivariate conditions and cultures in which cities developed have also produced infinite variety from the common theme which this chapter has attempted to trace.

Further reading

This chapter has covered a very wide range of material and the following list is highly selective.
First must come a classic work:
MUMFORD, L. 1961: *The City in History. Its Origins, its Transformations, its Prospects*. London. Also available in a Pelican edition.
Next there are two attempts to provide multi-volume histories of urban form. Both are valuable. The volumes by Lavedan are more in the form of a continuous history, whereas the books by Gutkind are more in the form of a gazeteer.
GUTKIND, E.A. 1964 cont.: *International History of City Development* (London). 1: *Urban Development in Central Europe* (1964); 2: *Urban Development in the Alpine and Scandinavian Countries* (1965); 3: *Urban Development in Southern Europe; Spain and Portugal* (1967); 4: *Urban Development in Southern Europe; Italy and Greece* (1969); 5: *Urban Development in Western Europe; France and Belgium* (1970); 6: *Urban Development in Western Europe; Great Britain and the Netherlands* (1971); 7: *Urban Development in East-Central Europe; Poland, Czechoslovakia, and Hungary* (1972); 8: *Urban Development in Eastern Europe; Bulgaria, Romania, and the USSR*.
LAVEDAN, P. 1952 cont.: *Histoire de L'urbanisme. Epoque Contemporaine* (1952); *Renaissance et Temps Modernes* (1959); *Antiquité* (1966); *L'urbanisme au Moyen Age* (1974). The last two volumes were written with Jeanne Hugueney.
Other, single volume, studies are:

BENEVOLO, L. 1980: *The History of the City*, trans. Culverwell, G. Camb., Mass.
BURKE, G. 1971: *Towns in the Making*. London.
HIORNS, F.R. 1956: *Town Building in History*. London.
MORRIS, A.E.J. 1972: *History of Urban Form*. London.
All the above books cover the various historical periods which have been reviewed but are predominantly European in their emphases.
The references in the text will provide a guide to reading on the specific areas and periods dealt with in the chapter.
For Greek town development the standard reference is:
VON GERKAN, A. 1924: *Griechische stadtanlagen. Untersuchungen zur Entwicklung des Stadesbaues im Altertum. Berlin and Leipzig*.
The most accessible general volume in English is:
WYCHERLEY, R.E. 1962: *How the Greeks Built Cities*, 2nd edn. London.
Two other basic studies are:
MARTIN, R. 1965: *L'urbanisme dans la Grèce Antique*. Paris.
KRIESIS, A. 1965: *Greek Town Building*. Athens.
For Roman towns the following are valuable:
CASTAGNOLI, R. 1971: *Orthogonal Town Planning in Antiquity*, trans. V. Caliandro. Camb., Mass.
WACHER, J. 1974: *The Towns of Roman Britain*. London.
The literature on medieval urbanism is vast but a beginning can be made with one of the classics:
PIRENNE, H. 1968: *Medieval Cities*. Princeton.
while Edith Ennen's book is available in translation.
Ennen, E. 1979: *The Medieval Town*, trans. N. Fryde. Amsterdam.
An exegenesis of Pirenne's themes can be found in:
BENTON, J.F. 1968: *Town Origins. The Evidence from Medieval England*. Boston.
while the basic exposition for the continent is:
GANSHOF, F.L. 1943: *Étude sur le Développement des Villes Entre Loire et Rhin au Moyen Age*. Paris and Brussels.
In addition a useful general treatment occurs in:
POSTAN, M.M., RICH, E.E. and MILLER, E. (eds.) 1963: *The Cambridge Economic History of Europe*, vol. III. Economic Organization Policies in the Middle Ages. Cambridge.
The best study of the bastide is:
BERESFORD, M. 1967: *New Towns of the Middle Ages. Town Plantation in England and Wales and Gascony*. New York and Washington.
Material on towns in eastern Europe and Russia is not so easily accessible and the volumes by Gutkind are the best source in English but:
BARLEY, M.W. (ed.) 1977: *European towns: their archaeology and early history*. London,
has sections on most parts of Europe.
For the USA the three books by Reps are most valuable:
REPS, J.W. 1965: *The Making of Urban America. A History of City Planning in the United States*. Princeton, NJ.
REPS, J.W. 1972: *Tidewater Towns. City Planning in*

Colonial Virginia and Maryland. Williamsburg and
Charlottesville, Virginia.
REPS, J.W. 1979: *Cities of the American West. A History
of Frontier Urban Planning*. Princeton, NJ.
A more general work is:
MCKELVEY, B. 1969: *The City in American History*.
London.

3
The Origins of the Towns of England

1 Introduction

The first chapter of this book sought to establish the conditions under which urbanism arose. The second traced the diffusion of urbanism laying emphasis not on the abstract concept of urbanization but upon the specific settlement form. That diffusion, it is implied, led to the origins of urban settlement in those parts of the world removed from the nuclear areas as conventionally defined. It is both necessary and appropriate, therefore, to turn to consider the origin of towns (a concept different from that of the origins of urbanism) in one specific area, thereby adding some specificity to the very general scale which has dominated to this point.

It is as well at the outset to qualify the title under which this chapter is presented. 'The origins of the towns' in an area suggests the existence of a discrete, well defined period when town life began and after which it was an enduring feature both of socioeconomic development and of the landscape. This is far from the case, a situation which in itself is a comment on the simplistic view of the origin of urbanism in a few areas and its subsequent transfer to the remaining parts of the world. This more detailed study, therefore, acts both as an extension of and a corrective to the study of the diffusion of the city undertaken in the previous chapter.

The problem of urban beginnings in England has a long and classic historiography. It was placed firmly in the context of continental work by Carl Stephenson in his influential book, *Borough and Town. A Study of Urban Origins in England*, which was published in 1933. As Stephenson fully acknowledged in the preface, the inspiration of his book was his period of study under Henri Pirenne, and the theme he adopted was the application of Pirenne's views on medieval city origins to England, 'The Norman borough', he wrote in the concluding paragraph of the book, 'may be considered new in all its essential features, no matter when or by whom its walls were raised. Divorced from the origins of the borough, the origin of town life in England thus appears in its true character – a problem, not of legal interpretation, but of social history' (Stephenson, 1933, 214). The pre-existing Saxon settlements were thus regarded as primarily military and administrative in function, pre-urban nuclei which were transformed only after the Norman conquest into functioning towns with commercial roles. 'The dominant features of the original settlement – agrarian, military, official – were entirely submerged. It was not from them that the town sprang, but from the exigencies of a new society' (Stephenson, 1933, 8). In many ways this was a neat and simple view. Towns would be viewed almost as physical transfers from continental sources, and a process which would now be called relocational diffusion, substantiated.

The stark view that there was no effective urban life, in a functional rather than an administrative sense, in Britain between the abandonment of the island by Rome in AD 410 and the establishment of Norman rule after 1066 was immediately challenged; the idea of the existence of town life in Anglo-Saxon England and of a gradual reinvigoration of the urban centres which had decayed with the collapse of Roman control has been gradually reasserted. This does not necessarily imply direct continuity of something which can be called 'town life' through from the Roman period. The conclusion of Wacher is an effective representation of such opinion.

Despite therefore the obvious continuity of settlement which took place in most, we must be forced to the conclusion that the towns themselves did not survive as institutions, and with them perished the culture that they had been foremost in sustaining. Town life had been reduced to life in towns and it cannot be emphasized enough that towns did not continue. . . . Yet an oral tradition kept alive the names of many, so that they became transmuted into the new language. If many were also resurrected in the late Saxon and medieval periods, it was because their sites, by accident of geography, were as suitable for the economics of these periods as they had once been for Roman Britain. (Wacher, 1974, 421–2)

In spite of the lack of continuity and because of the preservation of at least place names, it would seem appropriate to begin an enquiry into urban origins in England with the establishment of the Roman city system. But here, also, complexity is introduced for it has become more and more apparent that, within the preceding Iron Age civilization of Britain, settlements had developed which in functional terms demand consideration as having urban characteristics. The neat simplicity of Norman origins following a Roman phase which was clearly isolated at one end by means of a *de novo* Roman introduction and, at the other end, by a post-Roman collapse and disappearance, is no longer tenable. In consequence it is necessary to consider the evidence for pre-Roman towns in Iron Age Britain. Two non-urban periods – the pre-Roman Iron Age and the pre-Norman Dark Ages – can no longer be accepted, and both, therefore, have to be investigated as the origins of towns and the process of urbanization in England are considered.

2 Pre-Roman urbanization

The view that the hill-forts of western Europe had nothing that can be identified as proximate to the modern concept of urban functions is probably an inheritance from the dominance of the classical tradition in nineteenth-century learning. That tradition, accepting 'colonialist' evidence at face value, interpreted civilization as being either Greek or Roman and all else barbarian, the very word used by the Greeks to consign all non-Greek peoples to a universal, uncivilized category. Only now is learning freeing itself from the classical bondage, and it is being accepted that in the pre-Roman west a substantial movement had been made towards politically organized territories controlled from large central settlements. These, if they had no legal status in the later use of that concept as a settlement possessing a charter giving defined rights to the inhabitants, nevertheless functioned in many ways in an urban context.

This situation is most clearly demonstrable in pre-Roman Gaul. Daphne Nash has been able to show that a complex politico-urban system had developed prior to the Roman conquest. The key elements in that system were the *oppidum* and the *vicus*, the former being a fortified town, the latter a settlement of a non-defensive character. The *oppida* had three main features; 'their political and defensive characteristics, their character as ports of trade, and their predominantly non-agricultural population'. Nash goes on to the maintain that 'it can scarcely be doubted that the *oppida* were the highest seats of administration of the Gauls immediately before the conquest', and that, 'in addition, among the Celts there was an ancient traditional association of redistributive exchange with administration and the payment of tribute and taxes: it is not surprising therefore that they continued to be associated in the *oppida*' (Nash, 1976, 104). It would seem, however, that not all the locations used for exchange were settled and it is possible that small periodic markets operated at some of the small unexplained enclosures which characterize the area under discussion by Nash, that of east central France. These periodic markets were subordinate to larger regional markets which were conducted at permanently settled points. These were the *vici*. Nash demonstrates the elaboration of the system by showing that 'it was the largest and most central exchange and administrative

sites which became *oppida*, where the local nobility could attract foreign traders and conduct luxury exchange' (Nash, 1976, 106). All this evidence suggests a hierarchical structuring of markets and settlements. Moreover, the organization of territory reinforced the economic trends for by the first century 'the emergence of the state had made definite changes in Celtic society, and it is a near certainty that at some stage in the process of centralization the territory of each civitas, under the control now of a recently consolidated nobility, was formally delimited and subdivided on lines best suited to the efficient collection of tributes and the organization of the military levy' (Nash, 1976, 112). All this leads to the conclusion that the urbanization process had already begun before the Roman conquest, which took over and adopted an existing system of exchange and administration based on settlements which can only be considered as towns.

The association in this outline of ports of trade with political and administrative centres must be regarded with some reservation. The ports of trade, or emporia, were, perhaps, more characteristically located at the margins of politico-administrative systems where trade, especially the import of luxuries, was most likely. Hence they were divorced from such systems rather than central to them. Only at a later stage of development were the political and economic elements collapsed into one when the vitality of the internal market led to the atrophy of at least some of the ports of trade (Hodges, 1982, 47ff). This would modify but not greatly distort Nash's interpretation.

Gaul has been briefly considered because there the evidence is clearer than in England. But it is not unreal to look for parallel processes on both sides of the channel. There is every likelihood that a similar evolution took place, at least in the south and east of England. This is quite bluntly put forward by Barry Cunliffe. 'It is generally accepted by prehistorians that immediately before the invasion of AD 43 there existed in southeastern Britain centres of occupation which might reasonably be called towns, yet the significance of the pre-Roman urbanization to the development of Roman towns is frequently dismissed or misunderstood' (Cunliffe, 1976, 135).

The evidence which supports this contention is derived from the growing body of information about Iron Age Britain. On the one hand the examination of cultivation suggests a process of intensification which was accompanied by an increasing population. It is possible to infer a society which became more clearly stratified, with an aristocracy operating from large bases over defined territories. Again this sort of inference, for that is what it is, is supported by the evidence derived from coinage which, by the first century BC, it has been argued, suggests, the sudden rise of major marketing centres each within a network of satellite sites or sub-centres and a peripheral zone from which it draws its supplies (Collis, 1971, 1974). Even Rodwell, who was critical of the way Collis analyses numismatic evidence, concludes, the probability that the first order of pre-Roman settlements, both Belgic and non-Belgic, should be regarded as urban, or at least proto-urban, is rapidly gaining acceptance and reinforcement through current archaeological work. Judged on functional criteria . . . there can be little doubt that the more prosperous and complex centres of Belgic Britain merit recognition as urban at least three-quarters of a century before the Claudian conquest and perhaps much earlier. (Rodwell, 1976, 291)

These studies suggest a parallel to the developments already noted in France where major *oppida* rose to take on functions which were urban in nature.

Cunliffe has proposed a developmental sequence in a paper boldly entitled, 'The Origins of Urbanization in Britain' (Cunliffe, 1976). The critical elements are set out in diagrammatic form (Figure 3.1). The early hill-forts represent hill-top enclosures which had been constructed as early as 1000 BC and associate the Iron Age structures with earlier Bronze Age features. By the fifth century there seems to have been an abandonment of some of these smaller forts, with the survival of those occupying locations in well defined natural territories. These became the 'developed hill-forts' of Cunliffe's sequence, enclosures which were heavily defended. From the evidence of excavation at Maiden Castle, South Cadbury, Croft Ambrey, Moel-y-Gaer and Danebury it is possible to piece together the characteristics of these developed forts. They were central places for defined territories and had emerged as such after a period of development, possibly involving competition with neighbouring rivals. These centres supported a resident population primarily dependent on agriculture, but most certainly, part of the time or a section of the population was devoted to manufacturing goods which were produced in surplus and traded. The forts thus served as focal points for

redistribution. In addition there appeared to have been some internal functional differentiation, especially in the setting aside of areas for storage. These forts also seemed to have been religious centres, and the strong defences indicate the existence of some coercive power. Finally, they were the most complex form in a settlement hierarchy. All these characteristics match the evolutionary picture derived from the Gaulish evidence and clearly mark out the emergence of what can be called proto-urban functions, and from these beginnings urban settlements were derived. The subsequent developments are but inadequately attested by excavation but during the first century BC it would seem that, especially in the southeast, there was a modification of the old system, including the development of new sites which are analogous to the development of defended exchange centres in Gaul, and which Cunliffe has called '*enclosed oppida*' (Cunliffe, 1976, 148). Finally, in the last 100 years before the Roman invasion of AD 43 it would seem that a move to '*territorial oppida*' took place for a shift is evidenced from the highly defended fort to the more open nucleated settlements acting as territorial capitals. 'For Verulamium (St Albans), Canterbury and Winchester, therefore, there is some evidence, admittedly slight, to suggest that defensive measures were no longer thought necessary and the nucleus of the settlements, freed from these constraints, had shifted' (Cunliffe, 1976, 151.) Figure 3.2 indicates the relationship between the enclosure at Bigbury and the site of Canterbury, emphasizing a valley-ward shift, as true urban functions became dominant. The evidence from Silchester and Colchester is scrappy but 'there can . . . be very little doubt that sites like Colchester (Camulodunum) and Silchester (Calleva) had become major urban centres by the time of the Roman conquest, serving as the capitals of considerable tribal territories' (Cunliffe, 1976, 151). In all probability most of the other

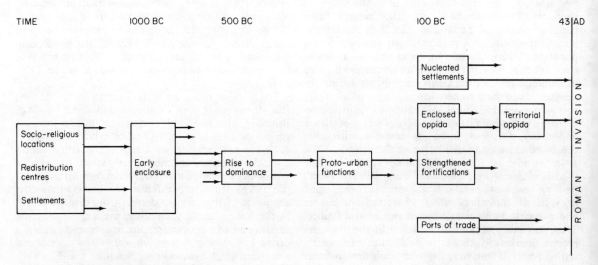

3.1.   The change of function of defended sites in Britain in the first millennium BC (after Cunliffe).

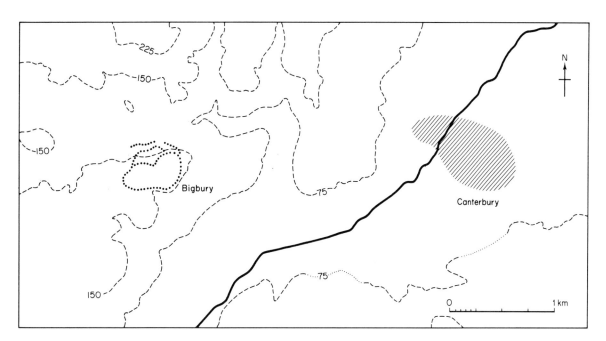

3.2.   Canterbury: related to preceding settlements (after
        Cunliffe).

comparable sites were of equal importance. Thus the
parallel with France is established and there is the
probability of a developed urban hierarchy, including the
ports of trade such as Hengistbury, operating at the time
of the conquest. 'Canterbury, Chichester, Silchester,
Verulamium and Colchester all became important cities
within a few decades of the Roman invasion'. That
invasion inaugurated not a process of the complete *de
novo* erection of an urban system, but rather the takeover
and elaboration of one which was in part already in
existence (Figure 3.3).

At this point it is worth reconsidering the bases for
urban origins in Britain which are now being
promulgated. Cunliffe has set out another diagram
(Figure 3.4) in which he has represented the interaction of
the various factors affecting the process of enclosure
which produced the hill-forts. If this interpretation,
together with all the evidence so far briefly presented in
this chapter, is related to the more general problem of
urban origins as presented in chapter 1 then it would seem
that a number of prime movers in urbanism are
confirmed. The first is the intensification of agriculture,
producing in this case not so much a surplus to be mani-
pulated as a population growth which triggered off
aggression and warfare. Even so, behind this explicit
need for enclosure, there is the implicit acceptance of the
centralization of coercive power which had to be reliant
upon the sort of surplus envisaged in those theories which
ascribe to it a critical role in town beginnings. Warfare
and military demands also are clearly represented, while
it appears that trade, even if in an organized form it came

later and is only represented in Figure 3.4 as a demand for
slaves, also played its part in the creation of proto-urban
nucleations. What seems not apparent is the critical
religious element. But here a rather closer scrutiny is
necessary. In Figure 3.4 the beginnings of a nucleation
are represented by the rather ambiguous word 'focus',
which apparently suggests the existence of some form of
central core prior to the metamorphoses of the last half-
millennium BC. Cunliffe himself has written elsewhere of
the possible origins of hill-forts and sees amongst them
the role of religious foci. He goes on to suggest that the
Neolithic causwayed camp could have served some form
of socio-religious role and that a theme of gathering
places for communities on religious festivals runs
through the entire span of British social development. It
is therefore possible that some hill-forts served such a
purpose, or developed from such beginnings. 'The
presence of temples or shrines is now well attested within
several defended enclosures, for example Heathrow
(Middlesex), South Cadbury (Somerset) and probably
Maiden Castle (Dorset), and a continuity of religious
observance might be thought to be reflected in the large
number of hill-forts which house later Roman temples'
(Cunliffe, 1974, 248). But the most fascinating site is
Danebury in Hampshire for there the hill summit is
marked by a series of pits, some of them containing
upright timbers of considerable dimensions and which
apparently date to the beginning of the first millenium.
Cunliffe asks the rhetorical question – 'Are we here
seeing the tail-end of the henge monument tradition?'
– and answers that if thus be so, then Danebury seems to
demonstrate a transition process from a ritual centre to a
permanent settlement. If this be accepted, and it is very

3.3.   Iron Age urbanization (after Cunliffe).

tenuous, then the origins of urbanism in England are set quite clearly within the context of urban origins in general. It is also significant that, in her study of the growth of urban society in France, Nash states that most *oppida* were also associated with, or actually contained, a religious cult site, whose significance sometimes extended well beyond the period of the occupation of the sites themselves. It could be argued that the first foci were generated by the need for religious or ritual centres which by virtue of their sanctity and control eventually were transformed into the emergent towns of immediate pre-Roman times.

3   Roman towns in England

The Roman occupation of Britain began in AD 43 and there followed a process of conquest and acquisition in which the foundation of towns was a crucial part. As has already been outlined (p. 32) there were three types of town (Figure 3.5) (Wacher, 1974). The first was the 'colonia', a town founded to house discharged legionaries, each of whom was given a plot within the town. The *coloniae* were therefore settlements of Roman citizens and each received a charter (*lex coloniae*). Colchester was the first *colonia* founded in Britain, in AD 49, and York, Gloucester and Lincoln also belonged to

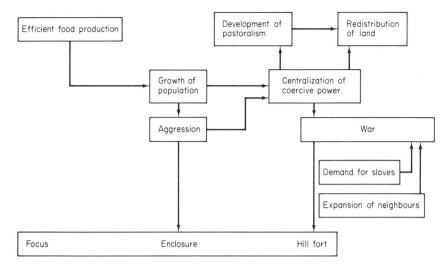

Focus | Enclosure | Hill fort

3.4.   Factors affecting the process of enclosure (after
        Cunliffe).

the group. The second category was the '*municipium*'
which was usually created by the upgrading of an existing
settlement. The *municipium* was only partly made up of
citizens, and had Latin rather than Roman rights.
Verulamium is the only town in Britain which was clearly
of such status, although Canterbury, Dorchester,
Leicester and Wroxeter may have been also. The third
group, according to Wacher, was the *civitas capitals* and
planned '*vici*'. The *civitas capitals* were the centres
established for the control of the civitates into which the
country was divided for effective administration and
which essentially corresponded to Iron Age tribal
groups. These are shown on Figure 3.5, together with the
colonia and the small towns or *vici* which can be assumed
to have been something more than villages, due to their
urban-type layout. Lowland Britain, what is now
England, was thus provided with a basic urban system on
the Roman model and the impact of Romanization was
sufficient to ensure its operation as an urban system
rather than as a series of separated military
encampments.

The point at issue in this chapter, however, is not the
way in which a hierarchy can be identified, for this is a
problem which will need to be considered at a later stage
in this book when the topic of the growth of city systems
is considered (chapters 4 and 5). The critical problem is
the extent to which the towns enumerated in the previous
paragraph can be considered to be continuations of pre-
Roman settlements. On *a priori* grounds this would seem
to be likely for it is much easier for an invading
conqueror to take over, and control through an existing
system adapted to population distribution and long-
standing usages of centrality, than to set up a new system.
Change over time might slowly, and eventually
considerably, modify the old system, but that is a
separate matter.

It is still possible to deny that any real urbanism existed
prior to the Roman conquest. Graham Webster writes,
'no evidence had yet been found in Britain that native
peoples organized themselves in urban communities on
the pattern of the Mediterranean world before the
Roman conquest. Their settlements in southeast England
appear to be no more than a scatter of round huts and
enclosures, but by the conquest some communities had at
least moved away from forest retreats and hill-top
fortresses to occupy more open ground by rivers . . .'
(Webster, 1966, 31). Two qualifications, the phrase
'pattern of the Mediterranean world' and the acceptance
of valley-ward movement, take much of the force out of
this objection. The general view would seem to be that of
A.L.F. Rivet, that a series of pre-Roman 'states' had
developed in England and that their administrative
centres were some of them very large indeed. 'Although',
he concludes, 'they cannot properly be called cities, some
of the Britons were already accustomed to central settlements on a truly regal scale' (Rivet, 1966, 103). This was
the theme developed in the previous section. Two
illustrations of the general process of development can be
given.

As has already been indicated, the Roman system of
occupation was to transform the old tribal territories into
self-governing districts of non-citizens, the *civitates
peregrinae*. A good number of the central settlements of
these civitates can be identified (Figure 3.6), among them
Calleva Atrebatum (Silchester), Corinium Dobunnorum
(Cirencester), Durovernum Cantiacorum (Canterbury),
Isca Dumnoniorum (Exeter), Isurium Brigantum (Ald-
borough), Noviomagus Regnesium (Chichester), Ratae
Coritanorum (Leicester), Venta Belgarum (Winchester),
Venta Icenorum (Caistor-by-Norwich), Venta Silurum
(Caerwent) and Viroconium Cornoviorum (Wroxeter).
To these Petuaria (Brough on Humber), Durnovaria

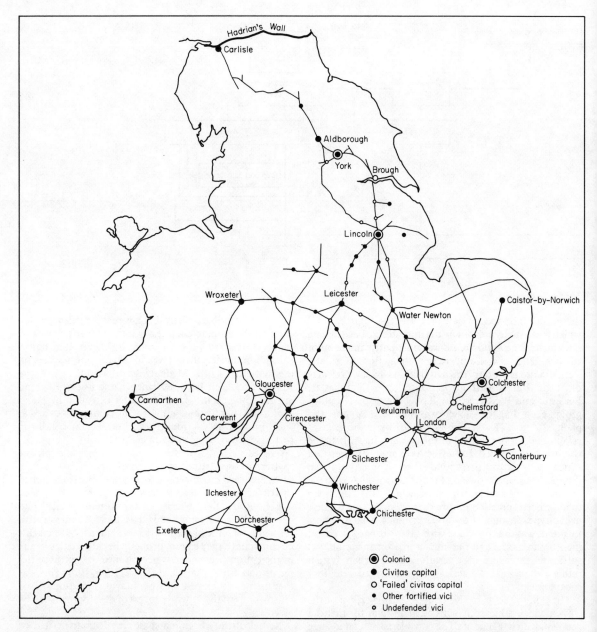

3.5.   The towns of Roman Britain (after Wacher).

(Dorchester) and Moridunum (Carmarthen) can probably be added. Corinium Dobunnorum, modern Cirencester, was the civitas capital of the Dobunni. The previous hill-fort caput of the tribal group was the oppidum at Bagendon some three miles to the north of what was to become the site of the Roman town (Figure 3.7). It is possible that Boduocus, king of the Dobunni, was one of the first to surrender to the invading Romans under Aulus Plautius in AD 43, and by so doing he was confirmed in his powers and remained as an ally of Rome. Even so, it was essential for the Romans to ensure

the military control of a crucial nodal point which secured a line of access from the Thames basin into that of the river Severn through the Cotswold Hills. If 'natural' nodality is an empty concept, the actual nodality of this location was created by the evolving Roman road system, for Fosse Way and Akeman Street intersected Ermin Street at this point. A fort was established in the lowland at the crossing point of the river Churn, controlling both the crossing and movement along the Cotswold Hills and across them. About AD 49 this fort was moved slightly to the north. The subsequent

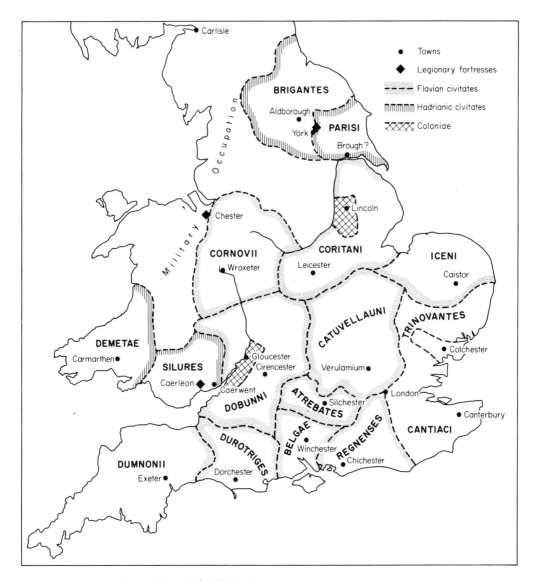

3.6.   Flavian and Hadrianic civitates (after Wacher).

process seems to have been one of 'natural' development. The fort provided a new and rich market for the oppidum at Bagendon, barely three miles away, and this probably induced permanent settlement close to the new centre of attraction. Growth took place immediately to the north of the fort. 'This civilian settlement seems to have been regulated almost from the first, no doubt under legal status of *vicus*, with streets laid out parallel to the axes of the fort' (Wacher, 1974, 294). As this growth took place there was a reciprocal decline of the hill-fort at Bagendon which was probably deserted by between AD 60 and 70. The new settlement was economically flourishing, had the strongest of links with the old tribal tradition and was in a most favourable location in relation to the road systems. It was the obvious settlement to become the

capital of Civitas Dobunnorum when it was established in the Flavian period. Redevelopment produced the standard grid-pattern Roman settlement with a central forum.

The narrative is, however, more complicated than has been presented here. The roles of Boduocus and of the neighbouring hill-fort at Minchinhampton are far from clear, but they do not greatly matter in relation to the development of the settlement pattern. Here is a characteristic case of continuity in location, if not *in situ*. *Oppidum* had given way to *civitas capital*, with a close and demonstrable relationship which fairly indicates both the transfer of an earlier system into that of Roman urbanism and the changes which took place during the transformation. As Mrs Clifford concludes,

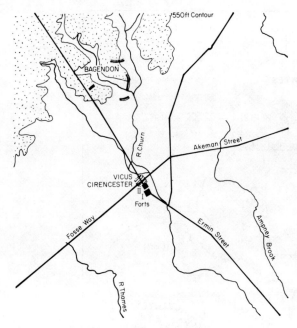

3.7.   Roman forts at Cirencester (after Wacher).

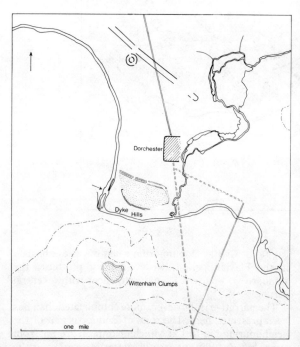

3.8.   Dorchester and Dyke Hills (after Rowley). The Iron Age Hill Fort is at Wittenham Clumps and the parallel banks at Dyke Hills the remains of a Belgic *oppidum*. The lines and circle to the north are the remains of a Neolithic cursus and henge.

At Bagendon the fourth period of occupation was the final one; and at this same time, between about AD 50 and about 60 at the latest, Cirencester was beginning its existence as a civilian settlement behind the Roman military front. The sequel there, whenever exactly it was brought about in due official form, was the raising of that settlement into Corinium Dobunnorum, the administrative capital of the Dobunnii as a civitas, or canton of regional self-government, in the permanent civil organization of Roman Britain. In this sense, and it is a very real sense, Cirencester was the Roman successor of pre-Roman Bagendon. (Clifford, 1961, 165).

A second example is representative of the small towns of Roman Britain. Figure 3.8 depicts the general features of the situation of Dorchester on Thames in Oxfordshire (Rowley, 1975). The Roman name of the settlement has been lost and it was first recorded by Bede in the eighth century as Dorcis and Dorciccaestrae. The first element of the name is British, although its meaning is not known. The whole area about Dorchester has a rich archaeological content. Only a kilometre and a half to the north were (until destroyed by gravel excavation) a Neolithic henge and cursus. But just a kilometre to the south of the present town, which is partly on the Roman site, is the Iron Age hill-fort of Wittenham Clumps, while to the immediate south of the town are the Dyke Hills. These parallel earth-works probably formed part of what is now believed to have been a Belgic *oppidum*. Trevor Rowley concludes, 'it seems probable that Dorchester began as a pre-Belgic settlement of indeterminate character' (Rowley, 1975, 116), and although the exact relationship between the Dyke Hills and the Roman settlements is not known, nevertheless the general process of settlement seems similar to that at Cirencester. A Roman fort was first constructed at the river crossing and from this initial foundation the small town developed.

It is now evident that at least some Roman towns were direct continuations, in location if not in actual site, of pre-existing *oppida* or hill-forts. A general valley-ward movement of settlement was the main consequence of local change, although even here such a change was already in progress, as already indicated at Canterbury (Figure 3.2), whilst excavations at Prae Wood have seemingly indicated a similar extension to the site of Verulamium (Frere, 1971). The Roman occupation of Britain proceeded, therefore, much as other occupations of new territory. Existing settlements, especially those with significant administrative roles, were capitalized on and towns developed on or near to their sites but rebuilt according to Roman form. This established a fundamental element of continuity, associating tribal *oppida* with Roman towns. On the other hand, a conqueror has to establish an effective system of control and an effective administrative system. To do this new lines of communication are established and new strong-points set up, initially as forts. Frere (1975) has attempted to quantify the various contributors to the small towns of Roman Britain. He estimates that some 56 per cent had a sure or possible military origin, that is, they developed from such forts. The small towns which developed from Belgic or other native sites Frere suggests were few in number, only some 13 per cent. But when the cases where a fort had first succeeded to a native settlement and where the military classification has been given precedence, are taken into account, the proportion rises to some 28 per cent, so that nearly a third of the small Roman towns had native precursors. As soon as military necessity becomes less dominant, differential growth begins related to economic and commercial advantage, and modification of the urban system takes place. The loss of direct military and administrative relevance means that some towns decline, decay and may disappear altogether (Carter, 1965). The Roman city system in Britain by the end of the period was a complex consequence of all these influences, but it must now be accepted that of critical relevance within that complex were the pre-Roman patterns of native hill-forts.

An assessment of the element of urban continuity causes as many difficulties at the end of the Roman period as it does at the beginning. If there are problems in relating Iron Age settlement to Roman towns, there are also obscurities in the relation between Roman towns and Saxon settlement. The prima facie evidence for a strong degree of continuity in the latter case is that of place names. If the creations of nineteenth-century industry are excluded, then a great many of the major provincial towns of England bear names which are of Latin or part Latin origin. The survival of so many urban sites suggests a continuity which cannot be dismissed by arguing for the permanent value of locations determined by what some historians call geographical advantages; it is hardly proper to invoke a geographical determinism when it happens to be convenient. The continuity is cultural, and man-made, not given by nature.

The earlier interpretation of a regime of invasion and physical destruction which simply obliterated the Roman towns, is no longer tenable. It was based largely on the tenuous evidence of Gildas, apparent evidence of fire and destruction from excavations at Wroxeter in 1860 (Wright, 1872), and a misconceived view of the Anglo-Saxon conquest as an earlier version of a coordinated nineteenth-century invasion of a foreign terrain. It now seems that the Roman city system simply decayed as the bases for its maintenance were removed. A system of cities can be imposed by a conquering power in a new area, but it can only be sustained as long as there are incoming supports in the form of population, power and wealth. It is, in this sense, parasitic in relation to the country. Once these external sources dry up, then each city must depend on its being able to act either as an independent producer of wealth (industry) or on functioning as a central place, as a market and exchange centre for a hinterland and a mediator for that hinterland with the outside world. This depends both on the stable wealth and productivity of the hinterland and effective local communications. With the withdrawal of the Roman army and imperial government the direct prop of the city system was removed. At the same time the economic system was in a state of chaos, while the intensity and organization of farming was never sufficient to carry a heavy urban burden. Collapse ensued, and cities were abandoned without any process of siege or attack. The major part of the evidence from Roman sites supports this interpretation. Most significant is that from those locations which were not reoccupied on an urban scale, such as Silchester, no signs of physical destruction were uncovered during excavation (Boon, 1957). Town life lasted on into the fifth century and Roman cities became Saxon settlements. Most of the sites seem to have remained inhabited in some form, and hence the major contribution made to the subsequent English city system, even though the Romano-British culture was itself replaced by an English one. Frere has reviewed evidence from Caistor, Canterbury, Exeter, Silchester, Catterick and Verulamium to show that, 'in one way or another the results of modern excavation, or of survey and research, have shown . . . that life continued in our towns, often on quite a civilized level, well into that fifth century. But it has also shown that this was possible only by hiring the services of Germanic troops, who sooner or later were likely to rebel. . . . The two worlds meet now before 400 in a preliminary phase of cooperative relations before the Saxon settlement proper began' (Frere, 1966, 98).

Wacher introduced a further element into the situation by arguing that widespread plague and pestilence, for which there is evidence, might have been a major contributory cause of urban decline (Wacher, 1974, 414–18). It was possibly, he contends, the character of the towns as centres of infectious disease which explains the Saxon tendency to keep away from them rather than adopt a policy of wholesale takeover.

This general picture of post-Roman town decay is by no means an unusual one. If the development of any area after a period of town-founding conquest is considered, then it will be seen that in order to survive beyond that period, towns have to take on economic functions. If they cannot do this, if they cannot achieve viability as centres for surrounding tributary areas, or if those areas are not sufficiently wealthy or economically developed to generate the necessary demand, then they decline into villages or disappear. They can survive parasitically as administrative centres, but this assumes the continued existence of a competent political authority, of power, and again the inflow of wealth. The aftermath of the Norman conquest of Britain provided large numbers of examples of towns founded and given charters but which failed to survive or even to start a sustainable economic life. The major difference at the end of the Roman period was the collapse of the whole imperial system itself. Even so, life continued at many of the urban sites, and continuity was ensured.

It is still possible partially, therefore, to accept the categoric conclusion of Wacher which was quoted earlier in this chapter. 'Town life had been reduced to life in towns and it cannot be emphasized enough that towns did not continue, and by no stretch of the imagination can they be thought to have done so. Any powers of recovery which they might have had, had also been effectively destroyed' (Wacher, 1974, 422). As he himself discusses at the outset of his book, all this largely depends on what is meant by the words 'town' and 'continuity', for, as has already been suggested, his subsequent sentence too easily throws onto geographical location the indisputable evidence of place-name survival. 'If many were . . . resurrected in the late Saxon and medieval periods, it was because their sites, by accident of geography, were as suitable for the economics of these periods as they had once been for Roman Britain' (Wacher, 1974, 422). A geographer may be less happy at accepting such 'accidents', and the view of Rivet may be a more cautious and relevant one, 'Roman Britain extended over 400 years and history does not happen in chapters . . . we too must see our period historically, considering all the possibilities of change and development in those four centuries, and, looking both backwards to the Iron Age and forwards to the Saxon kingdoms, seek out the material that is needed for a better understanding of the continuity which must be there' (Rivet, 1966, 110).

4 Saxon towns and Norman boroughs

The first critical point in relation to that continuity is the existence in Anglo-Saxon England of a city system and the abandonment of the notion of a non-urban hiatus between the collapse of Roman urbanism and the founding of Norman boroughs. 'One general result of recent investigation', writes Henry Loyn, 'is a growing sense of wonder that scholars could either seriously have held that the Anglo-Saxons outside London had no town worthy of the name. . . . There is evidence enough for the existence of towns, and firm and conclusive indication of varied and subtly complex urban growth' (Loyn, 1971, 115). The second point is the extent of continuity between Roman town and Saxon burh. An outline model of the Roman–Saxon urban transition has been suggested by Martin Biddle (1971), a model largely derived from the process of development at Canterbury. He suggests that the first stage is a replacement of their original Romano-British hirers by German mercenaries. This is followed by the emergence from among the mercenaries of a leader who establishes a 'royal' house. Further arrivals of Germanic populations reinforce this takeover. The leader builds a palace within the old Roman *enceinte* which, under the impact of a collapsed economy, has lost its commercial functions and might well be in a state of physical decay. Timber huts built by the German populations are set across the lines of the Roman streets producing considerable modification, though this varies from place to place. The Church, seeking focal points on which to base its territorial organization, uses these places which still preserve quasi-administrative func-

tions. There was no charter and possibly very little commercial activity. Into this scheme the role of the ports of trade, which has already been noted (p. 65), has to be fitted. These remained and developed outside the evolving polities but under the regulation of rulers. Possibly their activities provided the model for the creation of internal market systems which replaced the redistributive system (Sawyer, 1977). As market organization grew it reacted on the ports of trade, often to their detriment. Finally by the ninth and tenth centuries increasing trade and commercial growth is reinforced by the royal need to construct strong military defences. Formal planning is reintroduced, but towns are now created, not simply fortified strong-points. This is a tentative model applicable to one part of England only, but it meets all the immediate problems. It accepts a brief non-urban phase at the period of maximum disruption, but preserves that basic continuity of site which saw the translation of some of the significant Roman towns into significant English towns.

The process which has been traced above has parallels which help to confirm its essential credibility. If, again, the aftermath of the Norman conquest in England and Wales is considered, it is apparent that even where both potential and actual economic development were extremely limited, the urban status of many of the founded towns was preserved by the fact of administrative necessity. Government, in its varied forms and degrees of rigour of control, has to work. It was not until some four centuries after the conquest that many towns lost their administrative supremacy through its transfer to successful economic competitors. The final and formal extinction of the administrative pattern did not occur until the Reform Act of 1832, some seven centuries after the establishment of the basic features. Now, this parallel does not demand in any way a formal, far-reaching Saxon administrative system, either lay or ecclesiastic, or even one of an attenuated sort. But control has to be exercised from a point and those towns which had been Roman were the most obvious and impressive points. Moreover, this suggests a parallel with the general European pattern. As trade and commerce developed, and as protection was needed against the depredations of the Danes, so 'new' towns emerged on the foundations of the old.

The richest evidence of this process has been derived from the extensive excavations which have been carried out at Winchester (Barlow, Biddle *et al.*, 1976). There it has been clearly shown that the medieval grid plan within the city walls is not coincident with that of the Roman city (Venta Belgarum). Further, the grid of streets pre-dates the Norman Conquest. Biddle and Hill date the planning to the period probably before 904, and possibly between AD 880 and 886. The general development of Winchester has much in common with Canterbury. There is evidence of a royal palace from the middle of the seventh century, while the church, later to be known as the Old Minster, had been founded by Cenwalh of Wessex about AD 648. The town became greatly significant as a royal and ecclesiastic settlement but it was 'not an urban place in a full economic and social sense before the ninth century' (Biddle, 1971, 396). Earlier, by the fifth century, it appears that timber huts were built across Roman street lines and the palace and minster were constructed without regard to them. Even so, some elements remained. High Street linked the east and west gates, which were exactly coincident with the Roman breaks in the walled defences. It probably formed the main through artery of communication, swelling at its eastern end to form a market place. Building divergence, however, removed it slightly from the precise line of the Roman street (Figure 3.9).

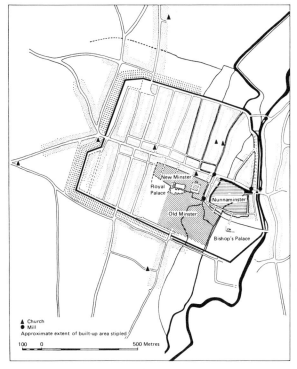

3.9. Winchester *c*. 933–1066 (after Biddle and Hill). Only parish churches known to be of pre-Conquest origin are shown.

The 'refoundation' of Winchester took place as part of a systematic fortification of towns by King Alfred against the Danish threat. This involved formal internal planning in which a grid system was used based on the axial High Street. Although that street approximates to the Roman line, the offset streets bear no relation to the earlier, obscured plan (Figure 3.9). Winchester's development shows the way in which, during a brief period of transition, both urban function, in its fullest sense, and urban form, were partially lost, but were rapidly restored in part conformity to what had gone before, for it should be remembered that the exact location is retained, as well as the exact perimeter of the defences and the approximate run of High Street. Of the

late Saxon burh Biddle and Keene write, 'Within the walls in the seventh to ninth centuries there seem to have been large open spaces, at least partly under cultivation, and three – perhaps four – components of settlement: a royal dwelling, the episcopal community, a limited number of enclosed private dwellings, and perhaps some service population along the eastern part of the axial route which later became *ceap straet* and is now High Street' (Biddle and Keene, 1976, 450) (Figure 3.9). From this pre-urban nucleus the Saxon burh was derived and by the conquest in 1066 it had become a thriving urban community – 'the variety of the crafts and trades practised in Winchester on the eve of the Norman conquest must have been one of the most strikingly urban features' (Biddle and Keene, 1976, 459). There were specialized markets in special locations and a wide range of trading contacts.

The discussion of the evolution of Winchester has noted that the layout of the Roman settlement was partially lost. In other towns it disappeared completely, in spite of a continuity in settlement from pre-Roman times. Canterbury is an appropriate example for it has already been used (p. 66) to demonstrate such continuity. With the shift from Bigbury it became a territorial oppidum and within decades of the Roman occupation it had become a significant administrative centre – Durovernum Cantiacorum – one of the first civitas capitals to emerge in Britain (Wacher, 1974, 178). N.P. Brooks writes, 'its role as the administrative centre of a tribal region was repeated in the Anglo-Saxon period when Canterbury was a *volksburg* – Cantawaraburh being the borough of the people of Kent. We do not yet know what (if anything) this meant for the economy, the buildings and the layout of the Dark Age and early medieval town. When Augustine arrived in 597 to convert the pagan English to Christianity, Canterbury is said to have been the metropolis of King Ethelberht's *imperium*. . . . To some degree therefore, it must have been the seat of secular power and residence. Until a royal residence or palace is located and excavated in Canterbury however, we cannot know whether the barbarian Anglo-Saxon rulers of Kent made use of Roman buildings or sought to continue anything of Roman civic administration' (Brooks, 1977, 489). Certainly significant physical elements of the Roman city survived to play a dominant role in the form of the later city. These were the defensive walls which were followed precisely by the medieval defences, and four out of the five gates. Topographically, therefore, the early medieval city was in its broadest outlines conditioned by the physical remains of the Roman settlement.

But that conditioning related solely to broad outline for, in complete contrast, nothing of the intra-mural layout has survived (Figure 3.10). That layout was the consequence of a process of severe contraction of settlement in the Dark Ages, and possibly a very rapid one in which the Roman street system was lost, and presumably, the general function as a town in the broadest sense. There followed the gradual emergence of

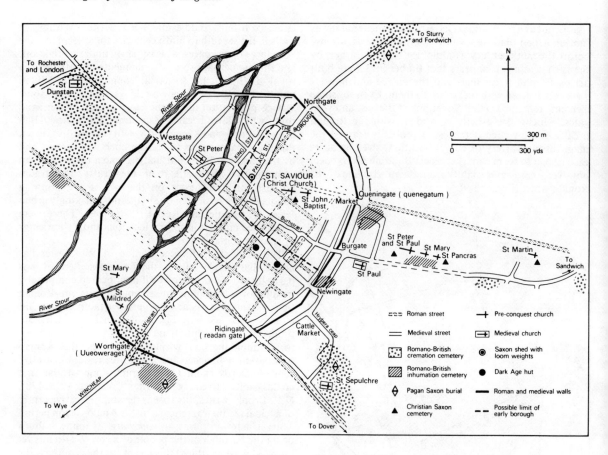

3.10.   Anglo-Saxon Canterbury (after N.P. Brooks).

a new pattern dominated by the cathedral complex in the northeastern quadrant. Using the evidence of street directions and names, Brooks suggests that the early burh, possibly with primitive defences, was restricted to that area (Figure 3.10), a situation generally parallel to that in Trier which has already been discussed (Figure 2.20, p. 39–40). Brooks argues that this newly emergent pattern was largely determined by the churches and especially by the cathedral. 'It is not until the laying-out of a new east–west street through the town, which involved the building of a new gate (Newingate . . .), and the development of a somewhat irregular grid of streets parallel and at right-angles to this street and Wistraet [Figure 3.10] that a more secular element enters the planning of the medieval city. The laying-out of the streets had certainly been accomplished by the twelfth century. Until direct archaeological evidence is forthcoming it is best understood as another example of late-Saxon planning, perhaps to be attributed to the early tenth century' (Brooks, 1977, 495).

This reference to late-Saxon planning immediately recalls the case of Winchester already introduced. Biddle and Hill have noted a rhetorical question posed by Asse in his life of King Arthur – 'What of the cities and towns he restored, and the others, which he built where none had been before?' (Biddle and Hill, 1971, 83). Two

problems arise therefore; the existence of towns with non-Roman bases and of formal grid planning. An association of these can be derived from pre-Conquest Hereford. At the outset it must be recorded that although there is no evidence of a formal Roman town on the site, there is evidence of occupation. 'Some kind of Roman settlement is indicated archaeologically at Hereford . . . where there are several Roman altars. These and other re-used material may indicate a Roman religious or military focus before the establishment of the town, palace or bishopric in the seventh or eighth centuries' (Rahtz, 1977, 110). So as Lobel asserts, 'the origin of the place is extremely obscure. There is a tradition that it was the centre of a British diocese and later the seventh-century seat of a bishopric of the kingdom of the Magonsaete, a Saxon people, but it is not until the early eighth century that there is reliable evidence for either a town called Hereford or for a bishopric there' (Lobel, 1969, 1).

Figure 3.11 indicates the major features of Saxon Hereford as they can be derived from a number of sources (Noble and Shoesmith, 1967; Lobel, 1969; Shoesmith, 1974; Biddle, 1976; Rahtz, 1977). Two pre-Norman enceintes can be tentatively identified. The earliest, on a gravel terrace immediately north of the

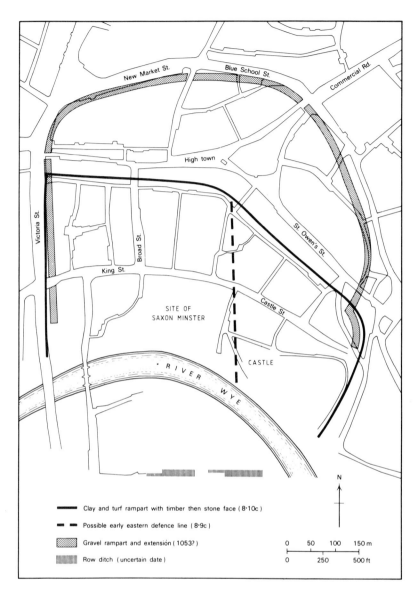

3.11. The early topography of Hereford (after Biddle, Lobel and Shoesmith).

New Market St.

Blue School St.

Commercial Rd.

High town

Victoria St.

Broad St.

St. Owen's St.

King St.

SITE OF
SAXON MINSTER

Castle St.

CASTLE

R I V E R   W Y E

N

Clay and turf rampart with timber then stone face (8·10c)

Possible early eastern defence line (8·9c)

Gravel rampart and extension (1053?)

Row ditch (uncertain date)

| 0 | 50 | 100 | 150 m |

| 0 | 250 | 500 ft |

river Wye, consists of an eighth-century gravel rampart which is topped by a further turf and clay rampart. This latter structure is interpreted as being early tenth century in date and constituted the defences of the burh which was known to have existed in AD 914 (Lobel, 1969, 42). The second enceinte consists of a gravel rampart probably built in 1055 by Harold Godwinson after the city had been destroyed by the Welsh. This consisted of a northern extension into what came to be called 'high town'. The layout of high town was largely consequent upon the intersection of the roads, along the lines of early tracks, leading into the town, but it is the construction of the street plan within the first enceinte which is of the greater interest here. Biddle writes, 'Within this enclosure main streets intersecting at right-angles joined the west gate to the supposed site of the east gate and the north gate to the river ford [Figure 3.11]. There were side-streets at right-angles to the main east–west street and an intra-mural street along the northern defences. . . . It must be emphasized that there is as yet no direct dating evidence for the internal layout just described. . . . Nevertheless the location of this layout within what appears to be the earliest enceinte suggests that the streets may be contemporary with the first true defences and thus belong to the ninth or even to the eighth century' (Biddle, 1975, 25–6). Biddle goes on to suggest that the early appearance of such a formally planned system of streets reflects the importance of Mercian influences in Anglo-Saxon planned towns, possibly the source of Wessex plans.

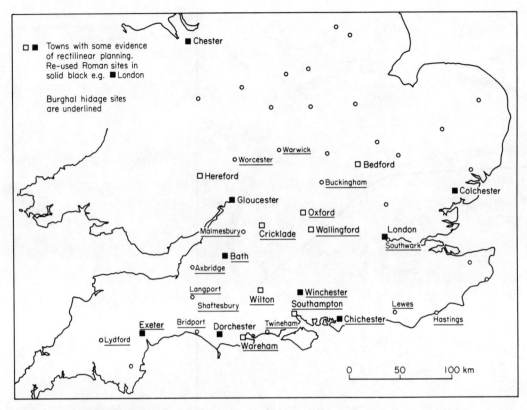

3.12.   Towns in existence in 930 AD which became
Domesday boroughs (after Biddle).

This discussion has moved away from the role of towns to that of internal layout but, nevertheless, the central control needed for formalized planning indicates the significance of Saxon urban development. It only needs to add that perhaps the best example of a port of trade was Hamwich, which lay fronting the Itchen and to the east of the later borough of Southampton. It was a characteristic gateway community. By the tenth century, however, it had declined as the internally directed city system came into being.

The broader picture is represented in Figure 3.12 which indicates towns in existence in AD 930 which became Domesday boroughs. Those which had re-used Roman sites are identified and their contributions to the emerging town system was considerable. It must again be stressed, however, that there were other sources from which towns developed. Even so, there is a discernible underlying stratum of Roman settlements. What above all is apparent is the great variety of ways in which, related to the exigencies of particular circumstances – and the threat of the Danes and the consequent towns of the burghal hidage is the clearest general one – Roman towns were revitalized and new burhs created.

The final phase, from which the complete pre-industrial system sprang, was the foundation of the Norman boroughs. It is possible to accept Stephenson's

view that by the latter half of the eleventh century the population of the borough was predominantly mercantile. After take-over and the generation of new towns, the primary process of economic sorting gathered momentum to elaborate a set of towns onto which the industrial period was to surperimpose yet another overlay and initiate another process of competition and sorting.

The characteristics of the emergent mercantile and planned towns of the Middle Ages has already been discussed in chapter 2 and there is little purpose in following the same trends in England. However, one example of a non-Roman burh transformed into Norman town can be cited in illustration of the general process. The exact origin of the Anglian burh of Nottingham is not known (Barley, 1969). Presumably it was a small village settled by the kinsmen of one Snot from whom the settlement takes its name – Snotingeham. This village, probably made into a fortified burh, occupied a strategic location at a ford across the river Trent, and a defensive site on a river cliff formed out of Bunter Sandstone (Figure 3.13). It was made one of the five headquarters of the Danish armies after the Scandinavian settlement in 873. Along with Derby, Leicester, Lincoln and Stamford it was raised to a significant status. The burh was captured by Edward the Elder in 921 and was refortified and strengthened. Barley's conclusion indicates its urban

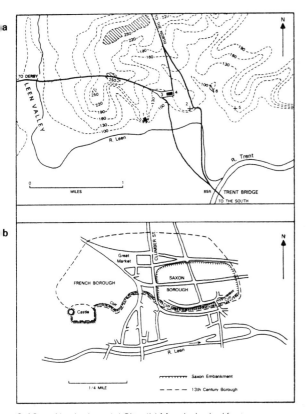

3.13.   Nottingham (a) Site; (b) Morphological features.

functions. 'There are indications that the Anglian burh
was a centre of administration and trade. Since the late
ninth century it had been the head of its shire and had
possessed a mint since at least the reign of Athelstan
(924–39). Membership of the loose confederation of the
Five Boroughs meant that Scandinavian influence with
its mercantile bias was strong. The Domesday account
provided unusual evidence of mercantile development,
with its emphasis on the passage of ships on the Trent and
on the road from Lincoln to York through the town. On
the other hand, the burghal population was small . . .'
(Barley, 1969, 2). After the conquest the significance of
the location was quickly appreciated and a castle
borough was established in 1068 on the edge of the
sandstone cliff, but to the west of the burh. New defences
were developed and some of those of the Anglian
settlement were deliberately filled in as they were no
longer relevant. There is no doubt that the new regime
provided a major stimulus to commercial development,
'Henry I's charter greatly encouraged the town by
recognizing the right to attract immigrants, by granting
freedom of toll on the river Trent and in the market, and
by giving the right to levy toll of others. . . . Before the
end of the twelfth century the town had acquired the
rights of self-government and such urban privileges as a
guild merchant and freedom from toll throughout the
land' (Barley, 1969, 3). The usages of the older Anglian

burh, however, remained and Nottingham was divided
into English and French customs, old and new. The
morphology of the town reflected these two elements for,
lying side by side, they still dominate the structure of the
town (Figure 3.13b). They symbolize those mutations of
burh into borough and borough into town which are the
critical changes of the period.

The Anglo-Norman borough derived its status either
from prescriptive rights or by the granting of a charter by
king or feudal lord (Donkin, 1973). The burgesses who
were given privileges, especially that of holding burgages
on freehold tenure, also provided financial returns in the
form of tolls. There was clearly an incentive both for king
and feudal lord to create boroughs. By the death of King
John in 1216, Donkin estimates, some 120 places had
secured charters either confirming rights or granting
new ones. About a half of these had been Domesday
boroughs. In addition there were the towns planted anew
in the process of conquest. It should also be noted that 'in
1294 a differential tax on movable property was
introduced. . . . But the list of 226 places described as
boroughs on the enrolled accounts . . . differs from that
of the chartered boroughs. On the other hand, over
40 seignoral boroughs never appeared as taxation
boroughs' (Donkin, 1973, 127–8). Such discrepancy was
probably due to local variations in the interpretation of
the trading activity which identified a taxation borough.
In spite of all the difficulties of interpretation which still
remain, it is clear that the account of urban origins in
England must end at this point. Figure 3.14 is R.A.
Donkin's summary of English boroughs between 1086
and 1334. However the detail might vary, this is a
composite map built up by the superimposition of layers
of settlement from different periods, each layer showing,
at least partially, an adjustment to the one that went
before. Above all, this review of urban origins in
England indicates the complexity of the problem. There
are no single and simple beginnings, but rather a slow
evolutionary process within which each stage is partly a
product of the previous one until a point is reached, by
the eleventh century, when an interactive system of towns
is acceptable. In essence, the developments through each
phase are constant and trends are replicated. This notion
of a constancy in the processes at work can be set out in
the form of a simple model.

1 Conquest and occupation	Adoption of the existing settlement pattern to provide control.	The emergence of politico-religious territories.
2 Administrative priority	Control exerted, partly based on external sources of wealth and power.	Gateway communities or Ports of Trade, i.e. long-distance import centres divorced from politico-administrative system.

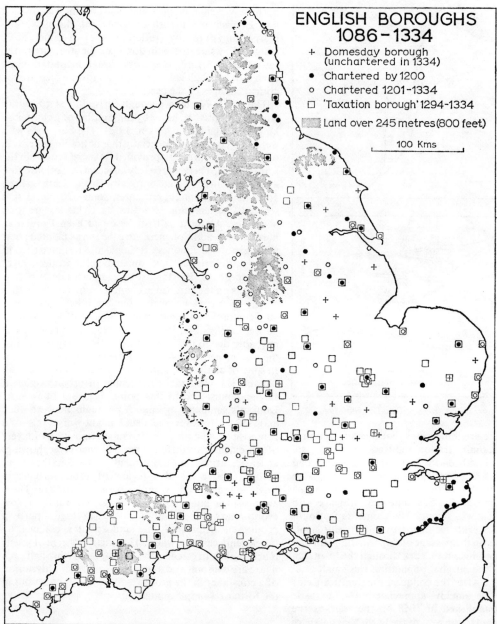

ENGLISH BOROUGHS 1086-1334

+ Domesday borough (unchartered in 1334)
● Chartered by 1200
○ Chartered 1201-1334
□ 'Taxation borough' 1294-1334

Land over 245 metres (800 feet)

100 Kms

3.14.   English boroughs 1086-1334 (after Donkin).

3 Economic competition	Sorting and grading based on locational advantages derived from circulation of people and trade – or without economic vitality, decline.	Integration of Ports of Trade into the 'national system' – the decline of those not so absorbed.	4 Administrative-economic convergence	The development of the urban places into a central place system. But with unconsolidated overlay as well as effective integration.
			5 Conquest and occupation	Adoption of the existing settlement pattern, etc.

This by no means applies with universal appropriateness but it does set out how, over a long period of incursions from outside the country, the town, as such, emerged. The Roman city system was partly an adaptation of the hill-fort precursor, but also substantially innovative. Moreover, at the end of the third phase in the above scheme economic decline had led virtually to disappearance. Again whereas the Roman system was initially maintained from without, the Saxon pattern of burhs evolved within the country, though both were at first concerned with military control, and then maintaining that by administration. It is significant too, that the first Danish boroughs became capitals of shires named after them, defining the political territory they administered and for which they became 'central settlements'. Ultimately, in some though far from all cases, the line leads back, as was suggested earlier, to the possible religious significance of assemblies at hill-forts or their earlier predecessors. Even at the end of the period reviewed the close association of church and town is apparent, although the prime initial motivation, as suggested in the above table, is the town as garrison. Land has to be won and retained before it can be exploited either for the cure of souls or the cultivation of the land and the marketing and distribution of products. Henry Loyn has written, 'we are all Taitians now' (Loyn, 1971, 116), and it is appropriate to conclude with a brief extract from Tait's great work *The Medieval English borough*. 'If it is not possible to draw a perfectly sharp line of demarcation in the development of the borough at the Norman Conquest, it is equally difficult to draw such a line at the settlement of the Danes . . . or indeed at any earlier date after the permanent reoccupation of the old Roman towns. It is all one story' (Tait, 1936, 138).

Further reading

The classic protagonists in the debate on the origin of English towns were:

STEPHENSON, C. 1933: *Borough and Town. A Study of Urban Origins in England*. Cambridge, Mass., and

TAIT, J. 1936: *The Medieval English Borough*. Manchester.

Modern summaries are given by Loyn and Biddle in their chapters in:

CLEMOES, P. and HUGHES, K. (eds.) 1971: *England before the Conquest. Studies in Primary Sources Presented to Dorothy Whitelock* (Cambridge), which are detailed in the list of references.

Useful summaries are found also in the various early chapters of:

DARBY, H.C. (ed.) 1973: *A New Historical Geography of England*. Cambridge,

and a general review in:

BENTON, J.F. 1968: *Town Origins. The Evidence from Medieval England*. Boston, Mass.

The main material on the Iron Age and concepts of urbanism are to be found in the work of Barry Cuncliffe, especially:

CUNLIFFE, B. 1976: The Origins of Urbanization in Britain. In CUNLIFFE, B. and ROWLEY, T. (eds.): *Oppida: the Beginning of Urbanization in Barbarian Europe*. British Archaeological Reports, Supplementary series, No. 11 (Oxford).

There is a great array of material on the Roman Towns, much of it detailed reports on excavations. The three most useful general sources are:

RODWELL, W. and ROWLEY, T. (eds.) 1975: *Small Towns of Roman Britiain*. BAR 15 (Oxford).

WACHER, J.S. (ed.) 1966: *The Civitas Capitals of Roman Britain*. Leicester.

WACHER, J.S. 1974: *The Towns of Roman Britain*. London.

On the urbanism of the Dark Ages a most valuable recent publication is:

HODGES. R. 1982: *Dark Age economics. The origins of towns and trade AD 600 – 1000*. London

The general material on Saxon and Norman towns has been indicated above, but two outstanding publications should also be consulted:

LOBEL, M.D. 1969: *Historic Towns. Maps and Plans of Towns and Cities in the British Isles with Historical Commentaries, from Earliest Times to Circa 1800*, vols. 1–3. Oxford.

BARLOW, F., BIDDLE, M. *et al.* 1976: *Winchester in the Early Middle Ages. An Edition and Discussion of the Winton Domesday* (Oxford). This is volume 1 in a series being published under the general title of Winchester Studies. The series will eventually build to the most complete study of the early development of any English city.

A general volume of value, which contains a good bibliography, is:

BARLEY, M.W. (ed.) 1976: *The Plans and Topography of Medieval Towns in England and Wales*. Council for British Archaeology, Research Report No. 14.

A short paper dealing with the origins of a city from Saxon nuclei is:

BURGESS, L.A. 1964: *The Origins of Southampton*. Dept. of English Local History, Univ. of Leciester. Occasional papers No. 16 (Leicester).

Part II. Urbanization: The City System

4

Size, Status and Region: The Micro Scale, The Static Condition

1 Introduction

Part I was concerned with the very general problem of how urbanism began, how it spread and, by reference to a specific example and invoking both indigenous evolution and the impact of extension from already urbanized areas, how it began in one selected country. After a section on urbanism it is proper to follow with one on urbanization and to consider the number of towns, their statuses or sizes and the relation between them, and the ratio of the urban fraction to the total population. These are difficult tasks. If status or significance is to be assessed rather than size, then the fact that the bases of that significance changed over time means that, even if the information were available, it would be impossible to identify a standard set of markers. Size, measured by population numbers not superficial area, has the advantage of being not only self-evident as a criterion but one which is inclusive and consistent over any time period and applicable to all cultural situations. But before the dates of the national censuses the populations of cities have to be estimated. The first aim of this chapter is accordingly to give some indication, mainly in relation to the Western world, of the sorts of data which can be used to establish city sizes, define functional statuses and identify complementary regions.

2 The Population of Towns

The beginnings of formal national censuses would seem to mark a clear break in the availability and reliability of urban population figures but this is far from being so. Censuses began in a local and sporadic fashion before they became both national in extent and regularly taken. Thus Corfield (1982,7) has noted some 125 local enumerations for English towns during the eighteenth century. However, general population counts are of limited value for the purposes of studying urbanization unless city populations can be separately and accurately identified.

It can be maintained that the earliest census counts of China date to the second millenium BC (Hollingsworth, 1976, 65), whilst the Bible notes a variety of Israeli counts, mainly of men of fighting age. The Roman census began in the sixth century BC but came to an end in the first century AD (Wolfe, 1932). What can be termed modern censuses date from the seventeenth century. Quebec had one as early as 1665, but regular systems began in 1749 in Sweden. Austria followed in 1754 and Norway and Denmark in 1769. In Britain a bill introduced into Parliament in 1753 to institute a census was defeated and it was not until 1801 that the first British census was taken. The prime motivation in the USA was the relation of Representatives in the House to population and the first census followed close on the establishment of the union in 1790. In contrast, although there were earlier attempts, the first census proper in Russia dates to 1897. In summary, therefore, European censuses start in the mid eighteenth century and all countries were involved by the end of the nineteenth. Outside Europe or European-settled areas, however, progress was much slower. The Indian census was begun in 1872 but only becomes reliable as late as 1921 (Hollingsworth, 1976, 74) while for the whole of Africa censuses date to the present century.

It can be seen from the brief review above that reasonably accurate urban populations, while obtainable for some cities for very early dates, only become universally available on a comparable basis during the nineteenth century. Comparability was, of course, always vitiated by contrasted bases of definition of what constituted the town or city. It is worthy of note that the first effective study of urban populations was that by Weber: *The Growth of Cities in the Nineteenth Century*. It was published in 1899 and was as much a response to the availability of data as to the problem it considered.

Before the period when census data provide a reliable source a wide range of surrogate evidence has been used to construct population totals. Hollingsworth in his *Historical Demography* lists 18 ranging from vital registration data to cemetery data, both from skeletons and tombstone inscriptions, but only the first five are of real value in compiling urban population figures and the remainder can be aggregated as other sources giving:

Vital registration data

Bills of mortality

Ecclesiastical records, such as parish registers and
   communicant lists

Fiscal documents

Military records
Other sources.

The first three have much in common for they are all concerned with the vital processes of births and deaths together with the ceremonies of marriage and baptism. Formal civil registration either coincided with, or post-dated, census taking so that it is of little relevance to ascertaining population totals. Ecclesiastical records, especially parish registers, have a critical role in demographic analysis but are somewhat less significant in the compilation of urban population totals. It follows that prior to census figures fiscal records are perhaps the most widely used of sources.

The raising of revenue by taxation is one of the earliest and most consistent of governmental activities – 'And it came to pass in those days, that there went out a decree from Caesar Augustus, that all the world should be taxed'. In order to carry out the process lists were necessary either of a specified section or of all the population. The most valuable lists are those, usually called poll taxes, where all the population was covered providing a head count. A widely used British example is the Subsidy Roll of Edward III of 1377 (Russell, 1948; Beresford, 1958) which, covering the whole of England apart from Cheshire and Durham, provides the major source for estimates of fourteenth-century population. There is still the problem of three omitted groups, children under 14, mendicant friars and the indigent or beggars. The latter two groups were comparatively small and the number of children form the main problem. To account for all these a multiplier of 1.5 is conventionally used but it is clear that considerable inaccuracies can arise.

Where graduated taxes were levied based on some measure of wealth rather than on a 'body', then even further error is likely to creep in; 'The use of taxation records to illuminate population positively invites confusion between numbers and wealth' (Reynolds, 1977, 144). Even so, one of the most valuable sources for the estimation of sixteenth-century populations in Britain is the lay subsidy surveys of 1524–5 and 1543–5 (Sheail, 1972). As the name suggests they, too, were made as the basis for taxation. The 1524–5 subsidy was levied 'on each man's most important form of wealth, as defined by the Act, namely personal property (goods), landed incomes and wages' (Sheail, 1972, 111). The definitions are only critical if the distribution of wealth is the main purpose of investigation. But the third category included wage-earners who earned at least £1 a year. If a man did not earn a pound or more in landed income or wages and did not own £2 or more in goods, then he paid no taxes. In consequence not only were children and house-wives omitted, but also those who paid no tax. 'The number of taxpayers cannot, therefore, be equated with the number of households in each vill' (Sheail, 1972, 112). In order to translate the lists into populations, therefore, one must suppose a constant relationship between people listed and the actual population. Sheail points out three sources from which distortions could arise. First, by definition, all those in holy orders were excluded. Second, children

below the age of 16 and women who were not household heads were exempt. Third, there is no guarantee that those who compiled the lists worked to a standard basis. Patten has reviewed the lay subsidy, and other similar sources which are more restricted in extent, and concludes, 'To get near approximations of population from these sources it is necessary for some sort of multiplier to be applied to represent the section of the population not counted in the records. For example, family size in the 1520s may be held to have been 4.5 persons per family so that the number of taxpayers times 4.5 together with an estimate of those not taxed gives a population total. But the figures derived from such calculations are of the most approximate kind. . . . Figures derived in this way are mere indicators of the relative order of size of towns, rather than exact totals' (Patten, 1978, 99). There is a still further set of problems in that not all of England was included and the lists are missing from some areas in all counties. What at first seems, therefore, a valuable source on scrutiny certainly does not lose its value but is revealed as having considerable problems in interpretation.

Perhaps the most widely used British pre-census source based on an assessment of wealth for taxation is the Hearth Tax returns for the 1660s. 'At the Restoration, the Convention Parliament calculated that Charles II would be able to discharge the ordinary expenses of peace-time government with an income of £1,200.000 a year. The failure of the financial settlement to produce this amount led to the need for supplementary taxation, one form of which was the Hearth Money. The Act of 1662 (14 Car 11 c 10) which established the tax created an annual due of 2s. for every hearth . . . unless the occupant was exempted on the grounds of poverty' (Howell, 1972, 1). The number of hearths was, of course, a crude measure of wealth. There was, again, as with all forms of taxation ancient and modern, considerable evasion so that the raw data have to be treated with reservation. In addition, in order to estimate population, the number of households or the number of hearths have again to be converted by the use of a multiplier into population totals. There is no accepted figure and, indeed, there would have been considerable regional variations. Suggestions range from 6.8 to 4.5 per household based on estimates of average family size (Howell, 1972) but most estimates have used the lower figure.

The fifth of the sources noted earlier was military records. In general terms the recorded sizes of armies have been used to assess total populations but unless specifically city armies these are of limited value in determining urban size. Again in a British context the Tudor Muster Rolls which were designed to identify those available for what would now be called 'military service' provide population listings, but only of those in the relevant age and sex groups. Multipliers can again be used to establish a total population, 'but it is obvious that the muster definition of "able" men actually allowed many men to dodge the roll, and later the payment of a mustering bounty would obviously tend to lead to inflated totals in the muster' (Hollingsworth, 1976, 231). In consequence the value of the rolls as a source of information is greatly impaired.

In addition to the sources so far discussed there is a wide range of other information which provides limited, much less certain and more circumscribed bases for estimating urban populations. Plans and surveys form one distinct group for from a count of houses or plots and an assumption of the number of inhabitants per house or plot an estimate can be derived. Still further removed in reliability would be the attempt to derive a population from the extent of a walled area where the line of defences is known but little of the internal detail. Thus as one moves away to general estimates from tenuous evidence so the results themselves are not only less reliable but become limited in that range which is essential for geographical study.

The degree of reliability can be illustrated from *3000 years of urban growth*, a book by Chandler and Fox (1974) which is one of the few studies which attempts to review the sizes of cities. In a section entitled 'methods' the authors record,

a demographic void seemed at first the case for Anhilvada. Back of 1197, it did not have any figures whatever, except one for distance around and another for the number of market places. Reluctantly we concluded we did not have a good ratio for market places. That left the area and the spotty data at 1197, when 15,000 were slain and 20,000 were captured. Those slain would be presumably be militia, and the captured, women. So 15,000 × the usual 6 for militia = 90,000. That does for 1197, but Anhilvada's height of glory was earlier. What of then? To then we could assign her area. This in turn could be compared to the area covered by Ahmedabad, a nearby city, when at its peak in the 1600s. And Anhilvada's peak was known to have been in the reign which went from 1094 to 1143. So we are able to assign a population of 125,000 in 1100 and, as the country was near its full size by 996, a further figure of 100,000 in 1000. (Chandler and Fox, 1974, 2–3)

This passage indicates just how tenuous estimates of early populations can be.

A further example of the unreliability of the results can be demonstrated in Table 4.1, which shows two sets of estimates for towns of France of over 20,000 people in 1500.

Even with the fairly wide bands used by de Vries there is agreement in only seven out of the nineteen French towns assigned populations of over 20,000 by the two estimates. This again indicates how the utmost caution is necessary when using pre-census urban population totals. In the next chapter discussion of city hierarchies based on population is undertaken but it must be remembered how unreliable the basic data are.

At this point one further factor needs to be introduced relating to areal extent and its use as a means of estimating urban populations. Map evidence can ensure

Table 4.1: Population of French cities in 1500

(a) Chandler and Fox[1]		(b) de Vries[2]
		Figures in thousands
Paris	225	100+
Lyon	80	50–99
Rouen	75	40–49
Tours	60	10–19
Marseille	45	30–39
Toulouse	40	30–39
Bourges	32	under 10
Orleans	28	20–29
Angers	25	20–29
Caen	35	20–29
Dijon	24	10–19
Troyes	23	10–19
Dieppe	20	under 10
Bordeaux	20	20–29
Montpellier	20	under 10
Amiens	20	20–29
Strasbourg[3]	24	20–29
Avignon		20–29
Boulogne		20–29

[1]Chandler, T. and Fox, G. (1974): 3000 years of urban growth (New York).

[2]de Vries, J. (1981): Patterns of urbanization in pre-industrial Europe in H. Schmal ed. *patterns of European Urbanization since 1500* (London).

[3]Strasbourg is given under Germany by Chandler and Fox.

that the whole of a settlement is included or that only part of a walled or defined area which is built-up is considered. Documentary evidence, including census data, often reflects formally designated administrative boundaries which need bear no relation to physical extent of settlement. Indeed, at times when towns were either growing or declining rapidly it was probable that no such relation appertained. The nineteenth century was a period of rapid urban growth and as a result settlement soon extended beyond pre-industrial borough boundaries. In the reverse situation new settlements grew within larger areas and population totals were recorded for those administrative areas and not for the individual settlements. Due to these situations considerable error can result from the careless use of census figure. For England and Wales during the period 1801–1911 C.M. Law has attempted to recalculate urban population figures so that they refer to comparable areas (Law, 1967). He adopted three criteria. The first was a minimum population of 2500. The second was a minimum density of one per acre adding suburban populations outside legal boundaries where that density was recorded. The third criterion was that of 'nucleation' determined by the examination of appropriate maps to ensure that discrete settlements were identified. The contrast between Law's figures and those of the census in terms of percentage urban are given in Table 4.2.

Although the differences are not great they represent considerable divergence in individual cases. These illustrations, from attempts to reconstruct early pre-

Table 4.2: Comparison of urban populations in England and Wales in the censuses and by C.M. Law between 1851 and 1911

	Census	C.M. Law
1851	50.2	54
1861	54.6	58.7
1871	61.8	65.2
1881	67.8	70.0
1891	72.0	74.5
1901	77.0	78.0
1911	78.1	78.9

census populations and from a demonstration of how census figures need to be scrutinized, show how insecure are the figures used for the past populations of towns. This section cannot be a manual with instructions for the derivation of such populations for all countries in all past times, that is manifestly impossible. What it has attempted to do is give some indication of the more widely used sources and to suggest the reserve with which they must always be treated.

Two further aspects arise derived from the estimation of urban populations. These are the sizes of historical cities and the urban proportion.

(i) The largest cities

Given the great problems of estimating totals any study of the largest cities in the world over time can only be speculative. There seems to be general agreement that the earliest cities, those which were discussed in chapter 1, had populations of some 30,000. It was because of the sudden appearance of such large settlements that Childe coined the phrase 'the urban revolution'. Again the population of Memphis at about 3000 BC has been estimated at 40,000. Even by the second millennium cities of 100,000 had appeared. Lagash, the Babylonian capital, probably reached that figure as did Memphis, while Babylon itself and Nineveh had populations of 200,000 (Chandler and Fox, 1974).

The first city to reach 500,000 was Rome around the year AD 1 and this increased to over 750,000. In complete contrast, the first city with a population of over a million is said to be Chaugan, the capital of China under the Tang dynasty. As the world's largest city it gave way to Baghdad towards the end of the first millennium AD. It was not until 1841 that a city reached two million, London, recording 2,235, 344 at the census of that year. This is well within that period when industrialization and especially new methods of transport had brought about a completely new situation where New York was to overtake London at some eight million in 1925 and Tokyo overtake New York at some 15 million in 1965.

However unreliable figures may be, two simple conclusions follow from them.

1   In spite of all the limitations on movement which characterized the pre-industrial city, considerable sizes were attained. These were directly the result of primacy (see p. 99) and, physically, were associated with very high densities.

2   The nineteenth century witnessed a great release from the constraints which limited the population size of cities and rapid growth quite quickly made the concept of a free-standing city with a defined population anachronistic. Regional populations replaced city populations as the meaningful basis of analysis.

(ii) The urban proportion

One of the standard conventions by which urbanization is measured is that of the proportion (percentage) of the total population living in cities or in settlements of a given minimum size. But any such figure is of little value unless the total from which the fraction is being derived is both obtainable and meaningful. Prior to the formation of the modern nation state, and with the national censuses which were in part the result of that formation, it is doubtful if anything with much meaning can be derived. As Reissman writes (1964, 196), 'the nation, rather than the city, is the meaningful unit for the analysis of urbanization', so until the emergence of modern nations the measurement of urbanization in a conventional way has little meaning. Table 4.3. reproduces the material assembled by Weber at the turn of the nineteenth century. From it some generalizations can be drawn

1   The urban proportion, prior to industrialization, was universally low; generally below 10 per cent. It is doubtful whether variations within that low fraction held any significance given all the problems of estimation and definition.

2   There is an obvious contrast between the very high populations reached by cities at early dates and the low percentage urbanization. This can only be explained by the condition called primacy where one very large city dominated a country with a retinue of only very small towns.

3   Given the low proportions and their nature it is difficult to use the urban proportion with much relevance in discussions of urbanization prior to the mid eighteenth century. Moreover fluctuations were so limited as to have little relevance at a gross scale.

4   The period of substantial transformation is the nineteenth century by the end of which proportions of over 75 per cent were being recorded.

3   The functional status of a town

Although estimates of population present difficulties a much more intractable set of problems arises if one attempts to follow standard procedures in the ranking of contemporary towns by the examination of the presence or absence of those goods and services which are indicative of functions performed. The whole corpus of work derived from Christaller's study of central places in southwest Germany was largely concerned with establishing ranked arrays of towns based on some form of

Table 4.3:   Percentage of population living in towns (urban population) during the nineteenth century (after Weber)

Countries	1800				1850			
	Year	100,000 +	20,000 +	10,000 +	Year	100,000 +	20,000 +	10,000 +
1 England and Wales	1801	9.73	16.94	21.30	1851	22.58	35.0	39.45
2 Scotland	1801	0.	13.9	17.0	1851	16.9	27.7	32.2
3 Australia (7 colonies)								
4 Belgium	1800–10	0.	8.7	13.5	1846	6.8	16.6	20.8
5 Saxony	1815	0.	7.7	8.9	1849	0.	9.9	13.6
6 Netherlands*	1795	11.5	24.5	29.5	1849	7.3	21.7	29.0
7 Turkey in Europe								
8 China								
9 Uruguay								
10 Prussia	1816	1.8	6.0	7.25	1849	3.1	7.8	10.63
11 Germany								
12 Argentina								
13 United States	1800	0.	3.8	3.8	1850	6.0	9.8	12.0
14 Cuba								
15 France	1801	2.8	6.7	9.5	1851	4.6	10.6	14.4
16 Denmark	1801	10.9	10.9	10.9	1840	9.6	9.6	9.6
17 Spain	1820 ca.	1.45	9.75	[1.40]	1857	4.4	9.6	[16.2]
18 Italy	1800 ca.	4.4			1848	6.0		
19 Bavaria	1800 ca.	0.	3.7		1849	2.4	6.12	
20 Ireland	1800 ca.	3.1	6.6	7.8	1851	3.9	8.7	10.1
21 Canada					1851	0.	7.4	8.5
22 Chile								
23 Norway	1801	0.	0.	3.3	1845	0.	4.2	5.3
24 Switzerland	1822	0.	1.3	4.3	1850	0.	5.2	7.3
25 British Guiana								
26 Persia								
27 Austria	1800 ca.	2.63	3.56	4.37	1843	2.8	4.2	5.8
28 Hungary†	1800 ca.	0.	2.31	5.35	1850	1.35	4.55	9.1
29 Egypt								
30 Ecuador								
31 Venezuela								
32 Newloundland								
33 Roumania								
34 Greece								
35 Sweden	1805	0.	3.	3.9	1850	0.	3.4	4.7
36 Central America								
37 Japan								
38 Turkey in Asia								
39 Mexico								
40 Philippines								
41 Transvaal								
42 Bornu (Soudan)								
43 Portugal	1801	9.5	10.3	12.7	1857	7.2	10.7	12.9
44 Peru								
45 Bulgaria								
46 Paraguay								
47 Brazil								
48 Colombia								
49 Russia	1820	1.4	2.4	3.7	1856	1.6	3.5	5.3
50 Algiers								
51 Cape Colony								
52 British India								
53 Bolivia								
54 Jamaica								
55 Natal								
56 Servia								
57 Bosnia-Herzegowina								
58 Orange Free State								
59 Abyssinia								

*The figures for 1890 refer to the agglomerated population; for comparison with 1795 and 1849, the basis should be the territorial unit (G) giving the percentages 17, 14.3, 31.3 and 43.0.

		1890				
	Year	100,000 +	20,000– 100,000	20,000 +	10,000 +	2,000 –
1	1891	31.82	21.76	53.58	61.73	72.05
2	1891	29.8	12.6	42.4	49.9	65.4
3	1891	29.1	9.7	38.8	41.4	
4	1890	17.4	8.7	26.1	34.8	
5	1890	22.6	7.4	30.0	34.7	64.5
6	1889	16.6	12.7	29.3	33.5	
7	1885	21.4	3.5	24.9		
8	1896	22.0				
9	1890	20.4	0.	30.4	30.4	
10	1890	12.9	10.1	23.0	30.	48.5
11	1890	21.1	9.8	21.9		47.0
12	1890	16.2	6.6	22.8	27.8	
13	1890	15.5	8.3	23.8	27.6	37.7
14	1887	12.3	16.2	28.5		
15	1891	12.0	9.1	21.1	25.9	37.4
16	1890	17.3	2.9	20.2	23.6	32.4
17	1887	6.8	11.2	18.0	[29.6]	
18	1881	6.9	6.4	13.3	20.6	[43.4]
19	1890	8.8	7.0	15.8	20.5	31.9
20	1891	10.6	4.7	15.3	18.0	26.4
21	1891	8.2	6.0	14.2	17.1	27.3
22	1885	11.6	2.7	14.3	17.1	
23	1890	7.6	6.2	13.8	16.7	22.2
24	1888	0.	13.2	13.2	16.5	
25	1892	0.	16.4	16.4	16.4	
26	1896	5.1	[7.0]	[12.]		
27	1890	8.	4.	12.	15.8	32.5
28	1890	3.23	8.03	11.26	[17.6]	
29	1882	8.6	2.6	11.2	15.7	
30	1889	0.	12.2	12.2	15.5	
31	1891	0.	8.	8.	14.7	
32	1891	0.	14.4	14.4	14.4	
33	1889–90	4.4	6.3	10.7	14.2	
34	1889	4.9	4.1	9.0	14.0	
35	1890	7.34	3.5	10.84	13.74	18.0
36	1889–92	0.	6.5	6.5	13.6	
37	1890	5.84	4.53	10.37	13.1	
38	1885	3.2	[7.0]	[10.2]		
39	1895	2.7	7.0	9.7	[13.0]	
40	1887	2.2	7.5	9.7		
41	1896	12.9	0.	12.9	12.9	
42	1896	0.	11.0	11.0		
43	1890	8.8	0.4	9.2	12.7	
44	1876	4.0	3.8	7.8	11.8	
45	1888	0.	5.2	5.2	11.2	
46	1890	0.	4.1	4.1	10.6	
47	1888	5.7	3.	8.7	10.2	
48	1886–95	2.7	4.	6.7	9.7	
49	1885	3.2	4.	7.2	9.3	12.3
50	1891	0.	6.0	6.0	8.3	
51	1891	0.	6.8	6.8	8.2	
52	1891	2.1	2.8	4.9	7.3	
53	1880–6	0.	3.9	3.9	6.4	
54	1891	0.	6.3	6.3	6.3	
55	1891	0.	0.	0.	0.	
56	1890	0.	2.5	2.5	5.1	
57	1885	0.	1.9	1.9	3.8	
58	1890	0.	0.	0.	0.	
59	1969	0.	0.	0.	0.	

analysis of functional content (Carter, 1981, 71–88). It would seem logical, therefore, that past hierarchies would also be more properly based on such content, rather than on population totals where adventitious elements could distort the central-place role. Immediately this approach is adopted three difficulties arise. The first is the identification and evaluation of the functions to be used, the second the sources from which they can be derived and the third the methods to be employed to establish ranks or grades of towns. These can be considered in turn.

(i) The identification of functions

This is a problem common to past and present analyses; but it becomes greater when related to the past and greater still when related to the remote past. Its crux is to isolate and identify those functions which are properly a measure of urban status. The difficulty in modern studies is to identify what, for example, a shop actually sells in order to include it within a classificatory system. A greengrocer might well also sell fish and qualify as a fishmonger. When this sort of analysis is taken back into the past two uncertainties are added.

The first is that specialization in retailing is a comparatively late development and even in the nineteenth century quite unexpected combinations of trades appear. Thus in Slater's Directory for 1895 one Jemina Bridgeman located at 1 Market Street, Newtown in Mid-Wales, is entered as 'fancy draper and servants' registry office' (Lewis, 1975a, 187–8). When the same problem is taken back beyond the date of town directories and other sources have to be used, even greater confusion arises. John Patten, who has written most penetratingly on this topic (1977) records in late sixteenth-century Ipswich of a man indicted as

> a profest glover by traed and had prentices att work att it and hee a stranger comed in town, and since is falen into generall other trades he seles nutmegs cloves and peper vinigere soap and starch candle and salte tobachoe Rebens allmaner of thred peres laces and inkles and other generall commodities which belong to the grocers traed and haberdashers traed then they seles peas buter and chees backon hereine, oatmeal, flower, eges, aples and other fruet as Roets, turnips, and all things else there is anything to be saved in likewise they sell all sorts of Breed. (Patten, 1977, 305)

As Patten comments, 'this may well be an extreme example of how bald an occupational designation like "glover" in a list of freemen could be'.

The second uncertainty is apparent in the above quotation. It was only during the nineteenth century that the modern shopping centre or central business district developed (see chapter 8). Before that, retailing was largely carried on through market stalls set up once a week in the high street on market day. It is unreal, therefore, to project back the modern concept of assemblages of central institutions. Indeed, insofar as that can be

done it would be more appropriate to select administrative functions rather than commercial, for a universal
central place activity was the operation of local and
national government. The fact that a town was the place
where the assizes were held was possibly more important
than the presence of a particular commercial function
which might well have been a consequence of the first
role. One has to adapt the array of evidence to the
primary role of the town at a particular period.

A way out of this has been to examine the total array of
activities, including those which can be called industrial,
as the best signal of urban status. This is a form of reaction to the situation just described. Prior to a system
of national transportation of centrally manufactured
goods, the concept 'shopping centre' had limited meaning. But, as a corollary, goods had to be produced
locally and the range of crafts, effectively the diversity of
occupations, can be used as a measure of the size and
significance of a town. Here, again, the major difficulty
is that of identifying occupations with any degree of
certainty. John Patten's discussions of urban occupations in pre-industrial England (1977, 1978) have already
been referred to and the example of the Ipswich glover
quoted. Ambiguities arise not only over scale – was a
'merchant' a great operator on a national or even international scale or a minor dealer? – but also over actual
activities – did a merchant make and sell, or only sell? If
difficulties exist in relation to individual trades and
occupations then classifications only compound the
possible errors. Moreover, while classification into
groups is used for the comparison of the relative social
composition of towns, it is not as valuable for the
establishment of a rank order, especially if the sources
from which the data are drawn are fragmentary rather
than complete. This introduces the nature of the data
sources used.

(ii) Data sources

When population figures were discussed the major
watershed was identified as the publication of the first
official national censuses. In relation to the analysis of
the functional status of a town the parallel break is the
appearance of trade directories (Norton, 1950; Lewis,
1975a). Once these are available, however inaccurate
they might have been, a uniform and consistent basis
exists for the compilation of the functional content of a
town. There was, of course, a direct relationship between
urban development, the maturing of central business
districts and the publication of directories. Two sets of
problems arise, the first relate to sources in pre-directory
times, the second to the use of directories themselves.

Patten's reviews of pre-industrial occupations (Patten,
1977, 1978) have already been utilized in considering the
nature of occupations, they also include considerations
of sources. Patten divided these sources into two; records
which include occupational descriptions because that
was their prime end and those which give such information in passing or a sufficient indication for inference of

occupation to be made. Prominent amongst the first
group are 'records of admission to town freedom (i.e. the
right to trade and/or manufacture freely within the
town); of enrolment into apprenticeships; and various
lists of households, of those in particular sorts of trades,
of aliens, of foreign workers . . . and sometimes
of the poor . . .' (Patten, 1978, 151). Amongst the second group there is a variety of material although wills
and probate inventories are perhaps the most fruitful.
Taxation and muster lists, as well as parish registers,
mentioned when population numbers were being considered, also provide occupational data.

The critical problem arising from all these sources is
that they are partial and probably inaccurate so that the
nature of the use which can be made of them is restricted.

The dilemmas which arise in the use of directories are
more widely known and appreciated. Lewis in his consideration of them as a data source in urban analysis
(1975a) sets out six limitations. These are (1) the accuracy
of compilation, (2) the lack of relation of entries to
specific places, (3) multiple entries, (4) classification of
outlets, (5) part-time outlets, (6) spatial coverage. These
are mainly self-explanatory. Accuracy increases during
the nineteenth century from the time when the compiler
was reliant upon local information – 'Here he begs to
solicit an Annual (say by the 10th of the month of
September) Return of Gentlemen, etc. gone out of
business, and a list of those who have newly entered into
commerce, in order to render each Town annual correct'
(Holden, 1811, vol I, n.p.) – to the latter part of the
century when formal surveys were made by full-time
employees. The relation to specific places refers to the
fact that occasionally small towns are grouped or a town
and its surrounding region presented together so that the
actual relation of entry to urban place cannot be
ascertained. Multiple entries are frequent, businesses
occurring both by their formal title and under the name
of the owner, but these can be sorted out by careful
scrutiny. The classification of outlets is the problem
already considered as the identification of functions
where a quotation from a directory was used in
illustration (p. 87). Part-time outlets introduce one of
the standard quandaries in present-day studies and
limited demand in the nineteenth century made such
entries as, 'open on Thursday from 12.30 to 2.30', fairly
frequent. In working up the data account has to be taken
of this situation so careful scrutiny for the identification
of part-time operations is essential. Finally, one of the
most irritating aspects relates to spatial coverage. In most
cases one is attempting to analyse a set of places in a given
area, but that area need not coincide with directory
publication so that lists when abstracted will refer to
different dates. At some of these dates the same set of
towns may not be available so that the evidence collected
may refer to differing arrays of settlements at varying
dates.

There are, therefore, numerous difficulties in using
trade directories but with care they do provide a resource
of inestimable value for the consideration of urban

character in the late eighteenth and nineteenth centuries.

(iii) Methods of analysis

Given that functions have been satisfactorily derived from the sorts of sources which have been outlined, the next problem is that of methods of analysis. At this point there is little purpose in entering into a full discussion of the methods by which town ranks can be established since that has been treated elsewhere (Carter, 1981). It is appropriate, however, to present some indication of procedures which are particularly relevant in the analysis of historical data for to a degree methods are conditioned by the data.

If the pre-directory period is considered then it is clear that, partly because numbers are impossible to ascertain in any case, a presence–absence matrix is the only feasible basis. Excellent examples occur in the work of Patten on East Anglia where all the information available has been collated and examined by means of scalogram analysis. 'Scalogram analysis is a very simple non-parametric ranking technique by which towns and occupations can be set the one against the other, providing both a good description of the urban hierarchy and a starting point for discussion . . .' (Patten, 1978, 252) (Figure 4.1). There are obvious limitations to the method, more especially the fact that numbers are ignored. It remains essentially a process of illustration and a basis of discussion rather than an analytical procedure designed to derive and characterize discrete or distinctive ranks of towns or even to probe whether these existed at the period under review.

A presence–absence matrix can, of course, be subject to more sophisticated forms of analysis, especially where the data are themselves more reliable so that the effort is worthwhile. Lucy Caroe in a study of the ranking of towns in East Anglia in 1846 used a grouping procedure called 'association analysis' (Caroe, 1968). Her data were derived from directories, newspapers and local histories. Some entries common to all towns, such as innkeepers and bakers for example, were omitted and a total of 61 functions compiled. One advantage of presence–absence entries is that nominal data, such as the holding of a Quarter Session Court, can be included, but as Caroe admits, the decision to work at this low level of measurement 'was necessitated by the lack of precision in the county directories'. The procedure adopted was one of 'dichotomous division' by which the universe of 76 settlements is successively divided. The method involves the use of principal components analysis to identify the largest single source of variation in a correlation matrix of all the functions, with the highest loading variable, that is one of the 61 functions, being characterized as that most sensitive to the established largest source of variation. The settlements are then divided on the basis of the presence–absence of that function and the resultant sub-groups subject to the same procedure so that a progressive pattern of division follows. The basis of the division can of course be either the functions or the

settlements and Caroe carried out the exercise for both giving groupings, or rankings, by both functions and settlements. Her results are shown in Figure 4.2. The highest-ranking group in 1846 included Norwich, Ipswich, Yarmouth, Kings Lynn, Colchester, Bury St Edmunds and Chelmsford, with Lowestoft as a marginal member. The distinguishing functions were those constituting group 11, where the professions seemed to have played a significant role. As a point of interest comparison can be made between Figures 4.2 and 4.3 and given the differences in definition of the areas studied, a fair degree of continuity between the sixteenth and the nineteenth centuries is apparent.

A widely used method of analysis is that derived by Davies (1967) using the formula

$$C = \frac{t}{T} \times 100$$

Where C is the location coefficient of function t, t is one outlet of function t and T the total number of those outlets in the area. If the derived coefficient is multiplied by the number of outlets in a settlement a centrality value is derived, that is the centrality given to that settlement by function t. If then all the centrality values are summed a functional index is derived. The main contrast to the methods so far described is that the measurement is ordinal and the numbers of each function are employed. This is only feasible where dependable evidence is available so that it tends to be limited to data derived from directories of the later part of the nineteenth century. Lewis uses this procedure in a study of the England/Wales border at seven dates between 1791 and 1891–5 in order to give a dynamic picture of change. His major problem is that not all the towns are included at each date, partly due to their changing importance, partly due to the different bases of directory compilation. This vitiates one great advantage of the method, the ability to calculate the percentage of regional centrality vested in a centre at successive dates. The only way Lewis can solve this is by reworking all his data for common sets of towns at each date.

In spite of its problems this last method would seem the most effective where the changes in status over time are to be measured and it is this dynamic which is the most interesting product of the examination of past hierarchies.

4 The urban field or the complementary region

Along with the identification of the statuses of towns in the past goes the establishment of their tributary areas. The critical issue here is the need to establish a system of urban tributary areas across a region, for one example is of little value when only analysis of the system of ranked towns and their spheres of influence makes any geographical sense. This means that the data must be universal and this condition sets considerable constraints.

When the area dominated by only one town is to be defined then a variety of evidence can be employed.

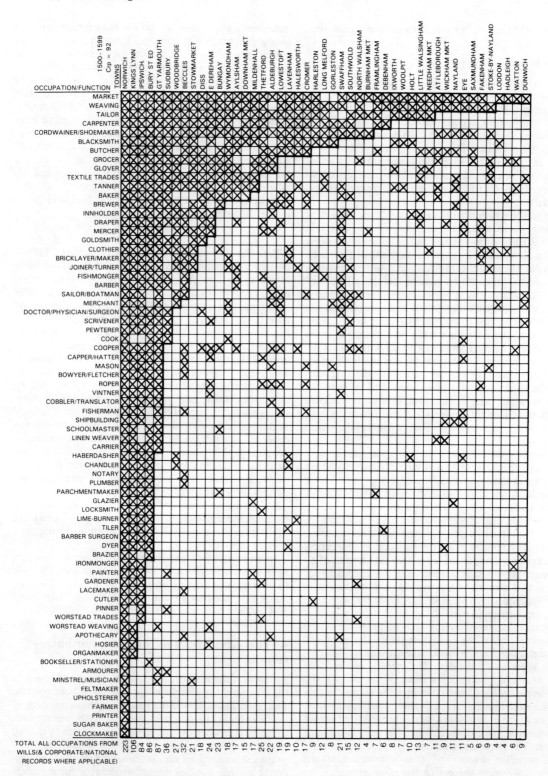

4.1. Scalogram of occupations for East Anglian towns
1500–1599 (after Patten).

Group 1   Group 2   Group 3   Group 4   Group 5   Group 6   Group 7   Group 8   Group 9   Group 10   Group 11

Column settlements (top, read vertically): Norwich, Ipswich, Yarmouth, Kings Lynn, Colchester, Bury St Ed., Chelmsford, Lowestoft, Saffron Walden, Woodbridge, Maldon, Thetford, Swaffham, Bungay, E. Dereham, Hadleigh, Stowmarket, Wymondham, Halesworth, Diss, Holt, Eye, Beccles, Gt. Dunmow, N. Walsham, Braintree, Wickham Mkt., Halstead, Wells, Coggeshall, Clare, Debenham, Kelvedon, Needham Mkt., C. Hedingham, Long Melford, Haverhill, Witham, Fakenham, Harwich, Cromer, Watton, Aylsham, Mendlesham, Stradbroke, Dedham, Hingham, Kenninghall, E. Bergholt, Stebbing, Southwold, Reepham, Thaxted, Lavenham, Nayland, Shipdham, S. Hedingham, Attleborough, Ixworth, Gt. Baddow, Wickhambrook, Wetherslield, Castle Acre, Hilgay, Martham, Fressingfield, Bures St. Mary, Grt. Waltham, Cavendish, Stanton, Walsham le W., Felstead, Sheringham, Coddenham, Stoke Nayland, Wenhaston

Row groups (trades/services):

Group 1: surgeon, carrier, carpenter, wheelwright, bricklayer, plumber, etc., cooper, saddler, chapel

Group 2: hairdresser

Group 3: maltster, ins. agent, basket mkr., hosier, glover

Group 4: auctioneer, chemist, druggist, solicitor, cabinet mkr., watch, clockmkr., builder, milliner, tinman

Group 5: banker, bookseller, vet. surgeon, ironmonger, china, glass dlr., market, coach mkr., currier, petty sessions

Group 6: brewer, wine, spirit dlr., surveyor, straw hat dlr.

Group 7: coal merchant, corn & coal mcht., corn merchant, livery stables, hatter, fruit, grngrocer, gunmaker

Group 8: cattle dealer, brickmaker

Group 9: fishmonger, land, house agt., agric. impl. mkr., fellmonger, union workhse.

Group 10: horse dealer, quarter sessions

Group 11: physician, accountant, w'sale grocer, dentist, pawnbroker, tobacconist, carver, gilder, cutler

Group 12: lodging house, straw plait dlr.

— Division significant at P = 0·001
— Division significant at P = 0·01
- - - Division significant at P = 0·05

4.2. East Anglian towns 1846. Association analysis: final grouping by trades/services and settlements (after Caroe).

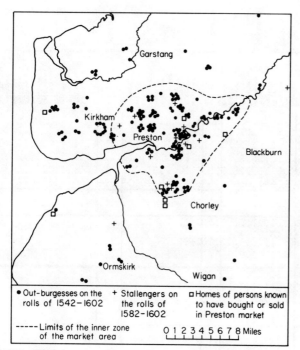

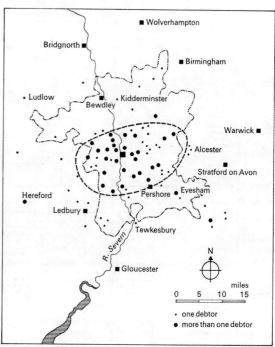

4.3.   The market area of Preston in the late sixteenth and
       seventeenth centuries (after Rodgers).

4.4.   Worcester's market region in the sixteenth century
       (after Dyer). The definition of the region is based on
       debt statements in probate records in which debts to
       Worcester shopkeepers are recorded.

Indeed, it would not be a great distortion to argue that the sources have been the stimulus and that the one-off studies of towns which have been published have been the results of exploitations of discovered sources rather than the search for and identification of sources for a region being studied.

A characteristic example is given in Figure 4.3 from a study by H.A. Rodgers of the market area of Preston in the sixteenth and seventeenth centuries, one of the earlier attempts to set out an urban tributary area in past times. Rodgers used three associated sets of evidence. The first was 'given by records of transactions in Preston in which the homes of the buyers or sellers are mentioned, though regrettably little of this material appears to have survived. Examination of the borough records, supplemented by a few chance discoveries, yielded only the cases plotted' on Figure 4.3 (Rodgers, 1956). The second set of evidence was the distribution of the homes of the *stallengers* of Preston between 1586 and 1602. These were people who had the privilege of setting up stalls in the market place and selling on equal terms with the townsmen. Finally the rolls of out-burgesses between 1542 and 1602, that is those who were usually resident outside the town, were used on the principle that they were entitled to buy and sell free of toll in the town's market. These distributions collectively enabled Rodgers to identify an inner zone of the market areas which was dominated by Preston, together with an outer zone where the borough shared trade with local centres.

Another basis for the establishment of a market region

is used by Dyer in his study of Worcester in the sixteenth century (Dyer, 1973). He examined the probate records of Worcester citizens and from them extracted debt statements on the grounds that these revealed the place of residence of the customers of Worcester shop-keepers (Figure 4.4). 'The map based on this evidence shows that these customers were drawn from an elliptical area about 25 miles from west to east and about 15 miles from north to south. Thus few people travelled more than 10 to 12 miles to the city to buy and sell, and this represents the core of Worcester's region. . . . The size of this region was determined partly by the distance which people could reasonably cover on foot with their produce and purchases (15 miles was approaching the maximum in this respect) and also by the presence of other market centres' (Dyer, 1973, 68).

Dyer goes on to examine the sources of animals brought to market at Worcester, but it is more interesting to consider a different source of evidence. Langton has examined the market areas of bell manufacturers for towns in the west of England and along the Welsh border (Figure 4.5). He uses this to demonstrate that although it is well established that urban craftsmen served both local and international markets, they also 'served market areas in bands of the spectrum in between. By the seventeenth century the home market had developed sufficiently to accommodate the existence of congeries of craftsmen serving with specialist lines regions much larger than the

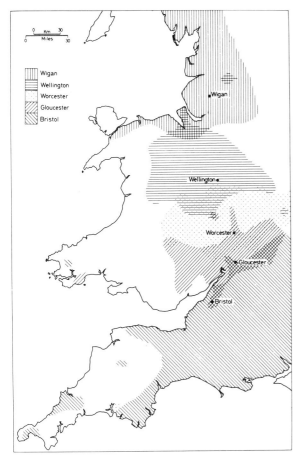

4.5.   Market areas of bell manufacturers in some west of
England towns *c*. 1550–1700 (after Langton).

normal market areas of the towns in which they lived'
(Langton, 1978, 188). Perhaps the use of a manufactured
product strays beyond the sort of criterion usually used
to establish conventional market areas, but in this case,
as at Preston, outer zones of quite considerable dimension seem to have developed suggesting that localisms
and the principle of separation, by which towns served
discrete, single areas, had long given way to the principle
of competition between towns bringing about a hierarchical structuring. But this anticipates the discussion of
the next chapter.

The search for a universal criterion which would
enable an extensive region to be divided into its
component urban fields leads to the only basis which was
general: administration. Even in medieval times it is
possible to construct market areas from town charters
and ordinances. Thus in Wales the ordinances of Edward
I, usually appended to the Statute of Rhuddlan of 1284,
define market areas. 'Edward's concern for the
prosperity of the English burgesses whom he had induced
to reside in North Wales is shown in his attempt to secure
for them a complete monopoly of the trade there. The

market districts of the boroughs . . . were definitely
established, and special injunctions encouraged the
attendance of buyers and sellers. One enactment
stipulated that one person from each house should visit
the weekly market of his district for the purpose of
buying and selling. This was hardly practicable, and after
a few years was modified by Prince Edward of
Caernarvon, who ordinated the presence only of those
having business to transact' (Lewis, E.A., 1912, 174).
Using these ordinances a system of market areas for a
considerable area can be constructed.

The elaboration of the administrative system in
nineteenth-century Britain means that the possibilities of
identifying town areas greatly increase. As early as 1955
Carter had proposed the use of Poor Law Unions, the
association of parishes designated for the operation of
the Poor Law (Carter, 1955). This was on the basis that
the Commissioners stated, 'the most convenient limit of
union we have found has been that of a circle taking a
market town as a centre and comprehending those surrounding parishes whose inhabitants are accustomed to
resort to the same market'. The unions, therefore, provide evidence of immediate market areas but do not allow
for any hierarchical grouping of areas at levels above
those of the designated market towns.

Another basis which gives a wider coverage is the
analysis of the journeys of carriers to market. Again this
was used by Carter in 1955 to establish higher-order associations. Figure 4.6a and 4.6b provide an effective insight
into urban fields in southwest Wales in the first half of
the nineteenth century using both types of evidence. The
two regional centres of Carmarthen and Haverfordwest
stand out at the head of the hierarchy, with the other
towns representing lower orders.

Finally movement of a different character, that of
finance, has been used by Conzen for the United States in
the nineteenth century exploiting bank administration as
his basis (Conzen, 1977) and, in particular, the correspondent system.

By 1840, New York State law required all country
banks to keep funds in New York city, mainly for note
redemption. Many banks in other states followed suit
. . . the 1863 National Bank Act established eight
'reserve' cities to aid New York in the geographical
management of a new national currency. New York
was elevated to 'central reserve' city status, thus con-
serving its national pre-eminence. The new reserve
cities were Boston, Philadelphia, Baltimore, Cincinnati, New Orleans, Providence, Chicago and St Louis.
An amendment in 1864 added Washington, Albany,
Pittsburgh, Cleveland, Detroit, Milwaukee,
Louisville, Leavenworth and San Francisco. The act
gave large regional cities formal sanction to channel
banking business in their hinterlands through their
own institutions. (Conzen, 1977, 92–3)

The significant point is in the last sentence for by establishing hinterland linkages it is possible to build up a
system of bank territories which can serve as a surrogate

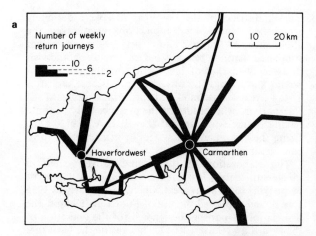

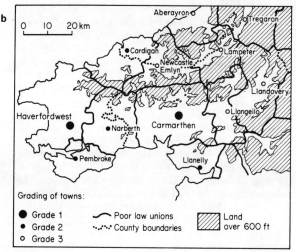

4.6.   (a) Regular journeys of carriers to market in southwest Wales, 1830.
(b) Market areas in south west Wales based on Poor Law Unions, 1835.

for urban regions. These are shown in 1881 and 1910 on Figure 4.7 and although only part of the USA is covered it is evident that such an analysis can be extended to cover the whole country.

This short section has demonstrated that there is a great variety of evidence which can, with a little imagination, be used to establish the boundaries of territories subject to central places, but there is as yet little in the way of consistent evidence being used widely and with consensus. Perhaps given the contrasted problems of both time and place this is not surprising.

5   Conclusion

In the Introduction to this chapter it was stressed that it would be quite absurd to pretend that even the most cursory survey of methods of establishing urban populations and city ranks and regions could be made. At best

only some indication of possibilities to be explored and exploited could be given. To a considerable degree those possibilities have not been particularly well or thoroughly used by historical geographers. Possibly their disparate nature has meant that mainly local studies over limited timespans are the only ones easily carried out and the scope of broader interpretation from these is limited. The more obvious of the bases is population and the next chapter will demonstrate that it is virtually exclusively on derived urban populations that most studies of city system evolution have been based. As one moves to the macro-scale and the dynamic situation the more complex methods of ranking towns are set aside in favour of the inclusive nature and the common basis of numbers.

Further reading

A book which attempts to set out the population of significant cities throughout time is:

CHANDLER, T. and FOX, G. 1974: *3000 Years of Urban Growth*. New York, but as indicated in the text it is an uncritical volume and needs to be treated with considerable reservation.

A scholarly book which treats a smaller area over a limited time-span is:

MOLS, R. 1954: *Introduction a la Demographie Historique des Villes d'Europe du XIVᵉ au XVIIIᵉ Siecle*, three volumes. Louvain.

Early British urban populations are considered in:

RUSSELL, J.C. 1948: *British Medieval Population*. Albuquerque, especially chapter XI, The boroughs and the distribution of population.

A more general work is:

HOLLINGSWORTH, T.H. 1969: *Historical Demography*. Cambridge.

The material on the use of functions to rank towns in the past is more limited and reference should be made to the works by Carter, Lewis and Patten in the list of references. A recent examination of the value of directory material is to be found in:

SHAW, G. 1982: *British directories as sources in historical geography* Inst. Brit. Geogrs: Historical geography research series, 8.

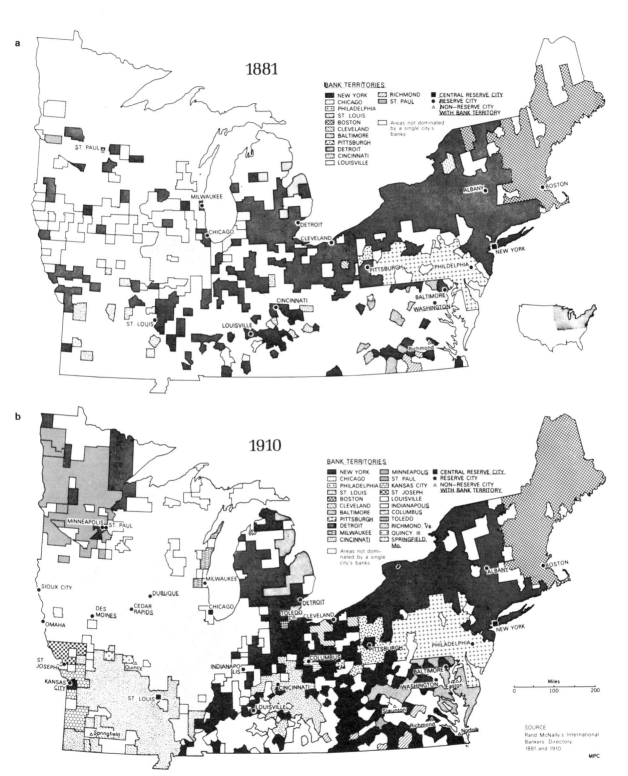

a

1881

BANK TERRITORIES

■ NEW YORK	▨ RICHMOND	■ CENTRAL RESERVE CITY
▢ CHICAGO	▨ ST. PAUL	● RESERVE CITY
⊞ PHILADELPHIA		△ NON-RESERVE CITY
▨ ST. LOUIS		WITH BANK TERRITORY
▨ BOSTON	▢ Areas not dominated	
▨ CLEVELAND	by a single city's	
▨ BALTIMORE	banks	
▨ PITTSBURGH		
▨ DETROIT		
▨ CINCINNATI		
▢ LOUISVILLE		

ST. PAUL △

MILWAUKEE ●

CHICAGO ●

DETROIT ●

CLEVELAND ●

ALBANY ●

BOSTON ●

PITTSBURGH ●   PHILADELPHIA ●

NEW YORK ■

CINCINNATI ●

ST. LOUIS ●

LOUISVILLE ●

BALTIMORE ●
WASHINGTON ●

Richmond ●

b

1910

BANK TERRITORIES

■ NEW YORK	▨ MINNEAPOLIS	■ CENTRAL RESERVE CITY
▢ CHICAGO	▨ ST. PAUL	● RESERVE CITY
⊞ PHILADELPHIA	▨ KANSAS CITY	△ NON-RESERVE CITY
▨ ST. LOUIS	⊠ ST. JOSEPH	WITH BANK TERRITORY
▨ BOSTON	▢ LOUISVILLE	
▨ CLEVELAND	▨ INDIANAPOLIS	
▨ BALTIMORE	▢ COLUMBUS	
▨ PITTSBURGH	▦ TOLEDO	
▨ DETROIT	▨ RICHMOND. Va.	
▨ MILWAUKEE	▨ QUINCY. Ill.	
▨ CINCINNATI	▢ SPRINGFIELD. Mo.	
▢ Areas not dominated by a single city's banks		

SIOUX CITY ●

MINNEAPOLIS ● ST. PAUL ●

DUBUQUE ●

MILWAUKEE ●

DES MOINES ●

CEDAR RAPIDS ●

OMAHA ●

CHICAGO ●

DETROIT ●

TOLEDO ●
CLEVELAND ●

ALBANY ●

BOSTON ●

ST JOSEPH ●

Quincy △

PITTSBURGH ●

PHILADELPHIA

NEW YORK ■

KANSAS CITY ●

ST. LOUIS ■

INDIANAPOLIS ●

COLUMBUS ●

BALTIMORE ●

WASHINGTON ● Easton

△ Springfield

CINCINNATI ●

LOUISVILLE ●

Staunton △

Richmond △

Norfolk △

Miles
0   100   200

SOURCE
Rand McNally's International
Bankers Directory
1881 and 1910

MPC

4.7.   Metropolitan county-level banking hinterlands in the
urban-industrial core of the United States, (a) 1881
and (b) 1910 (after Conzen).

5
The Evolution of the City System

1 Introduction

The consideration of the growth of individual towns is one of the oldest traditions in geography. Long before urban geography was recognized as a systematic study in its own right, degree examination questions in regional geography commonly asked for a discussion of the growth of specified towns in relation to site and situation. In complete contrast, analysis of the growth of the city system, that is of a set of towns and their interrelations, is a recent product derived from central-place theory. Such an introduction of an historical element into central-place studies, however, has not only been sporadic but has failed to produce any consensus. That is in part a consequence of the inability of classic central-place theory to sustain itself against other views of the relation between the sizes and numbers of towns in a given area. For example, in spite of attempts to demonstrate their compatibility, the rank-size rule must appear as an alternative to a hierarchically structured system. This lack of clarity and agreement over contemporary relationships obviously inhibits attempts to establish an historical process of universal application, for if the end-product is in dispute it is little wonder that the development sequence leading to it is not agreed.

It is not possible, therefore, at the outset of this chapter to present an accepted and over-arching theory or model of urban growth for the remainder of the chapter empirically to demonstrate. On the other hand, that does not imply a return to the study of unique cases, for that is too pessimistic a view of the contribution of central-place theory to historical urban geography. At least a number of generalizations can be selected out of the many attempts which have been made to establish general principles operative in the growth of city systems, and these can be examined, however short they may fall of being universal.

Before the theme of the general evolution of city systems is taken up, it is imperative to introduce a brief technical note for it is possible that some discussions of that theme have been clouded by an inadequate specification of what is being considered. Urban growth and the evolution of a system of central places may be two quite different concepts, the one referring to increments of populations from all sources, the other to the distribu-tion of a specified array of countryside-serving functions amongst contending centres.

2 Technical notes

(a) Measures of centrality and size

One of the great inconsistencies in the attempts to intro-duce a dynamic element into central-place studies relates to the measurement of centrality. In classical central-place theory, centrality, the significance of a settlement as a service centre for the surrounding countryside, is not necessarily related to size, or to use Christaller's word, importance, which is conventionally measured by population. As a result a considerable literature has been generated on methods of measuring centrality. Yet the moment studies of past situations are undertaken the dilemma of whether to invoke centrality by the accumulation of functions or size by population is dis-carded without hesitation and the two collapsed into one. There are but few studies which are specifically based on the examination of past functional complexes; popu-lation figures are virtually universally used.

The reason for the adoption of size or importance are easily realized for the practical problems related to any other procedure are considerable. In the previous chapter it was indicated that although prior to the era of modern population censuses it is not easy to generate reliable population figures, it is even more difficult to collect data providing accurate arrays of functions for settlements, even after the coming of the city directory.

One solution to this problem, as the previous chapter demonstrated, is to adopt a simple presence–absence classification for any trade or activity in a town. Barker claims that 'two advantages are that the relative magnitude of directory errors in abstracting data is substantially reduced and also, the problem of devising arbitrary counting procedures to accommodate com-binations of trades at a given establishment, is avoided' (Barker, 1978, 3). These advantages are greater the more remote the period and the less reliable the data. Patten, as the last chapter noted, in his studies of East Anglia between 1500 and 1700, adopted such a method as his basis of analysis constructing a scalogram of occupations and functions against towns (Patten, 1978) but where the subsequent analysis was by means of visual inspection. Barker in his work on southwest England adopted a more rigorous procedure constructing a matrix of similarities between all the trades identified and subjecting it to a principal components analysis, the first three components being rotated to an orthogonal solution using the varimax procedure. The functions with highest loading on the three components give an indication of related trades. Component One picked out the ubiquitous trades, such as bakers; Component Two a large group of trades associated with the larger places, such as banks and booksellers; Component Three identified highly specialized functions, such as carters. A grouping procedure was applied to the component scores to derive a hierarchical ordering in 1861. Barker has also presented similar orderings for 1889 and 1911, thereby deriving a dynamic study, although over a much shorter time period than other studies (Barker, 1980).

These late nineteenth-century analyses are based on one uniform set of directories so that data abstraction, especially related to a presence–absence situation is greatly simplified. Generally, however, few investigators have thought it worthwhile investing large amounts of time and effort in attempting to overcome the severe problem of gathering data; it has been far easier to fall back on population totals.

But, as already noted, population figures for past periods themselves pose problems. Apart from the obvious difficulty of establishing them, their main advantage has in-built problems for they are indivisible, inclusive totals which contain in their generation both central place and specialized functions. Certainly some of the more ambitious statistical manipulations have been vitiated by an inadequate comprehension of the basic input.

(b) Conceptual bases of hierarchies

A further problem impinges on the problem of past hierarchies and one which is conceptual in nature. In many parts of the world urban status was a thing administratively granted and rights and privileges so derived were often more significant than size. It is, therefore, difficult to identify what should be the basis of assessment. For example, when John Speed in his maps of England and Wales at the beginning of the seventeenth century used symbols of varying sizes and character to represent towns he was implicitly identifying an urban hierarchy. A careful analysis of his usage will reveal that the largest symbols were used for cathedral cities regardless of size, for some were minuscule in population counts (Bird, 1975-6). Speed was establishing a perceived hierarchy in terms relevant to his own times, but his maps indicate the dangers of accepting past presentations of hierarchical structures at their face value and turning them uncritically into twentieth-century terms.

It can be argued that Speed's ordering was no different from a perceived rather than a measured ranking at the present day, but perhaps the point at issue can be clarified by introducing the recognition of ranks of towns within the Roman Empire – colonia, municipium, for example. Here again there is a tendency, at a time when no other criteria are available, to take these at their face value as indicators of a hierarchical structure. It is, however, extremely dangerous to equate such a structure derived from very different conditions in the past with a contemporary central-place system.

(c) Simulation of change

One of the standard procedures in attempting to understand change over time is to employ simulation techniques by which patterns of change from a given situation can be generated under circumstances which are predetermined. The results can be matched with actual situations thereby providing a measure of the possible explanatory power of the predetermined circumstances. Anomalies will reveal unsuspected causal influences. The two best known examples in the context of urban growth are those by Morrill (1965) and Robson (1973) respectively. This chapter cannot digress into an exegesis of simulation techniques as such. Moreover, it can justifiably be contended that no great illumination has been provided by them in the field of city system evolution. Consequently, with the references having been set out, no attempt will be made to pursue simulation any further.

Setting aside simulation, therefore, it is apparent that these brief technical notes have revealed three quite different bases on which past rank-size relationships can be discussed;

1 Centrality assessments, varying the criteria to be used according to the period under review.
2 Populations, which are, however, most frequently estimates for accurate figures are generally unobtainable.
3 Contemporarily defined (perceived) status, where the bases will change greatly according to time and space.

With these difficulties as a background, but always to be borne in mind, it is possible to proceed to review notions of city system evolution.

3 City system structure and evolution

(a) Alternative structures

As a basis for the consideration of change over time it is necessary briefly to review the various possible structures which have been proposed for city systems and to set out some of the possible past situations in which they may have occurred.

(i) Separation. This is an unusual, even paradoxical, condition to include, although it is most certainly one that can be envisaged. All formal systems imply interactions between the constituent objects and hence it is odd to propose a situation without relations between the objects, or cities in this case, where there can be no

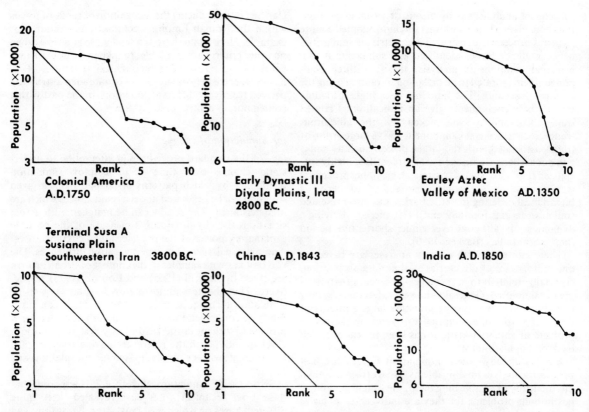

5.1.   Archaelogical and historical convex rank-size
distributions (after Johnson).

system. But in any territory there is no absolute necessity for interaction to occur and it is feasible to conceive of a condition of individual, separated and non-interacting settlements. The earliest colonial towns on the shores of a new land can be identified as of this type, as in Australia in the early years of the nineteenth century. Geoffrey Blainey in his brilliant book, *The Tyranny of Distance* (1966) heads his third chapter 'Isolation', his fourth 'Limpet Ports' and begins that fourth chapter with the comment that anyone circumnavigating Australia about 1830, 'would have come across isolated ports, flourishing or gasping or dead. The coast by then resembled a necklace with much lace and only a few beads haphazardly arranged' (Blainey, 1966, 70). The bastide towns established by invading medieval barons can be thought of as similar in their initial phase. Size would be locally determined or related to exogenous forces.

An alternative but theoretical view is of a situation where cities are complete mirror-images of each other, each with the same size and identical array of functions. Again in theoretical terms to cover a territory they would be equally spaced but since no interaction would be generated they would be effectively separated. It is worth recording that this was the view Sir Thomas More took of Utopia.

Under this same heading it is possible to introduce the situation which is referred to as convexity, that is where on a log population against log rank graph, settlements are not distributed on a straight line (see *iv*, page 99) in a rank-size rule relationship but where the shape of the graph is convex (Figure 5.1). Explanations usually advanced for this situation are either pooling, where two or more autonomous systems are combined in the same analysis, or partitioning, whereby a primate city of a complete system is excluded. These are specific problems, however, which could influence the outcome of any analysis and, since systems are seldom closed, usually does. G.J. Johnson (1980) reviewing the class of convex distributions relates them generally to a relatively low degree of integration in the wider system. Thus he contends that 'the area of the future United States was occupied in 1750 by a series of separate British colonies lacking an integrated political, much less economic system' (Johnson, 1980, 234). If the rank-size relationship is examined over the following 100 years then the pattern is a familiar one. 'The period from before independence to the middle of the nineteenth century was one of political unification, urbanization and economic development. The increasing integration of the system was associated with a marked decrease in rank-size convexity to a nearly log-normal distribution in 1850' (Johnson, 1980, 237; but see also Figure 5.2). These changes remain to be discussed but lack of integration can be seen as separation, a word which carries fewer problems of interpretation.

(ii) Primacy. This is the situation where one very large city predominates over all others. There is no precise specification of the relative sizes of those other cities in the system; they could be small but similar or have some varying size relationship with each other. The notion of primacy was derived from an early (1939) paper by Mark Jefferson who propounded 'the Law of the Primate City', arguing that, 'the largest city shall be supereminent, and not merely in size, but in national influence' (Jefferson, 1939, 227). Setting aside national influence which is difficult to measure, there remains the term 'largest', but even there no precise indication of meaning was established. Further justification of the 'law' was vague, even mystic when it was related to the translation of the 'Great Tradition' of the folk society into an urban context (Redfield and Singer, 1954).

Historically, it is possible to envisage three situations in which a primate city might emerge.

1 *The creation of the nation state about the city.* This was especially relevant to the European condition in the early modern period when the national states were created out of medieval particularism. These states were accumulations of territory by military or dynastic means into united kingdoms. The capital cities were the generating and predominant foci; the ascendency of the organizing core was reflected in the primacy of the city at its centre.

2 *The role of absolute rulers.* It can be shown how city layout epitomized the domination of absolute rulers (page 10). In a functional context the same situation led to the supremacy of one city as the ruler ensured the complete dominance of his capital over potential provincial rivals.

3 *Colonial centres of exploitation.* In many ways these primate cities were no more than the realization of 1 and 2 in territories external to the nation state. Points of entry and points of control of the colonial power were made into centres of absolute dominance where the authority of the colonial power could be made secure. In a post-colonial situation it is likely that a similar condition would last for a considerable period before a more widespread, national economic development would invigorate provincial towns, lead to a more general basis of hinterland service and offset the imprint of colonial times.

(iii) Hierarchy. This is a well known relationship between cities in a system, postulated by central-place theory, where settlements occur in a series of well marked size steps, the number in each lower step being greater, and in the purest interpretation there being a direct relationship between the numbers of towns in each of the steps, or ranks or grades as terms more frequently used. Central-place theory has been used to interpret periodic market systems in primitive economies, but in its standard form a developed economy must be envisaged. The hierarchical arrangement is a consequence of the

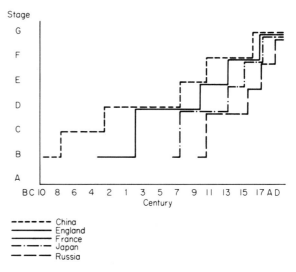

Stage

BC 10 8 6 4 2 1 3 5 7 9 11 13 15 17 AD
Century

----- China
——— England
—·—·— France
············ Japan
— — — Russia

5.2. The urban network view of periods of economic development (after Rozman). For interpretation see text p. 102.

interaction and competition between centres and they can only occur under conditions of active trade and easy movement. At this point, given the extensive literature on the urban hierarchy, no further development will be presented but in considering the growth of the system it will be necessary to return to the idea of a hierarchical ordering.

(iv) Continuum. This is the principle of the rank-size rule for cities which suggests a continuous and not a stepped-like arrangement of city sizes in descending ranked array. On logarithmic paper this would take the form of a straight line: the size of any city multiplied by its rank would be equal to the size of the largest city. Unlike central-place theory, which was based on deductive argument, the rank-size rule is claimed to be an empirically observed relationship. G. W. Zipf was largely responsible for bringing the rule into geographical discussion by way of his book, *Natural Unity and Disunity* (Zipf, 1941), but in it he only provided the most general of explanations. He contended that there were two sets of opposed tendencies operative on the city system. The first moved to diversification where a large number of communities benefited from being located near to raw material sources thereby minimizing transport costs. The other force was one of unification where a small number of large communities minimized the movement of finished goods to the consumer. From these opposing conditions a balance emerged which brought about the rank-size rule. Again this seems to demand a developed economy. It must be added that attempts have been made to show that hierarchical and rank-size arrangements are not incompatible.

(v) Disorder or disarray. It must be proper and legitimate to introduce into the discussion a situation of complete randomness, that is, where there is no discernible order in the sizes of settlements. Such a condi-

tion is said to be derived from the maximization of entropy. This idea comes from thermodynamics where entropy becomes maximized in any closed system, thereby generating a random condition where none of three ordered situations so far described would obtain. Robson's comments are pertinent:

> For the physical sciences, the concept of entropy derives from the tendency of a system to assume the most random molecular state. Systems, in other words, are likely to become disordered. The reason for the tendency is that random molecular motion more probably produces a disordered than an ordered state. Entropy is the property by which the disorder is described quantitatively so that a more disordered state has a higher entropy than an ordered state. In transferring such concepts to urban studies two problems stand out; how can one measure order and disorder and how can one translate the notion of molecular activity into the context of the 'performance' of the city? (Robson, 1973, 17)

Given these problems, together with the fact that city systems are never closed systems, that application of the concept of entropy is not likely to be greatly productive. Even so, in general and subjective terms, it can be envisaged that over a long period of time an area subjected to repeated phases of urban genesis and subsequent development based on a series of quite different stimuli, that is with contrasted functional bases, might well be characterized by a disordered or random arrangement as regards the sizes and locations of its cities. Such a vague and simple concept, it is true, debases the precise and measurable formulation of entropy, but it offers an effective descriptive interpretation and is in line with the processes and tabulation set out in chapter 3, pages 74–81.

It must be added, however, that it can be argued that entropy is maximized when the city system reaches equilibrium and that the steady-state equilibrium is the most probable. In turn, that state is similar to the rank-size rule. 'A city size distribution obeying the rank-size rule is the most probable distribution and represents the steady-state equilibrium in which entropy has been maximized' (Robson, 1973, 244). In the midst of these discussions which seem to multiply confusion rather than bring clarity one is tempted to paraphrase the well known example of meiosis 'its order rooted in disorder stood . . .'!

(b) The evolution of structures

It would undoubtedly be tidy and intellectually satisfying if the five interpretations of the structure of city systems could be viewed not as a range of possibilities but as succeeding organizations in an evolutionary process, as part of one theory of development. In general terms this is not difficult to do.

The earliest situation is one of separation at a time before mobility allows that interaction which is essential for systematic relationships. From this a primate city

arrangement comes about with the emergence of the modern nation state when the capital city becomes predominant over all others, creating national unity, epitomizing the national will and organizing economic development. This has been called a Solar central place system (Smith, 1976). At a more primitive level effective organization of a tribal territory can be considered as a parallel. Development pushing forward with confidence within the nation state, modifies the urban situation considerably for it is essentially urban based, whilst the regions have to be effectively served by accessible centres. Increasing mobility makes all this possible so that provincial towns become ordered into a hierarchy of centres below the level of the capital city (unless an artificial alternative is chosen to allay regional jealousies).

In the next stage an increasing array of economic activities promotes the tensions which arise between the growing number of smaller places required for effective exploitation of the country's resources, and the smaller number of larger places for distribution and these, together with regional variations in wealth and the integration of ports of trade, blur the incipient hierarchical structuring and convert it into an approximation to the rank-size rule. The earlier situations have implied towns growing mainly as service centres but with time a wider range of city-generating functions develops, many of which are unrelated to the service of an immediate hinterland. Mining and manufacturing towns grow, so do spas, resorts and educational centres; transport creates specialized towns. But these functions do not remain discrete and separate activities, they react on each other. The result is an increasing complexity, or put in another way, increasing randomness where no identifiable size relation holds. Entropy has been maximized.

(c) The evolution of structures and economic development

Speculation as to the evolution of structures, in the manner of the mythical lady herself, opens up a Pandora's Box with perhaps the sole consolation that Hope remains in that container. All this follows from the fact that it is implicit that a relationship must exist between any such evolution and economic development. Thus a link is established with those broad works which have speculated on development and, in some cases, ascribed to the city a particular role.

It is possible to begin with one of the most ambitious of works, Wallerstein's *The Modern World-System* (Wallerstein, 1974) even though the urban role is somewhat thinly treated. A review by Dodgshon raises points of relevance. He writes, 'Unlike a sixteenth-century World-System, the spatial structure of a late eighteenth and nineteenth-century World-System can actually be seen taking shape in response to the forces acting upon it . . . these forces were those of the self-regulating market system acting via an emergent city system to allocate worldwide resources in a manner consistent with a world-scaled von Thünen-type model' (Dodgshon, 1977, 16). In the evolutionary sequence of city-system structures sketched above, the 'emergent city system' marks the transfer from a primate toward a hierarchical order under the impact of the economic forces which were supplanting the military-cum-political forces which had brought the primate city into being under conditions of relative immobility. Again, Dodgshon records, 'Changes in the level of urban demand have been explored by a number of writers. Harvey and Frank, for example, have argued for its structural significance to the World-System, a well developed system or hierarchy being essential if the manipulative forces of the self-regulating market were to be communicated from the core to the periphery' (Dodgshon, 1977, 16). A further quotation can be added. 'There is little comparison between the scale of urban population as it emerged over the nineteenth century and that of the sixteenth century when barely 20 million people could have been living in the towns of Europe and when the size of towns or cities was measured in thousands . . . rather than millions. Since the difference between a town living off its local hinterland and one forced to look to a much wider world can be construed in terms of population mass, it follows that the appearance of a vast aggregate metropolis over the nineteenth century must have given an unprecedented impetus to the integration of a much more extensive space economy' (Dodgshon, 1977, 17). That 'integration' seems very close to the ideas generated by Zipf in a book which had as part of its title 'National Unity' and hence to the view of a city system corresponding to the rank-size rule.

The brief indication which has been presented of the association of city system structure with World-System state does little more than demonstrate that the two must be linked and accordingly studies of the evolution of the city system impinge upon a very large body of literature to which some reference must be made.

The most cogent review of this literature is that by Philip Abrams in his paper, 'Towns and economic growth: some theories and problems' (Abrams and Wrigley, 1978). Much of the controversy revolves around the view of an active and creative urban role in historical transitions especially that from feudalism to capitalism. Abrams uses the book by Maurice Dobb, *Studies in the development of capitalism* (Dobb, 1946), to support his main contention. Dobb considered the relation between the decline of feudalism and the growth of towns and asserted that 'so that as the growth of the market exercised a disintegrating influence on the structure of feudalism and prepared the soil for the growth of forces which were to weaken and supplant it, the story of this influence can largely be identified with the rise of towns' (Dobb, 1946, 70). The statement is somewhat loose but as Abrams concludes, 'By implication towns are treated as a generic social entity and attention is directed to the possibility of an important relationship between what might be called "townness" and the dissolution of social relations. But neither the structure and dynamics of the

implied relationship nor the specific properties of "townness" are ever articulated in clear unambiguous general terms' (Abrams and Wrigley, 1978, 11).

At the crux of this view is one familiar to geographers, and which has been considered in the Introduction, which urges those approaches, usually called structural, which demand a study not based on the urban phenomenon itself but on those deeper-seated socioeconomic forces which condition it. Abrams puts his view as follows:

> the tendency to attribute analytical significance to the form at the expense of the relational substance becomes very powerful. Even historians who theoretically should have known much better succumb, often in the face of the evidence of their own research, to the plausible hypothesis that the town as such, or the quality of urbanism abstracted from it, must surely be an independent social structural reality and a decisive agency or variable in the process of social change. . . . Nevertheless, it is as true now as it was when Wirth wrote 'Urbanism as a way of life', that, as he put it, 'in the rich literature of the city we look in vain for a theory systematizing the available knowledge concerning the city as a social entity'. It may be that one reason for this is that in an important analytical sense the city is *not* a social entity; that we have been the victims of the fallacy of misplaced concreteness in treating it as such; and that one object of urban history and urban sociology now might be to get rid of the concept of the town. (Abrams and Wrigley, 1978, 10)

Caught up in this rejection of much of the speculation on urban influences are two attitudes. The first is the historian's aversion to generalization and desire to remain with the particular. This must result in a rejection of a general view of city-system evolution. The second is the assertion that the city is not an independent variable (not a social entity) but the product of the operating forces, political, social, economic. In short, the city cannot be a process, there are no urban processes per se. Like many contentious issues this is little short of a truism.

At this point it is necessary to revert back to the generation of this issue, a view of the evolution of the city system. There it has been clearly implied that the system was not self-generating. Urbanism of itself was not setting up its own developmental sequence but rather the various structures were the product of politico-socioeconomic change. It is implicit that those changes themselves followed a pattern, but it would be extremely foolish to claim that a universal mode of city-system evolution can be established, although perhaps it is worthy of investigation. The way forward in this chapter, therefore, is not by pursuit of these nebulous ideas but rather by the examination of more specific transitions. Even so, these transitions are couched in urban terms, much as that might be opposite to the views of structuralists and historians. To the geographer the point of departure is legitimately observed differences in the structure of the city system over time. These differences are the relevant facts which demand analysis and call for interpretation.

With this conclusion it is appropriate to review an attempt which has been made to provide a 'periodization' of history based on urban development. This has been made by Gilbert Rozman in *Urban Networks in Russia, 1750–1800, and Pre-modern Periodization* (Rozman, 1976). He identifies seven levels of central places defined by two sets of definitions, the one relating to commercial and administrative functions, the other to population. In terms of the methods of establishing levels set out at the beginning of this chapter, functions or population, Rozman adopts, but equates, both. The levels are set out in Table 5.1. In relation to the gradual filling out of the full system of seven levels, Rozman proposes such stages labelled A to G as set out in Table 5.2.

The seven stages are defined in turn. Stage A is interpreted as pre-urban. Stage B is the first phase of urban development where 'generally isolated urban centres are loosely integrated into a national setting. Surrounding villages send tribute in support of military, religious and administrative functions' which are lodged in these centres. This seems to parallel the process of synoecism which has been introduced earlier in this book in the discussion of urban origins and the idea of 'separation' as a principle of distribution. At Stage C a formal administrative hierarchy appears. 'The existence of two levels of cities facilitates the regular movement of goods and manpower from scattered areas in which there are lower-level cities to a small number of higher-level cities' (Rozman, 1976, 35). Stage D represents a culmination of the process with 'an unusual concentration of population in one dominant city' (p. 35), a condition that bears strong echoes of a primate city situation. At this point there is a major switch from the dominance of administrative functions and where commerce was, however, important, still secondary, to the reverse where 'Stage E marks the beginning of . . . commercial centralization. . . . The widespread appearance of periodic markets in settlements miles removed from administrative centres is the mark of the onset of Stage E' (p. 36). Stage F sees the initiation of a new level of intermediate marketing centres, while finally at Stage G all seven levels of cities are present. 'Just as Stage B, C and D designate phases in the

Table 5.1: Definitions of the seven levels of central places

Level	Definition I	Definition II
1	National administrative centre	National administrative centre and more populous than any level-3 city
2	Regional centre or a capital of a decentralized state	Regional centre and more populous than any level-3 city
3	Elevated administrative centre or a major port linking a level-1 or 2 city to distant areas	Population: 30,000–299,999 and not classified at levels 1 or 2
4	Second lowest administrative centre or a major regional port	Population: 10,000–29,999
5	Lowest administrative centre	Population: 3,000–9,999
6	Intermediate marketing settlement	Population: fewer than 3,000 people and an intermediate marketing settlement
7	Standard marketing settlement	Population: fewer than 3,000 people and a standard marketing settlement or an administrative centre without a periodic market

maturation of an essentially administrative hierarchy. Stages E, F and G refer to the maturation of a commercial hierarchy, even though many of the major commercial nexuses are found in cities that also have administrative functions' (p. 37).

On examination, this schema has much in common with conventional views and the schema set out in chapter 3. It would be generally accepted that at earliest times administrative functions took precedence in the growth of cities as rulers extended their control over territories where the first necessity was government through an effective administration, even if its purpose was to extract wealth. Again, the break between Stages D and E would seem to correspond with the change from primacy to hierarchical ordering, with subsequent Stages F and G representing a maturing of the hierarchy.

When the schema is applied in detail, however, difficulties begin to arise. Figure 5.2 shows Rozman's interpretation of the way five countries have moved

Table 5.2: The seven stages of pre-modern urban development

Stage	Number of levels present	Usual levels present	Characteristic
A	zero	–	pre-urban
B	one	2	tribute city
C	two	1, 5 or 2, 5	state city
D	two, three, or four	1, 4, 5 or 2, 4, 5 or 2, 3 or 1, 3, 4, 5	imperial city
E	four or five	1, 3, 5, 7 or 1, 3, 4, 5, 7	standard marketing
F	five or six	1, 3, 5, 6, 7 or 1, 3, 4, 5, 6, 7	intermediate marketing
G	seven	1, 2, 3, 4, 5, 6, 7	national marketing

through these seven stages. Disregarding the pre-urban stage, as far as England is concerned Stage B is vaguely referred to 'early indigenous centres' (p. 78), made up of 'level-2 tribal centres about which little is known'. Then 'the absorption of . . . England into the Roman Empire resulted in a rapid transition from Stage B to Stage D' (p. 78) in which the 'imperial city' is Rome. 'Stage E and the early part of Stage F occurred during the late tenth and early fourteenth centuries' (p. 78). In order to accommodate urban decline centralized and decentralized phases of these stages have to be invoked . . . 'a decentralized phase of Stage F appeared in the aftermath of the bubonic plague' (p. 78). In brief, these simple, unidimensional phases do not work. In order to accommodate them quite inappropriate changes of scale are made. Thus at one time 'England' is seen as part of the Roman Empire, at another as an independent nation. This enables Rozman to put the transition from a primate situation (Rome, the imperial city) to a hierarchical one in England at the low point of urban decline in the Dark Ages. But revival was initially related to secular and ecclesiastic administration onto which commercial functions became attached. And surely as far as England is concerned London was the primate and imperial city even into the eighteenth century? The sharp division between administrative and commercial functions cannot be made. In order to offset the problem of the primacy of London Rozman again invokes a centralized phase. 'Stage F in England . . . as Stage D before it, can

readily be divided into a centralized and decentralized phase. During Stage D the centralized phase based predominantly on administrative controls had yielded to the extremely decentralized conditions of the period known as the Dark Ages. The reverse pattern occurred in

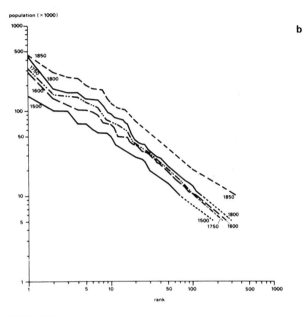

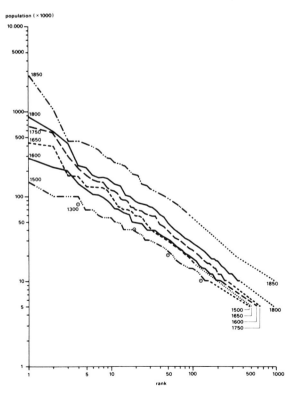

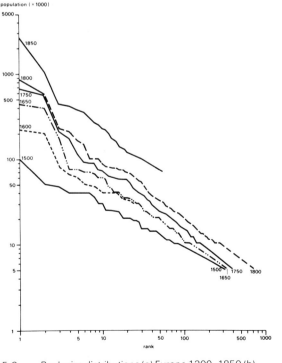

5.3. Rank-size distributions (a) Europe 1300–1850 (b) Southern Europe 1500–1800; (c) Northern Europe 1500–1800; (after de Vries).

. . . the Stage F society when decentralized patterns were replaced by new heights of centralization' (p. 82). But this is mere sophistry. The situation is far more complex than Rozman's schema allows for, with periods of urban growth and decay, and a wide variety of urban roles being characteristic, the various stages recur for it is not one simple process of change.

A further attempt to review broad categories of city system change can be found in the study by de Vries of 'Patterns of urbanization in pre-industrial Europe, 1500–1800' in the volume *Patterns of European urbanization since 1500* (Schmal, 1981). De Vries begins by discussing the critical data sources and from them the three rank-size distributions, for Europe and two broad subdivisions, northern and southern, which are shown in Figure 5.3. In interpretation he identifies a situation in 1500 where the distributions show a small slope coefficient with what he calls a 'flat' top. These suggest that the largest cities at that date were smaller than would be predicted, and this is particularly so in northern Europe if Paris be excepted. In turn this situation is interpreted as demonstrating 'a lack of integration', for 'the summation of many small relatively autarkic urban systems – which seems a good description of medieval urbanism – is likely to generate a flat-topped curve with a shallow slope' (de Vries, 1981, 93).

Some 100 years later, by the period about 1600, the slope of all three curves is steeper and that for the whole of Europe is more regular, indicating progress towards economic integration and this in spite of the emergence of nationalism and politically separated identities. The flatness of the earlier period in northern Europe is replaced by a steeper slope 'shifting unmistakably toward a situation where the largest cities are the most populous. . . . By 1650 this new structure is achieved, while the rest of the distribution is quite regular, and much steeper in slope than any earlier distribution' (de Vries, 1981, 94).

De Vries's general review of change is worthy of recording in full. 'The process of urban growth in Europe as a whole as well as in the two great zones treated here can be summarized by a rank-size curve which, step-by-step from 1500 to 1750, straightens out (loses its flat top) and rotates to achieve gradually steeper slopes from the pivot of an almost stable number of small cities. This is an abstract way of saying that urban growth in this long period was heavily concentrated in the large cities (and cities that became large) and was not characterized by the birth of numerous new cities' (de Vries, 1981, 94).

After the middle of the eighteenth century the situation changes fundamentally with the Industrial Revolution initially reversing the 'centuries-long process of urban population concentration in the largest cities'. New towns and small towns are created although eventually economies of scale lead to the largest again dominating growth.

From his survey de Vries identifies three dominant phases (Figure 5.4).

1   The long sixteenth century, 1500 to 1600 or 1650.

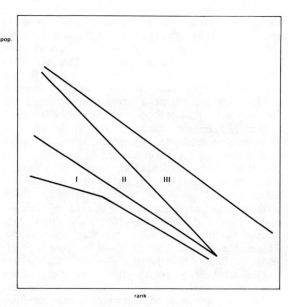

5.4.   Three periods of pre modern urbanization in Europe (after de Vries).

2   The age of the rural proletariat, 1600 to 1650/1750.
3   The new urbanization, 1750 to 1800/1850.

De Vries's notions can be set against the present author's earlier formulation of the growth of the Welsh city system, given the necessary scale changes (Carter, 1969). There a phase of urban genesis was seen to produce an unintegrated city system (if that is not an impossibility by definition) dominated by a principle of separation. Economic development resulted in competition during which towns rose or fell within the rank order. The eventual product was one of relative stability until a new phase of genesis was once again initiated. The two phases of genesis were the medieval and the industrial. De Vries's analysis is not greatly different. What is surprising, however, is that although the post-medieval period of urban decline is invoked to explain the transition from his first to his second phase, there is no apparent recognition of the great phase of Renaissance town foundation. This was noted in relation to the Welsh study, but since the area was so slightly affected it was treated as 'minor exogenous interpolation'. For the whole of Europe a rather more certain impact would have been expected.

It is now proper to move on to look at rather more detailed studies of the controls of and influences on change in the system.

4 The state of the city system: Controls and influences

(i) Primacy and hierarchy

The relationships between the various structures of the city system have received a great deal of general comment and analysis, but there has been much less in the way of detailed studies of specific periods. Britain and the USA can be considered in the exploration of the relationships between a primate and an hierarchical condition.

Although the dominance of Paris within France is the most frequently cited example of primacy, the clearest case in pre-industrial Europe was that of London. Not only was London larger than Paris (575,000 as against 500,000 at the end of the seventeenth century; 900,000 as against 550,000 at the end of the eighteenth), but also London contained a considerably larger proportion of the country's population (7 per cent in 1650, 11 per cent in 1750 as against 2.5 per cent for Paris at both dates) (Wrigley, 1978). The primate nature of London can be seen most clearly by comparing its population at successive dates between 1600 and 1850 with that of the next largest town in England.

Table 5.3: Populations of London and next largest English city, 1600–1801 (after Daunton, 1978)

Date	London	Next-largest city	Multiplier
1600	250,000	15,000 (Norwich)	17
1750	655,000	50,000 (Bristol)	13
1801	960,000	84,000 (Manchester)	11
1851	2,400,000	376,000 (Liverpool)	6

According to the rank size where $R^n S_R = M$, where R is the rank of a city, S_R the population of a city of rank R and n and M constants, then the second-ranked city should be half the size of the first ranked; that is, in Table 5.3 the multiplier should be 2. It is even possible to take the measure of London's primacy further back into the past if figures such as those suggested in Russell's *British Medieval Population* (see chapter 4, p. 83) are adopted. The figures are far too tentative to put on a graph of the multiplier to create a moving picture of the next-largest city divided into London's population against time, but its general form would seem to be clear. From Domesday on it would appear to change little until the fifteenth century when a very rapid rise took it to a peak in the seventeenth century. This was followed by a corresponding decline as industrial cities took off on their growth. Even so London retained its primacy well into the nineteenth century. This situation is in line with that which was discussed in the last section and where an early condition of many small autarkic systems is replaced by an effective national system dominated by the primate national capital.

Consideration of the levels below London, however, will reveal structures more akin to a hierarchical ordering representing the smaller autarkic systems. These would

appear to have been present from late medieval times. The clearest exposition of such a situation is fortunately available in the work of John Patten (1978). Given the difficulties over data his study of the urban system is confined to East Anglia, but he is able to deploy both population figures and analyses of the range of economic activities present in the various towns. Reverting to the earlier technical notes it must be added that Patten's work is perhaps the most impressive demonstration of the use of functional data in an historical context.

Patten presents the urban hierarchy for three periods, the sixteenth century, the early seventeenth and the late seventeenth century. He asserts that a quite clear fourfold ranking of towns can be established for East Anglia in the sixteenth century. 'At its top and standing by itself was Norwich in Norfolk; a great provincial city; the next level was of the four county and/or port towns of Kings Lynn and Great Yarmouth in Norfolk, Ipswich and Bury St Edmunds in Suffolk, with their noted marketing or manufacturing specialities' (Patten, 1978, 259). Below the two top ranks there were some 40 lesser towns which are divided into two grades 'though it is difficult to draw a clear line between them'. By the early seventeenth century there had been little change. 'The four county towns and ports remained clearly differentiated from Norwich, and from the major and minor local towns that lay below them in the urban systems' (Patten, 1978, 274). The same situation is identified in the later part of the century, although Norwich, the capital of the region, had distanced itself still more clearly from the four towns of the second order in population numbers, although not in terms of a multiplier which remained fairly constantly at between 1.7 and 2.0.

The conclusion from this review of Patten's work, as from other surveys, is that below the primate city of London there had developed from an early date a structured hierarchy of towns reflecting the early economic maturity which was achieved in western Europe.

It is a widespread view that a primate city is parasitic, sucking into itself the surplus wealth produced in the rest of the country. Possibly, images of the profligacy of the French court have contributed to such an attitude. E.A. Wrigley has attempted to demonstrate how in the case of London the opposite was true (Wrigley, 1978). Figure 5.5 is his interpretation of the links between London's growth and the Industrial Revolution in England, of the way in which the demands set up by the primate city through its drive and size triggered off those changes which are now considered to have constituted an industrial revolution. If Wrigley's model, which he suggests is intended to aid further thought rather than to encapsulate the whole of the changes taking place, is considered then the central boxes between London and the precipitated changes in the provinces can be interpreted as having critical influences on the regional sub-systems. Improved transport, better commercial facilities, higher real incomes, agricultural change, all these were the stimuli which promoted the hierarchical

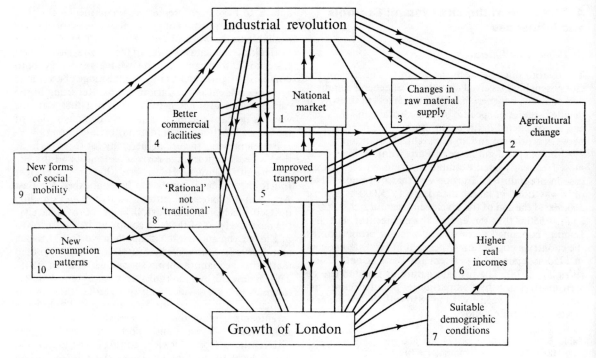

5.5.   Links between London's growth and the Industrial
Revolution in England (after Wrigley).

structuring of towns within the regions as they permeated down the system. It was this process which was to generate the explosive growth of towns, significantly in most cases they were not new towns but those with an already established commercial basis.

The hierarchical ranking of the pre-industrial period was, therefore, completely overtaken by industrially based growth to create a different set of relationships. As far as the primacy–hierarchy relationship is concerned, prior to industrialization it is apparent that these could coexist and that at an early date a series of regional sub-systems developed linked mainly through their capitals to London, the primate coordinator of the regional sub-sets.

The city system in the USA has been the subject of much general examination but little detailed study of limited time periods. Borchert's major phases of metropolitan evolution have already been referred to in the consideration of the diffusion of urbanism in the United States (Borchert, 1967). It can also be adapted to relate to the dominant principles controlling the structure of the system. The earliest colonial phase before 1763 can be regarded as one of separation where a series of virtually discrete enclaves were controlled from the coastal towns. After 1763 a phase which can be called hinterland expansion took place and a second urban frontier was established along the lines of the Ohio and the Mississippi. This was the period when New York became the primate city, even though it never approached anything like the dominance of London. Nevertheless, the primacy of

New York can be regarded as one taken over from London, for in the colonial periods the ports of the eastern seaboard can be regarded as extensions of the British system, isolated minor sub-systems. The next period after 1820 can be called one of 'spatial extraversion' (Brook, 1975) as the whole of the territory was occupied and where instant cities (Barth, 1975) sprang up. By this means a hierarchical structure was established under the leadership of New York.

The last period has been considered in some detail by Michael Conzen who, as chapter 4 noted, has tapped an unusual and interesting data source, the system of bank correspondents which arose from the need to channel business between the rapidly extending number of banks throughout the country. 'The pattern of correspondent accounts represents the accumulated structure of tens of thousands of channels voluntarily set up between banks in large commercial centres and those dispersed across the country, and provides a first approximation of the flow of capital through the financial system. A correspondent relationship in the nineteenth century involved a bank in a small community maintaining a deposit account with a bank in a large city' (Conzen, 1977, 91). The city bank used the funds to gain interest and, in turn, provided an array of services. Within this relationship Conzen identifies a four-level hierarchy which had emerged by 1870. At the head of this was New York with Boston and Philadelphia making up a second and lower level. Below, and distinguished by having annual clearing of over $200 million, was a third level (see

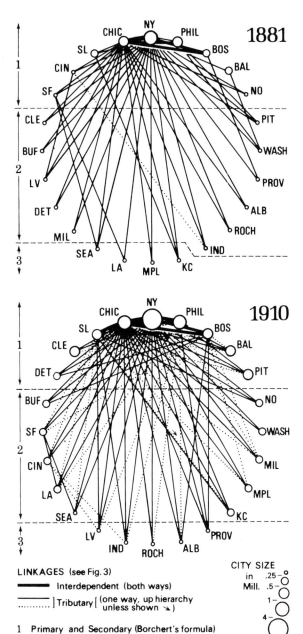

LINKAGES (see Fig. 3)

▬▬▬ Interdependent (both ways)

──── ⎤ Tributary ⎡ (one way, up hierarchy
··········· ⎦   ⎣ unless shown ↘)

1 Primary and Secondary (Borchert's formula)
2 Tertiary (do.)
3 Other (incl. in Duncan and Lieberson's group)

CITY SIZE
in   .25 – ○
Mill. .5 – ○
         1 – ○
         4 – ○
                    MPC

5.6.   Large city banking interdependence in the USA in
        1881 and 1910 (after Conzen).

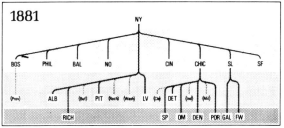

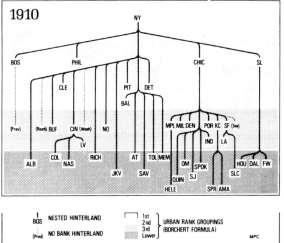

5.7.   The regionalized urban hierarchy in the USA based on
        bank hinterlands. 1881 and 1910 (after Conzen).

Figure 5.6). The rest constituted the lowest, fourth level, but the period was one of rapid urban growth and hence there was movement between the levels or ranks: Chicago, notably, joined the second level during the 1880s. This process continued as shown in Figures 5.6 and 5.7. The contrasts between 1881 and 1910 are particularly significant as the simple hierarchical structure of the mid-century became more complex, and perhaps less clearly stratified with the addition of centres. Conzen concludes, 'Between 1840 and 1910 the urban system as a whole evolved from a primate order to a modified hierarchical one with high-level interdependencies' (Conzen, 1975, 108).

It is both difficult and unwise to try to relate the American pattern of development to that outlined for England at an earlier date and under different conditions. But the parallels intrude. New York was, to an extent, a primate city and during the century it changed from exercising control over segmented subsystems to being the head of a national and integrated system. There are great differences in that London was a generator of impulses, New York was in part responding to an extending array of cities. But certain regularities in the transformation of a primate city into one which is the head of a more complex and growing system seem to emerge.

108   *The evolution of the city system*

(ii) Locational advantages, competition and change

The major quality which characterizes the city systems of
both countries and regions over most of their histories is
stability and resistance to change especially in the higher
orders. This is to be expected since substantial forces
would be required to shift established relationships and
displace entrenched advantages. The studies by Patten in
East Anglia between 1500 and 1700 and of Lewis in the
English–Welsh border in the nineteenth century both
emphasize the stable nature of the ranking of towns.
That change does take place is testified to by the rare
formal revisions of status as in the Municipal
Corporations Act of 1835 in England and Wales when an
attempt was made to adjust legal status to economic
reality following a period of substantial change. There
are always fluctuations taking place within the structure
of the city system, some purely local, others reflecting
more general trends.

Local examples must always have limited interest but it
is proper to include one such case which can be fitted into
discussions already presented. The stable position in East
Anglia was presumably the outcome of earlier shuffling
between competing centres and an illustration of such
movement can be derived from the Welsh borders with
England in the late medieval period. Radnorshire was
created a county at the Act of Union of 1536. Within its
confines were six borough towns (Figure 5.9), Rhayader,
Knighton, Presteigne, Painscastle, Cefnllys and New
Radnor. The last, shifted from a nearby older site, gave
its name to the county. If the number of burgages be
taken as a measure then New Radnor was of significant
size in the early fourteenth century and dominant in that
area which was to form the county in the sixteenth. Two
hundred and sixty two burgages were recorded in 1304
making it seventh in a list of 48 given by Beresford and
comparing with 162 at Knighton, 50 at Painscastle and 20
at Cefnllys (Beresford, 1967). At the Act of Union the
status of the town was apparently confirmed – 'the said
Towne of Newe Radnore shalbe named accepted reputed
used had and taken hede and Shire Towne of the saide
Countie or Shire of Radnore. And that the shire Courte
and Counties of and for the saide Countie or Shire of
Radnore shalbe holden and kepte one tyme at the saide
Towne of Newe Radnore and the nexte tyme at the
Towne of Rather Gowye (Rhayader or Rhaiadr Gwy) in
the same Countie or Shire and so to be kepte in the same
two townes alternis vicibus forever and in none other
place' (Rees, 1948, 60).

Already, however, particular events and environmental conditions were beginning to tell against New
Radnor. In 1404 the castle and town had been besieged by
Owain Glyndwr in the course of the revolt he led against
the English crown. Camden recorded in 1586 (the English
version is from the translation of 1610), 'After that Owen
Glendowerdwy, that notable rebell had burnt it, it
beganne by little and little to decrease and grow to decay'
(Camden, 1610, 623), whilst George Owen described it at
the beginning of the seventeenth century as 'poore and

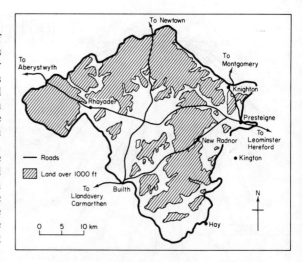

5.8.   Radnorshire towns and communications in the
seventeenth century.

ruinous' (Owen, 1902). But it was not only particular
events which undermined New Radnor. The town had
been an admirable base in Mortimer land during the
process of occupation but it was situated in a bleak and
unproductive area, the larger part of its hinterland being
composed of the high moorland of Radnor Forest.
Economic significance shifted eastward to the more
fertile lowland fringe. Presteigne, in the words of
Camden, was 'a very little village within the memorie of
our grandfathers' but had 'growne now to be so great a
market town and faire withall, that at this day it
dammereth and dimmeth the light in some sort of
Radnor' (Camden, 1610, 623). Presteigne was also more
favourably located in relation to the growing communication system so that a later topographer at the beginning of the nineteenth century could record that the town
'is now the chief town in the county of Radnor' and that
'the neighbourhood for five miles around is principally
supplied with grocery, drapery, ironwork and shop
goods in general, from this place, which has become a
central depot for these articles of trade' (Lewis, 1833,
n.p.). It had also taken over the role of assize town from
the two named in the Act of Union.

This example has been introduced as a specific illustration of local change in the status of towns. But it carries
broader implications. Similar changes were taking place
across Wales as the towns founded for primarily military
reasons competed for status in the new condition of providing services for surrounding territory. Out of this
competition towns assembled suites of functions, at first
primarily administrative such as assize and county
towns, but later and slowly predominantly economic. In
this way a hierarchical ordering was brought about forming the variety of sub-systems under the primacy of
London. But if a hierarchical structuring did emerge it
was based on the way some towns could exploit a favourable location, more often to preserve a status. Indeed, the

continuity of settlement in certain locations from prehistoric times to the present day does suggest that there are advantaged locations which even under fundamentally changing economic conditions still benefit from the dominance of distinctive areas or lines of movement. Everitt has introduced the concept of primary towns in England (Everitt, 1974), that is towns which are ancient in origin and still survive. It is true that the reasons he ascribe are largely associated with general character; they tend to be religious centres often with royal or ecclesiastical estates associated, and were trading centres before the conquest. A relation to prehistoric and Roman roads does suggest a long-lasting association with dominance of movements. One of the concepts which has often been propounded in part opposition to central-place theory is that of the gateway city, the settlement dominating a significant line of movement especially of entry into a territory. The term gateway city seems to have been coined by R.D. McKenzie as early as 1933 (McKenzie, 1933; Bird, 1977).

Gateway cities rose at entrance points to producing regions and functioned as collecting centres for the basic products from surrounding settlement and as distribution points for manufactured goods brought in from outside territory. These gateway centres maintained contact with tributary territories through a community hierarchy of villages, towns and cities established on the basis of railway transportation. Thus the basic pattern of modern American settlement was formed. (McKenzie, 1933, 4–5)

The hypothesis of the gateway city was given its modern form in a study by A.F. Burghardt in 1971 of the growth of Winnipeg (Burghardt, 1971). It has subsequently been developed by Bird who argues that the whole gateway concept is much more than a variation on that of central place (Bird, 1977, 115–27). As such it carried clear locational overtones. London (or Edinburgh or Dublin) in this sense is not a central place, it is clearly eccentric within the kingdom it united about itself, but it is essentially a prime gateway into lowland England and as such reached economic, if not administrative, supremacy in Roman times and subsequently retained it.

Such contentions introduce no new principle. In his study of capital cities written in the 1930s Vaughan Cornish identified a group he called frontier-based capitals characterized by an eccentric, that is an out of centre, location. Such situations came about partly because the city was an advanced forward base protecting that which lay behind, partly because of the operation of a gateway role. Dublin is an example of one scale, while Vienna is another virtually at a continental scale. All this is in itself part of a more general view that urban places are seldom generated by central-place functions. That the surrounding countryside sets up demands which must be met at a central point is a statement of functional relations, not of historical evolution for which it seems to have been taken. Towns are generated by specific reasons and only later do they become central places. This much

Burghardt accepts – 'the final state, after a long period of time, will be an approximation of the classical central-place distribution and hierarchy of centres' (Burghardt, 1971, 272). Once again, reference back to the origins of towns in England dealt with in chapter 3 will provide exemplification.

The hierarchy, therefore, is subject both to change as locational advantages change and to resistance to change due to the major advantages of some locations. But the perpetuation of these advantages is as much a result of cumulative causation in an economic sense as of the permanent merits of some situations.

(iii) Cumulative causation, agglomeration economies and rank stability

In the previous section changes in rank were illustrated but in conditions which appertained to small towns or related to a formative stage in city system development. The 'boom and bust' period of American history left behind as many ghost towns as did the failure of boroughs planted by medieval barons. But once the system was established there were strong forces maintaining stability, especially among the larger towns, a point which was emphasized in section 4(ii). Prime amongst these were cumulative causation and the value of primary advantages sites. This section will discuss the former, for the latter were discussed in the previous section.

The main exponent of the significance of cumulative causation has been Allan Pred. In his book *City-Systems in Advanced Economies* he synthesizes much of his earlier work. There he begins by maintaining that, 'one of the most striking features of the historical growth and development of city systems in those countries which can currently be classified as economically advanced is the long-term stability in the national or regional population rank of their leading metropolitan complexes. Typically, over very long periods of time, the presently most important metropolitan complexes of the city-systems of broadly defined regions and entire 'post-industrial' countries have experienced either no shift in population rank at all, or an upward or downward shift of one or two ranks' (Pred, 1977, 33). Table 5.4 reproduces Pred's data for the leading urban complexes of the northeastern United States in 1810 and 1970 which demonstrate very little change over 150 years.

Table 5.4: Population and regional city-system rank of leading northeastern USA complexes, 1810 and 1970 (after Pred, 1977)

Urban complex	1810 Population	Rank	1970 Population	Rank
New York	100,775	1	16,894,371	1
Philadelphia	87,303	2	5,317,407	2
Boston	38,746	4	3,388,795	3
Baltimore	46,555	3	2,700,558	4
Providence	10,071	7	905,558	5
Albany	10,672	6	777,793	6

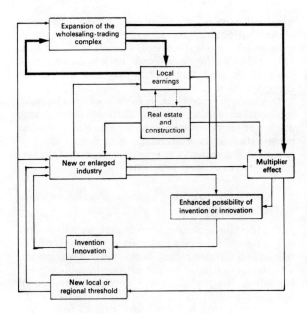

5.9.   The circular and cumulative feedback process of local urban size-growth for a single large US mercantile city. 1790–1840 (after Pred). Heavier lines indicate the most important relationships.

5.10.   The circular and cumulative feedback process generating large city stability in national and regional city systems (after Pred). C_1, C_2, C_n, refer to comparatively large mercantile cities.

Myrdal's cumulative causation notion (Myrdal, 1957) can be closely associated with that of agglomeration economies. Pred in generating his empirical study of the United States before 1840 sets out two essential features. The first of these was that specialized economic information circulated in a spatially biased manner, that is it was available in the largest cities first. The second was that 'two-way economic interdependencies of some significance early manifested themselves between the largest cities of both the national system of cities and newly formed regional systems' (Pred, 1977, 37). Both of these are concerned with information flows and innovation which are functionally related to each other and firmly attached to the highest urban levels hence providing the self-reinforcing mechanism of cumulative and cyclical causation which can be expressed for the single city in terms of the model in Figure 5.9. This is largely self-explanatory with any expansion of the wholesale-trading complex leading to a 'spiralling-up' based on the multiplier effect. Figure 5.10 transplants this from the single-city context into that of a dominant group of cities (C_2, C_3, C_n) where interactions occur and interdependencies result in bringing about the biases in the circulation of information and the two-way economic interdependencies noted as essential features above. Moreover, once these large cities had lifted themselves into dominance change was unlikely. Pred writes, 'once manufacturing became spatially concentrated in large cities, it was unlikely to shift because business management was much more prone to augment existing facilities than to relocate and repeat large initial capital expenditures' (Pred, 1977, 97), a principle well known in the early days of economic geography as geographical inertia.

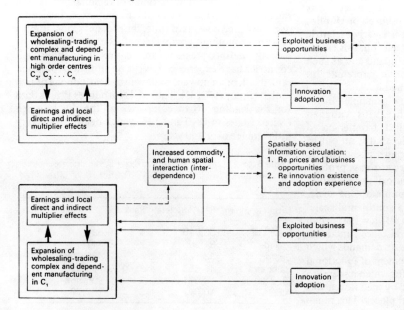

Pred effectively demonstrates his argument by a mass of empirical evidence relating to city system growth in the USA, laying particular stress on the way in which information and innovation are cornered by the large cities. These bases are, of course, very similar to those which are advanced to explain divergence in regional terms where contrasts between core and peripheral areas become accentuated over time. Certainly these are the sorts of reasons which must be advanced to explain why the upper levels of the hierarchy have remained stable over such long periods.

(iv) Transformations of the city system

Although this chapter has been concerned with the evolution of the city system, and by implication with changes within it, much of the emphasis has been on stability and the resistance to change especially in the higher levels. Local change in the lower ranks of the order has been demonstrated and it has been noted that it was part of a more general process. Even so, stability has been the main theme. To some degree stability can be over-emphasized since effective measurement of relationships depends on accurate census data and this has only been available for most countries from the beginning of the nineteenth century. Moreover, the literature has a considerable American bias and hence a relatively short historical period has been reviewed. Undoubtedly the immediate reaction of the non-specialist might well be the opposite of an assumption of stability with the major transformation of the city system by industrialization cited in evidence. The British census, beginning as it does in 1801, misses the critical years of change when the late-medieval system was totally revolutionized. This is best illustrated by considering the six highest-ranked towns in Britain in 1650 and 1801.

Table 5.5: Six highest-ranked cities, 1650 and 1801

City	1650 Rank	City	1801 Rank
London	1	London	1
Norwich	2 (8)*	Manchester-Salford	2
York	3 (17)	Liverpool	3
Bristol	4	Birmingham	4
Newcastle	5 (14)	Bristol	5
Exeter	6 (15)	Leeds	6

*Figures in brackets give the 1801 ranking of those not in the first six at that date.

After 1650, probably from about 1730, a period of stability was replaced by one of quite fundamental change. If London be excluded, only Bristol retained its place among the six largest towns in 1801. Norwich had moved down to eighth, Newcastle to fourteenth, Exeter to fifteenth and York to seventeenth. The newcomers which had displaced them rested unequivocally on industry as a basis for their growth. Manchester and Liverpool, the first the regional centre of commerce, the second the

port, were the cities created by cotton textiles; Birmingham was the largest of a group of West Midland towns concerned with metalware and miscellaneous engineering products; Leeds was the capital of the woollen manufacturers of Yorkshire's West Riding. Each of these was associated with an aureole of smaller towns the sizes of which were closely related to their industrial development. This is best illustrated from Lancashire where the smaller cotton townships grew as rapidly from 1801 and 1821 as the larger centres.

Table 5.6: Population growth of cotton towns in Lancashire, 1801–1821 (after Chalklin, 1974)

Town	Population 1801	1821
Wigan	10,989	17,716
Bury	7,072	10,583
Oldham	12,024	21,662
Blackburn	11,980	21,940
Bolton	12,549	22,037
Preston	11,887	24,575
Stockport (Cheshire)	14,850	21,726

B.T. Robson in his book *Urban Growth* has carried out an intensive study of these changes, including the standard types of analysis, though necessarily restricting himself to the period when census data were available. In these, rank order was plotted against population size for decennial censuses (Figure 5.11) and also the rank changes of individual towns between censuses were plotted. The progressive horizontal shift to the right in the rank-size array (Figure 5.11) demonstrates the simple addition of extra members into the array, while the

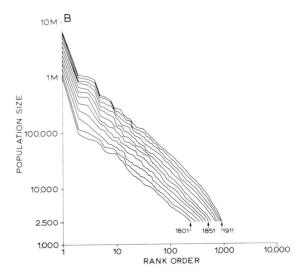

5.11.   Size array of cities over time: England and Wales, 1801–1911 (after Robson).

vertical shift indicates the growth of the size of individual members. The general form of the graph remains surprisingly similar, thereby reflecting some form of allometric growth, that is, there is a relationship between the addition of extra cities and the size of cities. This confirms the conclusion noted earlier regarding the concentration of growth in the upper ranks of the settlement array, but it does not signify that a structural transformation was in progress. As regards those towns which were the largest in 1801, the examination of change in rank supports the view that there was comparatively little shift of rank order amongst the top places, but that fluctuation became greater the further down the hierarchy of towns one moves. Robson writes, 'All of these larger places (London, Liverpool, Manchester, Birmingham), indeed, show relatively little change in their rank orders over the whole period. On the other hand, with the smaller places there is a tendency for increasingly large fluctuations to occur at smaller city sizes. Some places move rapidly up the rank hierarchy: Leicester, for example, was twenty-first in 1801, had moved to thirteenth by 1891 and retained this rank up to 1911. Other places moved rapidly down the hierarchy: Exeter, for example, being at twentieth position, and had fallen to sixty-fifth by 1911' (Robson, 1973, 38). Exeter effectively illustrates those cities experiencing quite catastrophic decline. 'Exeter in 1700 was the finishing and market centre for the local serge industry.' That industry declined in two stages, the first from about 1714 to 1748 and then in the mid 1790s. 'By 1800 the industry was insignificant in the economy of the town, and with the industry went Exeter's commercial function. The town experienced severe relative decline . . . [becoming] a centre for shopkeeping and services, a social and regional capital, and market for an agricultural hinterland' (Daunton, 1978, 269–70). W.G. Hoskins has written, 'The town which had once extended its entrepôt trade from Holland to Newfoundland, and from Norway to the Canaries, was now a small market town collecting and distributing for only 20 miles around' (Hoskins, 1935, 150).

These analyses, therefore, suggest that over a short time period the largest cities captured, in direct and simple terms, a disproportionate amount of growth, thereby maintaining their highest ranking and confirming an allometric growth characteristic. At the lower end of the scale there was considerable change and jockeying for position.

This 'change and jockeying for position' must be interpreted as towns, constrained by the threshold populations needed to generate services and by the limited range over which they could operate, eventually achieving a settled relationship in the context of the total population distribution. Thus, two forces which have already been noted were at work, in addition to the direct, aggregating influences of industry and mining. The first of these was those agglomerating economies in the offering of goods and services which favoured the largest settlements. The second was those constraints of the traditional central place concept, threshold and range, which sorted out the smaller centres. The end-product was a system which locally showed evidence of a hierarchical structuring but which nationally, in population terms, did not. Haggett, Cliff and Frey (1977) in *Locational Models* briefly review historical changes in city-size distributions. They concluded that although the Industrial Revolution administered a severe shock to the system, there may be a tendency for the urban system to move towards a dynamic equilibrium, maximum entropy, distribution. The bases for contending that such a distribution is similar to the rank-size rule have already been indicated. 'A city size distribution obeying the rank-size rule is the most probable distribution and represents the steady-state equilibrium in which entropy has been maximized' (Richardson, 1973, 244). The transformation of the British system would accord with such a process.

5 Conclusion

The consideration of detailed aspects of change considered in the last section must have gone a considerable way to undermine the simplistic view of an evolutionary sequence in the form of the city system: yet some substance remains in the idea of such a sequence. Certainly separation, non-competition, is the most primitive of conditions and can be identified in a variety of historical contexts, medieval Europe and colonial USA amongst them. Primacy is not easy to identify other than in descriptive terms, but again it is most easily associated with the relatively early stages of economic development and particularly under the political and administrative situations which have been discussed. Primacy is a product as much of the process of political development as it is of economic organization. Again it is not difficult to argue that a hierarchical situation is most likely to occur where economic development is advanced and the political system relatively mature, but where the prime urban role remains service for a countryside where the activities are primarily agricultural and evenly spread rather than industrial and a consequence of point production.

The coming of industry disrupts any structure based on central-place spatial relations, although the constraints of threshold and range still apply. Locally therefore, it is still possible to trace orders or ranks of towns though these may not hold nationally. At that level the collapsing of hierarchical sub-systems into one produces an approximation to a rank-size condition, or what perhaps is more honestly accepted as a random distribution. In the end the distinction is so dependent on definition and measurement that it is hardly possible to sustain in a meaningful way. It is likely in any case that in situations of advanced economic development hierarchy, rank-size relationship or randomness may be reflections of the scale of analysis rather than of the degree of development, that is of an historical sequence.

In spite of all the reservations which must surround attempts to derive a standard succession of differing relationships between sets of cities dependent upon stages of economic development and political organization, such attempts must remain a proper and legitimate field of enquiry. If a period of separation be excluded, and that in itself is significant, cities do not exist *in vacuo*; they interact. The nature of that interaction and its consequences are critical to the whole field of urban growth and its understanding and an essential adjunct to the comprehension of the nature of urbanization. If it is true that the nature of the relationships between towns must be related to political integration and economic development, it must also be true that these relationships reveal insight into the processes which have produced them.

Further reading

For discussions of the structuring of city-systems most texts in urban geography can be consulted, for example:

BERRY, B.J.L. and HORTON, F.W. 1970: *Geographic Perspectives on Urban Systems*. Englewood Cliffs, NJ, where chapter 3, The distribution of city sizes, 64–93, is an effective discussion.

CARTER, H. 1981: *The Study of Urban Geography*, 3rd edn. London.

A particularly useful exposition occurs in Robson (1973), while Rozman (1976) relates historical periodization to urban growth.

A more advanced consideration is:

RICHARDSON, M.W. 1973: The theory of the distribution of city sizes: review and prospects. *Regional Studies* 7, 239–51.

For the problem of constructing past hierarchies see Barker (1978, 1980), Lewis (1970) and Patten (1978). An early paper was Carter, H. (1956): The Urban Hierarchy and Historical Geography, *Geographical Studies* 3, 85–101.

On the evolution of structures and economic development apart from Abrams (1978), Dobb (1946) and Wallerstein (1974), see also:

BRAUDEL, F. 1967: *Capitalism and Material Life*. London. Chapter 8 deals with Towns, 363–440.

Apart from his paper on the maturing urban system in the USA, Conzen has also written on:

CONZEN, M.P. 1975: Capital flows and the developing urban hierarchy: state bank capital in Wisconsin 1854–1895. *Economic Geography* 51, 321–8.

The stability of the city system in the USA was the subject of a widely quoted paper:

MADDEN, C.H. 1956: Some indications of stability in the growth of cities in the United States. *Economic Development and Cultural Change* 4, 236–52,

but Pred has been the most prolific writer. In addition to the book noted in the text (1977) other works are:

PRED, A. 1966: *The Spatial Dynamics of US Urban Industrial Growth 1800–1914*. Cambridge, Mass.

PRED, A. 1973: *Urban Growth and the Circulation of Information: the United States System of Cities, 1790–1840*. Cambridge, Mass.

6

In Whose Image is the City Made? The Physical Form of Urbanism

1 Introduction

In the first three chapters of this book, in which urban origins and the diffusion of urbanism were discussed, it was apparent that city layout involved something far more profound than a search for the most functionally satisfactory arrangement of streets. As Rykwert argues, the rite of town founding

> touched on one of the great commonplaces of religious experience. The construction of any human dwelling or communal building is in some sense always an *anamnesis*, the recalling of a divine 'instituting' of a centre of the world. That is why the place on which it is built cannot arbitrarily or even 'rationally' be chosen by the builders, it must be 'discovered' through the revelation of some divine agency. And once it has been discovered, the permanence of revelation in that place must be assured. The mythical hero or deity attains the centre of the universe or the top of the cosmic mountain by overcoming epic obstacles. The ordinary mortal may find this place anagogically through the agency of ritual. (Rykwert, 1976, 90)

In the Roman world, to which the bulk of Rykwert's book is devoted, the ritual procedures, which controlled both the identification of site and especially the plan of the town, were derived from myth and religion. In succeeding phases of town founding the same principle holds, but the mythical hero is replaced by priest-king or god-emperor and eventually by secular ruler. With a more complete secularization, and the rise of mercantilism and industrial capitalism, the organizing lead passed into the hands of competing individuals who created towns which reflected the ethos of an uninhibited striving for wealth. In short, the plan and built form of the town are direct reflections of the nature of culture on the large scale, and using that word in its anthropological sense, and of social organization on the smaller scale and in a more direct sense. It is a truism that the town epitomizes in its physical nature the complex of political, economic and social forces which characterized the period of its creation.

In being a 'made form' a town is also a piece of art, not in the direct sense of something necessarily and deliberately created to induce an emotion or create a sense

reaction, but rather in that it must reflect the spirit of an age and be as much part of that age as its poetry, its music or its philosophy. Ewart Johns (1965) in his book *British Townscapes* has been one of the few writing in English to pursue this theme. In his contrast of classical formalism with Gothic disorder and exuberance, however, he adopts too simple a model by which to interpret the immense complexity of forces and impulses that have played a part in the creation of townscapes. This chapter is an attempt to demonstrate that great variety of ways in which the ethos of a period or culture is caught, in that cliché of an analogy, like a fly in amber, in what are at least the quasi-permanent forms of urban layout. Unlike works of art which can be preserved in museums, towns are the propagators of real-life change, the centres of innovation, which is why they are such ready touchstones of fashion. But this also means that they are subject to redevelopment and successive rebuilding, a process which destroys the physical remnants of the past. Only occasionally is the total evidence preserved, more often it is a fragmentary but valued relict in the present townscape.

There is no intention of achieving the end set above by presenting a complete narrative history of urban form. Four episodes, each representing a contrasted view of the city, have been selected in order to illustrate and substantiate the major thesis which this chapter seeks to advance.

2 Renaissance and baroque towns in Europe: The city as an aristocratic estate

It is conventional to regard the form of the post-medieval town in western Europe as being derived from three influential groups, although their distinction is quite artificial and the degree of overlap considerable. The first group was 'the architects', profoundly influenced by the revival and the publishing of the manuscripts of the Roman architect Marcus Vitruvius Pollio and various exegeses upon them which were produced (Morgan, 1914). The second group was the urban theorists who wrote in somewhat more abstract terms and whose Renaissance polymathy was marked by overlap not only with the architects but also the sculptors and painters. The third group was more clearly distinct and was the military engineers, who had more direct functional ends in view and were responding to basic changes in the nature of warfare which were taking place. From the activities of these three groups novel urban forms appeared which, under the political control of absolute rulers, were to make a distinctive contribution to the urban landscape of Europe.

It is not easy to make any clear distinction between the architects and the urban theorists for to a large extent the groups merged. The architects, however, derived their inspiration from the Ten Books on Architecture of Vitruvius which appeared in Rome between 1484 and 1492 as *De Architectura*. A reading of the work will reveal very little that is precisely related to town plan, apart from a short section which makes up chapter VI of Book I. In that section Vitruvius dealt with 'the direction of the streets'. His basic argument, contrary to all the views as to a ritual basis for town layout, is a simple physical one – 'the apportionment of house lots within the wall and the laying-out of streets and alleys with regard to climatic conditions'. The critical control was the direction of the prevalent winds. 'Some people have held', wrote Vitruvius, 'that there are only four winds . . . . But more careful investigators tells us that there are eight'. The prime aim of the plan is, therefore, to provide maximum protection and the instructions given suggest an octagonal shape with the 'directions of your streets and alleys . . . laid down on the lines of divisions between the quarters of two winds. On this principle of arrangement the disagreeable forces of the winds will be shut out from the dwellings and lines of houses.' Vitruvius included no diagram or plan of his notional town and a wide variety of interpretations resulted. Indeed, it has been argued that the popularity of Vitruvius was in part related to a situation where any author could produce his own design under the authority of a classical source. In general terms the writings of Vitruvius gave support to a radial-concentric model which was emerging as a highly favoured, though by no means universal, theme in Renaissance town planning.

The architects were also strongly influenced by an innovation in the concept of space which owed nothing to Vitruvius but much to Renaissance art. This was 'perspective' which, as Giedion points out, is etymologically derived from 'clear seeing' (Giedion, 1954, 31). Perspective was not simply a technological change but represented a fundamental alteration in the view of the world. Universalism had been represented in medieval times by the Catholic Church and the Holy Roman Empire. Protestantism and nationalism represented a break-up of the old monolithic system and the substitution of a fragmented and individual view, a new perspective. 'To the fifteenth century the principle of perspective came as a complete revolution, involving an extreme and violent break with the medieval conception of space, and with the flat, floating arrangements which were its artistic expression' (Giedion, 1954, 31). If the terms 'flat floating arrangements' are envisaged as city plan then there is a strong suggestion of grid blocks,

whereas perspective implies focality and the control of lines of vision so that a scheme which is concentric and radial emerges.

At this point the overlap of architect and theorist becomes apparent, for the urban theorist was thinking in terms of the town as a three-dimensional object designed to give pleasure to the eye, as well as to provide an efficient functioning mechanism. This was the theme of one of the most noted of the group, Leon Battista Alberti (Gadol, 1972). His major work was presented to the Pope in 1452 but was posthumously published in 1485 as *De Re Aedificatoria*. Alberti was much concerned with the effective operation of the town, but he also demanded that the built form should give aesthetic pleasure. 'He introduced a new concept which, developed, amplified and taken to the extreme, even to excess, was to bring out a radical transformation. This was the aesthetic nature of the city. The city must not only be efficient functionally, it must be a thing of beauty' (Lavedan, 1959, 12). Alberti stressed the pleasure and significance of the visual scene and by that, as well as the importance he attached to the radial-concentric system and the need for the notion of unity within the urban whole, he anticipated the classical urbanism which was to come.

The military engineers had more practical aims. The critical conditions were the widespread use of gunpowder and the rapid development of artillery. These meant that a curtain wall, however strong, was an ineffective defence against siege. The reaction was to set out systems of bastions which became more and more elaborate reaching a climax in the work of Vauban. In many cases the superficial area covered by a great complexity of outworks was much larger than the town itself which was a small kernel within a very thick shell. These defences did not of themselves condition the plan of the town which, however, responded to the same military need. It is difficult to deploy cannon in a grid plan for there is no dominant line of fire, and the point of fire can be outflanked. But cannon at a central 'place' can fire effectively along the lines of radii. At the same time, before the defence lines have been breached, the internal force can be rapidly dispatched to the perimeter walls along the same radii. Here again, therefore, a form of radial-concentric scheme was favoured (Grodecki, 1965).

The most revealing summation of all these influences is the design proposed for a city to be called Sforzinda which was drawn up by Antonio di Pietro Averlino, who is usually known as Filarete. He was an architect and sculptor whose life spanned the Quattrocento for he was born in 1404 and died in 1472. His major work was an unpublished treatise called *Trattato d'Architectura* which was completed in the early 1460s (Lazzaroni and Munoz, eds., 1908). His ideal city was to be called Sforzinda after Francesco Sforza, Duke of Milan, who had commissioned the design. The proposed layout was a complex piece of geometry made up by superimposing two squares upon each other to create an eight-pointed star with sixteen sides (Figure 6.1). At each outward-pointing acute angle there was to be a tower, whilst at

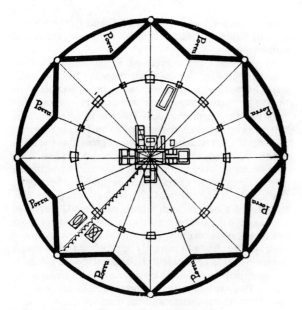

6.1.   Sforzinda. The plan devised by Filarete.

each of the inward pointing obtuse angles a gate was to be located. 'The streets', wrote Filarete, 'should lead from the gates to the centre of the city where I would place the main square, which ought to be twice as long as it is wide. In the middle of it I would build a tower high enough to overlook the whole surrounding district' (Lazzaroni and Munoz, eds., 1908). There was to be a further series of eight streets leading from the towers to the central plaza, thus making a series of sixteen radials. There was also to be a dominant circular street and where this crossed the radials sixteen minor squares were to be established. The eight of these on the roads leading from the gates were to be devoted to markets for various commodities, while churches were to be built in the squares on the roads from the towers. The main square for the merchants was off-set from the central piazza or plaza whilst at the two ends of the length of the main piazza were to be the Palace of the Duke and the Cathedral. Locations were also fixed for a hospital and a theatre.

An examination of this proposed city will suggest that in its conception there were five contributory sources.

1   It was essentially a Vitruvian derivative. Although the simple octagon has been made far more elaborate, it still remains in the form of the eight-pointed star. Moreover, there is careful attention paid to the city as an effectively functioning unit in the elaborate provision of markets and of advanced urban services.

2   It was fully in line with the views of the urban theorists. It was conceived 'all of one piece' and care-fully allows for a variety of perspectives. It appears as a unified if elaborate work of art, the work of the sculptor dealing in the shaping and arrangement of tangible forms.

3   It had a philosophic base in political terms in that it

symbolized the central and autocratic control of the ruler who was to build it. The location of the palace at the central position of authority to which all aspects of the town's life led and from which all facets of the town's being were derived, was a critical and key feature. Judith Moholy-Nagy in discussing Sforzinda writes, 'Thomas Aquinas, the master of Scholasticism, had said in his *Summa Theologica*: 'The city is the perfect community . . . and building cities is the duty of Kings'. The Sforza of Milan com-missioned the architect Filarete in 1457 to construct 'an ideal city for a tyrant', seeing obviously no con-tradiction in terms' (Moholy-Nagy, 1968, 68). It is difficult to see under the contemporary sociopolitical conditions why any contradiction should have been perceived. What Filarete produced was an appro-priate design, compatible with strong central control, and where the 'tyrant' physically and symbolically operated from the centre of a web-like structure. It marks the beginning of that stress on the castle-palace of the ruler which was to grow into a standard feature as the power of individual secular rulers increased and absolutism became part of the political system.

4   In her commentary Moholy-Nagy adds, 'The two superimposed squares form an eight-cornered star, signifying planetary constellations. The palace stronghold has the plan of a gnomon, above which would have arisen a stepped tower, a world moun-tain' (Moholy-Nagy, 1968, 68). This suggests that a more ancient symbolism was also a contributor to the design. From the account by Filarete, which is in the form of a dialogue between architect and prince, there is every justification for such an interpretation. The town was to be made safe for the tyrant in all ways so that its prosperity was guaranteed not only by physical defences but also by its form being adjusted to those astrological influences which were benign. James Curl takes this view further and argues that the symbolism struck more deeply (Curl, 1970). The town plan was essentially a mandala form. The circle or sphere is the symbol both of completeness and of perfection. In Zen Buddhism, for example, the circle divided into eight represents the entire cosmos in its relation to divine powers. 'This circular form, with basic subdivision from the centre of the circle, is known as a mandala form and is interpreted in Jungian terms as an archetypal image from within the human unconscious. . . . It is seen as the awakener and preserver of life' (Curl, 1970, 6). In the more limited and mundane reference to the terri-tories of a secular prince the basic meaning was the same. The completeness of dominance, the perfec-tion of order and the ruler as the giver of life, are all symbolized. There is no reason to believe that all this was not part of the basis for the layout of Sforzinda.

5   After the more fanciful, it is appropriate to add that although there were no fortifications, the towers were so arranged as to give completely overlapping

fields of fire. The necessities of physical defence were well taken care of, even though the town itself was not a fortress.

Sforzinda has been presented as an epitome of Renaissance town design. Although the town itself was never built it is possible to identify many of its characteristic features which, at least in part, appeared both in the completely new towns which were built and in the sections which were added to existing towns. Many were, like Sforzinda, named after their overlords so that a good number of European towns commemorate their founders: Phillipeville, Vitry le François, Marienburg, Charleroi, are all standard examples. The most useful classification of these towns is that provided by Lavedan (1959, 76–118). He suggests three characteristic situations in which these towns were founded. The first group had a locational basis in that it was made up of towns established on military frontiers as a consequence of the widespread insecurity and warfare which characterized the period. The second group had a more functional basis in that it was made up of towns founded for religious reasons, usually to provide refuge for persecuted minorities at a time when wars of religion

were prevalent. The third group had a political basis for it contained those settlements established as capitals or residences by many of the petty rulers of a Europe which had still to be organized into a system of nation states. There is no point here in entering into a descriptive account of a plethora of examples, most of which are treated in nearly every history of town plan which has been written. Figure 6.2 provides a standard example of the first type, Palma Nuova, founded by the Venetians in 1593 as a defensive outpost against the Turks, is the nearest in shape to Sforzinda. Freudenstadt was established in the Black Forest in 1599 by Frederick I of Württemberg as a town for Protestant refugees, whilst Charleville, as its name reflects, was a capital set up by Charles, Duke of Nevers and Mantua, between 1608 and 1620, complete with a Place Ducale and a dominating statue.

The heading of this section is the town as aristocratic estate and it is this condition which is exemplified by Charleville. The succeeding Baroque period was to emphasize, even caricature, these features. As the

6.2.   Palma Nuova. Braun and Hogenberg, *Civitates Orbis Terrarum*, 1598.

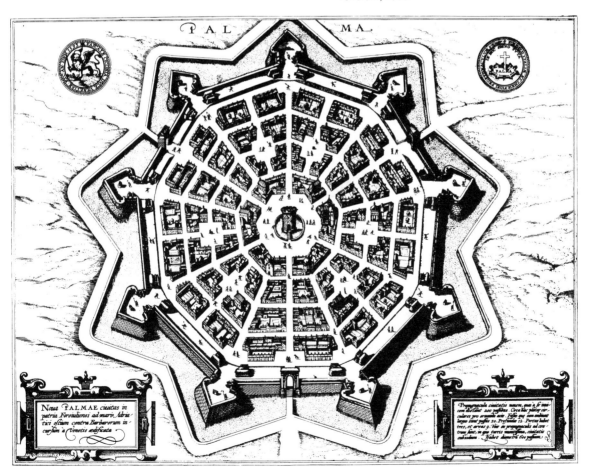

Renaissance merged into Baroque so the rich symbolism which western Europe had inherited was formalized with a more rigid and ordered treatment. The fundamental control is to be found in the political scene for the Age of Absolutism reached its apogee not only in the courts of the great monarchs but in those of the multiplicity of minor states and lesser nobility. Perhaps the court of count Almaviva is one to quote, while the Droit de Seigneur, satirized in the Marriage of Figaro, is an example of the completeness of the control of the autocrat. In philosophy a world controlled by the inscrutable ways of Providence was giving way to the concept of a universe as set out by a Newton or a Descartes, where rational laws interpreted the comprehendable and predictable operation of natural forces. In the arts, too, balanced structure and control were things to admire; those

> Pleas'd with a work where nothing's just or fit;
> One glaring chaos and wild heap of wit;

were to be condemned. The couplets of Pope were as polished and balanced as the façade of Blenheim Palace.

All these forces were brought to bear on the type of ideal plan, which the Renaissance had fostered, in those 'great days of aristocracy, when the perfect pearl of the Renaissance was mishapen by a rigid manner and the Baroque was born of that tension between nature and artifice' (Vidal, 1953, 16). The result was the creation of towns which are the most effective summations of the ethos of an age. Richelieu by its name, and Versailles by its reputation, speak for themselves. St Petersburg, constructed at the beginning of the eighteenth century, is a further admirable example (Bater, 1976). Moholy-Nagy writes of the original plan illustrating, 'clearer than most other absolutistic schemes the cosmic-dynastic grand illusion, the great palace sending its surveillance and benevolence into the far corners of the geometrically disciplined urban universe' (Moholy-Nagy, 1968, 72). But perhaps most extravagant in its form if not in its size or political power, was Karlsruhe founded by the Margrave Karl Wilhelm of Baden Durlach in 1715.

The original plan is shown in Figure 6.3. A description of what is adequately conveyed by a plan is hardly necessary but the critical elements need to be stressed. The key to the whole layout was a circular clearing in a completely wooded area. At first this was intended to be the location only of a palace and the idea of an associated town was subsequently developed. A tower marked the geometric centre of the circle and from it 32 radii in the form of cleared avenues were set out. A section of nine of these, forming a southern sector, made up the area where the town itself was established. The palace extended partway

6.3.   Karlsruhe in 1834. The earlier star-shaped settlement north of the Langestrasse can be contrasted with the area to the south developed at the beginning of the nineteenth century.

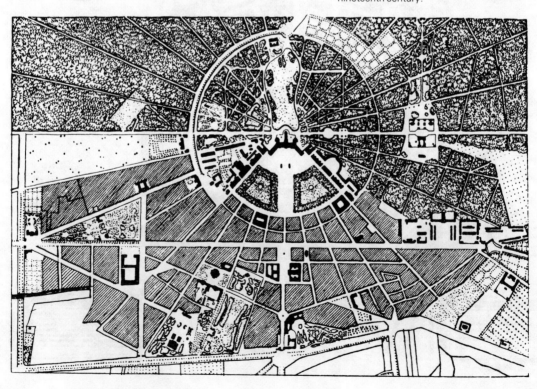

along the two arms of the outer of what can be called the nine urban radials. Beyond the palace parts of two concentric circles were described across the nine radials and this gave the basic layout of the town. A major commercial street, the Lange Strasse, was provided by a line drawn at a tangent to the outer circle. The town was in that way given two major axes, the one composed of the central of the nine urban radii and leading due south from the centre of the palace, the second being the tangential main street. Where these intersected a major square with a church was to be built. The town was never completed in the absolute form of its initial design. In particular the church was eventually replaced by a market square and the regularity beyond the Lange Strasse partly modified. Even so, it is the supreme example of the Baroque town. It is difficult to better Gutkind's comment.

> Symbolically, aesthetically, socially and economically, the town was the appendix of the palace. . . . French and Italian influences, theoretical designs for ideal towns, geometrical landscape architecture, and the new techniques of military engineers – all manifold and new conceptions – played a part in shaping the rigid geometrical layout of park and town. It was a veritable pattern-book of ideas and prototypes ranging from the radial pattern of Palma Nuova, the starlike design of new fortresses, and the diagonal streets of the Piazza de Populo to the Gardens of Versailles. It was a drawing-board plan, rigid, logical and somewhat disingenuous, but it was a perfect symbol of the time, of the *l'état c'est moi* spirit of the absolute rulers. (Gutkind, 1964, 300–4)

It was a sunburst and the sun-king was patterned in urban form, but in doing this the marvellous discovery of perspective had become degraded into mere stage setting.

Here then is the first answer to the question, 'In whose image is the city made?'. An earlier chapter has pointed out that the city was conceived as a representation on earth of another world, a microscopic reflection of the macrocosm. But as the secularization of culture and society took place the symbols of the older order were taken and reshaped to epitomize the control of earthly rulers who nevertheless still saw themselves as 'priests' divinely set on the earth to wield authority. That authority took the form of transforming the disorder of the natural world into a civilized and civic form. All this was reflected in the layout of towns, created in the image of their makers. It was only where control was not absolute that failure ensued. Had it not been for the fact that Charles II lacked the power, and perhaps more pertinently the finance, of other European rulers, then the present-day city of London, restored after the Great Fire of 1666, might have been one of the major and standard examples of Baroque planning (Reddaway, 1951). It was left to the aristocracy as they developed their estates in west London to bring piecemeal into that growing city the characteristics which appertained to European urbanism.

3   The grid plan and urban America: The democratic city

It is the simplest of themes to place in opposition the grand design of the aristocratic and regal cities of Baroque Europe and the humble grid on which the new cities of the rapidly growing United States were being built. After all, in his exegesis on the origin and growth of the grid-plan town Stanislawski argued that one of the factors predisposing the adoption of the grid is the equal division and disposition of land (Stanislawski, 1946). By this argument the grid is, therefore, the symbolic opposite of the radial-concentric scheme for the latter separates ruler and ruled, master and man, and exalts the supremacy of authority, while the former allocates land equally to all and, in its neutral subdivision of space on *a priori* grounds predicates no preferred social order. But hesitation arises immediately over this somewhat facile truism for in medieval times the equal division of land was the consequence of a landlord providing urban sites in return for money or services. This might suggest that the grid was not so much the symbol of democratic and egalitarian systems, but rather of mercantile capitalism, for it was the simplest, cheapest and most rapid way of exploiting urban land. But before returning to this basic theme of symbolism it is necessary briefly to consider the system of American land division.

The basis for the division and disposition of what was the public domain, after the gaining of independence from the British crown, was one of the major tasks of the Continental Congress. In 1785 the Land Ordinance was promulgated and it established a system which was to be applied to all public land. This land was to be subdivided and developed as a series of townships each of which was to measure six miles by six (Figure 6.4). Each township thus covered 36 square miles and was to be divided into 36 sections, each of one square mile. The land was to be auctioned both by townships and sections at a minimum price of one dollar per acre plus survey costs. There was a number of provisions included; some of the sections in each township were reserved for the national government; one was reserved for the maintenance of schools; some were set aside for the redemption of land certificates used as payment for soldiers in the revolutionary war. Even so, the general effect was to provide a universal base for land subdivision and hence for the layout of towns. John Reps summarizes the impact as follows:

> The survey system adopted by the Continental Congress and the policies for disposal of western lands established in 1785 governed the settlement of America during the next century until the closing of the frontier. Today, as one flies over the last mountain ridges from the east, one sees stretching ahead to the horizon a vast chequerboard of fields and roads. With military precision, modified only on occasion by some severe topographic break, or some earlier system of land distribution, this rectangular grid persists to the shores of the Pacific. America thus lives on a giant gridiron

imposed on the natural landscape by the early sur- veyors carrying out the mandate of the Continental Congress expressed in the Land Ordinance of 1785. (Reps, 1965, 216–7)

Reps also goes on to make the assertion so widely held, that the result of this universal grid base to cities was dullness and mediocrity in planning. This, in a rather more controversial interpretation of the symbolic terms this chapter has introduced, may be seen as the expression of the greyness and lack of distinction which follows from egalitarianism and the adoption of the standards of the lowest common factor. If elitism has its spatial measure, so too does egalitarianism.

Almost any American city of the land which was yet to be occupied in 1785 will show the features outlined and little needs to be said about the grid. But one example of

In 1804 when the lands west of the Ohio river passed into national ownership, Congress provided for its survey into quadrangular units, each 6 miles 'square', and containing 36 sub-units each of a square mile, known as sections. These units were bounded by north-south lines (Prime Meridians) and east-west lines (Base Lines) and were numbered by reference to them. Thus T.1.S. stands for the first 'Township' to the south of the base line and R.1.W. stands for the first 'Range' west of the Prime Meridian. Clearly, as in the British Grid Reference system, these 'town- ships' and 'ranges', can be used to locate any 36 square mile area, thus T1N.R2E is shaded in fig. 6.4a. Note in Fig. 6.5, which follows, Natrona is located at T20N.R10W (of the 3rd Prime Meridian) and on section 14 and the grid plan is determined by this system.

The townships are *always* numbered according to fig. 6.4b, beginning with section one in the NE corner. Sections 8, 11, 26 and 29 reserved for the federal Government and Section 16 for the main- tenance of public schools.

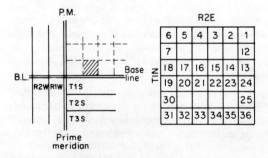

6.4.   The American grid as established by the land ordinance of 1785.

an unsuccessful development illustrated by Reps can be used to make some further comment on the city as a democratic product. Natrona in Illinois was laid out by Conklin and company in 1857 along the Chicago, Alton and St Louis railway (Reps, 1965, 392). As the accom- panying plan (Figure 6.5) shows, it was developed within Section 14 of a Township and laid out precisely along grid lines. But the numbering of the streets provides addi- tional interest. In 1874 the outermost streets in a west–east direction were Eleventh and Sixteenth Street, while the limits in a north–south direction were marked by I Street and P Street. The promoters had obviously provided room for massive expansion before all the letters of the alphabet were used and the problem of what to do beyond First Street arose. So the grid could be easily and indefinitely extended and it is in that the signi- ficance of the street identification system lies. But the actual system is itself symbolic of time and place. In this democratic country city streets could not be named after princes and prelates (although towns were named after individuals). There could be no Rues Royales or Place Ducales nor was there the possibility of Regent Streets, Albert Terraces, Victoria Avenues or Alexandra Roads. Moreover, in such new territories of a new country, there were no cultural traditions to fall back on, certainly not those of the Indians which were in any case hardly appro- priate for cities. The solution was simplicity itself and the epitome of anonymous democracy. To First Street and Second Street, or Eleventh and Sixteenth Street no one could take objection, and if the cross streets seemed too mundane as A Street and B Street or I Street and P Street, then the names of trees were neutral enough. Oak Streets and Walnut Streets, Cherry Streets and Sycamore Streets proliferated, as neutral in their names and their cultural content as the streets of the grid they identified.

It is a mistake, however, to over-emphasize the regularity and monotony of the grid. 'Urban critics', writes Grady Clay, 'particularly those hung up in the per- spectivist tradition, insist that the American city is unvarying and monotonous in its addiction to the grid. But it is not enough to echo this stale lament; for to understand an American city on first contact, one must look beyond the individual grid to its interface or fracture zone with the next, and to variations within the grid. One need not swallow the line that all grids are alike, nor accept whole hog the assertion that one break is as good as another' (Clay, 1973, 42). While the metaphors may be mixed, Clay has a valid point. He proceeds to illustrate it by showing how, in fact, distinctive breaks do occur in recurrent situations; on lines where an earlier, local grid meets that of the national system; where older diagonals slash their way across later grids as in the classic case of Broadway on Manhattan; where changes take place from older grids to newer suburban road alignments. All these bring both variety and significance in detailed examination. The sharpest breaks, however, are often located at the edge of the CBD. 'Time and time again, as one travels outward from old downtowns – as in Denver, San Francisco,

Township
Twenty N. Range 10 W. 3ᴰ P.M.

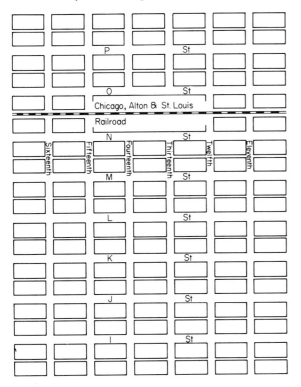

6.5.   Natrona in 1857.

New Orleans, Seattle, Fresno, Las Vegas or Minneapolis – one confronts confusion: the grid turns angular and odd-cornered; it slopes off in a new direction. And along this zone of fractured intersections one encounters a new framework with different densities, architectural styles, building setbacks' (Clay, 1973, 44) (Figure 6.6). This new framework is, of course, a direct reflection of changes in historical evolution which find their way into the layouts even of the most standard of grid-plan towns.

In the context of 'in whose image was the city made', which is the theme of this chapter, grid variations are a little less significant and the critical association, once the egalitarian point has been made, is paradoxically with the very opposite of fair shares for all. A good example is set out by Sam Bass Warner (1968) in his book on Philadelphia, significantly called *The Private City*. At the beginning the broad, straight and handsome streets of the city were regarded as one of the best examples of urban planning in the United States, but as the city grew rapidly during the nineteenth century other qualities of the grid came into prominence. 'The rectangular survey of open farmland, the laying-out of streets and blocks into even rectangles, the subdivision of blocks into narrow house lots, this was the simplest, cheapest and clearest way of dividing land for rapid development. It

was an ideal method since it treated all land similarly, for a real estate market composed of hundreds of land speculators and home builders, and thousands of petty landlords and small home buyers. . . . Thus, falling in with the rest of the nation, Philadelphians extended their street grid indefinitely along their urban frontier (Warner, 1968, 52). Warner's theme of privatism and the private city epitomizes the predominant theme of self-interest and the possibility of 'making it rich' which characterized the American way of life. This was even the burden of William Penn who in 1685 wrote, 'The improvement of the place is best measur'd by the advance of Value upon every man's Lot . . . the worst Lot in the Town, without any Improvement upon it, is worth four times more than it was when it was lay'd out, and the best forty' (Still, 1974, 17). What was urged was both democratic and individualistic, but to those two concerns public welfare was sacrificed. The grid was extended further and further into the surrounding country, and there were no principal controls to enforce standards in terms of street width or building lines. Nor was any attention directed towards the relation of the grid to the demands being generated by traffic flows growing ever denser. Within the grid itself there was no attempt, and indeed no opportunity, to organize an effective distribution of urban service functions. There was no centrality, no focal points, given by the plan, so that institutions, such as schools and police stations, were scattered haphazardly and shopping centres were in fact not 'centres' but 'strips' as street fronts were adapted. 'The effect . . . was a city without squares of shops and public buildings, a city without gathering places which might have assisted in focusing the daily activities of neighbourhoods. Instead of sub-centres the process of building created acres and acres of amorphous tracts. . . . This weakly structured physical form proved a serious handicap. Whatever community life that was to flourish from now on would have to flourish despite the physical form of the city, not because of it' (Warner, 1968, 55–6).

To derive the social consequences is not the purpose of this chapter, but rather to reveal the underlying socioeconomic and cultural influences. The image of nineteenth-century urban extension in Philadelphia was the image both of democratic government and of a capitalist system. The aristocratic vice of ostentatious focality was debarred since it was counter to the way of life in the New World; but the vice, if such it be, of the acquisition and exploitation of property was not. The grid was at once, therefore, testimony to an egalitarian system which made no distinction between men other than their ability to compete. That competition was best organized on the grid, on the basis of which transactions in property lots were most easily carried out. Perhaps it is symbolic that so many competitive games are based on a chequerboard.

It is of the greatest significance that the one major city where such a system was not only wholly adopted was the federal capital. There, as the symbols of the federal principle, appropriate buildings were needed; the White

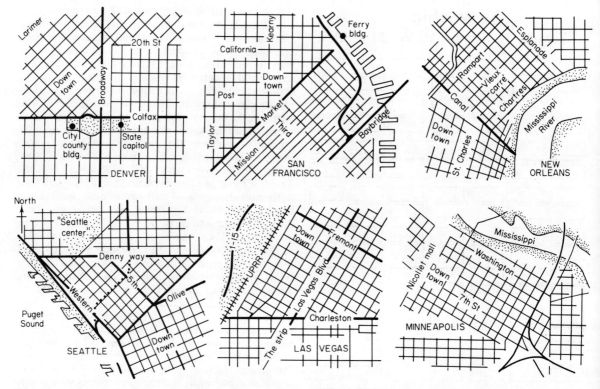

6.6.   Breaks in the grid pattern of some cities of the USA
(after Clay). Note how frequently the initial grid was at
right-angles to a water landing.

House, the home of the President, the individual who
represented unity; Congress on the Capitol, the symbol
of the unity of government. These national buildings
could not recede into the anonymity of the grid, the
White House could not just be 1600 Pennsylvania
Avenue however democratic that might sound, so onto
the grid was superimposed a radial scheme raising the
significance of the buildings at the radial centres. If the
capitalist *mores* of America show in the grid, so too does
the federal determination in the layout of Washington
DC.

4   The towns of colonial India: The city of
the two cultures

The third example of the cultural determination of
urban historical form can be presented quite briefly,
although in many ways it represents the most absolute
and spectacular case. In North America, as in Australia
or South Africa, the European colonials were moving
into an area with no indigenous urban tradition, but such
was not the case in Asia where intrusion occurred into
culturally alien areas with high densities of population
and long-standing urban cultures. The two cultures of
colonizer and colonized continued side by side, certainly
interacting, but engendering a distinctive urban form

made up of the two elements. In writing on 'comparative
urban ecology' London and Flanagan (1976) have proposed a typology of cities as set out in Table 6.1.

Table 6.1: A typology of cities with differing ecological
structures (after London and Flanagan, 1976)

---

1 Pre-industrial cities influenced by colonialism
2 Pre-industrial cities uninfluenced by colonialism having
   indigenous invention of industrial technology
3 Pre-industrial cities uninfluenced by colonialism *not*
   having indigenous invention of industrial technology
4 Cities reflecting the 'pure' impact of industrial technology

---

Although the 'types' are based on ecological structure
they can be as appropriately used for the examination of
physical structure. In such a context no better example
exists of the first type than that brought about by British
colonial rule in India (Brush, 1962). That the interaction
was not only one-way can be seen in the many terms
which found their way back to the colonizing country. In
the physical or built structure of the town what in the
USA is called a 'ranch style' house still remains in
Britain, the term derived from colonial Asia, a
bungalow. This whole problem of the colonial city in
India has been the subject of an excellent and thorough
study by A.D. King (1976) in his book entitled *Colonial
Urban Development*, and accordingly only a brief
outline is presented here based largely on that source.

A most effective introduction to the colonial city is a consideration of the linguistic terms which were used to describe the various parts of the city. King sets these out in a table which is reproduced, in part, below (Table 6.2).

Table 6.2: Key terminology in the language of colonial urbanization (after King, 1976)

Urban	Scale of Level Urban sector	Urban unit
Civil station	Bazaar	Barracks
Civil lines	Colony	Bungalow
Cantonment	Esplanade	Chummery
Lines	Mall	Club
Circuit House		Compound
Dak (bungalow)		Lodge
		Quarters
Residency		Rest House

These words represent 'physical-spatial-social' elements in the urban system which are expressed in the metropolitan rather than in the indigenous language (i.e. English rather than Hindi). Such terms, however, are either not found in the system of urban nomenclature in the metropolitan society (e.g. civil lines, civil station, cantonment, chummery . . .) or, if they do exist, are used with different meanings to those prevailing in the ex-colonial society (e.g. compound, bungalow, bazaar)' (King, 1976, 71). Perhaps the most common word which King does not mention, since it has no physical connotation, though most definitely a social one, is the word 'pucca' which described a bungalow of masonry construction, brick or stone with tiled roof, and which brought a widely used adjective into English. The location of the berth on the ships taking the representatives of the colonial power to India also provided a keyword. Port Out, Starboard Home gave not only a location away from the heat of the sun but, in the mnemonic POSH, a lasting social categorization also. A review of these terms describes the major spatial elements of the colonial city. They can be grouped about three elements critical in the morphology of Indian urbanism. The first was the garrison, the basic physical representation of military control. The second element was the civil administration developed by the colonizing power 'to run' the country, whilst the third was the native city which pre-dated the colonial grafting-on of the newer parts.

The key military area was known as the 'cantonment', the all-embracing term for the garrison base. It is, perhaps, significant that the internal division of the cantonment was very much on the lines identified by modern studies of social areas in western cities. The two fundamental dimensions were ethnicity, which simply divided the European from the Indian (although the Anglo-Indian did provide problems), and social class which, at least within the cantonment, was represented

by an obvious and well-marked line which separated the officers and gentlemen from the other ranks (although here, too, gentlemen rankers provided an embarrassing intermediary group). The life-cycle dimension was not as marked but there was a clear difference in the accommodation demands of the married and those of the large numbers of single males. The cantonment itself, therefore, apart from the city, was laid out in a way which faithfully reflected the *mores* of military society. The ethnic contrasts were represented by quite separate areas for Europeans and for the native troops. Since the barracks of the European soldiery and the bamboo and matting huts of the Indians were set out in parallel lines the word 'Lines' was universally used to an extent where it became a synonym for accommodation. The European Infantry Lines and the Native Lines were distinctive spatial components of the cantonment. Each race, too, had its own hospital, parade ground and other facilities. Perhaps the main motive behind this segregation, or system of apartheid, was as much reliability as ethnicity, for British troops were presumably more trustworthy than native recruits and could not be diluted by mixing. But even in death the distinction was maintained and most cantonments had a separate burial ground for the interment of the European dead. In this general situation the word 'native' itself had taken on a pejorative significance, one which to a large extent still remains in English.

The ethnic divide was paralleled by a social class divide. The European other ranks lived in barracks in the military lines but the officers lived in bungalows each set in its own compound which was usually at least half an acre and sometimes a good deal more. King presents an extensive study of 'The bungalow-compound complex as a study in the cultural use of space' (King, 1976) in which he demonstrates how the system was a socio-cultural response to a specific environment. In a climate that was both hot and wet the protection which was provided by tall buildings very close to each other in the native settlements was not available so that a substitute was achieved by extensive spacing and the provision of verandahs. The verandah-surrounded bungalow was to be 'diffused' back to Britain where it became a well defined element of late nineteenth and early twentieth-century urban extension.

One non-military function was to be found residing in the cantonment. This was the bazaar defined in the Government of India's *Cantonments Code* of 1899 as 'any land in a cantonment which has been set apart for the purposes of trade or the residence by natives . . . and the boundaries of which have been demarcated by pillars or posts . . . under the authority of the General Officer of the Command'. It contrasted with the European shop, which was usually found in the Civil Lines and stocked an extensive range of European goods. As this implies, the civil administration was spatially separated from the military, although it took its name from the military context and was known as the Civil Station or the Civil Lines. Within the area was a close society of civil servants, doctors, clergy and traders and that society engendered a whole range of distinctive urban features. Amongst these was the Mall, a standard central promenade devoted to social interaction and display, although occasionally it was characterized by a nucleus of European shops. The 'foreigners' had to create their own social 'way of life' and the key to it was 'The Club'. Where this had recreational, as well as purely social, facilities it was often called the Gymkhana Club. But the society, both military and civilian, was a transient one and accommodation for those on the move in a distinctively European environment was necessary. This was met at the Club or at the special Dak Bungalow, in the larger centres by a European hotel. Finally, a life-cycle dimension was added to this primarily socio-ethnic division, by the demands of the large numbers of single males. For these residential accommodation in rooms with communal kitchens was provided at the 'chummery'. Like the word Gymkhana it is redolent of both an age and a society.

Figure 6.7 shows how many of these elements characterized the city of Allahabad during the nineteenth and early twentieth centuries. The settlement was located at the confluence of the Ganges and the Jumna rivers and was a sacred site, the ancient city of Prayag. It was also supposedly at the confluence of the legendary Saraswati, the lost river of the Punjab (Spate and Ahmad, 1950). The Mogul emperor Akbar had built a fort at the angle where the two rivers met and this was taken over by the British to form the Fort Cantonment. It constituted, however, a very limited area, far too small in extent for the effective deployment of the military arm of the Raj. The site of Allahabad was itself constricted, for it lay between the Ganges and the Jumna. The latter was bordered by steep bluffs while the Ganges was characterized by moving sandbanks liable to inundation. A more extensive old cantonment was developed within the confluence core, but eventually a much more extensive site was developed to the west, called the New Cantonment. The demand for space, derived both from

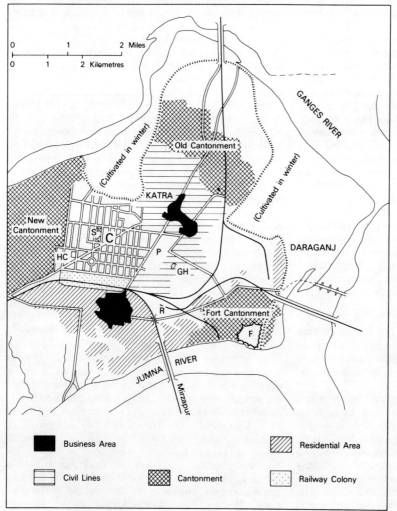

6.7.   The structure of Allahabad in 1931.
C = Cannington (part of Civil Lines),
HC = High Court,
GH = Government House,
S = Secretariat,
P = Alfred Park,
R = City Railway Station.

basic military needs and from the large compounds in which the bungalows were set, is well illustrated by this development. A map of the city in 1931 from the Imperial Gazetteer of India clearly shows the distinctive elements (Figure 6.7). The New Cantonment was lavishly laid out in spatial terms. The core was dominated by the Brigade HQ which was surrounded by the European Infantry Lines, the Cavalry Lines and the Artillery Lines. Tucked away from these and well segregated to the northeast were the Native Infantry Lines. Adjacent to them was the Bazaar. The burial ground was located well away from the living areas, from which it was separated by Macpherson Park.

The Civil Lines were situated to the east of the New Cantonment and were established on an extensive grid plan cut through by the main route which was related to the axis of the old Mogul city. Within the area were all the standard representatives of English culture in India: the Government Offices, the Law Courts, the Hotel, Hospital and the Allahabad Club. It was neatly segregated: to the north was the river Ganges while the New Cantonment was to the west: to the south were the railway lines and to the east Alfred Park provided a break. The native city was to the south, nearer the Jumna river and on the other side of the tracks. It was a densely populated and unplanned maze of narrow streets in complete contrast to the Civil Lines. Not only the railway, but the Junction Station and the accommodation for the railway staff set out in severely rectangular fashion, separated Indian city from European quarter. Brush points not only to the ubiquity and the formal layout of the railway settlement, but also to its internal social distinctions.

> The most distinctive features of the railway towns are the perfectly uniform grid of streets and the monotonous rows of brick dwellings, graded and rented strictly according to the wage scale and occupational status of the employees. For the lowest-paid semi-skilled workers, who were from the start invariably Indians, a single room with attached kitchen and enclosed courtyard was considered sufficient. These dwelling units are built in contiguous rows of 10 and 12, or multiples thereof, allowing little or no open space between street and entrance. The quarters designed for the intermediate grades of personnel, often including Eurasians as well as Indians, have more rooms, some in a second storey, and are set back farther from the street. The two-storey bungalows built for the employees with the highest technical skills or managerial capacity and receiving the highest salaries, who at first were mainly British, stand amid spacious landscaped grounds with small-row houses for the servants at the rear. (Brush, 1962, 62–3)

In Allahabad the railway area was effectively deployed to block access to the north, there being no crossing for wheeled traffic for more than a mile. The railway thus completely shuts off the crowded and irregular Indian city from the broadly planned rectangular Cantonment and Civil Lines, a district of large bungalows and public offices in spacious compounds and gardens. (Spate and Ahmad, 1950, 267)

There is no need to labour the point. Society in nineteenth-century India had a distinctive character and organization of its own. That organization with all the crudities and niceties of its ethnic and social distinctions was quite faithfully reflected in the forms of the towns it developed.

5 The city as social conscience: The planned industrial town

The narrative history of urban development during the nineteenth century has been presented many times (Ashworth, 1954; C. and R. Bell, 1969; Burke, 1971; Cherry, 1972; Tarn, 1973). Britain can be considered as an example for it was where the Industrial Revolution began, and where some of the worse excesses of slum housing were created (Engels, 1892; Chapman, 1971; Gauldie, 1974; Sutcliffe, 1974), as well as those movements, associated with the name of Robert Owen at the beginning of the century and Ebenezer Howard at the end, which did most to introduce new concepts of town planning. The crux of this planning movement is that in reaction to the abysmal conditions created in the great industrial towns, there was a stirring of the social conscience even of the most determined and profit-maximizing of the industrialists. In consequence, it is possible to view nineteenth-century layout as a constant battle ground between the forces of profit and those of welfare. This was not, as is often implied, fought over by two completely distinct groups of individuals in some sort of moralistic western epic complete with 'goodies' and 'baddies', but rather the whole conflict was a part of everyman's character. But if it is the argument of many modern geographers that the content of the politico-economic system is the key to the processes that shape the occupation of space, then the period was one unashamedly dedicated to the creation of material wealth in a competitive context on a scale greatly different from that of past periods. In turn the political will shaped the religious credo which through a legitimizing function allowed the reality of industrial growth to be supported by the tenets of faith. The result was the creation of a material standard of living which in time rose markedly over the whole range of society. But, of course, it arose differentially. At a period dominated by the creation of wealth, rather than its distribution, the extent and justification, even the moral acceptability, of the differential only slowly became a central theme, although even a Tory Disraeli seeking to ally aristocracy and workers against the great class of entrepreneurs, was fully aware of the Rich and the Poor which he enshrined in the phrase, The Two Nations (Disraeli, 1845). From the beginning of the century both the massive inequality and its support by established religion were attacked, as for example, in the work of Robert Owen. But the entrepreneur, too, had a conscience and an awareness of the bitter world he was creating. Perhaps, also, there was an element of self-interest as writer after writer warned of the enormous pressure of resentment being built up in the city slums. 'What is true of London, is true of Manchester, Birmingham, Leeds, is true of all great towns. Everywhere barbarous indifference, hard egotism on one hand, and nameless misery on the other, everywhere social warfare . . . everywhere reciprocal plundering under the protection of the law, and all so shameless, so openly avowed that one . . . can only wonder that the whole crazy fabric still hangs together' (Engels, 1892, 58). Engels could take heart, however, in the belief that that the severance of patriarchal relationships between employer and workingman would release the latter to produce a revolutionary working-class movement and to overturn the system. That such an end-result did not occur was probably due in part to the fact that, in crude terms, capitalism 'delivered the goods', in the form of generally rising living standards, contentious as that issue is (A.J. Taylor, 1975). But it was also partly related to the fact that pressure was always being slightly relieved by political progress towards a democratic system of government and by the fact that philanthropic notions of a paternalistic kind were usually to be found even in Mr Gradgrind and Mr Bounderby. It was in this fashion that the notion of the 'ideal city' came back once more into the realm of urban development. It was not now, however, conceived in the form of design to give artistic unity and aesthetic pleasure, as a work of art as in the Renaissance, but rather it was considered almost as a piece of industrial machinery which, although it might have its own beauty, was designed to function efficiently and last long. If the ideal towns of the Renaissance gave an environment for despots and celebrated their domination, those of the nineteenth century were more mundane exercises in the effective location of industry and the reflection of the Victorian social order.

One example will be sufficient to develop the equation of the structure of nineteenth-century society with the physical characteristics of urban planning. But before discussing Saltaire, a preface is necessary in which a brief consideration of theory can be outlined. This is best set out in that lengthy work by James Silk Buckingham which was published in 1849 and appropriately called, *National Evils and Practical Remedies* (Buckingham, 1849).

The line of descent of Buckingham's ideas leads directly back to Owen and his Village of Cooperation. The intermediate stage in this transition process was represented by John Minter Morgan who, with a group of Anglican clergy, prepared a scheme for a Christian Commonwealth where laissez-faire competition was to be abolished, where the pursuits were to be primarily rural and where all the vices of urban areas, as for example public houses, were to be excluded (Ashworth, 1954, 123). Buckingham, himself, associated the Self-Supporting Village Society of Morgan with Owen's work, suggesting that 'Owen's plan was practicable but

had failed because of the omission of religious instruction and public worship' (Ashworth, 1954, 125). Like so many Victorians, Buckingham was greatly concerned with the current evils of society, especially crime, drunkenness and prostitution, although like so many others he was not prepared to trace the symptoms, beyond the immediate cause of the urban environment, to the nature of the socioeconomic system. Even so, the notion which on the playing fields of public-school England was reflected in the tag of *mens sana in corpore sano*, had enough in common with that great tenet of atheistic, socialist faith that evil dominantly derives from the capitalist system and the environment it engenders, corrupting as it does the innocence of the new-born, to allow Buckingham to claim descent from Owen. A village of cooperation or a sanitary town had at least some generating elements in common, however superficial they were. But Buckingham was no critic of the social system, he was a reformer who dealt in the management of the environment within the whole panoply of the existing social structures.

Buckingham proposed that his town should be called Victoria, thus firmly declaring his allegiance at the outset. It was to be made up of a series of some nine squares one within the other (Figure 6.8). The outer square was to have sides of one mile in length and the whole town was to contain 10,000 people at, therefore, a very low density. The use of each square was carefully allocated to reproduce the existing social order. Manufacturing industry was to be located beyond the outer urban limits in order to reduce pollution. The outer peripheral square was to contain the houses of the working class and as one moved in towards the centre so

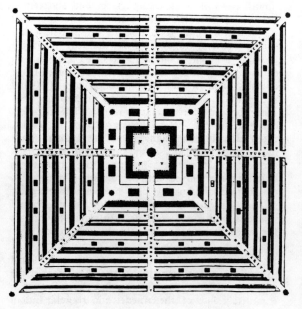

6.8.   Victoria: the plan proposed by J.S. Buckingham.

one moved up the social scale, although each square devoted to residence was separated from the next residential square by one devoted to a specific urban function. Thus, next in from the working-class housing and in reasonable proximity to it in what was still the walking city, was to be a square of workshops. The working class were thus sandwiched between the industries beyond the periphery and a craft and workshop square. The next square, the third in from the periphery, provided residences for the class next up in the pecking order from the labourers and artisans. These were the 'superintendents of the different departments of labour and persons in charge of the general stores for the distribution and supply of all the articles required for the use of the town' (Buckingham, 1849, cited in Stewart, 1952, 170–1). Appropriately the next square contained the shops which were not part of a central business district but distributed about this square. Again moving towards the centre, the next square, the fifth, provided houses for the professional classes, while the sixth was in turn a non-residential square. This time it was to take the form of a public promenade where 'the youngest and most delicate' could exercise and where the town band would each evening provide appropriate musical entertainment. The professional class was appropriately located between the shops and the promenade. The seventh square accommodated the upper ranges of the professions and wealthy capitalists. Within this, and surrounded by trees, lawns and flower gardens, were to be the main public buildings, whilst at the centre, in the innermost square were to be housed members of the town government and 'the more opulent capitalists'. At the centre of this inner square, and of the whole town, was to be a great octagonal tower rising to about 300 feet and providing not only lighting and viewing galleries but the great symbol of Victorian municipal building and reminder of the virtue of punctuality and hard work, a clock.

The concentric squares were broken at the central points of the sides and at the corners by eight radiating avenues. These, too, were appropriately named – Faith, Hope, Charity, Justice, Unity, Peace, Concord and Fortitude – an admirable roll-call of publicly acclaimed virtues even if private, and at times public, conduct did not always live up to precept. The moral welfare of the inhabitants was to be sustained not only by surrounding them by uplifting symbolic street names, but also by the exclusion of all intoxicants, of tobacco and of all weapons of war and explosives. Physical comfort was to be aided by minimizing pollution, the equipping of all houses with flush toilets and by siting public baths at convenient locations.

It is, perhaps, too easy to treat this enlightened plan facetiously, for in relation to its date it was far-seeing and concerned. All the noxious elements of the contemporary urban environment were carefully excluded and the bases for a decent life for working-class people laid down. Perhaps the most interesting feature anticipates a discussion which will have to be extended later (chapters 9 and 10) and relates to social space. The segregation which Buckingham proposed was essentially that of the pre-industrial city, with the wealthy towards the centre and the poor at the periphery. Again the location of administration and public buildings, rather than of shops, at the centre is indicative of a situation which looks back to the past and the pre-industrial period, rather than anticipates the emergence of the central business district of the latter part of the century. On the other hand, whereas a specific location is given for workshops and crafts, larger-scale industry is also anticipated. Again, the proprietors of the shops are located away from them indicating a forward view of the divorce of workplace and residence that came with the lock-up shop (chapter 8). Buckingham's Victoria has considerable interest, therefore, as a town envisaged just at the point of transformation of the old pre-industrial order into the industrial town of the early twentieth century.

Here, then, is a fascinating exercise in Utopian city planning, as idealized in its structure as any *città ideale* of the Renaissance.

If James Silk Buckingham was an epitome of Victorian social thinking on urban problems, then Sir Titus Salt was the paradigm of the Victorian industrialist. In an evocative paragraph Cecil Stewart records the critical facts of his life. 'Titus Salt was born of poor parents in a cottage seven miles from Bradford on September 20, 1803, at 4 o'clock in the morning, according to a record in the family Bible. Sir Titus Salt, Bart., died on Friday afternoon, December 19, 1876, at twenty to one, leaving an estate valued at about half a million, a large number of testimonials expressing the satisfaction of his employees, a bust of purest Carrara marble weighing just under two tons, a couple of full-length portraits, a monument in Bradford, derived in its style from the Albert Memorial, and a bereaved family of eleven children' (Stewart, 1952, 148).

Salt had made his fortune, to use a phrase appropriate to the age, by being the first to realize the potential of the wool of the llama, alpaca. He had been determined to retire at 50, but on reaching that age decided to continue his firm, partly in the interest of his sons. But this was not to be in the overcrowded conditions and the polluted and disease-ridden environment of Bradford. He chose a site on the River Aire near Shipley, outside the borough limits of Bradford and, therefore, free from its rates levy and its building conditions (Dewhirst, 1960, 140). There he began the construction of Saltaire. There is no evidence that he was in any way aware of, let alone influenced by, Buckingham's extravaganza, but rather by a somewhat contrasted source for he was a great admirer of Disraeli and had read his novel, *Sybil, or the Two Nations*. In that there is a brief description of what a model industrial town might be like – 'when the workpeople of Mr Trafford left his factory they were not forgotten' – and that appears to have been his most direct inspiration.

Salt's aim was to build a factory first and, when it was operating, to move his workforce to his town (Stewart,

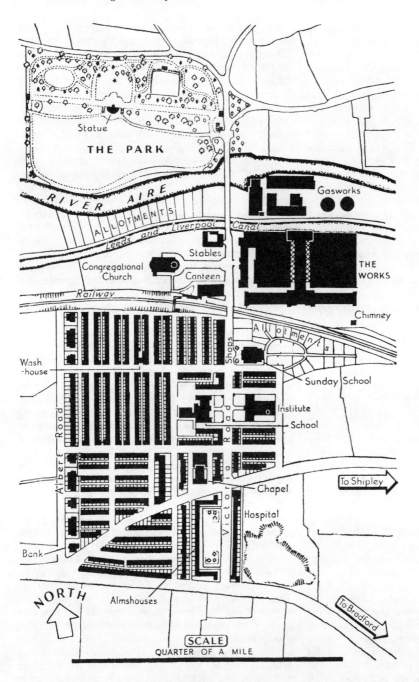

6.9.   The plan of Saltaire (after Stewart).

1952; Dewhirst, 1960). But he was determined to get the planning right so he conducted a survey among his workforce to find out how many were single, how large were the families and how many were elderly so that the numbers of houses of varying sizes, including almshouses, could be properly adjusted. It was not public participation for his was a strictly paternalistic view, but at least it was a unique attempt to adjust housing provision to housing need. There was nothing very distinguished about the actual layout of Saltaire. It was apparently devised after lengthy consultation with the Bradford architectural firm of Lockwood and Mason, who had designed among other buildings Bradford's impressive Town Hall. But they were architects rather than planners and there was nothing Gothic about the layout they conceived, for the town was nothing more than a standard grid pattern of terraced rows of cottages, which gave a gross density of about 16 houses to the acre, or 20 if the land devoted to the mill and open land be discounted. The houses were very ordinary structures with parlour, kitchen, pantry and cellar and three or four bedrooms. Each of the houses had a yard with a coal store, privy and ashpit for the water-closet had not achieved a wide distribution by mid-century. Even so, the houses were a vast improvement on the back-to-backs which were being built at exactly the same time in Bradford. The fair comparison is with contemporary housing, rather than with that of the later part of the century or the present. In complete contrast to Victoria this town was built purely to house mill workers and there was no great range of social classes. Even so, 21 houses of a superior quality in groups of two and four were built for 'overlookers and managers' and they were the only ones to have small front gardens. They were located along one of the main streets called Albert Road, where the bank was also appropriately sited (Figure 6.9). The other main street was named Victoria Road and along it the main public buildings were placed. It is this lavish provision of public facilities, all of them donated by Salt, that distinguished the town. The Institute, for reading and recreation, faced the school across Victoria Road and the shops were arranged nearby. There was a hospital and almshouses, and baths and wash-houses where clothes could be washed and dried were provided. Allotments were available, even if the houses had no gardens, and across the River Aire a public park was laid out in 1871. There were opportunities for boating and fishing in the river. Finally, Salt was a member of the Congregational Church and a church, 'the most effective of Lockwood's work' (Stewart, 1952, 158), was placed between rail and river and facing the mill. There was also a Sunday School, and since he was no bigot, an impressive array of other religious buildings developed. Stewart's (1952) summary of the motivation behind Saltaire – salvation, education and sanitation – neatly encapsulates the sorts of ideas of cleanliness (in mind and body) and godliness which dominated Victorian philanthropy. Perhaps Tarn's apophthegm – five per cent philanthropy – adds a further necessary element (Tarn, 1973). The whole of Victorian industrial paternalism, as well as its social conscience, is made manifest in the layout of Saltaire.

6 Conclusion

Although four separate examples have formed the bulk of this chapter, they have been illustrative of one basic principle, that the form of the town is an expression of the cultural values and social order of its creators. Most histories of town planning, explicitly or implicitly, adopt this theme, but it often gets lost in the chronological narrative that is the standard basis. This chapter has sought to make the generalization real and substantiate the principle with reference to contrasted times and places.

Further reading

Reading on the material dealt with in this chapter falls into three sections, the first concerned with the general principle, the second with general histories of town plan, the third with the four examples which have been used. In relation to principle the most useful studies are:

CURL, J. 1970: *European Cities and Society. A Study of the Influence of Political Climate on Town Design.* London.

MOHOLY-NAGY, J. 1968: *Matrix of Man. An Illustrated History of Urban Environment.* London.

RYKWERT, J. 1976: *The Idea of the Town: the Anthropology of Urban Form in Rome, Italy and the Ancient World.* London.

There are now a great number of histories of town plan. Those by Bell, C. and R. (1969), Burke, G. (1971) and Cherry, G. (1972) have been noted in the chapter. The most complete and lengthy are:

BENEVOLO, L. 1980: *The History of the City*, trans. G. Culverwell. Cambridge, Mass.

GUTKIND, E.A. 1964 cont.: *International History of City Development* (London); 1: *Urban Development in Central Europe* (1964); 2: *Urban Development in the Alpine and Scandinavian Countries* (1965); 3: *Urban Development in Southern Europe, Spain and Portugal* (1967); 4: *Urban Development in Southern Europe, Italy and Greece* (1969); 5: *Urban Development in Western Europe, France and Belgium* (1970); 6: *Urban Development in Western Europe, Great Britain and the Netherlands* (1971); 7: *Urban Development in East-Central Europe* (1972); 8: *Urban Development in Eastern Europe* (1972).

LAVEDAN, P. 1926–52: *Histoire de l'urbanisme*: 1: *Antiquite*; 2: *Moyen Age*; 3: *Renaissance et temps Modernes*; 4: *Epoque Contemporaine*.

The references given in the four examples provide the basis for further reading. The three books by Reps on town planning in the USA are particularly impressive studies.

REPS, J. 1965: *The Making of Urban America. A History of Town Planning in the United States.* Princeton, NJ.

REPS, J. 1972: *Tidewater Towns. City Planning in Colonial Virginia and Maryland.* Williamsburg, Va.

REPS, J. 1979: *Cities of the American West. A History of Frontier Urban Planning.* Princeton, NJ.

7
Suburbs, Estates and Fringe Belts: The Structure of Urban Extension

1 Introduction

The construction of a growth plan is the oldest geographical procedure in the investigation of urban extension but, although innumerable descriptive accounts of individual towns based on such growth plans have been produced, surprisingly, little has been written in conceptual terms on the general nature of that extension. A vague assumption is usually made that it was annular and that, in consequence, a section across a city would reveal a structure similar to that derived from cutting across a tree for both cases would display a series of growth bands, varying in thickness, it is true, according to the circumstances of succeeding time periods but depicting a process of regularly maintained outward extension. Such an analogy is completely inapposite, for urban growth is neither regular in occurrence nor simply circular or annular in form.

The poverty of analysis is revealed by the fact that there are but two concepts which have been used in the analysis of extension. The first, the suburb, is both ancient in derivation and general in its meaning; the second, the fringe belt, is recent in introduction and specific in its reference. In addition, a good deal of work has been devoted to the way in which personal estates in urban areas were exploited. Around these three pivots the present consideration is developed.

2 Suburb

Even in its medieval Latin form – suburbium – the meaning of suburb was broad. At the extreme Ennen noted, in her study *The Medieval Town*, the link between the Germanic 'Oppida' and the various types of Carolingian fortress; 'one of a castle proper and suburb outside it' (Ennen, 1979, 47). Again she records that the fortresses of Saxony, as described by Widukind, consisted of a castle and a civic settlement, that is of urbs and suburbium, which are called 'oppida' by that author. In short, here are cases where virtually all the settlement, effectively the town, apart from the fortress, is being called 'suburbium'. The same is true of the merchant quarters which were added to the pre-urban nuclei during medieval times and which were sometimes termed suburbs. This is made all the more complex when these

'suburbs' were surrounded by a defensive wall and thus incorporated into the city. Consideration of the growth of Hereford will indicate the way in which the northern suburb was eventually included within the city where it became the high town and the main market centre (Lobel, 1969) (See Chap. 3).

At the other extreme, and in complete contrast, the term was sometimes used for an extensive area about the town, including other settlements. Thus tenth-century Winchester was surrounded by a 'terra suburbana quae indique adiacet civitati', constituting an area of some five miles radius in which there were other towns (Keene, 1976, 71).

From the outset, therefore, the word suburb has had no precise connotation. This has been made worse by its modern transformation into a verb – suburbanize – which has acquired a meaning almost synonymous with urban extension itself, although carrying overtones of social processes as well. 'The modern suburb', wrote H.J. Dyos in a classic study of one of them, 'is clearly less of a geographical expression than it is an attitude of mind and a species of social as well as of economic behaviour' (Dyos, 1961, 26). Although, therefore, the notion of the suburb and suburban growth needs to be explored, it has to be carried out in the context of a term carrying little in the way of specific meaning and one which has changed over time.

(i) The medieval suburb

It is quite impossible to provide an adequate definition even of the medieval suburb. The simplest path is to identify the suburban as essentially extra-mural, but although this makes more geographical or spatial sense than conventional historical discussion over whether jurisdiction was separate or not, it fails to take into account the problems which arise over those cities which lacked walls altogether and, at the other extreme, those which were multivallate and where suburbs were progressively included within the walled city. This somewhat unsatisfactory definition accepted, a number of suburban situations can be identified.

(a) The portal suburb. Locations outside the town gates were the most characteristic of suburban situations.

The gate was the point where traffic was delayed on entering the city, it was a waiting place. It was the point at which journeys began and ended. The result was the collection of activities and trades associated with movement. At Southampton, 'outside Bargate to the north, Above Bar Street was called at this point the Street (or land) of the Carters' (Burgess, 1964, 19). The ubiquity of smiths in suburbs outside the gates will be considered later (chapter 8, p. 153). Where roads met at these points inns were established and markets developed. These were often no more than extents of the main roads leading to the town gate. Also outside the town were located the less pleasant and the more dangerous trades, such as the tanneries, or those demanding particular raw materials, such as the potters. In this way thriving suburbs came into being, in some cases their success resulting in their taking the lead and becoming the largest and creative part of the settlement.

The collection of such miscellaneous activities led to the suburb becoming one of the less desirable areas. Patten writes, 'Suburbs spilled out beyond the town walls of Canterbury, for instance, and became a haven for the work-shy, the vagrant and the lawless. . . . Complaints about suburban competition were continuous, and in Leicester suburban dwellers were characterized as "like drone bees to the hyve, paying neither scot nor lot, lye lurking in the suburbs and other secret places, in and about this town, and robbe your suppliants of the work" ' (Patten, 1978, 156–7).

(b) The ribbon suburb. This was usually a special case of the portal suburb where one major and predominant route characterized entrance to the city, and where trade was particularly active. In consequence the suburb extended in ribbon-like fashion. A prime example was Lincoln (Figure 7.1).

(c) Churches and religious foundations. The main creator of the nucleated extra-mural suburb was a church or religious foundation. It has already been indicated (chapter 2, p. 37) that burials were not permitted within walled areas and hence the graves of martyrs and those who had served the faith lay without the cities. In addition religious houses required a good deal of land which was not always available without disturbing existing buildings within the city and land was most easily available at the margins. As well as being the direct aim of pilgrimage, these establishments were also 'hospites' where the traveller could rest. Secular buildings grew about them and it was greatly in the interests of the clerics to obtain the right to hold a market and fairs. Once this was gained the suburb became a significant nucleus of semi-independent growth.

(d) The bridgehead suburb. In many ways this is a special case of the portal suburb since most points of access into a town across bridges were barred by gates. Where such situations occurred bridgehead suburbs were virtually universal. They presented a number of problems to the main cities. Their capture provided a major protected foothold for an attacker from which an assault could be launched while their separate jurisdictions,

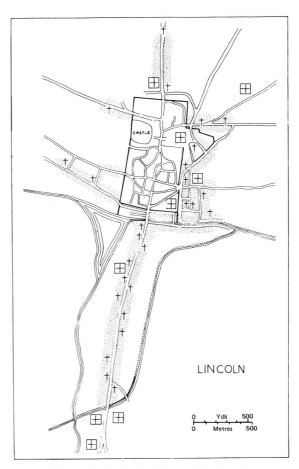

7.1. The medieval suburbs of Lincoln (after Keene).

together with the tendency for aliens to collect within them, meant that they were insecure. In many cases, therefore, both the jurisdiction and the physical defences of the town were extended across the bridgehead to the far riverbank and these became the first suburbs to be taken into the town.

Southwark on the south bank of the Thames, and linked to London by the only bridge across the river until the eighteenth century, was a typical bridgehead suburb (Figure 7.2). It had a range of religious foundations, including Bermondsey Abbey, and also of inns and lodging houses used by those who came to attend London fairs. But it was also a place of warehouses for river trade, of minor alleys and tenements, and also of prisons for the original Clink was located in Southwark. There was, therefore, always the trend towards the lower status which was the suburban characteristic. 'One of the most magnificent houses was Suffolk House. . . . Henry gave it as compensation to the Archbishop of York for the loss of Whitehall . . . and it was sold when the new York House was bought near Charing Cross. Suffolk House gave place to "many cottages of great rents to the

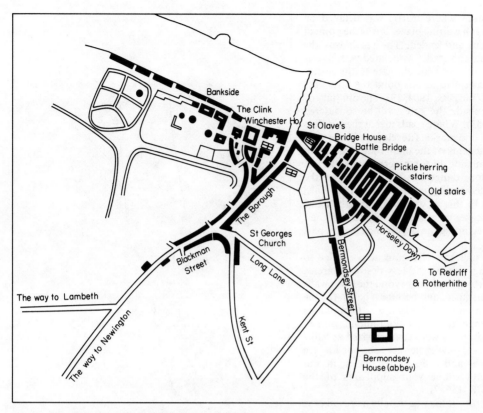

7.2.   Southwark and the southern suburbs of London in
        1600 (after Brett–James).

increasing of beggars in that borough'' ' (Brett-James, 1935, 157). Being removed from London it also became the centre for amusement. 'The Surrey side was well known in medieval times for pleasures of a degrading character, seemingly winked at by episcopal landlords' (Brett-James, 1935, 461). Amongst these were bear gardens, bull-baiting and, of course, subsequently theatres, including the Globe. Like such areas it presented the problem of separate jurisdiction so that in the reign of Edward VI it was made into the twenty-sixth ward of the city.

(e) The marginal suburb.   Although it has been stressed that growth was rarely annular or ring-like, nevertheless one of the typical modes of extra-mural suburban extension was along the streets which followed the town walls. These were later to become the boulevards. The compression into such a form was particularly strong when the city grew by a series of walled enclosures. Figure 7.3 shows Frankfurt-on-Main in 1552. Two suburban elements are plainly visible. The first is the walled and protected bridgehead suburb of Sachsen-hausen, notably by name the settlement of the Saxons. The second is the division of the city itself into two, the *altstadt* within the earliest fortifications, and the *neustadt* or new town which had been walled in 1333.

This protective surround had not only enclosed the earliest suburbs which had grown about the religious foundations, but also encouraged development within it producing a surrounding zone of extension. The nearest approximation to successive rings of suburban growth appear when a series of walled enceintes were constructed providing the mould for the suburban form.

It is clear from the brief review of Frankfurt that in most cases no one type of suburb occurred, but rather a complex mix of all the types. This can be illustrated from Paris where the initial kernel, the pre-urban nucleus, was the Ile de la Cité to which the post-Roman Lutetia had contracted. Subsequently commercial development concentrated on the right bank, initially about the Place de Grève, and it was to that location that the marketing role was transferred with Les Halles being established before 1137. Out of this developed the municipal basis of Paris, symbolized by the Hotel de Ville.

In contrast the left bank began its traditional role when, at the end of the twelfth century, largely due both to the physical and intellectual restrictiveness of the Ile de la Cité, Abelard established himself and his pupils there. Others followed and by 1210 a formalization into a university took place.

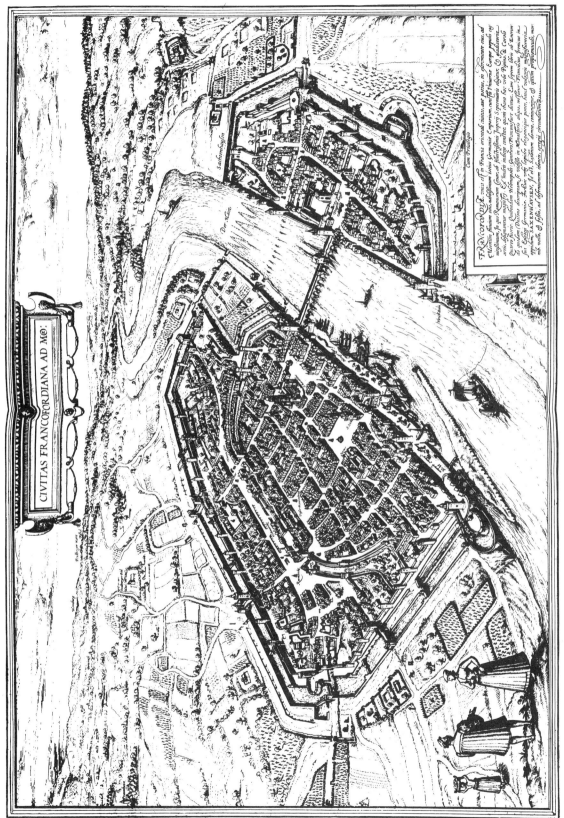

CIVITAS FRANCOFORDIANA AD M☉.

7.3. Frankfurt-on-Main in 1552. Braun and Hogenberg, *Civitates Orbis Terrarum* 1.35.

Paris in 1569. Braun and Hogenberg, *Civitates Orbis Terrarum* 1.7. Originally published in Münster's *Cosmographia*.

When in 1575 Braun and Hogenberg included a map of Paris (Figure 7.4) in the French-language version of their atlas, it was entitled 'La ville, cité et Université de Paris' thus including the three elements, two of which can be regarded as suburban extensions. Even by that time, however, further growth was in progress and to the north the suburb of St Germain des Prés, outside the walled area of 1190, is clearly visible. The Abbey, founded in the sixth century by a son of Clovis, had been the burial place in the eighth of the body of St Germain, Bishop of Paris. The Abbey was fortified, though not the settlement which grew about it, which by 1176, when it is first mentioned, was the location of a fair (Lavedan, 1960, 20).

One further example can be cited (Figure 7.5). Troyes, the Roman Augustobona, had grown on dry ground above the marshes of the Seine valley. It became through the standard process of evolution, the site of a bishopric and an administrative centre in Carolingian times when the Counts of Troyes gradually came to exercise a dominant secular control, building their castle within the old city. After the twelfth century, however, the Counts of Troyes began to develop commercial interests based on what were to become the fairs of Champagne, that at Troyes being first mentioned in 1114. The result was complete topographic transformation, for a new town grew about the fair location, forming the commercial and industrial, and hence the growing, core. The whole was fortified in the 1230s. Chapin's summary is 'the twelfth century saw Troyes, which by origin had only been a small episcopal centre, transformed into a relatively large town with new quarters to the south, to the east and especially to the west. This last quarter was rapidly developing into an important industrial town and taking the place of the old city' (Chapin, 1937, 34). In this case suburb turned itself into the centre, while effectively the old centre became relict.

This last example of Troyes demonstrates the great variety of suburban conditions. Classification can attempt to put suburbs into categories, the new town at Troyes was initially a portal suburb grown beneath the castle of the counts, but in reality situations were greatly varied as growth pushed beyond bounding walls and the first stages in the disappearance of the free-standing, discrete urban settlement began.

7.5.   Medieval Troyes (after Chapin).

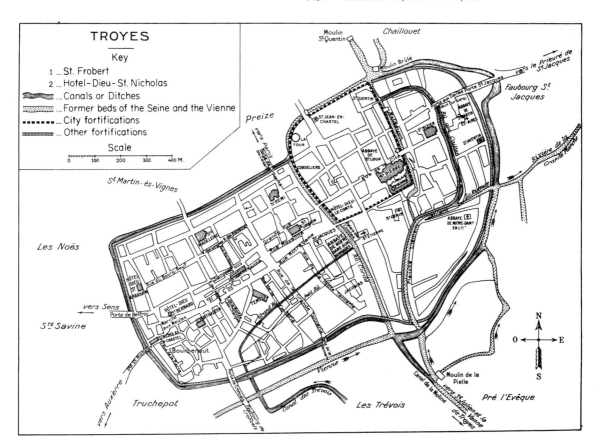

(ii) The suburb in late medieval and early modern times

There are fewer references to suburbs during this period than there are in the earlier medieval age and in succeeding times. Indeed, the word suburb itself seems in current usage to have restricted application and to be properly used only in relation to medieval towns or to those of the industrial period. Few would categorize the development of aristocratic estates of western London in the eighteenth century as a process of suburban extension. There are good reasons for the limitation of the use of the term in this period.

The first is that 1500–1700 was, if not, as many would argue for Britain, one of urban decline, certainly it was not one of ebulliant growth. Towns were often contracting and were being described as 'ruinous', rather than extending and being praised for their vigour. Suburbs, therefore, were not greatly in evidence since they were not being created.

The second reason is that where urban growth was in evidence, and this is surely the great period of Renaissance town founding, then there was a major inhibition to suburban extension by the great elaboration of defences. Given the vast extent of fortifications with great complexes of redoubts and strong-points often much larger than the settled area itself, then a suburb could not develop immediately adjacent to a city gate. Any building would have to be far removed from the defences, and from the traditional zone 'non aedificandi', to give clear lines of fire and to prevent attackers from approaching defence lines. Under these circumstances the traditional suburb could not form.

The third reason is that to create a new and distinctive generation of suburbs a new mobility was essential to distance the new settlement from the old. But this was not to come until the nineteenth century with street-car and railway. During this period, therefore, the dominant trend was the extension of the old and existing rather than the creation of new suburbs, or the building of completely new towns.

A fourth and final reason is that the bulk of towns at this time still had large areas of open space within them, made up both of common lands and gardens, so that there was ample space for infilling given the constraints of the friction of distance. Before effective transport came into being the most direct process was to build on the available land within the city confines rather than to extend beyond them.

All this does not mean that there was no outward growth. Indeed, these were the times when monarchs were actively trying to restrict the growth of London and Paris. But what growth that did occur was largely a matter of extending existing suburbs or the foundation of new towns; Versailles, after all, belongs to this period. The general tenor, however, can be taken from the Historic Atlas of British Town Plans (Lobel, 1969) where comparatively little growth is registered. Thus Harvey writes of Banbury, 'Increasing evidence of Banbury's

trading activity in the sixteenth and early seventeenth centuries may reflect increasing population. In 1545 it was said that there were 1400 communicants in the parish, but if this was so it is difficult to accept the statement in 1628 that there were only 300 houses in the town, implying a total population of about 1500. Certainly, however, the town had not expanded physically beyond the limits that it had reached by the late thirteenth century' (Harvey, 1969, 6–7).

(iii) Common lands and great estates

It is perhaps idiosyncratic to include urban extension on to common lands and private estates under the general heading of suburbs. Moreover, the context is exclusively British, though European and American equivalents will be introduced. In all these cases construction took place close to the city centre and constituted a direct continuation of the built-up area. They can be called inner suburbs and unless that word is to be given a very restricted definition, these extensions can be properly included as suburbs.

If attention at this stage is limited to Britain there were three situations where development could occur when urban growth was resumed during the eighteenth century. The first was the large open spaces which existed within the towns. The second was the common lands belonging to the municipal corporations and the third the private estates which lay adjacent to the towns and cities, sometimes small but very often large and in the hands of a small number of owners. These last two situations contributed to extension, to the creation of new suburbs. Since the style and fashion were led by the private estates it is these which will be examined first.

(a) Urban estates. The basis for the exploitation of estates, large and small, which lay at the margins of the towns as they then were, was the resurgence in town growth which characterized the eighteenth century. The mercantile prosperity which generated it was to lead directly into the Industrial Revolution, that most massive phase of extension. It is the nature of that extension and the types of control exercised over it which are the concerns of this chapter. The controls were twofold. In the first instance they were derived from the system of land holding or tenure, the way land was released for development, the role of the developer and the part played by the building trade. In the second instance there was a body of political or institutional constraints which greatly increased during the nineteenth century. All these had roles to play in shaping what are now the inner suburbs of cities.

The starting point of an assessment of the role of estate development is that characteristic of the capitalist system by which land was privately owned and within which often large estates had been successfully built up. Certainly, as far as London was concerned, one of the great fillips to that process had been the dissolution of the monasteries and the acquisition of their lands by the crown. 'In 1536 Henry VIII acquired by purchase or expropriation most of the land that today comprises the West End. He was especially eager to control the property, since it provided the water supply for his new palace at Whitehall. In later years he and his successors leased or sold chunks of the land, either to acquire funds or to reward court favourites. By the seventeenth century the freehold of most of the area was in private hands' (Olsen, 1964, 7). Thus, for example, the Covent Garden estate had belonged to the Abbey of Westminster but had been granted by Edward VI in 1553 to the first Earl of Bedford. The Russell family had further acquired the Bloomsbury estate by the marriage of the second son of the fifth earl, later the first Duke of Bedford, to a daughter and co-heir of the fourth Earl of Southampton whose family had bought it from the crown in 1545. In such ways were estates assembled.

When the possibilities for development became apparent there was a complex series of ways in which it could be carried out. The first was by outright sale of the freehold to developers. Chalklin has estimated that this accounted for at least half of the land made available in the provincial towns of England (Chalklin, 1974). The alternative procedure was to lease the land to a developer or builder for a period specified in the lease. That period varied greatly. In the eighteenth and early nineteenth century it tended to be shorter, 40 years being characteristic. During the nineteenth century, however, the period became longer and the 99-year lease was perhaps the most frequent. Other forms of lease were for a number of 'lives', the names of the individuals usually being specified or, indeed, in perpetuity at a fixed annual rent, the so-called fee-farm rent. Once a lease was granted, however, the landlord, who clearly had an interest in obtaining maximum value on reversion, by no means relinquished his ability to control the character of development. This could be exercised by means of restrictive covenants which again during the nineteenth century became longer, entering into the most specific detail not only as to type of building but also as to the maintenance of it and the uses to which it could be put.

The variation consequent upon the type of lease can be illustrated from the contrast between the Bedfords' development of the Covent Garden estate and of their Bloomsbury estate. Parcels of land on the Covent Garden estate were leased on the fee-farm system, that is in perpetuity. 'The owners of such property became for all practical purposes free-holders; so long as they continued to pay the fixed annual rents, the Earl and his heirs had no control over their buildings' (Olsen, 1964, 40). One street, Bedfordbury, was leased completely on that system so the steward of the Bedford estate in 1887 described with the greatest disapproval the process which had occurred. 'Every grantee became his own freeholder, and his plot of land was under his own absolute control, with this result; that Bedfordbury commenced its career by every man doing what was right in his own eyes in the way of building . . . a man would put two or three or four or it may be half-a-dozen houses or cottages, or anything he pleased upon it, and that went on in perpetuity. . . . It

was a perfect by-word and a proverb for everything that was disorderly and disgraceful . . . every man being his own master and under nobody's control' (Town Holdings Committee, 1867, quoted by Olsen, 1964, 40–1). It is somewhat ironic to find such freedom being condemned by the steward of a great capitalist family, but even by the late seventeenth century the Bedford estate had abandoned fee-farm leases. The Bloomsbury estate development contrasts in every way. Thus the building agreements for Bedford Square of 1776 meticulously specified the type of development, including the façades of the houses. 'The agreement went on to enumerate the dimensions of each storey, and the quality of materials for the different parts of the houses' (Olsen, 1964, 46). The unity and style given to Bloomsbury derived from the effective control exercised by the estate over development through covenants on the leases granted.

The westward extension of London through the process of estate development from the mid-seventeenth century into the nineteenth century has been recorded in detail by John Summerson, Donald J. Olsen and in the monumental *Survey of London* (Summerson, 1945; Olsen, 1964; Greater London Council, 1980). This process will not be followed in detail in this chapter. Two further examples can be used, however, to show the same processes at work in the large provincial city and the small town.

Birmingham has been used by David Cannadine in one of the most illuminating studies of estate development, that of the Calthorpe estate at Edgbaston at what was at the time the southern fringe of the city. Chalklin's discussion of the earlier growth of Birmingham in the eighteenth century mainly relates extension to the release of land from two estates (Chalklin, 1974). The first of those belonged to the Colmore family which was initially native to Birmingham, although it had long left Birmingham by the time of its development. The second estate consisted of the demesnes of the manor of Birmingham and had devolved into the hands of a Suffolk family called Gooch. A private act of 1746 made the Colmore estate available for development with leases being granted for up to 120 years. The main area of extension consequent upon the development of these lands lay to the northeast of the city as it was in 1750 (Figure 7.6). The Gooch lands were given over to development under an estate act of 1766. These lay mainly to the south and southeast of the settlement. Chalklin writes 'that there is no evidence that the failure of these two estates to supply building land before 1746 and 1766 respectively held up the physical expansion of Birmingham. Rather was it the case with each estate that land was made available just when it began to be needed' (Chalklin, 1974, 84). To a large extent the owners of these estates acted as developers. 'The Colmore Estate leased plots from a few hundred to 2000 or 3000 square yards in size, with a front between 5 and 20 or 30 yards. . . . The smaller plots were wholly built on by the lessee; some of the larger pieces were partly used by the lessee, and partly assigned to another builder' (Chalklin, 1974, 84).

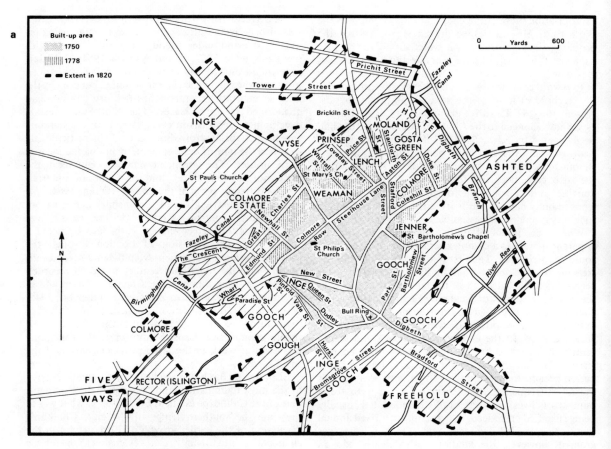

7.6.   Estates on the settlement edge of Birmingham
1750–1850. (based on Chalklin and Cannadine). (a)
The centre of Birmingham 1750–1820. The names
refer to landowners; (b) The Calthorpe estate at
Edgbaston about 1840. These two maps are to
different scales but the location of Five Ways can be
used to relate them. It is named on (a) and indicated by
a cross on (b).

As demand grew so other estates were developed, notably that of the Holte family of Aston where between 1788 and 1820 some 100 acres were used by builders. At these earlier dates there were but few restrictive covenants on leases. In Birmingham, as generally, they increased with time and the development of the Calthorpe estate in the parish of Edgbaston was subject to the greatest control. The estate had been built up to cover some 2000 acres but the main period of development was under the third Lord Calthorpe between 1807 and 1851. 'The details of the scheme were outlined in 1811–13 by John Harris, Lord Calthorpe's agent, and were immediately accepted and implemented. He proposed "a general and well considered plan" in order to attract "the gentlemen and tradesmen . . . at the expense of the farmer", on the grounds that such people would take land "rather for amusement than profit" '

(Cannadine, 1977, 468). The whole aim was to meet the demands of the wealthy who wished to leave the increasingly unattractive city centre for a greener and more attractive area. In order to achieve this, considerable sums were spent on constructing roads, sewers and tree-planted avenues. In addition, any incompatible land-uses, the obvious one was industry, were excluded and the strictest of covenants employed. Cannadine quotes one which prohibited, 'any small dwelling house or houses of the description of labourers' or poor persons' houses or which shall be occupied by labourers or poor persons, nor any workshop or workshops or other kind of shop or shops, nor any place or places for carrying on any trade or manufacture, nor any beer shop, ale house, tea garden, public strawberry garden or any other place of public resort or amusement whatsoever' (Cannadine, 1977, 470). All building plans were scrutinized before construction was authorized and the estate reserved the right to inspect each house twice a year to ensure that maintenance was effective.

Cannadine's main purpose in his study of the estate and its development is to reveal the way in which the social character of an area was created and how it subsequently developed. But for the purposes of this chapter it indicates the way in which the outward extension of the

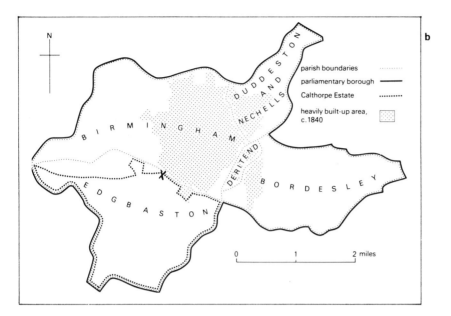

city was dependent on the willingness of land-holders to release their land for development and thus to create what were 'new towns or suburbs'. ' "Edgbaston is unquestionably the most important suburb in Birmingham", observed *Edgbastonia* on the occasion of its first issue in 1881' (Cannadine, 1977, 471). The nature and direction of extension were thus in the hands of the land-owners and the control they exerted was critical no matter what the size of the settlement; indeed the smaller it was the greater the influence.

The impact of the estate ownership on the small town can be demonstrated by Slater's study of Cirencester, which clearly illustrates the impact of the willingness to develop. During the nineteenth century the town became the market centre for much of the south and east Cotswolds and accordingly in two major phases, one between 1800 and 1840 and the other between 1860 and 1880, its population doubled to reach some 8500 by the end of the century.

There were two dominant landowners, the Earls of Bathurst and the Master family. 'By the end of the eighteenth century the Bathurst estate, containing some 10,500 acres, stretched west from the town for over five miles, adjoining the Master estate to the north and to the south the remaining town manor, Chesterton, a significant proportion of which was also part of the Bathurst estate. At the beginning of the nineteenth century, therefore, . . . Cirencester was enclosed on almost all sides by the continuum of the Master and Bathurst estates' (Slater, 1976, 147) (Figure 7.7). Only at Stratton to the north and Chesterton, to the southeast, were there any other landowners and they were largely prosperous local families who used the land to build large mansions for themselves.

Here, then, was a situation where although the impulses for growth came from the larger external rela-

tions of the town, the physical expression in terms of urban extension was dependent upon the policies of the two major estates. The Bathurst estate, concerned mainly with rural affairs, was unwilling to release land for residential development, although a large area to the southwest of the town was alienated for institutional and public-utility use. The major source, therefore, was the Master estate and part of its lands known as the Watermoor Nursery was laid out for building in 1853 although the sale of plots was delayed until 1859. The area lay to the southeast and consequently thus became the main direction of urban extension (Figure 7.7 a and b (i) and (ii)) with new streets, Corin Street, New Road, Chester Street and Church Street being added between 1859 and 1861. 'Sales of plots continued regularly throughout the 1860s, most of the land going in small lots for the construction of substantial villas, large semi-detached houses and short terraces aimed at the considerable lower middle-class, professional and commercial market for whom conditions in the older parts of the town were now becoming less and less desirable' (Slater, 1976, 153). In short, the same processes were operative in the small country town as in the large industrial city, even if the results were less spectacular. Indeed, just as the Calthorpe estate had in the end to compromise over its exclusive policy in order to realize its programme of development, so too the southern section of the Watermoor Nursery estate was developed for small working-class dwellings which were to add to a nucleus already established on Watermoor Common.

(b) Common lands. This introduction of Watermoor Common brings into the discussion the process of enclosure of common lands which was such a widespread feature of urban extension in the nineteenth century. These lands had been provided for the grazing of animals

a

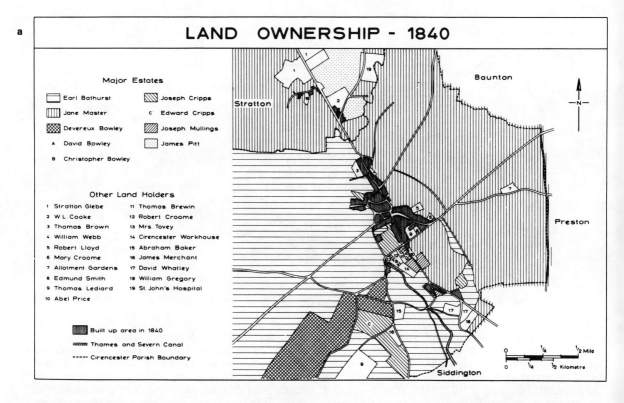

LAND OWNERSHIP - 1840

Major Estates

☐ Earl Bathurst   ▨ Joseph Cripps
▥ Jane Master   c' Edward Cripps
▨ Devereux Bowley ▨ Joseph Mullings
▲ David Bowley   ▦ James Pitt
ʙ Christopher Bowley

Other Land Holders

1 Stratton Glebe   11 Thomas Brewin
2 W.L.Cooke   12 Robert Croome
3 Thomas Brown   13 Mrs. Tovey
4 William Webb   14 Cirencester Workhouse
5 Robert Lloyd   15 Abraham Baker
6 Mary Croome   16 James Merchant
7 Allotment Gardens   17 David Whatley
8 Edmund Smith   18 William Gregory
9 Thomas Lediard   19 St.John's Hospital
10 Abel Price

▥ Built up area in 1840
═══ Thames and Severn Canal
----- Cirencester Parish Boundary

Baunton

Stratton

Preston

Siddington

and the cutting of peat at a time when food had to be provided by the burgesses themselves long before a system of local, let alone national, distribution had developed. By the nineteenth century that role had been lost and in many cases the land had been leased. Generally, however, the commons provided a source of building land immediately at the settlement margins and as cities began to grow the pressures for development became considerable. The classic case in England is Nottingham.

Figure 7.8 shows the extent of Nottingham in 1480 with the common lands of Sand Field and Clay Field to the north and of The Meadows and East Croft and West Croft lying on the valley lowlands of the Trent. In addition, in private hands, there were the Forest and the Duke of Newcastle's park of 150 acres, most of which was open and let out for grazing to local farmers and butchers (Edwards, 1966, 370). As the city prospered as an industrial centre all the development had to be accommodated within the old city. The result was appalling congestion and squalor through infill (see p. 142) but the burgesses and freemen consistently opposed development of the common lands partly because they would lose their rights but also because they anticipated a fall in rents if expansion took place. It was not until after the Reform Act of 1832 and the election of a new Borough Council in place of the Charter Corporation that the Nottingham Enclosure Act was promoted and passed in 1845. 'The town at last broke its bounds and entered on a

new phase of growth' (Edwards, 1966, 370). The whole pattern of subsequent development has been so comprehensively and incisively described by J.D. Chambers that it is worth quoting at length.

With the Enclosure Act of 1845 began a phase in the development of Nottingham to which the key . . . [is] the Enclosure Award drawn up by the three commissioners appointed under the Act of 1845, and it gives the distribution of the allotments of the various owners and their names, and also the layout of the new streets. The plan drawn up by the commissioners is substantially the plan of a very large part of Nottingham today. It took them 20 years to complete their work, for it was not until 1865 that they laid down their office and handed over the area which they had marked out to the jurisdiction of the Corporation. In the meantime, development had taken place in many parts, although the roads were not made up, and bitter complaints were made that communications were almost impossible owing to the roads being reduced to a sea of mud in winter time. This, as we might expect, was especially serious in the case of the Meadows and above all Arkwright Street, the condition of which in times of flood can be imagined. But the commissioners were unperturbed, and continued on their leisurely way, not merely laying out new streets, but conditioning the development of Nottingham in the Meadows, the Sand Field and the Clay Field from that

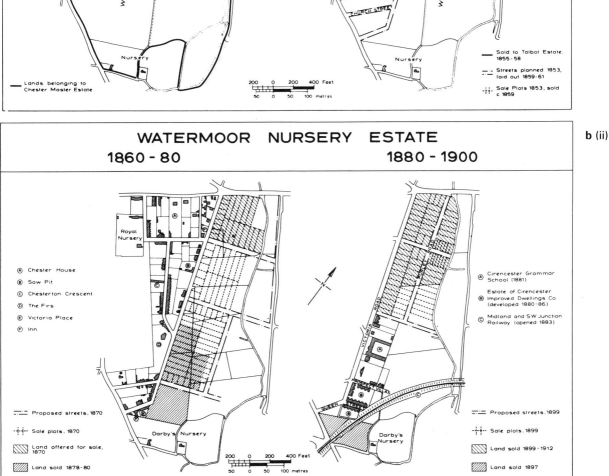

7.7. Landholding and urban development in Cirencester in the nineteenth century: (a) Land ownership in 1840;

(b) The Watermoor Nursery Estate, (i) 1850 and 1850–1860, (ii) 1860–1880 and 1880–1900 (after Slater).

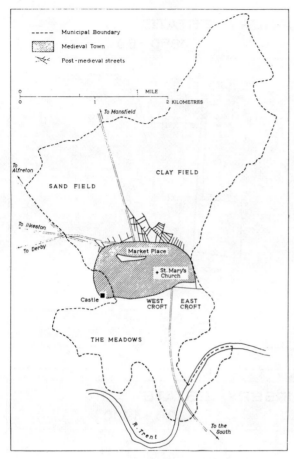

7.8.   The open-fields of Nottingham in the fifteenth century.

day to the present. Briefly, their method was to get out allotments according to the claims of the various owners, of whom there were about 400. They had to arrange the allotments according to the road plan which seems generally to have followed the pre-enclosure field paths; and these go back to the Middle Ages and beyond. . . . Within the pattern thus laid down by history or by nature the allotments of all shapes and sizes were set out, each in the possession of a separate owner. This system was followed over the entire area of the Meadows and the Sand Field and Clay Field; and of course each one of the new owners had an unfettered right to develop his allotment subject to the provision of the Enclosure Act. Since there were about 400 owners there were, in effect, 400 little town planners at work, each busily engaged in the development of his allotment according to his own ideas and without reference to what was taking place on the allotment of his neighbour . . . the streets were laid out without design or intention – except to get the maximum number of houses on the available land. . . . The new Nottingham was drab and depressing beyond description to the modern eyes; but

it was vastly more healthy and not less intimate than the old. . . . So the Lammas Lands and Meadows were enclosed and a wilderness of Victorian bricks and mortar took their place. (Chambers, 1952)

Although it means reverting to estate development it is worth noting that at Nottingham, too, there was a parallel to the western residential squares of London and the wide avenues of Edgbaston at Birmingham. This was the Park Estate which, as has been already noted, belonged to the Duke of Newcastle. Its development was undertaken by the fifth duke beginning in 1854. To the west of the castle a distinctive area of high-quality residences for the successful entrepreneurs of Nottingham was initiated. By 1877 some 650 houses had been built and a prestige area created.

This brief section, however, is concerned with the exploitation of common land and the development of the open fields of Nottingham is an effective symbol of a process which characterized the nineteenth-century extension of many cities.

(iv) Infill: a corollary of extension

At this point it is essential to counter the assumption that growth in population necessarily implies extension in area and, in consequence, the creation of suburbs. Increased numbers can be accommodated by raising densities and particularly by the infilling of open space. It might seem odd to include a comment on 'infill' in a section devoted mainly to suburban extension but functionally the role of infill and extension are the same. The early town was seldom completely built over and in most cases there were extensive open areas, most frequently the large gardens which, like the common land, were an essential part of the primitive urban economy. Even from early times, however, a process of gradual infill was established as towns grew in population. For a number of reasons, however, it was during the late eighteenth and nineteenth centuries that the main period of infill occurred, the obvious one being that it was a major phase of urban population growth.

Given that growth, there were a number of critical controls. The first was that the city was still the walking city, especially as far as the poor were concerned to whom neither horse nor carriage was available. Again the nature of much urban employment, predominantly in the service trades, and casual in nature, meant that accessibility to the city was critical. Both the nature of jobs and immobility imposed their own necessities of concentration and hence high-density occupation. A further factor was that most of those willing to develop estates at the margins of the built-up area were eager to maintain the highest quality and thereby keep land values, and reversionary values, high. This triggered the first movement of the wealthy out of the city centre leaving their vacant houses available for division and their grounds for building on. Both accommodation and land were released at the time when demand was increasing.

Under these circumstances the greatest advantage to

any land-holder was gained by maximizing densities. The process of infilling tended to degrade the environment for where quality could not be maintained the substitute was quantity; returns were best gained by crowding as many rent payers as possible onto a unit area. The ways in which this was done in Britain created classic elements of working-class housing in the eighteenth and nineteenth centuries. They can be divided into two, those which exploited the residual structures and those which were new constructions. The residential buildings, those left by the exodus of the better off, were subdivided and converted into tenements. The tenement itself as a constructed element was much more common in Scotland, but the 'Rookeries' of London were the epitome of urban slums. At the basement of these buildings there were the cellars, habitations beneath street level, barely illuminated by their windows and the destination of all that drained from higher levels.

One of the main features of new construction was the back-to-back houses, although they were used for extension as well as infill. 'They are built back-to-back; without ventilation or drainage; and, like a honeycomb, every particle of space occupied. Double rows of these houses form courts, with perhaps a pump at one end and a privy at the other, common to the occupants of about 20 houses' (Chadwick, 1842, 240). Where a narrow alley (or gully or gunnel, there was a variety of local names)

separated two rows of houses, the term 'tunnel back' has been used. The court was the simplest way of exploiting the narrow street-fronted but lengthy urban burgage or lot, for rows of houses could be built about a narrow central court (Figure 7.9).

A description of the plan of these methods of infill is a bland way of presenting what were the filthiest and most abject of slums. In Liverpool alone in 1840 there were some 2400 courts inhabited by 86,000 people and 7810 cellars with a population of 39,000 (Ashworth, 1954, 17). But from Engels to Booth and on (Booth, 1968; Engels, 1892) there have been innumerable accounts and descriptions of British working-class housing, none better than in the pages of the many Reports of government committees on public health and housing. It is now one of the most well studied topics and social conditions have been vividly portrayed (Tarn, 1971; Chapman, 1971; Gauldie, 1974; Burnett, 1978). The purpose of this brief diversion into housing conditions has been to indicate the extent and nature of the infilling process that went along with suburban growth as towns increased in size.

7.9. Patterns of housing infill in the nineteenth century. This is a section of Merthyr Tydfil (South Wales) in 1851. The way in which courts are gradually filling in the blocks is clearly apparent. Numerous back-to-back terraces are identifiable.

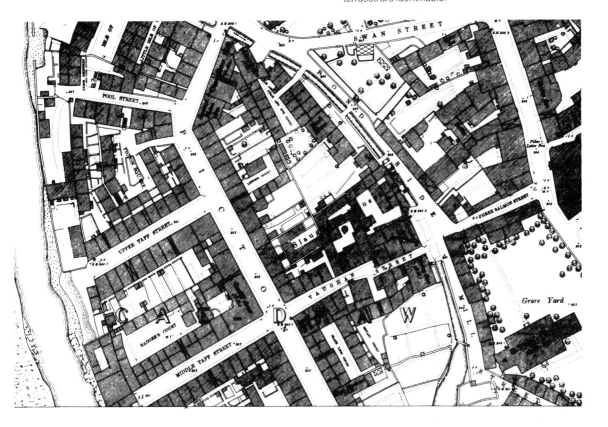

(v) Public control and urban growth

The review of the development of private estates for urban extension introduced the operation of the restrictive covenant which was written into leases so that the type of development was controlled and the actions of the lessee constrained. During the nineteenth century in areas where no such covenants existed working-class housing of the lowest possible quality and of the type just considered was erected and, as has been stressed, it was built at the highest possible density. For example, much of the development of the Nottingham common lands was of this sort. The eventual result was that public legislation began to do for these sorts of developments what restricting covenants did for the wealthier suburbs. It would be wrong to relate this too easily to a real concern for the housing conditions of the poor rather, initially, the generating impulse was a fear derived from the rapid spread of disease, especially cholera, in the poorest areas. Legislation began with public health before it became more particularly concerned with housing and, thereby, critically influenced the nature of urban extension. The main period of activity was from 1850 to 1880. 'During these years over 40 acts dealing with public health were passed. . . . But in these years parliament also came to appreciate that working-class housing constituted a set of problems quite distinct from those associated with public health, and gradually housing legislation began to embrace a concept of coherent slum clearance and urban renewal' (Wohl, 1977, 73). In the present context renewal or redevelopment is not the main concern but rather the control of new building, but there, too, the legislation was critical. '. . . it moved from permissive to compulsory power, from a reiteration of the autonomy of local government to an emphasis upon the coercive and the executive powers of municipal and national governments, and from an emphasis upon the rights of municipal government to cleanse and demolish houses dangerous to health to an acknowledgement of municipal authorities' right to become both builder and landlord' (Wohl, 1977, 73–4).

From such legislation two critical elements in the pattern of British urban extension followed. The first was municipal building of residences, council housing as it became known. It was not until the end of the century, however, in the Housing of the Working Classes Acts of 1885 and 1890 that any real progress was achieved and even then the activities of authorities were greatly limited until after the First World War. The second element is bye-law housing. During the century the various Public Health Acts, culminating in that of 1875, together with a variety of local improvement acts, enabled local authorities to pass bye-laws which set out controls on the nature of house building. These related to details such as the materials to be used, the size of rooms and their ventilation. But, also, they controlled the minimum width of roads and hence the density of building. An extract from one set of bye-laws can illustrate their nature. 'A new street shall be 36 feet in width if intended for a carriage road. Any new street constructed exceeding 100 feet shall be constructed for use as carriage road. There must be at least 24 feet space in front of every building. At the back an open space must be provided exclusively belonging to such a building and of an aggregate of not less than 150 square feet free from anything except water closet, privy, ash pit etc.'. 'Such an open space must extend throughout the entire width of such a building and the distance across such an open space from every part of such a building to the boundary of any habitation or premises immediately opposite or adjoining the site of such a building is to be not less than 15 feet'. These are extracts from the Ystradyfodwg Urban Sanitary Authority's bye-laws of 1879 but they are a standard if late representation of a general movement across Britain.

(vi) The extension of cities in the United States

There is no doubt that the extension of cities in the United States took on a much more regular pattern than it did in the Old World. There were two basic reasons. The first was the grid by which land was apportioned so that everywhere the standard block and lot dominated. The second was the complete absence of the aristocratic or large landed estate which had such a fundamental impact in Britain. In a strangely paradoxical way in the country of freedom, individual rights and speculation there was a much greater degree of uniformity.

The northward extension of Manhattan can be considered as a parallel of the westward extension of London. There were considerable areas in public ownership, partly derived from the common lands of the English charters, partly consequent upon the Act of Confiscation of 1782. These lands had been surveyed in 1785 and again in 1796. By 1806, however, the conclusion had been reached that the only solution to the problem of control of street widths and development was via a neutral Commission which was appointed in 1807 and reported in 1811. 'In considering the subject', the commissioners write, 'they could not but bear in mind that a city is to be composed principally of the habitations of men, and that straight-sided, and right-angled houses are the most cheap to build and the most convenient to live in. The effect of these plain and simple reflections was decisive' (Bridges, 1811, 24–5). The result was also plain and simple, 12 avenues crossed by 155 streets which was to provide the inviolable physical frame on which Manhattan was to grow.

The extension of Philadelphia took place on a similar basis. Warner comments, 'The rectangular survey of open farm-lands, the laying out of streets and blocks into even rectangles, the sub-division of blocks into narrow house lots, this was the simplest, cheapest, and clearest way of dividing land for rapid development. It was an ideal method, since it treated all land similarly, for a real-estate market composed of hundreds of land speculators and home builders and thousands of petty landlords and small home buyers. . . . Thus falling in with the rest of the nation, Philadelphians extended their street grid indefinitely along their urban frontier' (Warner, 1968, 52).

Some attempt has already been made to indicate that the grid was much more variable than at first might appear (chapter 6); there were quite clear breaks where grid was added to grid. But the inner suburban areas of most American cities are little more than extensions of that universal grid which, whatever the variations played, was still the predominant theme.

(vii) Street-car suburb

One of the standard features of industrialism was the growth of the industrial suburbs, new areas of settlement usually grown about a single major installation and developing a semi-independence. Often the industrial entrepreneur built his own residence adjacent to the works. Thus grew those settlements which have been called multi-nuclei. Merthyr Tydfil in Wales, which will be discussed further in chapter 10, is the perfect example composed as it was of a number of iron- and steel-works based communities each with its iron master's mansion – or castle in one case – and to a degree its own shopping and business districts. But all were within walking distances of each other and especially of the town centre. They were, therefore, like the vastly greater proportion of suburbs and extensions so far considered, contiguous to the main settlement. The constraint of adjacence was a product of relative immobility and the necessary limitations of the walking city. It was the breaking of these bonds by the coming of the street-car and the railway that was to bring into being a whole new generation of suburbs greatly different from those which had gone before. The street-car suburb could be completely detached from its parent city; contiguity was no longer a necessary condition.

There are two well known studies of the impact of suburban transport, the first of Boston by Warner, the second a more restricted study by Ward which takes comparisons between the American and the British experience. The critical contrast was the much earlier and more thorough adoption of rapid-transit systems in the United States so that the low-density and detached suburb was a feature of the late nineteenth century in the USA but more nearly of the inter-war period in Britain. The contrasts are effectively summarized in a comparison of public transport facilities in Leeds and Boston. (Table 7.1)

Even with these contrasts, however, the street-car suburb became a feature of the extension of Leeds and Figure 7.10 demonstrates the close relationship between local transport and building development which characterized the years between 1890 and 1919.

From this brief consideration of Boston and Leeds it follows that two major consequences for urban extension followed the coming of street-car and railway. The first was rapid physical extension so that the unconstrained city, especially in the USA, spread out with spectacular rapidity. Zane Miller has detailed this process for Cincinnati. 'The appearance of substantial residential

Table 7.1: The expansion of public transport facilities in Leeds and Boston, 1870–1920 (after Ward, 1964)

	Boston Passengers*	Track+	Leeds	Passengers*	Track+
1871	34				
1881	68				
1887	92	212	1894		27.5
1895	155	275			
1899	191	338			
1904	242	445	1902	48	71
1909	281	484			
1914	343	515	1916	94	114
1919	325	535			

*in millions
+in miles

suburbs on the hilltops occurred only after the introduction of the inclined plane, a steam-powered device that raised the horse-drawn street cars up the sharp grades of the hillsides and led to the rapid extension of the street railway system. Introduced in the 1850s, it had over 76 miles of track by 1880. The conversion of this system to cables and then electricity between 1880 and 1900 provided the means for the completion of the invasion of the highlands' (Miller, 1968, 6). The electricity-powered street-cars with their added speed and power intensified the outward push of urban growth and by 1912 there were 222 miles of track. In 1850 the city covered six square miles; by 1880 that had increased to 22.2 square

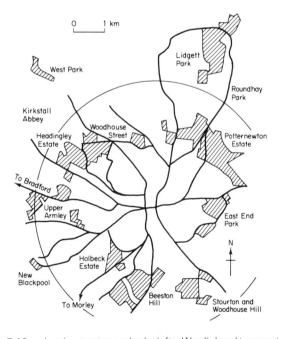

7.10.   Leeds: street-car suburbs (after Ward). Local transport and building development in Leeds, 1890–1919. Circle is 2.5 miles or 4 km from the city centre.

miles, by 1900 it was 35.27, by 1910 50.26 as annexations took place. 'Population growth, the increasing importance of industry in the city's economy, a successful annexation policy, but, most of all, technological innovations in the means of intra-city transportation, constituted the dynamics behind this urban explosion' (Miller, 1968, 6).

In this manner whole new suburban regions were created. Typical was 'Metroland', the area developed outside London along the Metropolitan railway line and so beautifully characterized by John Betjeman.

> Smoothly from Harrow, passing Preston Road,
> They saw the last green fields and misty sky,
> At Neasden watched a workmen's train unload,
> And, with the morning villas sliding by,
> They felt so sure on their electric trip
> That Youth and Progress were in partnership.
> All that day in murky London Wall
> The thought of Ruislip kept him warm inside. . . .

With the electrification celebrated by Betjeman the railway itself began encouraging development. 'It encouraged settlement not only by frequent services and low fares but also by advertising and by land-building speculation. It christened the railway hinterland "Metroland" and in its advertising posters associated it, not too precisely, with beech trees and the Chilterns' (White, 1971, 5).

This introduces the second consequence, social or class segregation. Segregation had always been a part of city residential structure but with the growth of rapid-transit systems those who could afford to do so were the first to remove themselves from the increasingly noisy, dirty and violent city and distance themselves from environmental decay. This established segregation on a completely new scale. At this point problems related to the evolution of social areas in the city intrude and these must constitute an issue for discussion in its own right. Before doing so, however, it is essential to consider attempts which have been made to discern patterns or structuring within the areas of extension with which this chapter has dealt.

3 Fringe belts

In the review of urban and suburb extension which has constituted the bulk of this chapter certain unwarrantable assumptions have been made.

The first of these is that the growth process is simply additive so that a narrative account of extension is sufficient. This is not so, for every addition necessarily has repercussion on what already exists, and with the whole city. In this way a constant restructuring takes place which is greatly more complex than a process of accumulation.

The second assumption is that the houses added are unvaried in their nature except insofar as they respond to different income-level demands. But this was not so. It

has been stressed that changes in transport technology were critical, so too were changes in housing technology and also in fashions of style and appearance. The outward extension has to be associated with innovations in house building and with the demand for new fashions both in structure and surrounding grounds.

The third assumption has been that all growth has been predominantly residential. It is true that the industrial suburb has been briefly mentioned but, further than that, no attempt has been made to examine land-uses in the process of extension.

The challenge which has been made to a set of assumptions indicates that here is no simple process of addition, like, to revert to the simile with which this chapter started, the growth rings in a tree-trunk. Rather there is a highly complex structuring and it is to reveal that structure that the notion of the fringe belt has been developed in urban geography. It is a concept introduced into the English literature by Conzen (Conzen, 1960) and elaborated by Whitehand in a series of studies (Whitehand, 1966, 1972, 1974, 1981).

The basic tenet on which the concept is based is that urban extension is rarely continuous, but is rather cyclical with periods of rapid outward growth alternating with periods of still-stand. The time of stability or little movement is often defined by a fixation line which can be either a physical barrier such as a steep slope or river, or a human-made obstacle, such as a town wall. But the basic constraint on growth must come from a lack of economic dynamism, a downswing in the building cycle, a period of slump. From this type of situation two distinctive features follow.

The first is that there tend to be greatly contrasted patterns of land-holding on either side of the fixation line. The most obvious situation is the long period of quiescence in urban development in the late medieval and early modern period which has already been identified in considering the growth of the city system and in suburban extension in this chapter. Many towns failed to expand beyond their medieval walls for a considerable time so that the extra-mural area became effectively a fringe belt. Under those circumstances there was a major contrast between the burgage plots within the walls and open fields or common land which lay without. From the contrast a major difference in the grain of land patterning becomes apparent as the fringe belt begins to be developed.

The second feature which follows is probably the more important. During the period of stability the town still creates the need for extensive land uses on its margins. These fall into two categories. The first is the demand for large land areas which are clearly not available within a fairly intensively built-up area. Such are cemeteries and hospitals, the latter especially at a time when those with infectious diseases needed to be isolated. Later examples are water and sewage works, cattle marts, public parks, playing fields and golf courses. Perhaps the earliest example would be the extensive defences with which early modern towns surrounded themselves. The

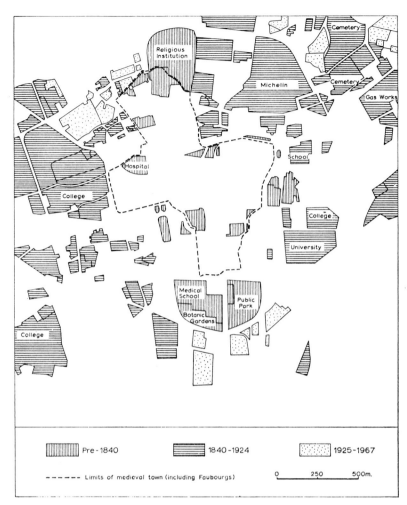

7.11. The inner fringe belt of Clermont Ferrand (after
Whitehand). The uses and plots are those of 1967;
beyond the medieval limits most of the areas left blank
are post 1924 residential accretions.

second category consists of those uses which could be
construed as nuisances or pollutants and which were
therefore eventually dismissed from the city. Even in
medieval times although leather workers such as glovers
carried on their trade within the walls, the tanners and
dyers were soon pushed out to locations where their
offensive trades created fewer problems. In the
eighteenth and nineteenth centuries heavy industry can
be classified in this category and Burgess's third zone of
workingmen's houses and heavy industry is a representation of its exclusion from the city centre, largely because
of space demands rather than its offensive character.
Figure 7.11 depicts a characteristic fringe belt developed
around a French city.

It will be apparent that any one town will demonstrate
not a single fringe belt around a primitive kernel, but a
succession of such belts related to phases of active

growth. Dependent on the nature of that succession these
are usually referred to as inner, middle and outer fringe
belts.

The main contribution of Whitehand has been greatly
to extend the fringe-belt concept which in origins is
related to urban morphology. He has argued that essential to its character is the replacement, in a phase where
residential extension is not dominant, of house building
by the placement of institutional uses. Once this is
accepted then the tradition of the bid-rent curve is
brought into consideration. That curve, which shows
uses with less need for central locations being outbid in
toward the city, is essentially static. But the existence of
booms and slumps, of a building cycle, must mean it
should be a dynamic feature since the willingness and
ability to bid will vary over time. It is only because bids
for residential development fall that a fixation line
emerges with a bordering fringe belt where institutional
uses demanding extensive land areas can effectively and
successfully bid. In this way the fringe belt emerges not

only as a morphological feature but one closely related to the evolving land-use pattern of the city.

The fringe belts which come into being as given over to marginal uses do not of course remain in that condition. As demand swings up land within them is taken over for residential purposes. Just as houses were built on the tail-ends of burgage plots, so too are the grounds of the older institutions used for development, as indeed can be playing fields and nurseries. These uses are then pushed out to form further fringe belts.

Whitehand has introduced a further feature into this situation. Each major phase of residential extension tends to bring with it distinctive building styles and housing fashions as well as more tangible improvements in domestic equipment. These have already been referred to as one of the generators of outward growth as they are demanded by the wealthier sections of the population at the leading edge of development. It follows that it is possible to identify innovations in house building and to integrate their diffusion and adoption into the process of fringe-belt creation, so that a holistic view of suburban character emerges at a much deeper level than the additive one with which the chapter began. The real difficulty is the practical one of achieving the integration of all the contributory elements to that character.

4 Conclusion

It is proper that a consideration of the manner in which town growth is expressed in physical terms should form a part of an historical approach to urban geography. That physical expression is, however, complex. It includes the annular accretions which especially were produced by a series of circumscribing walls, as well as the conventional concept of a suburb. But, also, it must cover the infilling of open areas which has taken place. Moreover, in detail these are all under the control of landowners and developers, public and private, and related to the willingness of these individuals and corporations to make land available on the bases of a variety of motivations. Again, extension and infill are not solely made up of housing for both involve a wide range of land utilization. In the early days of the development of urban geography A.E. Smailes wrote, 'as the urban core develops, the surrounding tracts appear as integuments of differing character, the products of successive phases of urban growth and the accompanying functional changes. The growth of every town is a twin process of outward extension and internal reorganization' (Smailes, 1953, 92). Perhaps because morphological studies have been so unfashionable, little progress has been made in the study of this twin process and it is still possible to quote Smailes as an indication of what has to be done rather than as an early pointer to a task which has been accomplished.

Further reading

There have been few attempts to consider the topic of urban extension as one in its own right and most publications on suburbs or the urban-rural fringe tend to deal with very recent and contemporary times. The best British source is:

JOHNSON, J.H. 1974: *Suburban Growth*. London.

An American parallel is:

MASOTTI, L.H. and HADDEN, J.K. (eds.) 1973: *The Urbanization of the Suburbs* (Beverley Hills). Urban Affairs Annual Reviews No. 7, where Part 1 deals with historical perspectives on suburbanization.

At a more detailed level the classic study of a suburb is:

DYOS, H.J. 1961: *Victorian Suburb. A Study of the Growth of Camberwell*. Leicester, which contains a general introductory discussion, while a somewhat more general study of Paris is:

BASTIE, J. 1964: *La Croissance de la Banlieue Parisienne*. Paris.

Most of these studies concentrate on the modern period and there are only rare examples of specific consideration of suburbs although most general works have some reference, for example:

PATTEN, J. 1978: *English Towns, 1500–1700*. Folkestone, and

CLARK, P. and SLACK, P. 1976: *English Towns in Transition 1500–1700*. Oxford.

One of the few direct works is:

KEENE, D.J. 1976: Suburban Growth. In BARLEY, M.W. (ed.): *The Plans and Topography of Medieval Towns in England and Wales*. Council for British Archaeology, Research Report 14.

With regard to the development of urban estates in West London the two best sources are the books by Summerson, J. (1945) and Olsen, D.J. (1964) which are given in the references. At much greater detail the appropriate volumes in:

GREATER LONDON COUNCIL (1900–1980 continuing): *Survey of London*. London. 39 volumes to date

can be consulted.

For the provincial cities the work by:

CHALKLIN, C.W. 1974 is an admirable study.

For the United States the best general volume is:

REPS, J. 1965: *The Making of Urban America*. Princeton, while

LAVEDAN, P. 1926–52: *Histoire de l'urbanisme*, 4 vols. Paris,

contains material covering European cities.

Nineteenth-century working-class housing in Britain is covered in a number of volumes. Those by Burnett (1978) and Chapman (1971) in the list of references are valuable and in addition there are:

GAULDIE, E. 1974: *Cruel Habitations. A History of Working-Class Housing, 1780–1918*, London.

SUTCLIFFE, A. (ed.) 1974: *Multi-storey Living. The British Working Class Experience*. London.

which deals especially with tenements, and a more general volume:

TARN, J. 1973: *Five Per Cent Philanthropy. An Account of Housing in Urban Areas Between 1840 and 1914*. Cambridge.

Middle and upper-class housing has received much less consideration but:

BURNETT, J. 1978: *A Social History of Housing, 1815–1970*. Newton Abbot,

is an excellent, wide-ranging volume.

Street-car suburbs are best considered in relation to the classic study:

WARNER, S.B. 1962: *Street Car Suburb: The Process of Growth in Boston, 1870–1900*. Cambridge, Mass.

Fringe belts have been largely considered by two authors – Conzen, M.R.G. and Whitehand, J.W.R. – and the works by them in the list of references should be consulted but Whitehand has presented an effective summary in:

WHITEHAND, J.W.R. (ed.) 1981: The Urban Landscape: Historical Development and Management. Papers by CONZEN, M.R.G. *Institute of British Geographers Special Publication, No. 13* (London).

8

The Internal Structure of the City: The Central Area

1 Introduction

Many urban geographers would probably consider that the emergence of a distinctive and specialized shopping centre is the key process in the patterning of the central area of the city. This is so because the development of the wide range of other specialized areas was functionally related to it, for it was the prime generating influence monopolizing the most valued land at least insofar as its core coincided with peak land values. The priority of the shopping centre is derived from the presumed ability of retailers to pay the highest prices for city-centre locations. Historically, however, that priority lacks conviction for, to use Sjoberg's categories, it is a feature of the industrial rather than of the pre-industrial city (Sjoberg, 1960). In the latter political and religious elements were predominant in shaping the centre, arrogating the most prestigious locations. It follows that it is impossible historically to retain a constant significance for the role of the retail area and the shopping function. To a degree this echoes Vance's argument for a pre-capitalist rather than a pre-industrial city (Vance, 1971). Vance contends that before the growth of modern capitalism land was not owned and regarded as a property investment, but rather it was held and evaluated in terms which were primarily social. In the town in particular it gave access to the guilds which initially had mainly a social and convivial basis and only later became trade associations. In this way participation in city life was a consequence of land-holding. Moreover, given their origins, the location of the guilds within the city was fortuitous and specialized trade areas developed bearing no relationship to any economic order based on a central point or peak land-value intersection which are products of the later capitalist order. If pre-industrial or pre-capitalist cities present a different suite of forces controlling their central area land-uses from those of later cities then it is sensible to divide examination of those uses into two sections. The break-point is a matter of some debate for pre-industrial and pre-capitalist refer to different points of inflexion, but in most general terms it is possible to contrast the evolution of retailing with the later evolution of shopping and use it as a preliminary basis.

Figure 8.1 sets out a more complex scheme proposed by Bucklin (1972) and used by Shaw and Wild (1979) in their study of 'Retail Patterns in Victorian Cities'. The level of economic development, within which pre-industrial and industrial stages are identified, is set against average retail operating costs. Where purchasing power is both low and diffuse then the retail system is dominated by periodic markets where operating costs, in such a context, are lowest. With economic development, however, purchasing power becomes both greater and more concentrated and hence the operating costs of the fixed dealer fall and the market becomes permanent, at first in structural and then in operational terms. Craftsmen-retailers can now establish fixed shops. With further economic advance the production of consumer goods becomes larger in scale and concentrated in regional location so that the local small-scale craftsman is undercut. This gives rise to the specialized retailer whilst, in turn, still further increases in scale bring the large-scale retail institutions into being. These progressive changes acted on the city centre and ultimately transformed it but as the diagram suggests the process was a continuous one rather than one which can be divided into neat phases, while one may perhaps doubt the coincidence implied in Figure 8.1 between industrialization and the dominance of large-scale retail institutions.

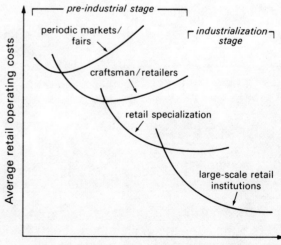

8.1.   Stages in British retail development (after Bucklin).

A further source of difficulty arises if Figure 8.1 is interpreted as representing some universal or world-wide progression. Although the centres of classical cities, the agora and the forum, were dominated by religious and administrative functions they also became market places and characterized by shops, that is the craftsmen-retailers stage had been reached. In the following discussion the evolution of the retail centre is limited to western Europe in post-classical times.

2   The evolution of retailing and commerce and the city centre

In the most primitive situation of periodic markets no such thing as a shopping centre existed, indeed the whole notion was alien. A widening of a main street gave sufficient space for temporary stalls to be set up on market days. Even that amount of adaptation was not essential for mats or cloths could be laid out on the floor, or on a trestle within any open space; the church-yard was a typical one, since it was a meeting place. To such a minor physical locale the weekly market was limited. Under such conditions many of the activities now related to the city centre were carried on within the household. Personal services were only demanded by those highest in the social order and performed by retainers. Retail trade was operated by pedlars, or ambulatory merchants, as Sjoberg terms them to indicate their somewhat greater significance. 'The existence of the ambulatory merchants is in part a reflection of the familial organization of the pre-industrial city, specifically the restriction of "respectable" womenfolk to the home' (Sjoberg, 1960, 202).

Under these conditions there was no formal price system and, although guilds could intervene, haggling or bargaining was the means by which a price was determined. Haggling is derived from an incomplete knowledge of the market, the absence of fixed weights and measures and inattention to time as a scarce commodity (Sjoberg, 1960, 206–7). It is evident that none of these has completely disappeared. Market days, certainly fair days, in many parts of the western world, result in stalls and booths being erected on main streets or adjacent grounds. There are itinerant traders who, if they do not indulge in classical haggling, at least sell by means of an extended patter which fulfils the same function. The delivery of newspapers, and in Britain of milk, is perhaps the last remnant of the sale direct to the household, so that the British milkman is the last ambulatory merchant, although the mail-order business may be the more appropriate descendent. The main issue here, however, is the influence of this sort of system upon the central area. The demand for buildings was minimal, the power of the trader or merchant limited, and hence the city was dominated by the centres of political and religious control. Castle, or town hall, and cathedral or church, were the major buildings and retail trade only incidental to these formative elements.

One of the standard sources of early town plans is the atlas by Braun and Hogenberg entitled 'Civitates orbis terrarum'. It was published between 1572 and 1598, with a final, sixth volume in 1617 and has been called 'the first serious attempt to give graphic representation of the main cities of the world, with a wealth of factual detail' (Skelton, 1966, v). To turn the pages of the atlas is to realize the complete dominance of religious and military structures. Figure 8.2 reproduces the plate which illustrates Bonn (already used as an example in chapter 2), together with the other Rhine towns of Neuss, Bruhl and Zons. The profiles bear out the dominance noted above, while the market place, although essential, is a secondary element and usually merely an open space. At these early times, however, the right to hold a market was a privilege granted by overlord or monarch. In this way both the success of a town was promoted and the local economy firmly placed in the hands of the controlling authority. Accordingly a symbol, usually a cross, was placed at the appropriate open space to give some formal indication of both right and location. In some cases the cross was derived directly from the church's desire to shift the market away from the churchyard, and it often provided the cross in the process.

Within the town the two groups most jealous of the right to control trade and industry were the corporation, in whom the privilege of holding markets and fairs was vested, and the guilds, which, as already noted, beginning probably as convivial associations, became concerned with the regulation of specific occupations. The buildings these two groups erected, town hall or guild hall, became the seats of markets – often carried on beneath them, since the structures were raised. These were the first permanent buildings associated with retail trade.

It is difficult to provide empirical locational evidence to support the generalizations which have been made. Indeed, it has been pointed out how inherently difficult it is to identify urban occupations with any degree of clarity for not only were several activities often carried out by the one person but the nature of the occupations changed over time; the surgeon was the descendant of the barber (Patten, 1977). With this reservation made, there are, however, two sources which, although very different in the scale of the work undertaken, do provide insights of a spatial character. The first of these is composed of two surveys of Winchester dated *c.* 1110 and 1148 which have been published as the first volume in the Winchester studies series. The second is a brief paper by Langton which analyses a fifteenth-century rental of Gloucester.

Writing of the markets of Winchester in the tenth century Biddle and Keene state unequivocally, 'The streets of Winchester were its market place. The commercial pre-eminence of High Street is emphasized by the name *ceapstraet*, by which it was known already at the beginning of the tenth century' (Biddle and Keene, 1976, 285). By the late Middle Ages market functions had become localized within particular parts of High Street (Figure 8.3).

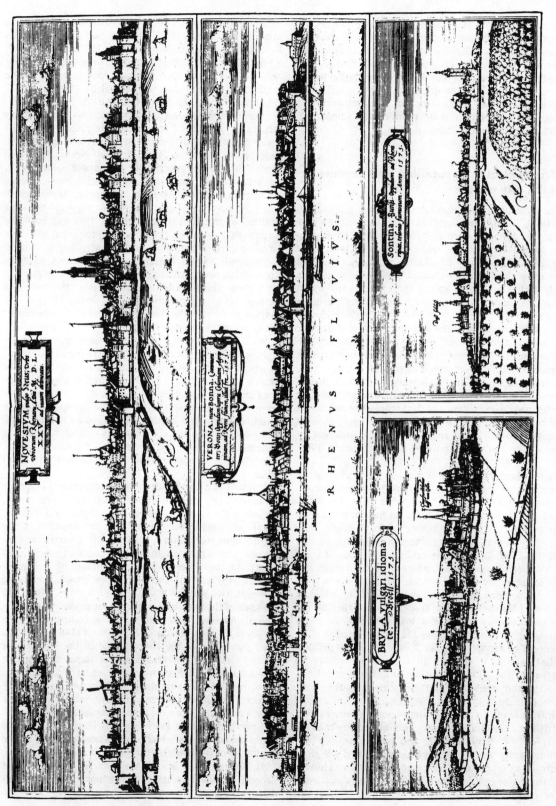

NOVESIVM vulgo Neuss Orbis vbiorum Romani, Ann. M. D. L. XXV ad nutum delineata

VERONA, nunc Bonna, Comunis ter; Bonni Oppidum supra Coloniam Agrippinam, ad Rheni flumen, illud Fr. 1575.

RHENVS FLVVIVS.

Sontina, Zuns, Oppidum ad Rheni ripam, resionis fumosum. Anno 1575.

BRVLA, vulgari idioma te. Broell. 1575.

8.2.   Rhine towns in the sixteenth century: Bonn, Neuss, Bruhl and Zons. Braun and Hogenberg, *Civitates Orbis Terrarum* 2.33.

Of the victualling trades the butchers were the most localized, for their stalls were only recorded on the north side of the High Street, principally in the neighbourhood of the entries to Alwarnestret and Flesmangerestret. . . . The butchers had perhaps originally congregated near the entry to Flesmangerestret, but by the beginning of the twelfth century had already set up their stalls further to the west in High Street, a movement which eventually became a migration and at the end of the thirteenth century resulted in the change of the name Alwarnestret to Flesmangerestret. (Biddle and Keene, 1976, 432)

At the earliest stages, therefore, an association of shops was evidently creating distinctive micro-regions, which are now recalled in characteristic names such as Butchers Row or The Shambles. The latter name, and all its associations, perhaps partly explain the reason for concentration.

Clear locational controls are apparent in another trade, that of the blacksmiths (Figure 8.4) for they were mainly engaged in shoeing horses and clearly positioned adjacent to the main town gates where journeys started and finished. Leather workers present a somewhat more complex pattern. Tanning was not only a noxious trade but it also required extensive water supplies. It can be suggested that its possible initial location in Tannerstret met the locational preconditions since it was removed from, and to the lee of, the centre and seamed by water courses. But by the late Middle Ages cloth workers, always requiring clean water, had displaced the tanners. The users of leather had no such constraints and the shoemakers were located mainly in High Street, although with representation in the western and southern suburbs (Figure 8.4). Again the only saddler recorded was outside the city walls, possibly reflecting the same controls as the blacksmiths.

Biddle and Keene record that

in the provision of raw materials and the organization of production the cloth trade was probably one of the most complex in the city. Most of the necessary entrepreneurial activity was presumably undertaken by the greater merchants of Winchester, those *prudeshommes* who, at least by the early thirteenth century, were members of the merchant guild and enjoyed the freedom to buy and sell in the city and elsewhere. Unfortunately men of this standing can rarely be identified in the surveys, although Chapman's Hall with its market for linen cloths and its church on the north side of High Street, probably served some of them as both a commercial and a social centre in the twelfth century. (Biddle and Keene, 1976, 435)

One further group can be considered, the moneyers (Figure 8.5) and goldsmiths (Figure 8.4). 'By the reign of Stephen the concentration of moneyers' interests upon the central area of High Street was even more strongly marked than in earlier periods . . . the tendency for moneyers to have an interest in the workshop area on the

south side of High Street . . . is confirmed and appears to reflect the separation between the industrial aspects of coining and the residences of the moneyers . . .' (Biddle and Keene, 1976, 416). Also on the south side of High Street were located the goldsmiths, in the southwestern quadrant of the walled city close to the former site of the royal palace and the cathedral, 'and among the houses of royal officials, barons and magnates'.

At this point it is sufficient to note that much of the discussion has been of craftsmen-retailers since it is impossible to separate making and selling, and this remains so until the nineteenth century. It would be mistaken, therefore, to write of a retail area, but one can accept the summary of Biddle and Keene that 'as a whole the distribution of named trades in Winchester in 1148 points to the well defined character of certain areas of the city' and to add that those hinged about the central axis of High Street which itself demonstrated areas of specialization.

Langton's study of late medieval Gloucester is based on a rental of 1455 where, he asserts, there is 'enough description of types of properties and their locations, rents, patterns of land-holding and occupations of inhabitants to yield a reconstruction of Gloucester in 1455 at a level of detail rarely possible for an English medieval town' (Langton, 1977, 260). Figure 8.6 records the distribution of the 75 . . . properties listed in the rental (which can be loosely categorized as business premises), comprising 46 shops, 11 inns, 5 bakeries, 5 forges and a farrier (mapped as a forge) . . . and a workshop'. Besides some industrial premises some diverse tenements associated with crafts have been added to the list (Langton, 1977, 265). Reviewing this distribution Langton notes that 'the shops entered in the rental clustered tenaciously around the High Cross' (Langton, 1977, 265). This inevitably gives the impression of a retailing core gathered at the main intersection, although again it must be repeated that it would be a mistake to interpret this from the viewpoint of the modern shopping centre. Langton also records that 'the specialist retailers and victuallers generally occupied the most central sites on the main streets: seven butchers still congregated in the Butchery and six mercers in the Mercery, though there were one or two others in each craft elsewhere in the centre. The manufacturer-retailers on the whole lived slightly further out, those in the cloth and clothing trades were strung out along Westgate between Lych Lane and Archdeacon's Lane, whilst those in the leather clothing trades were scattered along Northgate, Eastgate and Southgate, with notable concentrations of cordwainers by the South and North gates and of glovers along Eastgate and up against the High Cross. . . . Those cloth and leather craftsmen who did not manufacture for retail sale lived noticeably further away from the centre' (Langton, 1977, 273–4). The same tendencies characterized the metal trades, the cutlers being located nearer to the centre, the smiths further out.

The Chapman's Hall at Winchester has already been noted, and a further extension of the process of specialization was the emergence of wholesale markets. In his

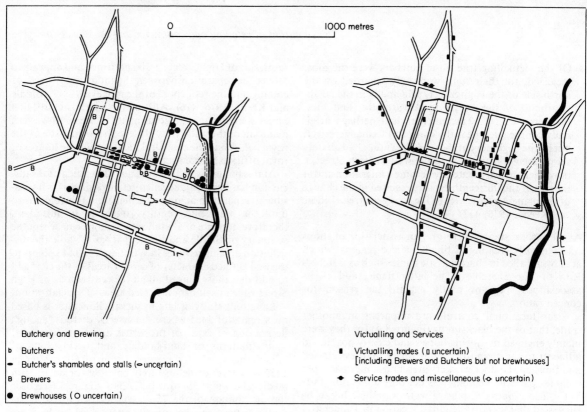

Butchery and Brewing

b   Butchers

⊷   Butcher's shambles and stalls (⊷uncertain)

B   Brewers

●   Brewhouses (O uncertain)

Victualling and Services

■   Victualling trades (□ uncertain)
[including Brewers and Butchers but not brewhouses]

✦   Service trades and miscellaneous (◇ uncertain)

8.3.   Winchester 1148: the distribution of butchery, brewing, victualling and services (after Biddle).

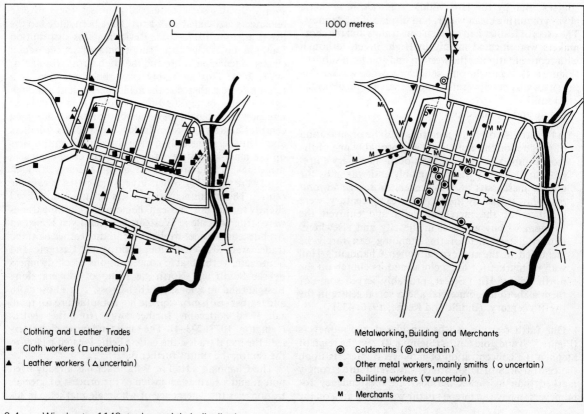

Clothing and Leather Trades

■   Cloth workers (□ uncertain)

▲   Leather workers (△ uncertain)

Metalworking, Building and Merchants

◉   Goldsmiths (◎ uncertain)

●   Other metal workers, mainly smiths (o uncertain)

▼   Building workers (▽ uncertain)

M   Merchants

8.4.   Winchester 1148: trades and their distribution.

study of Exeter between 1540 and 1640, W.T. MacCaffrey traces the development of its merchant hall. 'Already in 1533 an order of the Chamber had provided a place in the Guildhall, kept at the charge of the city, where foreigners bringing linen and woollen cloth were to carry on their business' (MacCaffrey, 1958, 75). It was on the initiative of the mayor and some friends that in 1538 a market building for wool, yarn and kersies was constructed. In 1555 the city leased the New Inn and converted it into a 'common hall for all manner of Clothe lynnen or wollyn and for all other merchandises and which shalbe called the merchauntes hall' (MacCaffrey, 1958, 76). In 1569 a separate yarn market was built in the parish of St Mary Major and eventually the wool and cloth market was moved to the old St John's Hospital building (MacCaffrey, 1958, 76). In this fashion a variety of wholesale markets developed, for at these 'strangers', that is merchants from outside Exeter, were allowed to sell to freeman of Exeter only and in gross, that is wholesale. It is significant that many of the ideal plans for cities during the Renaissance took up this theme and allowed for the location of a set of commodity markets about the central market square. Filarete's Sforzinda discussed in chapter 6 (see p. 116) is a good example.

At this point it will be apparent that in spite of the long period from which the evidence presented has been drawn and one which is usually adjudged to be of considerable significance in relation to urban development (Bridbury, 1962), many common characteristics are revealed which suggest that it may be possible to present a crude model of commercial land uses in the late medieval town in England (Figure 8.7). Along the main street, so often the High Street, and about a widening within it and a market cross which identified it, were located the main shops dealing with immediate demands, such as meat, or luxury demands in the larger towns. It would be wrong to imply any break between maker and seller, but at this point that division was nearest.

Specialization had already demarcated micro-regions of which the Shambles was probably the most universal. Within this same area a town hall or guild hall also provided a focus for trade, a market as well as a marker. Surrounding this centre was a zone characterized by retail-crafts, that is where making and selling were somewhat more intimately and directly related. On the one hand the product was of a less immediate variety than in the Shambles but on the other the raw materials were usually part-processed. Leather workers and clothiers worked on a prepared material whilst goldsmiths similarly were concerned with craftsmanship and reworking

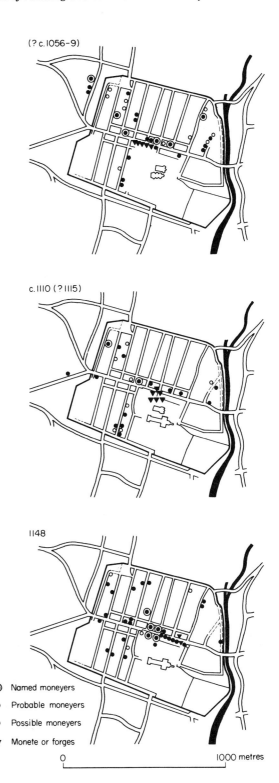

8.5.   Winchester: mints and moneyers' interests *c.* 1056–9, 1110–1115 and in 1148. Figure (a) includes the five *monete* on the south side of High Street destroyed *c.* 1070(?) for the Norman extension of the royal palace. Figure (c) includes moneyers of Henry I who still seem to have had interests in Winchester as late as 1148 as well as future moneyers of Henry II who appear already to have had interests in the city by that date.

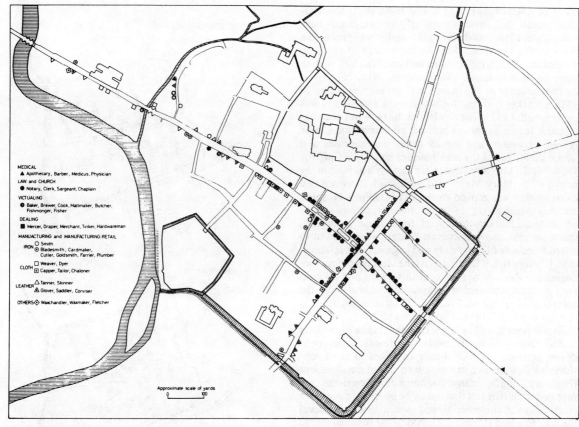

8.6.   The distribution of occupational groups in Gloucester
in 1455. (after Langton)

rather than basic production. Outside this again lay the
outer zone of craft-industries where primary processes
were undertaken, such as tanning or weaving and dyeing.
Often these activities had particular locational controls
such as the availability of water supplies or the creation
of unpleasant or noxious conditions. Metalworking with
its fire danger was of this latter order.

Within this generalized situation there were activities
with specific spatial demands. The smiths themselves
were usually located near to the city gates or in suburban
extensions, partly because of the problems noted above
but partly due to their seeking a sales point at a place of
immediate demand. In contrast, whereas the butchers
were concentrated the bakers were dispersed. Most large
houses had their own bakery and demand from the
poorer sections was best met by locations amongst them.
Finally wholesale markets developed, often at the
margins of the retail areas and the craft industry sections
reflecting the way that transactions were turned in both
directions.

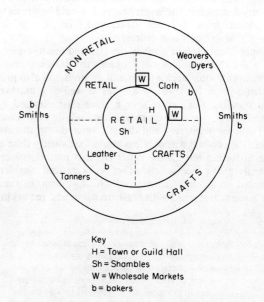

Key
H = Town or Guild Hall
Sh = Shambles
W = Wholesale Markets
b = bakers

8.7.   A model of central land-uses in the medieval city.

3 An intermediate stage: The market hall

The complete contrast to the system described above
– mass fixed-shop retailing – only emerged late in the
nineteenth century for earlier it had been confined to the
sale of specialist products to the 'upper class'. There was,
however, an intermediary in the market hall which provided a permanent structure at a time when the profits on
individual enterprises were insufficient to do so. It is also
an intermediary in the temporal sense in that although
market day represented a trading peak the market hall
was open for two or more days or even throughout the
week and hence bridged the situations of temporary stalls
in the High Street on market day and permanent shops
permanently open. Moreover, the market hall saw the
growth into dominance of the retailer, as against the
producer-retailer who brought goods for sale on market
day only. In this way the market hall represented a true
transition between the pre-industrial and the later
industrial condition, between street market and
permanent shopping centre.

In England, London, the primate city, led the way.
John Summerson, writing of Georgian London, noted
that at the time, 'the distinction between wholesale and
retail distribution was not [as] marked, geographically
and architecturally, as it became in the nineteenth
century. It was still an age of bargaining, and the market
was often a centre where wholesale and retail commerce
proceeded side by side' (Summerson, 1945, 248). A long,
arcaded market was built over the Fleet river in 1737,
although nothing as substantial was to be attempted in
London until a century later when Covent Garden
market was built in 1828–30. In the USA a similar pattern
can be traced in Boston. In 1742 Peter Faneuil constructed at his own expense the market hall which still
bears his name. It was reconstructed after a fire in 1761
and enlarged in 1805. By the early part of the nineteenth
century, however, pressure generated by open street sales
led Josiah Quincy, the Mayor of Boston, to undertake 'a
major piece of city planning that involved filling in the
Town Dock and building over the two wharves between it
and the Long Wharf, thus creating space for a new two-
storey granite market house. . . . The cornerstone of the
market was laid on 27 April 1825 and on Saturday
morning, 26 August 1826, the first customer bought his
leg of lamb' (Whitehill, 1959, 96).

Much of the controversy over early nineteenth-century
retailing is related to the view that specialized shops
served the well-off while the 'working classes' used these
market halls and that it was not until after 1850 that this
situation changed. Certainly those higher in the social
scale used market-halls of a sort for they were dignified
by the alternative name of arcades. Most well known of
these, and most long-lasting, was London's Burlington
Arcade constructed between 1815 and 1819. Roger Scola
has considered those lower in society in a study of food
markets and shops in Manchester between 1770 and
1870. Certainly he provides evidence for the significance
of the market hall.

In 1770, Manchester's Market Place in the centre of
the town was the main general market. Over the next
50 years or so, a number of smaller markets, some specialized and some general, were opened in an attempt
to relieve the pressure on the centre, and in 1803 a large
butchers' market opened in Bridge Street, off
Deansgate [Figure 8.8]. The 1820s saw further activity,
partly extending and partly replacing the existing
facilities, with the opening in Manchester of Brown
Street Market, London Road Market and a fish
market in the old Market Place, and for the first time
in 1827, a market in Salford. Of particular importance, however, was the opening in 1822 of Smithfield
Market at the top of Shudehill, not far from the old
Market Place. There were of course in the next 50 years
a number of changes; part of the Market Place and
Smithfield were covered and two market-halls were
opened, in Smithfield in 1858 and London Road in
1862. . . . Until 1846, butchers and fishmongers were
forbidden by manorial law to open a shop in the township of Manchester outside the allotted market' (Scola,
1975, 159–60).

This review, illustrated in Figure 8.8, is a good indication of a standard process. There were few towns, however small, that did not have an early nineteenth-century
market hall. Moreover, the growth of retail trade was
ultimately bound up with these halls. Michael Marks
started in Leeds as a pedlar or packman and by 1884 had
a stall in the Open Market at Leeds which then operated
on two days a week. From there he moved to the covered
market which had been opened in 1857 and which was
open every day of the week. By 1890 he had five such
penny bazaars and in 1894 started his partnership with
Thomas Spencer (Rees, 1969). Again, 'stalls in open
markets did a large part of the total men's outfittings
trade at that time, and also of the drapery trade in provincial cities and country towns. William Edgar used to sleep
under his stall at night, and John Swan had a nearby stall.
That is how Swan and Edgar met', and provided a name
which 'has been written in large letters over Piccadilly
Circus for over 150 years' (Adburgham, 1964, 15).

The evident conclusion from the foregoing discussion
is that there was a considerable and extended period of
change during the nineteenth century and that whereas
shops did serve those lowest in the social scale early on in
the century, the market lasted on until the end and, of
course, to the present day. One can accept the general
argument of Scola 'that the markets at Manchester and
Salford are frequented by a number of different traders
for a number of different reasons. To put forward, therefore a mono-causal explanation of the role of markets in
the distributive system conceals more than it reveals. The
logic however, of our argument is that market retailing
will inevitably decline as the consumption of meat, fish,
fruit and vegetables rises to the threshold point at which
the market retailers feel confident enough to leave the
central market and open shops' (Scola, 1975, 167).

The thresholds which Scola notices, however, were

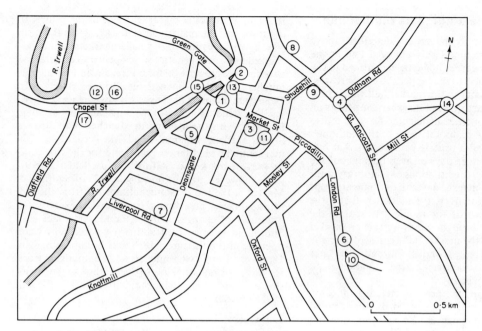

8.8.   Markets of Manchester and Salford, 1770–1870
       (showing year of opening and closing if appropriate)
       (after Scola).

1. Market Place including Smithy Door (later called
   Victoria Market)
2. Fennel Street (1769–1846)
3. Poolfold (1781 1803)
4. New Cross (1802–19)
5. Bridge Street (1803–73)
6. Bank Top (1804–24?)
7. Alport (opens 1804)
8. Miller Street (opens c. 1815)
9. Smithfield (opens 1822)
10. London Road (1824–78)
11. Brown Street (1827–40)
12. Salford Town Hall (1827–48)
13. Fish Market (opens 1828)
14. Bradford Street (c. 1830–46)
15. Salford Trinity (opens c. 1830)
16. Salford Central (opens 1840)
17. Salford Borough (1848–57)

obviously attained at different places at different times, earliest in the largest cities with the wealthiest populations, latest in the smallest towns with the poorest populations, so that the process was dragged out across the nineteenth century. Even so, Alison Adburgham writing of shops and shopping between 1800 and 1914 builds her book around the proposition that the year 1815 marked the beginning of a new pattern of retail distribution. 'At the beginning of the nineteenth century, the pattern of shopping was much as it had been for the whole of the previous century. The goods were sold by individual shopkeepers, who were proprietors of their own shops and lived on the premises, and who were often craftsmen making the goods they sold. Their customers came to them through word-of-mouth recommendation,

and for the most part they lived in the locality. There was no clear demarcation between retailers and wholesalers. After 1815, a change began' (Adburgham, 1964, 11).

As has been indicated, one cannot accept as sharp a change as Adburgham proposes, pivoted about one year, but her conclusion accords closely with that of Summerson and urges the view of the early nineteenth century as a period of transition. Before, the shopping pattern was based on weekly markets and periodic fairs; the shops that did exist were basically residential, house, workshop and retail shop being all combined under one roof; the streets were unlit and unpaved and shopping, or perhaps it is better termed, marketing, was an activity for those lowest in the social scale, the servants and domestics; shops did not advertise and were identified by signs for the illiterate, one of the last survivors being the pawnbroker's three balls; the clientele was primarily local. On the other side of this period of change a very different situation developed. Permanent shops, open throughout the day, and owned by specialist, non-resident retailers offered goods to a regional market. The clear advantages of association, to minimize travel and encourage purchases, led to well marked shopping areas coming into being. Part of this process was the displaying of goods behind especially designed windows. The streets were paved and lit by gas (Jones and Falkus, 1979). Shopping became a pleasurable, indeed an exciting, activity in which the middle and upper classes took the lead in making it fashionable. Tea rooms and restaurants allowed for rest and recuperation. All this, of course, is related to the great increase in manufactured goods, replacing those of the craft industries, and supplied from special warehouses; to the railways and the facility to distribute goods quickly and effectively; to the growth of wealth and the fashion of display amongst the new middle classes. In short, the industrial, economic and social transformation of the late eighteenth and early nineteenth century brought the shopping area with its attendant services into being, it created the central business district.

This transition is epitomized in London by the contrast of the old city with the new West End. The eighteenth century had seen the exploitation of the aristocratic estates as London grew westward. In the early part of the century the Grosvenor and Cavendish-Harley estates had been developed, in the economic upsurge after 1763 the Portman, Bedford and Southampton estates were capitalized. It was the demand that sprang from these new residential areas, as much as the need for an axis of movement, that brought Regent Street into being and transformed it and Piccadilly into the heart of the West End as a shopping centre. In contrast the city of London had been the domain of the old school of wholesaler-craftsman-retailer and as the shopping element was abstracted to its new location so that city became specialized in the relict elements, business and finance, and the East End in industry.

But it would be a mistake to interpret even the London watershed as a sharp and ridge-like divide. It is interesting to note Daniel Defoe in his *The Compleat English Tradesman* of 1726–32 recording, 'I have heard that some ladies, and these, too, persons of good note, have taken their coaches and have spent a whole afternoon in Ludgate Street or Covent Garden, only to divert themselves in going from one mercer's shop to another, to look upon their fine silks and to rattle and banter the shopkeepers, having not so much the least occasion, much less intention, to buy anything' (Defoe, 1726–32). As Lewis Mumford comments in quoting this extract (Mumford, 1961, 435), Defoe was obviously shocked by the practice. In contrast even at the beginning of the nineteenth century 'no lady . . . shopped after dark; nor did she shop in daylight except accompanied by her maid, her footman or her page. Even those streets which were not regarded as actually dangerous or unsavoury were, for a gentle woman, considered unseemly; and it was considered indiscreet for a lady to be in Bond Street in the afternoon' (Adburgham, 1964, 7). Defoe's disapproval, and the conventional restriction on women shoppers contrasted, were 100 years apart and again indicate a longer period of transformation than might be at first assumed, beginning perhaps in the early eighteenth century under the commercial stimulus of mercantilism and not being completed until the end of the nineteenth century.

4 The mid nineteenth century: An empirical example

Merthyr Tydfil was in 1851 the largest town in Wales with a population of 46,378. It had been a very small village but the growth of the iron industry transformed the settlement. Four iron-works nuclei grew about the village at Dowlais, Penydarren Cyfarthfa and Pentrebach (Figure 8.9). The result was a considerable stimulus to the central area which responded in a phase of extremely rapid growth attested by Alexander in his book *Retailing in England during the Industrial Revolution* (Alexander, 1970). In his study of selected towns he derives rates of growth as shown in Table 8.1.

Table 8.1: Percentage increase in number of retail shops, 1822 to 1848–51

	Per cent of increase of shops	Per cent of increase of population
Merthyr Tydfil	584	165
Manchester	500	146
Bolton	315	96
Leeds	305	104
Nottingham	305	42
Liverpool	270	100
Leicester	240	135
Norwich	130	36
York	75	60

In spite of its growth Merthyr still had the highest number of people per shop, 400 in 1822 and 145 in 1845–51 compared with York's 70 and 60. Alexander notes that in 1851 Merthyr and York were towns roughly equal in size; but the number, range and quality of retail facilities were very different. These differences can be attributed in part to the relative sizes of the towns 50 years earlier, their rates of population growth, and the small middle and upper-class consuming groups at Merthyr' (Alexander, 1970, 95). This reinforces the point already made as to the relationship between size, social class and the development of a permanent shopping centre. Merthyr was still growing as a retail centre and a shopping area had barely emerged. A critical stage was the building of a permanent market hall.

The Merthyr Market Act was passed in 1835 and was followed by erection of a market hall whilst a parallel Act of 1837 led to the building of the Dowlais Market Hall. These were the foci of newly emergent business districts. The market hall in Merthyr Tydfil itself was located to the north of the old village and to the west of High Street and bordered by streets appropriately named Wellington and Victoria! The correspondent of the *Morning Chronicle* pointed out that these were private not corporate ventures and the profits did not accrue to the town – 'They were established by private speculators, and are no doubt abundantly remunerative. The local act for Merthyr vests the property in the market in two private gentlemen whose shrewdness suggests the value of such a project; that of Dowlais belongs to the Dowlais Company. Thus owing to the want of a corporation in this town of 40,000 inhabitants . . . the tolls, producing . . . a very handsome yearly income, which might have

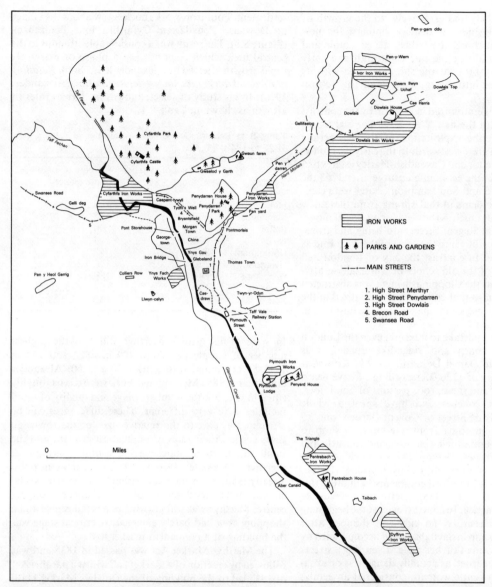

8.9.   Merthyr Tydfil: settlement structure. M indicates the
       site of the market hall

been appropriated to draining, cleansing and lighting this
dark, unsewered and filthy town, have been forever
alienated . . .' (*Morning Chronicle*, 1850). But
regardless to whom the profits went, around the market
and the streets adjacent to it and the corresponding
section of High Street, a thriving retail area had
developed. Again, the correspondent of the *Morning
Chronicle* provides a contemporary description –

> The shops of Merthyr are numerous, well furnished,
> and show all the bustle and activity of a thriving trade.
> The market-house, which is very capacious, may be
> termed a 'bazaar of shops'. The scene from six to ten
> o'clock on Saturday evening is one of the most

extraordinary I have ever witnessed. In this interval
what one might suppose the entire labouring population of Merthyr passes through its crowded halls. . . .
It is not only the field of supply, but evidently the promenade of the working classes. . . . One division of
the market is appropriated to butcher's meat; another
to vegetables; a third to poultry and butter; a fourth to
dried stores of bacon, cheese and herrings; a fifth to
apples, eggs and fruit. . . . There are also stalls of
every description and hardware and other shop goods.
Hatters, drapers, shoemakers, tinmen, ironmongers,
and even booksellers, here drive an active and thriving
trade. . . . Outside the market-house are booths
and shows, with their yellow-flaming lamps, flaunt-
ing pictures, and obstreperous music. (*Morning*

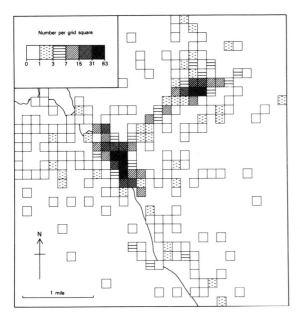

8.10.   Merthyr Tydfil 1851: Household heads employed in dealing.

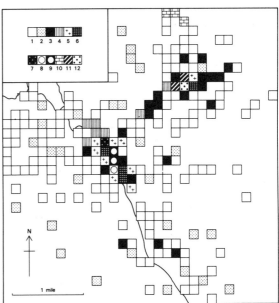

8.11.   Merthyr Tydfil 1851: clustering of grid squares. For explanation see text below.
Note: the area shown in Figure 7.9 covers the northern square of the two in cluster 6 to the south of the town centre.

Chronicle, 1850)

A somewhat more precise characterization of this area can be obtained by plotting by 200-metre grid square the numbers described as dealers in the 1851 census (Figure 8.10). Since these dealers were also resident a clear picture of a business core can be identified. Its base lay in the old village but it had extended north along the High Street and was anchored about the market hall. The 1871 census reveals intensification and a further northward drift. Similar evidence can be derived from directories (Carter and Wheatley, 1982) and both census and directories record permanent shops and not the stalls of country people travelling in on market day and Saturday to sell their produce. The shopkeepers proper were specialists in retail trade, many attracted by the opportunities offered by the rapid growth of the town. Welsh towns had been small and restricted in development so that enterprise, too, was limited in the retail field. This vacuum was filled by immigrant tradesmen, largely from England with the counties of the southwest predominant. Nearly a quarter of the household heads in the key enumeration district of the retail core were born in England (24.4 per cent). It is significant that in his consideration of housing the correspondent of the *Morning Chronicle* recorded, 'The better class of tradesmen have advanced a little, raising their houses to a second floor. . . . A tradesman named James, who had lived in Manchester but who is opening a business here, is building a house in the High Street on the same model as good houses in English towns' (*Morning Chronicle*, 1850).

Here then by mid century is a clear central shopping area, based on the market but containing an assemblage

of permanent shops about it. Here, too, lived those engaged in the professions so that at a time before residence and business were separated it was also the area highest in the social scale; it was still very much a mixed central area. But some variation can be discerned. For analysis the settlement was divided into grid squares for each of which scores on 39 variables were recorded. These were subject to a grouping procedure (Clustan) and the 12-cluster stage is shown in Figure 8.11. Cluster 5 occurs on the margins of the densely populated core of the town and is characterized by variables which indicate older and foreign-born heads of households and those engaged in 'other manufacturing', that is other than the main iron and coal industries. Cluster 6 is identified mainly by pauperism and employment in low-level occupations, including domestic service and building. Cluster 7 is characterized by Irish-born labourers while in contrast Cluster 8 is identified by those variables related to employment in dealing and birth in SW England. Cluster 9 is the highest-status area with its main association with those in the professions and in retail trade.

Taking the evidence from this analysis, and that from an 18-group cluster stage, it is possible to suggest a general model for the town. Around the market hall and the immediately adjacent areas was the intensive core. It was dominated by retailing and by a strong immigrant element of shopkeepers and those in the professions who had built for themselves the most elegant houses on the High Street. About this was an inner area where although retailing remained significant it was joined by craft workshops and diversified small-scale industry, including a tannery, slaughterhouse, a woollen mill, smithies and a number of breweries. The public/professional element was much less in evidence, while the birthplace range was extended. In short, a small intensive area gave way to a more general surround. This process was continued in an outward direction, for a further zone can be postulated where retailing was no longer a significant element and the craft-industry aspect had taken over. This is accompanied by the emergence of two areas, one to the north and one to the south of the centre, where, in close adjacence to that centre, sections characterized by the poorest physical conditions had 'dropped out'. As Gwyn Williams writes,

> . . . a rising tide of squatters flooded after them, camping in shacks and shanty towns, living between the arches of the canal bridges, overflowing into the cheap lodging houses around the bridges, as even the hastily thrown-up cottages of the middle-class speculators failed to cope with rising demand. This was the natural home for marginal people, receivers, sharpers of infinite variety, with the recreation centre of the Glebeland nearby, quick get-away routes over Aberdare Mountain and the Beacons to hand and two county borders within reach. Such pockets developed in every settled area, Dowlais included, but nowhere else did they grow into no-go areas such as those on the Taff. The Pont-y-Storehouse district and Caedraw further south on the east side became notorious. (Williams, 1966, 54–5)

It is possible from the evidence examined to suggest a' further marginal zone where less vicious 'drop-outs' from society, especially widowed females, survived by working as domestic servants and taking in lodgers. But this was broken by the extending sector of the well-off which in the 20 years between 1851 and 1871 broke through to create Thomastown (Figures 8.11 and 8.12). Perhaps it is inappropriate to represent this situation as a series of discrete zones, for reality was certainly not like that; but a pattern of transition out from the market core is certainly identifiable.

In reviewing the detailed situation in Merthyr, and the model derived from it three features stand out:
1 There is a parallelism with the model proposed for the medieval period. Even in 1850 the succession outwards from the centre of retailer, retailer-producer and general manufacturing or production still retained echoes of a much earlier situation in very different urban conditions.
2 The Market Hall at Merthyr, which was to remain until the 1960s, played a characteristic, intermediate and centralizing role.
3 A whole array of retail shops was already present by 1850 and if the term shopping centre, or even central business district, was inappropriate because of the substantial residential component, the emergent character was apparent.

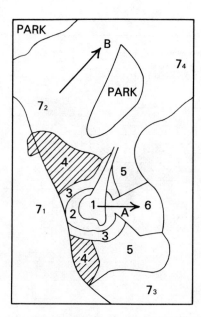

8.12.   The structure of Merthyr Tydfil in 1851: a generalized interpretation. The figures on the map represent:
1. Retail/Professional Core
2. Retail/Craft Inner Area
3. Craft, Diverse Light Industry & Warehouse Zone
4. Lowest Quality Residential Areas
5. Marginal Areas
6. Developing Area of Higher Quality Residence
7. Iron Manufacturing Nuclei:
      1. Ynysfach; 2. Cyfarthfa; 3. Plymouth;
      4. Penydarren
A. Direction of extension of higher quality residence area 1871
B. Later, end-of-century, extension of higher quality residence.

5 The development of the central business district

Perhaps the most comprehensive view of the emergence of the contemporary central business district is that by David Ward. He starts at a date which fits in reasonably well with the time-scale which has been identified in this chapter. 'Until the mid-nineteenth century, apart from the small exclusive residential quarters of the rich, the functional specialization of urban land uses was only weakly developed. Most industrial and commercial activities were conducted on the premises of the producer or merchant, and local purchases or services were obtained on a custom basis directly from the producer' (Ward, 1971, 87). Ward then presents both a model of the emergence of the central business district in the USA and a specific illustration using Boston as his example (Figures 8.13 and 8.14).

In his model (Figure 8.13) Ward identifies two stages, the first between 1840 and 1870 and the second from 1870 to 1900. In the first of these stages the dominating feature

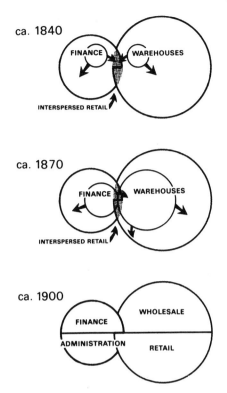

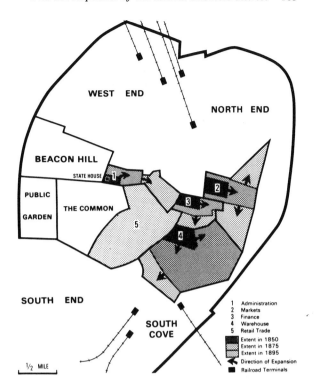

8.13. Generalized stages in the emergence of the Central Business District as set out by D. Ward.

8.14. The expansion of Boston's Central Business District, 1850–1900 (after Ward).

is the appearance of a distinct warehouse district, a consequence of increasing commercial activity. Storage space was in demand once a commodity or product was handled by a middle-man between producer and retailer and once manufactured goods were distributed on a regional or national basis. Integral with such developments were the financial and insurance interests on which trade relied and hence a small but distinctive financial area appeared. Between 1870 and 1900 the main process was specialization within these earlier areas. The financial sector both grew and threw off a distinctive administrative area, itself a response to the growth of urban government. Retail trade, which had tended to be scattered and interspersed among the commercial and financial areas, became the predominant activity in a specialized shopping area. In this way from the mixed and intermixed uses of the early part of the century a complex central business district developed, itself characterized by quite distinct sub-districts with closely associated uses.

It is worthwhile comparing this simple chronology with that put forward by Whitehand in a study of Glasgow. One of the main criticisms of Ward's outline is that it is not based on specific mapped or measured criteria, it is a descriptive survey and model. Whitehand's work is more specifically based on an analysis of rates of redevelopment. He concludes that 'Victorian redevelopment was dominated by the shop and the warehouse, the

form taken by the latter representing in townscape terms a dramatic innovation, being in almost all respects a pronounced departure from previous dwelling-like designs. Except for bank buildings, redevelopment for offices was comparatively rare. . . . In the large-scale renewal of the main shopping streets the nature of the buildings involved . . . strongly suggests both an enormous increase in floor-space requirements and pronounced changes in shop architecture associated with a changed conception of the scale and, in some respects, the nature of retailing' (Whitehand, 1978, 88). This generally agrees with Ward's work on Boston though the less chronologically specific 'Victorian' period used by Whitehand makes direct comparison difficult. Whitehand reports of the Edwardian period, 'the rate of redevelopment in the shopping areas fell, both absolutely and relative to that in the warehouse, office and institutional areas, all of which reached their highest rates of development at this time' (*ibid*). Again there is broad agreement with Ward, but the growth of the retail area does show some contrast apparently developing somewhat earlier in Glasgow, in line with all other British evidence. The general pattern can be summed as the earlier growth of the warehouse area, followed by later financial and office areas together with administration establishing distinctive regions, while the central shopping areas appear with increasing clarity throughout the nineteenth century.

The above succession is illustrated in Ward's map of the expansion of Boston's central business district between 1850 and 1900 (Figure 8.14). Local detail controlled the particular pattern. Thus administration grew from the dominance of State House, while the warehouse and market areas were related to the docks and the infilling process. Ward notes that although between 1835 and 1855 seven railway terminals were established they apparently had only a limited influence on the emerging central land-use pattern.

It will be apparent that the larger the city and the more rapid its growth then the greater will be the tendency for the general central area to give place to a series of interlocking specialized sections. It is appropriate to review at greater length the patterning of central London which has already been introduced. In London the separation of functions began in medieval times, for the city of London to the east was quite distinct from Westminster to the west. The former had an early history common to many medieval successors of the Roman towns of England: the latter was unique. That latter site was first used (ignoring fragmentary Roman evidence) as the location of an abbey on what was Thorney, or Thorn Island, with the first reliable record dating from 970. Royal associations date from the eleventh century for the Abbey was rebuilt by Edward the Confessor and the royal residence was moved from Winchester to Westminster in the same century. This addition of the royal palace and seat of 'national' government transformed the path of development. At a later date the Tudor monarchy which effectively united England and Wales added considerably to the area. In the early 1530s Henry VIII built St James Palace as well as beginning the development of Whitehall.

From early medieval times, therefore, the functions of central London were located in two separate areas which even by the late sixteenth century, as Hogenberg's map of 1572 demonstrates, were only linked by the thin line of the Strand (Figure 8.15). To the west was the Court and centre of national government which was to attract prestige residences (they could already be found in the Strand) and all that was to become associated with it in the way of shopping and personal service and entertainment and which was to become identified by the term 'West End'. To the east was the 'city', the base of the independent London burgesses and of the merchants out

8.15.   Land-use areas in London in the eighteenth century (after Spate).
 1. Aristocratic residential sector
 2. Government offices
 3. Middle class and professional residential areas
 4. Amusement and vice area
 5. Legal area
 6. Industrial areas and artisan dwellings
 7. Wharfs, warehouses, waterside trades, including labourers' dwellings
 8. 'The City' – commerce and finance
 9. Boundary of the City Liberties
10. West End shopping and hotel centres about the Haymarket and Charing cross
   The principal markets are shown
   S – Smithfield (meat, hay)
   L – Leadenhall (meat, provisions, leather)
   G – Covent Garden
   Q – Queenhithe (corn, meal, malt)
   B – Billingsgate
   R – Roomland (coal)
The boundaries are obviously approximate and the built-up area is about 1750.

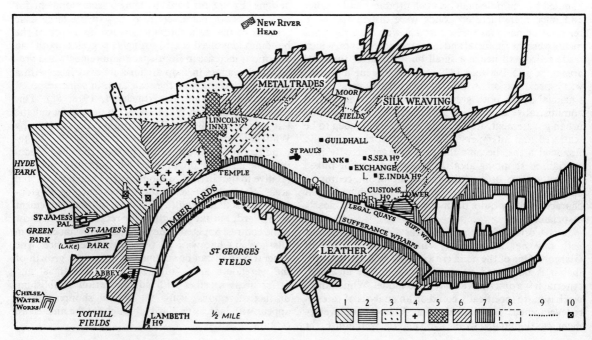

of which was to grow the financial centre, the trading interests, and the warehouses and industry of the 'East End'. It is of interest to observe that this completely reversed the characteristic pattern of continental development where the Roman castrum, the pre-urban nucleus, became the *cité*, the centre of administration, while the attached areas was the merchant section, the bourg.

Even in the Middle Ages a further distinctive area had appeared. Already in the fourteenth century the Order of St John, which had succeeded the Templars on the Temple site in 1324, had leased it to students of law. Lincoln's Inn was also left as a residence for lawyers by the Earl of Lincoln. Thus, appropriately located on the divide between the Court and the city, a legal area was early apparent.

Those strong forces which were to create modern London are perhaps first apparent in the Tudor period. The increase in trade and wealth led to population growth and an extension which the monarchy tried vainly to contain. The dissolution of the monasteries freed large amounts of land in and around the city. Characteristic was the Convent Garden, given to Sir John Russell in 1553 and in 1630 translated as Covent Garden into the first British 'piazza', a symbol of the western growth, to be followed by Soho Square in 1681.

Economic changes also began to operate. The trader or the dealer began to play a bigger role especially related to overseas trade and thus began to exert pressure on city sites so that land values rose. Craft industry, not able to meet the rising values, was displaced to the surrounding villages, especially Spitalfields and Clerkenwell, so that a northern and eastern industrial fringe was created. This was accentuated by the way in which maritime trade created a riverside area from the Tower to Limehouse concerned with the handling, repairing and provisioning of ships and with warehousing, the storage of bulk goods. An industrial and warehousing eastern end begins to develop, both activities largely extracted from the 'city'.

Oscar Spate attempted a reconstruction of the main 'occupational' areas of London in 1750 and this is reproduced in Figure 8.15. The structure reflects the early development together with the first impacts of the massive western movement of the highest-class residences which were to characterize the eighteenth and nineteenth centuries. It can be briefly divided into three:

1 East London.
(a) *The City*. A core of merchants and traders grouped about the Bank, the Exchange and the houses of the great companies, East India, South Seas, Hudson Bay.
(b) *Industrial areas*, with three sections.
  (i) Clerkenwell, characterized by metal working and jewellery.
  (ii) Spitalfields, characterized by silk weaving.
  (iii) The River Front, with a wide variety of activity with maritime connections.

2 West London.
(a) *St James and Westminster*: the seat of the Court and of government.
(b) *Aristocratic residences*, largely on the great estates which had been developed before 1750, including the Cavendish-Harley estate and the Grosvenor Estate.
(c) *Shopping*. The beginning of the extraction of retailing from the city, mainly by this period collecting about Charing Cross and the Haymarket.

3 The Strand.
This still remained as the connecting link between west and east, but with its own distinctive associations largely related to its intermediary location.
(a) *The legal area*, as has been indicated grown about the Temple northward from the river.
(b) *Amusement and vice*. This role is partly related to older 'parade' areas such as Lincolns Inn Fields which had fallen into disrepute as sites for what would now be termed 'pick-ups'; to the transformation of Covent Garden into a market; to the coffee-houses of the legal area; and to the theatre area epitomized by Drury Lane, one of the minor alleys off the Strand which became characterized by these functions.
(c) *Shopping*. Again an intermediary between the old city and the new western end.

It was onto this situation that the massive growth of the nineteenth century was impressed driving forward both eastern and western growth and accentuating specialization of areas. Kellett in his study of the impact of railways on Victorian cities writes,

> Because they set in motion a whole chain of operations in manufacturing, warehousing, transporting and selling, and because they depended to such a marked extent, even in the days of the telegraph and efficient postal service, upon the personal meeting, the dealers on the Exchange, and their associated offices and credit agencies, were able to bid for central location against all comers. Land values in the City of London were six to eight times as high as even the most elegant West End residential addresses. They were even two or three times as great (for the smaller sites required) as the prices the railways were able to bid for central land. The core of the central business district, therefore, must be taken as immovable by direct railway pressure. Residential areas, historic buildings, graveyards, hospitals, craft workshops, even, where necessary, factories, could be traversed or swept away, but not the central Exchange area. (Kellett, 1969, 298–9)

Although this is written in specific relation to railways the implication is wider. In London, the Royal Exchange, rebuilt between 1841 and 1844 and the Bank of England, built between 1788 and 1808 (rebuilt 1921–37) were the critical anchors of the highly specialized financial core which crystallized about them. Trading in commodities was filtered out and characterized appropriately

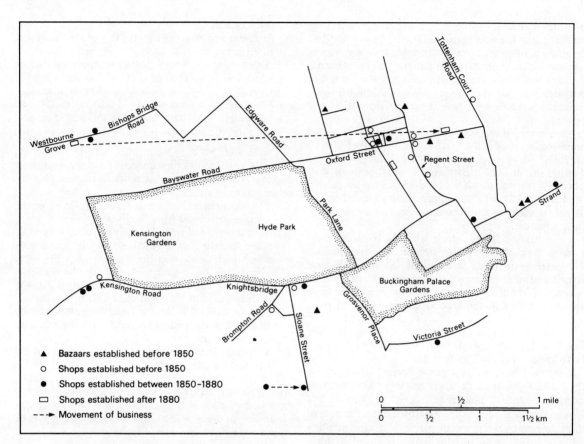

8.16.   The evolution of department stores in London's
        West End (after Shaw).

the area to the east more immediately in contact with the
warehouse and industrial areas of the dockland which
had been extensively developed after 1800 with the
beginning of the West India Dock.

It is noteworthy that Kellett ascribes the highest bid for
land to 'dealers on the Exchange', thereby negating the
principle with which this chapter began that the retail
trade bid highest and thus led change. In this case, however, London was a unique city and comparisons with
smaller towns are not easy to make.

Between the mixed margins of the financial core about
St Paul's and the legal area to the west a further specialized area emerged taking its name from an east-west
street which crossed a small tributary of the Thames, the
Fleet. The growth of a literate public and the increasing
ease of national distribution, rapidly enlarged the
printing and publishing business while legal publishing,
an even more specialized activity, had already occupied
the intersection of the areas. Again to quote Kellett,
'Mercery . . . was virtually chased into the West End by
the expanding printing business; first the professional
publishers of legal and other documents in Paternoster
Row, then the newspapers of Fleet Street' (Kellett, 1969,
300).

The continued extension completely transformed the
western margins after the 1815 date already discussed
(p. 158). The leader was retailing and especially the
department store. Shaw has identified three phases in this
process (Figure 8.16). The first was the construction of
bazaars in the 1830s and 1840s, virtually the market-hall
stage identified earlier. Shaw notes that there were 10 in
early Victorian London with Oxford Street, a new axis of
extension, being one of the major locations. The second
phase was the increase in shop size by amalgamation with
the intention of establishing 'island' sites dominating
a whole block. The third phase after 1880 was the construction of purpose-built stores reaching its peak with
the opening of Selfridges in 1909 (Shaw, 1979, 286).
Adburgham reproduces the list of properties as set out by
Hollingworth in order to acquire the Oxford Street island
site of Bourne and Hollingworth. It is set out exactly as
he wrote it:

1 pub	1 brothel
1 dairy	1 private residence
A branch of Finch's	A wholesale lace market
A barber	A nest of Polish tailors
A coffee house	A sweet shop
A carpet layer	Doan's Backache Pills
A costume	A cigarette factory
manufacturer	(Savory's)

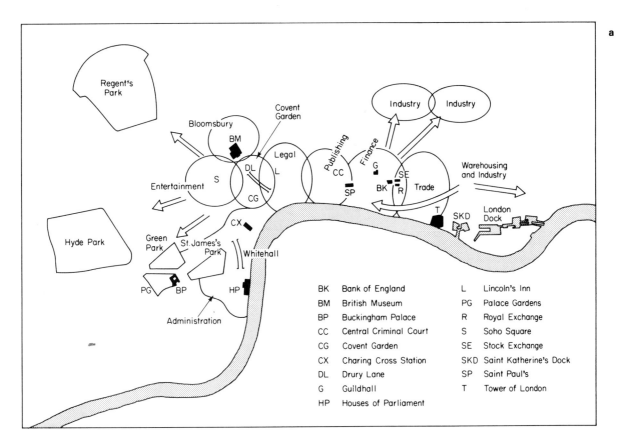

A wholesale milliner
A retail milliner
A music publisher
A musical instrument
  shop (German)
A palmist
A beauty parlour
British headquarters,
  New Columbia
  Gramophone Co.

A wholesale blouse maker
  (Frances)
A wine-merchant's cellar
A soda-water manufacturer
A jeweller
A baby linen manufacturer
A wallpaper merchant
An estate agent
2 solicitors
1 chapel.

The purpose of reproducing this list is not only to indicate the difficulties of building up large sites but also to demonstrate the way in which at the cores of evolving specialized areas uniformity was achieved by replacing a great mixture of uses.

As the retail area extended so, too, were other land uses dragged west, especially amusement and entertainment which became focused on Soho Square and included the area to the south where London's theatreland came into being. Again, to the north the section around the British Museum and the University of London developed a character partly derived from its intellectual environs, partly from the nature of the area to the south, and best summarized by the name of one square, Bloomsbury.

National administration pushed north from Westminster along Whitehall to meet the western extension at

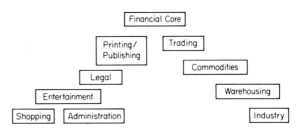

8.17. London: the development of specialized areas. These are shown in the most general terms. The diagram b indicates the way in which specialized areas progressively broke away from the commercial and financial core.

Charing Cross, thus establishing an extensive governmental and administrative region in the area between the river and the royal parks.

As these various extensions took place, core areas became clearly identifiable but the interstitial areas were much less clearly characterized and great mixtures of uses and occupations occurred. But the general picture by the end of the nineteenth century is summarized in Figure 8.17.

6 The railways and the central area

It has already been recorded that Boston's central area was bordered by seven railway terminals between 1835 and 1855, 'but apparently (they) exerted only limited influence on the emerging central land use pattern. Although the two clusters of terminals attempted to locate close to the centre by filling waterfront land in the Mill Pond and the South Cove, they were still at a considerable distance from the advancing fringe of the business quarter' (Ward, 1971, 93) (Figure 8.14). Kellett's general conclusion in relation to British towns is similar. 'The railways in the five cities studied (Birmingham, Manchester, Liverpool, Glasgow, London) were able on occasions to drive wedges into the central business district, or to define and circumscribe the area; but it must be frankly stated that their perceptible effect, even in the long term, upon the location of central business district functions was smaller than has sometimes been suggested' (Kellett, 1969, 269). Thus the building of the West End stations in London at Victoria and Charing Cross can be viewed as a response to those trends observed in the last section of this chapter rather

than an instigator of them. The ribbons of the railways and the knots of railheads and goodyards were significant elements in themselves, therefore, but apparently not pre-eminent among factors causing change.

The one British exception which Kellett allows is Liverpool (Figure 8.18) 'where there was perhaps more evidence than anywhere else of a re-centring of certain elements in the central district, although the heart of the central business district – the exchange and office area – remained impregnably fixed in its old location inland from the Pier Head and Castle Street' (Kellett, 1969, 304). This confirms the role of financial institutions identified in London. As land values there rose other users began to move out from the old town and eastwards. Site competition may have driven these other users out, therefore, rather than that they were attracted by the railway station but, even so, given the possibility of a wide range of choices they mainly congregated about Lime Street Station, 'with a unanimity which it is hard to assign to coincidence' (Kellett, 1969, 305). The retail area along the Lord Street–Bold Street axis added an extension towards Lime Street in Renshaw Street, while the entertainment and hotel area gathered about the station. 'An even greater change took place in the location of the administrative area – the Law Courts, municipal and public buildings, the Post Office – as expansion and reconstruction took place in the mid and late nineteenth century. Once again it was oriented to Lime Street, forming a species of platform or avenue between the office and exchange quarter and the terminal which, for many years, was the only exit for Manchester, Birmingham and London passenger traffic' (Kellett, 1969, 305) (Figure 8.18). Even here, however, it is possible to maintain that the main pull was to that part of the city which was most attractive in terms of social status and that the movement of retailing was as much related to that as to the railway station.

Perhaps the most significant role of the railway was not in the internal reorganization of central city uses as such but in the clearance of large areas of housing, usually of the poorest quality, and in the impact on tracts of better quality housing where deterioration can set in. The result was to hasten the process of inner city decline and suburban extension which is the subject of chapter 10.

The impact of the railway station upon central uses was probably of some, but varying, significance in most towns. In large, rapidly growing cities other forces were stronger, but in the smaller towns the railway was often a pre-eminent feature in the organization of central land uses (Carter, 1958).

7 The central area and vertical extension

Nineteenth-century changes in the central area were largely the result of specialization, segregation and consequent horizontal extension but the most significant transformation was to occur near the end of the century with the beginning of vertical growth. The appearance of

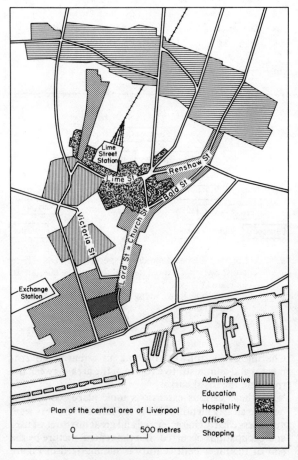

Plan of the central area of Liverpool

0   500 metres

Administrative
Education
Hospitality
Office
Shopping

8.18.   The central area of Liverpool 1910 (after Kellett).

the skyscraper was to initiate a major change in both the physical appearance and the functional character of the city centre.

Two technical developments were basic to the high-rise building. The first was the iron or steel-frame building which gave the essential strength without the weight of conventional forms of construction. The external or visible 'walls' became merely an infill, but, even more, much larger areas of glass could be used to give greater light within the buildings. The second innovation was the lift or elevator which provided the essential vertical access just as the street-car was providing it horizontally.

The first building based on a frame or skeleton is usually identified as a chocolate works built by Jules Saulnier at Noisel-sur-Marne in 1871–2 but it was apparently unknown in America and had no influence there. There are various claimants to be the first developer of the steel-frame building in the United States but certainly the first building actually erected, rather than planned or proposed, was the ten-storey Home Insurance Company Building in Chicago in 1883–5. The architect was William Le Baron Jenney, the founder of the so-called Chicago School.

Lifts or elevators had been used to raise goods but the first solely passenger elevator was devised by Elisha Graves Otis. It was demonstrated in 1853 and installed in a New York department store in 1857. This early version was based on hydraulic power and the rise limited by the physical laws of the pressure of the water column (Gottman, 1967). This meant that the maximum was some 20 storeys. This limitation, however, was removed by 1887 with the invention of the electric elevator. Steel-frame building and electric elevator meant that there was little limitation on the height of buildings. 'During the eighties a whole colony of buildings suddenly sprang up in Chicago – to heights of 12, 14, 16 and 23 storeys. These buildings were not erected in isolation, as they were in other cities, but in close proximity to each other. Each had its own individual appearance and its own name, and yet the aggregate appearance was not chaotic' (Giedion, 1954, 366–7). In short, a new type of urban skyline had appeared before the First World War. In Manhattan, the Flat-Iron Building of 1902 is regarded as the first skyscraper but by 1913 the new Woolworth Building reached 60 storeys. The American innovation was eventually to have a profound influence on European cities. As early as 1905 Auguste Perret, the pioneer of concrete construction, was outlining ideas for tall buildings around Paris. But it was Le Corbusier in the 1920s who was to bring tower blocks into the forefront of planning and architectural discussion and initiate the trend which was to transform city skylines in Europe (Evenson, 1979, 170–98).

The change in functional character of the city engendered by the skyscraper was epitomized by the first to be built for it was erected for the Home Insurance Company. 'The skyscraper is not only a landmark and an art form; it is also the expression of a social and intellectual revolution characteristic of our era. Skyscrapers are, in fact, highly functional buildings. It is noteworthy that the first skyscraper in Chicago and some of the early ones in New York were built by insurance companies – that is, by companies whose business is entirely bureaucratic. Their work is all on paper and in transactions' (Gottmann, 1967, 437). The early skyscraper marked the incipient predominance of transactional operations at the city centre and the emergence of the office sector as the prime mover in the evolution of the central business district.

The skyscraper had two related and critical effects. The first was to enable the city to function effectively on limited horizontal space by piling it up vertically; it provided that concentration essential to the transactional character of the post-industrial city. The second was to accentuate outward residential spread by making the accumulation of large numbers of workers at the city centre possible. Central height was a corollary of marginal spread.

Given the arguments which have been briefly set out, it could well be maintained that those major changes which brought the contemporary city into being were marked by the coming of the skyscraper and its incidence provides an appropriate point at which to end the discussion of the historical evolution of the central area.

8 Conclusion

This chapter has sought to demonstrate the processes and stages by which the modern city centre has evolved. The fact that the forum and agora of the classical city were, if only in part, commercial centres has been ignored in the pursuance of the central theme of continuous development. Conventionally that continuous development is broken into stages signalled by predominant buildings. Cathedral and castle or palace gave way to warehouse and town hall which in turn gave way to the multi-storey office block. Retailing, which was apparently the dynamic element, never achieved such significant physical form; the market hall and the department store, important as they were, never became the creators of characterizing skylines. Maybe that suggests that the real wielders of urban power, and those with the resources to remain resistant, were princes and prelates, merchants and merchant bankers. Retail trade has always been not only more fluid, but more in need of close and continuous adaptation to change. As the specialized uses have pulled apart it has not only developed its own clear urban regions but remained the matrix in which the remainder are placed.

Further reading

A general volume on retailing is:

DAVIS, D. 1966: *A History of Shopping*. London and Toronto.

However most histories of retailing deal with more recent times, two examples are:

ADBURGHAM, A. 1964: *Shops and Shopping 1800–1914*. London.

ALEXANDER, A. 1970: *Retailing in England during the Industrial Revolution*. London.

There are few geographical studies but two are:

SHAW, G. 1978: Patterns and processes in the geography of retail change with special reference to Kingston upon Hull. *Univ. of Hull Occ. Papers in Geography*, No. 24.

SHAW, G. and WILD, M.T. 1979: Retail patterns in the Victorian city. *Transactions of the Institute of British Geographers*, New Series, 4, 278–91.

Even studies of the development of the central area over a considerable time span are limited. The most widely quoted are those by Ward:

WARD, D. 1966: The Industrial Revolution and the emergence of Boston's central business district. *Economic Geography*. 42, 152–71.

WARD, D. 1971: *Cities and Immigrants. A Geography of Change in Nineteenth Century America*. New York.

A further paper is:

CARTER, H. and ROWLEY, G. 1966: The morphology of the central business district of Cardiff. *Transactions of the Institute of British Geographers*. 38, 119–34.

The most detailed study of a medieval town in terms of the distribution of functions at the centre is:

BIDDLE, M. (ed.) 1976: *Winchester in the Early Middle Ages. An Edition and Discussion of the Winton Domesday*. Oxford.

A much more limited but valuable study is:

LANGTON, J. 1977: Late medieval Gloucester: some data from a rental of 1455. *Transactions of the Institute of British Geographers*, New Series, 2, 259–77.

A paper which covers the transition from medieval to modern is:

VANCE, J.E. 1971: Land assignment in pre-capitalist, capitalist and post-capitalist cities. *Economic Geography* 47, 101–20.

while the role of the market hall is discussed in:

SCOLA, R. 1975: Food markets and shops in Manchester 1770–1870. *Journal of Historical Geography* 1, 153–67.

There is a vast amount of material on London but the best summary is still:

SPATE, O.H.K. 1948: The growth of London, AD 1660–1800, Chap. XIV in DARBY, H.C (ed.), *An Historical Geography of England Before 1800*.

The impact of railways is best dealt with in:

KELLETT, J.R. 1969: *The Impact of Railways on Victorian Cities*. London,

while the skyscraper is considered in:

GOTTMANN, J. 1967: Why the skyscraper? In ELDREDGE, H.W. (ed.) *Taming Megalopolis* (New York), Vol. 1, Chap. 10, 429–47. The paper was first published in *Geographical, Review* 56, 1966.

9

The Social Areas of the City: 1 The Pre-Industrial City

1 Introduction

Any review of the social areas of the city prior to the onset of industrialization must be largely conditioned by Gideon Sjoberg's book *The Pre-industrial City* published in 1960. Although few critics have accepted his delineation of the characteristics of a pre-industrial city without considerable reservation or modification (Wheatley, 1963), it still remains an acceptable point of departure. Sjoberg's work was wide-ranging; it included all aspects of the economic and social life of the city while its subtitle – 'past and present' – indicated that it was not in any way solely an historical study; rather the reverse for much of the exemplification was from the more accessible evidence from the undeveloped countries of the contemporary world.

From the viewpoint of the historical geographer the critical chapter is the fourth on 'Demography and ecology' and especially that section of it headed 'spatial arrangements'. In that section Sjoberg begins by stressing the presence of a defensive wall as a critical structuring element and then proceeds to discuss the internal arrangements in relation to it. He proposes 'three patterns of land use wherein the non-industrial city contrasts with the industrialized type'. These are:

1 The pre-eminence of the central area over the periphery, especially as portrayed in the distribution of social classes.
2 The existence of certain finer spatial differences according to ethnic, occupational and family ties.
3 A low incidence of functional differentiation elsewhere in the city.

2 Social status and intra-city locations

At this stage (2) and (3) can be set aside for later consideration and attention devoted to the first which has become the most widely quoted, largely because, in simplest terms, it demonstrates the existence of the reverse of the accepted modern or industrial pattern of social areas in cities where the inner city is in decay and suburbia is the home of those of highest social status. Sjoberg elaborates his proposition thus:

> The pre-industrial city's central area is notable . . . as the chief residence of the elite. Here are the luxurious

dwellings, though these often face inward, presenting a blank wall to the street – a reflection of the demand for privacy and the need to minimize ostentation in a city teeming with 'the underprivileged'. The disadvantaged members of the city fan out toward the periphery, with the very poorest and the outcasts in the suburbs, the farthest removed from the centre. Houses toward the city's fringes are small, flimsily constructed, often one-room, hovels into which whole families crowd. (Sjoberg, 1960, 97–8)

Sjoberg adds that still farther out and well beyond the limits of the city, the elite would possess country houses and estates.

The explanation for this situation is twofold, partly related to the need to control a power base, partly related to the technology of transport. If the elite were to maintain their absolute control long before representative democracy had come into being, then it could only be done by having 'ready access to the headquarters of the governmental, religious and educational organizations. The highly valued residence, then, is where the fullest advantage may be taken of the city's strategic facilities; in turn these latter have come to be tightly bunched for the convenience of the elite' (Sjoberg, 1960, 99). Much more pertinent in Sjoberg's view was transport and the need to minimize the need to travel locally at a time when it was slow, uncomfortable and inconvenient. Moreover, in a combination of both aspects of the explanation, residence outside the defences meant exposure to attack, while the journey into the city was itself dangerous. It followed that the elite sought the security, comfort and control of the centre, thereby relegating the lower orders to the urban periphery.

There were obvious disadvantages of central residence even at an early period. These were the twin dangers which were to assail London in the 1660s, plague and fire. The former could be avoided by fleeing to country houses, the latter became the main cause of the earliest legislation relating to building.

At this point it is useful to consider the generalizations that have been set out at a fairly gross level. This can be done by reviewing two sets of evidence. The first is a study of Exeter by W. G. Hoskins which was published in 1935 long before *The Pre-industrial City* was published and which is not referred to by Sjoberg (Hoskins, 1935). The second is the evidence on the nature of early suburbs to which some reference has already been made in chapter 7.

Hoskins's book, *Industry, Trade and People in Exeter 1688–1800'*, was derived from a study of the woollen industry of southwest England. However, the greater breadth of treatment of the city of Exeter allowed the inclusion of a chapter on 'The people of Exeter' which was based on the Hearth Tax Assessment of 1671–2 (see chapter 4, p. 83). It is perhaps necessary briefly to repeat that the tax dates from an Act of 1662 which was introduced to supplement the governmental expenses of Charles II. 'The tax created an annual due of 2 shillings for every hearth . . . unless the occupant was exempted on the grounds of poverty. Exemptions were made for those whose poverty already excused them from paying poor and church rates or whose house was less than 20 shillings per annum' (Howell, 1972, 1). A large number of hearths implied a large house and hence a wealthy household; the exemptions from poverty indicated the poorest households. Where the evidence is extant and sufficiently detailed (and it is not always so) the distribution of wealth within a city can be mapped either by street or by parish. This Hoskins pioneered in 1935 and the map of Exeter in Figure 9.1 is based on that in his book together with other statistical evidence given there in tabular form. The mean number of hearths per household for the city was 2.59 but there were 62 with over 10. The average number of hearths per household on a parish basis varied from 5.00 in St Stephen to 1.80 in St Sidwell, the mean being 3.1 and the standard deviation 1.07. There were five parishes out of the total of 20 with an average number over mean plus one standard deviation and if two additional parishes are added, where the figures were only a fraction below that total (4.17 and 4.09), then Hoskins's own words can be used to present the conclusion.

> The seven richest parishes form a compact nucleus in the heart of the city, though mainly to the eastern side of the Carfax, while the five poorest parishes all lie against or outside the line of the medieval walls. In the rich heart of the city we have a population of merchants and craftsmen, with a flavouring of 'esquires' who have, for the most part, made their money in trade, and it was from here that the city was governed and had been governed from some unknown time in the past. . . . On the other hand, the outer parishes, larger in area and far more populous, consisted for the most part of a labouring population dependent on the trades and crafts and personal service of the city. In St Sidwell, Holy Trinity and All Hallows-on-the-Wall, for example, more than half the families in each parish occupied houses with only one hearth, and very few families had more than two. (Hoskins, 1935, 116)

The actual percentages of households with more than two hearths were 12.4, 22 and 19.7 respectively, compared with 84.4 per cent and 66.7 per cent for the two central parishes of St Martin and St Petrock.

Here, then, is apparent evidence of the elite located at the centre and the poor at the margin set out long before the generalized presentation by Sjoberg. Moreover, in the reference to the government of the city, and in the fact that the Cathedral Cross was amongst the 'seven richest parishes', is a suggestion of that element of control which Sjoberg was to put forward.

The nature of the urban margin in pre-industrial time has already been partly considered in chapter 7. There the suburbs of medieval and early modern towns were identified as being characterized by the poorest sections of the population. In this chapter the work cited on Exeter by Hoskins has given the same result. In his general discussion on suburbs Dyos quotes evidence from Chaucer's 'Canterbury Tales' (Dyos, 1961, 20).

> 'Where dwelle ye? if it to telle be'.
> 'In the suburbes of a toun', quod he,
> 'Lurkynge in hernes and in lane blynde,
> Where-as thise robbours and thise theves, by Kynde
> Holden hir pryvee, fereful residence'.

This adds the associated features of the early suburbs as areas of lawlessness and violence. The reasons for such a condition are not difficult to enumerate. The suburb was outside the wall and, therefore, outside the protected and guarded section of the community, especially at night. Possibly it was also outside the jurisdiction of the town and of the control it operated. Again, in some cases, the suburb was the area where aliens without the right to hold land in the city were segregated and where the transitory elements of the population were lodged. It was also the area to which obnoxious, polluting and dangerous trades and industries, such as tanning and metal working were relegated. For all these reasons the suburb developed a less desirable character hence there gravitated to it both vice, thus avoiding urban control, and entertainment, particularly that of the more cruel sort. If the elite exercised their control and organized their government from the centre then as a straightforward matter of distance decay, a minimum of control and the least effective government occurred at the urban periphery.

A wider range of evidence to strengthen and broaden that so far presented can now be introduced. For Britain this has been done by Langton by adding consideration of the distribution of wealth in Dublin and Newcastle to that of Exeter (Figure 9.1) and by reference to a study of London by Glass (Langton, 1975; Glass, 1968). Langton concludes that the maps reproduced in Figure 9.1

> display strikingly similar patterns. In all cases houses of various sizes were unevenly distributed, and quite marked peaks occurred in each city. In all three, these peaks were located in proximity to the castle, either between the castle and the main place of worship as in Exeter and Dublin or, as in Newcastle, between the castle keep and the Guildhall. This location did not correspond with the main 'Market Square' or place of business. Indeed, such topographical 'centres' did not always exist in pre-nineteenth-century cities. . . .

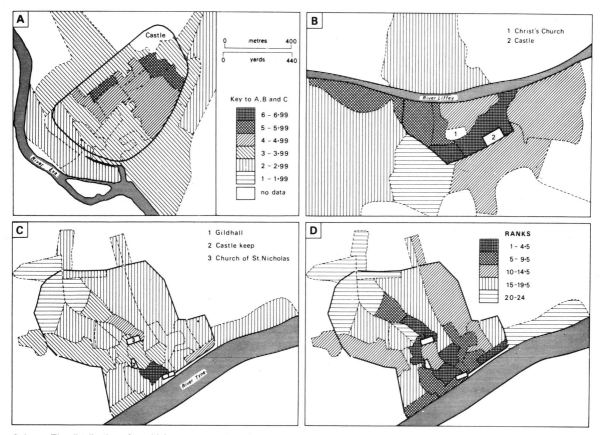

9.1. The distribution of wealth in some seventeenth-century British cities. A–C: average numbers of hearths per taxed household in Exeter in 1671–72, Dublin in 1671, and Newcastle in 1665, respectively. D: the ranks of Newcastle wards in 1665 on an index combining the average number of hearths per house, the percentage of tax payers in each ward, and the percentage of houses with six or more hearths (after Langton).

These patterns ostensibly go a long way to corroborate Sjoberg's hypotheses. So, too, does the prevalence of a sharp decline in wealth away from the peaks toward the walls or outskirts of the cities. . . . An entirely similar pattern is portrayed by the map of London prepared from 1695 data by Glass. (Langton, 1975, 8–10)

Glass concluded that 'London was an area with a fairly distinctive pre-industrial topography. The proportions of upper-status households were higher in the centre, and the lower-status households showed the greatest relative frequency on the periphery and in many parishes without the walls' (Glass, 1968, 583).

Langton concludes, 'Thus, three of the five largest English cities of the late seventeenth century, and Dublin, which was second to London in size in the British Isles as a whole, all displayed patterns of wealth distribution similar to those postulated by Sjoberg' (Langton, 1975, 10). The same can be said for very much smaller, provincial towns (Carter and Wheatley, 1979).

Work by Viggo Hansen on the pre-industrial city in Denmark (Hansen, 1976) can be used to extend this analysis to Europe. Here two medieval planned towns, Assens and Faborg, were examined by reference to land registers and the two Danish censuses of 1769 and 1787. Given the available detail, Hansen was able to plot data at the household level as against that of the parish or ward employed in the English examples. From the occupational evidence of the census Hansen divided the town population into four social classes. From his analysis of Assens he concludes, 'it is clear that Class 1 plays a dominant role in the main street Ostergarde, . . . where it occupied more than 25 per cent of all addresses. Class 2 is more dominant in the back lane to the north of the main street, where more than 50 per cent of the occupants belong to the artisans' class, as is also the case in the north–south running street. Class 3 dominates the street running to the port, where many seamen lived, while Class 4 covers most households in the back lane to the south. . . . Here the poor . . . lived on land belonging to the church' (Hansen, 1976, 55).

Two conclusions can be abstracted from this study. The first is the reiteration of the dominance of the wealthy at the centre. The second is that a scale element is added. There was segregation by social status in the pre-industrial city and at the crudest scale this was centre over against periphery. But at the finer scale, when a plot is made at the household level, the segregation appears at the finer front street–back street scale. Even in Exeter in the central parishes there was a representation of the less well off. Sixteen out of the 60 households in the parish of St Stephen had only one or two hearths and the same was true for 14 out of 42 in St Petrock. It is crucially important to comprehend the significance of scale when dealing with segregation. It would be totally wrong to think of the central areas which have been discussed as exclusively the preserve of the elite, indeed the elite needed a good array of labourers and servants close at hand. It would also be incorrect to reject the concept of segregation in the pre-industrial town because of the presence of the poor near the city centre. In the end it is a matter of scale and 'visibility'.

A further dimension can be added to this discussion, as well as a wider geographical area, by considering an example from the USA in John Swauger's study of Pittsburgh's residential pattern in 1815 (Swauger, 1978). Although the date is somewhat late the author maintains the city can be considered as pre-industrial in its characteristics, particularly since although manufacturing was significant it was carried on by independent artisans rather than in factories which had only just begun to appear and its population was a mere 8000. The communication system, or more precisely the quality of the roads, was of the lowest order; it was a walking city.

For the purpose of analysis Swauger divides the city into core and periphery and then subdivides each into three districts. The data are derived from a directory of 1815 compiled by an attorney. James M. Riddle's Directory contains 'the heads of families and persons in business' and is not the most ideal of sources. It certainly under-represented those in the lower social groups and presumably omitted slaves, indentured servants, the unemployed and the transient. 1314 households were named and to 1140 of these Swauger can assign an occupation and hence place them in seven 'occupational ranks'. The residential distribution of each of these groups between the core and the periphery is shown in Figure 9.2. Reviewing this evidence Swauger concludes, 'In sum, Pittsburgh's residential pattern in 1815 approached closely to the theoretical model of the non-industrial city. Classes sorted themselves out according to their rank, segregation being most striking at the extreme ends of the social scale. Elite citizens appropriated central housing sites, compelling middle and particularly lower-class Pittsburghers to locate on the town's outskirts' (Swauger, 1978, 274–5).

There are, however, two exceptions. The first, and the most obvious, can be seen in Figure 9.2 where it is apparent that those of private means were over-represented in the periphery where 61 per cent of the independently wealthy chose to live. Swauger's interpretation is that 'what set independently wealthy citizens apart from the rest of the upper stratum was that they did not work. No matter where business and professional people would have liked to live, inconvenient transportation left them little choice but to live in or near their job sites in the core. Because people of private means did not have to travel to

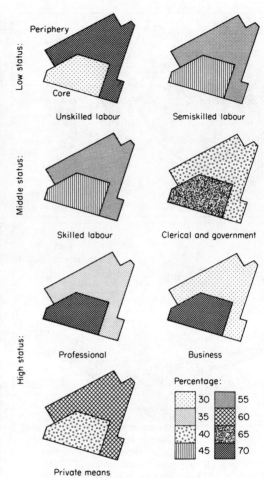

9.2.   Pittsburgh, 1815: the residential distribution of occupational groups between core and periphery (after Swauger).

places of work daily, they were comparatively free to exercise their residential preferences. And the housing options they chose reflected not the non-industrial elite's desire for central residence but the industrial elite's high valuation of peripheral homes' (Swauger, 1978, 275). It should be stressed that although those in the higher social group occupied a peripheral location this did not mean lack of segregation, for those of private means and the unskilled occupied very different districts of the periphery.

The other exception, however, by no means confirms Swauger's general conclusion which asserts the dominant role of transport and mobility. Out of the seven clergy listed in the Directory six did not live adjacent to their churches – 'long journeys to work were the rule amongst them'. Five lived on the outskirts, evidently willing to face the problem of travel for the benefit of social cachet. Seemingly class identification for the group out-weighed transportation problems.

This American example again confirms the broad

hypothesis with which this chapter started but some reservations remain over the interpretation of the necessary minimization of the journey to work as the main determinant, 'that the central location of the elite is best explained by a desire to avoid tiresome journeys to their jobs rather than by any high valuation of central housing' (Swauger, 1978, 277). Already by 1815 there was a significant manufacturing element in Pittsburgh, an incipient factory basis, which might well have been enough to push out those who had not urgent necessity to retain central contact. What this study shows is, perhaps, not the classic pre-industrial city but the first phase of transition from that category. Again, a much closer consideration of the political circumstances is needed – who controlled the city? Certainly at this date in Britain, before the Reform Act, the oligarchical nature of urban government demanded that residential presence should give weight to a control which was inherited from the medieval period. Once that control was lost to the democratic process, however attenuated, then the attractions of central residence were greatly diminished.

Some confirmation of Swauger's general thesis and some further elucidation of change can be derived from an example greatly contrasted in geographical location and cultural background. St Petersburg in the eighteenth and nineteenth century reveals at first a classical pattern of the Sjoberg type. After the fires in the city of 1736–7 a central area, the Admiralteyskaya district, had been reserved for the nobility and courtiers. In contrast, the periphery was characterized by low social status. 'In the peripheral boroughs . . . external appearances provides a much more reliable reflection of interior conditions and probable social-class composition. For instance, to the east across the Bol'shaya Neva was Okhta, a shabby suburb peopled almost entirely by peasants. To the north, on the same side of the river was the district of Vyborg. . . . Anybody conscious of his social position would not have considered living there: "Vyborg! Why, they say wolves roam the streets there in winter! It's such a dull place – a wilderness, no one lives there"'! (Bater, 1976, 80). The quotations from Goncharov's novel give an apt summary of why those of high social status did not occupy suburban locations in the pre-industrial city.

The implication of simple segregation, however, is not a true one. The initial low densities of population and the demand for services from the nobility, soon sucked those low in the social scale into these central areas and in the late 1820s Bater considers that 'admixture of classes, rather than segregation was quite evident even in the so-called fashionable areas . . . social-class heterogeneity, not homogeneity was the norm in what was generally regarded as the "court end of town" ' (Bater, 1976, 79–80). This was, however, related to a different scale of segregation which operated within buildings. The poorest occupied the cellars, commerce and craft industry the ground floor, while those of high status effectively isolated themselves on the second and upper floors. Bater presents a schematic view of change between 1760 and 1910 (Figure 9.3) and in interpreting it he writes that by 1860

the central city had been invaded by the lower classes, cellars and garrets were being converted. . . . These were still the preferred residential areas; . . . however, as the model shows, the territory so assigned a century earlier has been dismembered with the intrusion of industrial-commercial functions and their attendant work-forces . . . [By] . . . the early 1900s upper-class residential areas were no more than discontinuous pockets within the urban environment. They consisted of areas of living space on the second, third, and sometimes fourth floors of the built environment. They tended to be more ubiquitous than spatially segregated – and so, therefore, were their affluent occupants. Cellars had long since been occupied by the poor. A fairly rigid social-class system helped to maintain a sense of place amidst the seeming confusion of classes and activities. (Bater, 1976, 406–7)

Although following this example has taken the argument into the late nineteenth century which the next chapter will consider, it has also revealed apparently a situation where there is little suburbanward movement of the elite because of the absence of an effective transport system. Considering the social unrest and the extent of criminal activity one might have expected a strong tendency to move out. But two other factors held the elite in the centre. The first was that they left the city altogether in the summer for country residences so that a form of seasonal suburbanization made conventional suburbanization irrelevant. The second was the nature of the elite, still made up of the aristocracy and the landed gentry, who could afford to ignore the pestilential summer conditions of a city to a far greater degree than the merchants and traders of the Victorian city in England, but who still needed to exert authority in control of the centre. In short, although at first it is possible to argue for an interpretation related to transport systems, further consideration throws up a whole nexus of influences all related to the nature of the pre-industrial city.

3 Occupations and intra-city locations

This introduction of an aristocratic elite as against a mercantile interest is an appropriate prelude to the second way in which land-use in the pre-industrial city contrasted with 'the industrialized type' according to Sjoberg. This was the existence of what he termed finer spatial differences according to ethnicity, occupational and family ties. The first two of these are certainly capable of assessment.

That occupational bases for intra-urban spatial differentiation existed has already been shown in the consideration of the evolution of the central area when the tendency for trade groupings to occur was observed. Out of this two critical questions arise. The first is whether the elite, which has been shown to have occupied the centre of the city, was made up of an independent patriciate as implied in the St Petersburg example, or was it simply composed of the wealthiest merchants? The second is, if

Schematic and dynamic cross-sections of socio-economic functions

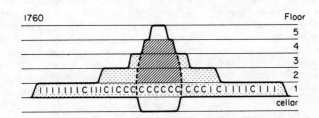

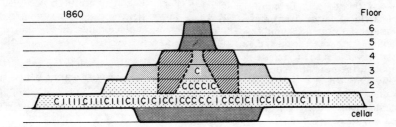

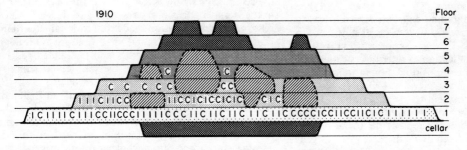

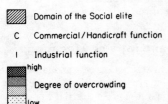

Domain of the Social elite

C   Commercial / Handicraft function

I   Industrial function

Degree of overcrowding (high / low)

9.3.   St Petersburg: schematic cross-section of socio-economic characteristics 1760–1910 (after Bater).

the latter was the case, did these merchants hive off from the distinctive trade areas to form a separate core to which success and wealth were the essential entreés? To some extent the answer to these questions lies in what would now be termed 'the class structure' but there considerable difficulties reside. Susan Reynolds in her book on 'English Medieval Towns', writes,

A society stratified by wealth is different from one stratified by groups defined by their occupations or their functions in a market economy. Though the social stratification in medieval towns may well have been formed by an unconscious muddle of both principles, we shall not be helped to understand it by using merchant, craftsman and servant as synonyms of rich, middling and poor. Other factors, too, influenced contemporaries' views of the social hierarchy. Long settlement probably conferred prestige on a family and the influence of noble values helps lend weight to descent and land-ownership. What exacerbated class divisions and class consciousness seems to have been less the direct conflict of the differing economic interests of merchants and craftsmen than the control over local taxation and government which municipal independence gave to the dominant men in a town, whether they were craftsmen, merchants or landowners. (Reynolds, 1977, 76)

In a way this begs the question since it becomes essential to identify the group exercising 'control', for if they were independent of particular trades they effectively constituted an urban patriciate. Again, in discussion, Reynolds writes, 'At the end of the period London had a prosperous elite, who were distinguished from their fellow citizens by wealth, municipal influence and less measurable elements of social prestige, rather than by their practice of any particular trade. The same may hold good for the twelfth century, and even for the eleventh too for all we know, though whether as many members of the elite were then merchants is less likely: at present it cannot be proved either way' (Reynolds, 1977, 78).

The need to enter these rather muddy waters is reinforced by the proposal of a pre-capitalist city which has been made by Vance (1971). This has already been introduced in chapter 8 in considering the evolution of the city centre. Essentially Vance argues for the holding rather than the owning of land and access to guild membership derived from land holding. Through the guilds the merchants dominated. What Vance is working towards is a rejection of the notion of an urban patriciate, alienated from trade, and exercising influence by way of descent and nobility. This is in line with standard views as to control in medieval towns. Vance tends to create obscurity by accepting that the wealthiest merchants tended to constitute an effective patriciate so that, in effect, a central, controlling and, what is more important, residing group emerged. This tends to vitiate his main contention that the pre-industrial (or pre-capitalist) city consisted of a series of occupationally distinct areas in which all groups (or classes) concerned with the activity resided so that there were no class-based sections of the city. This matter is dealt with in Langton's study which has already been quoted (p. 172) (Langton, 1975). There, like Vance, he argues that Sjoberg proposed an elite divorced from the economic functioning of the city which dominated its government and occupied the high-status core – a situation which might be identified in pre-industrial St Petersburg. Langton attempts to show that such was not the case in Newcastle, but given the comments by Reynolds cited above or the study by Hibbert on 'The origins of the medieval town patriciate' or the qualifications of Vance, the whole exercise seems chimerical. True, if the Pirenne thesis introduced in chapter 2 is accepted then the incoming traders of the medieval town were set apart from those already in occupation. Perhaps there was a true feudal town to set against the pre-industrial city. But the evidence is so tenuous that there is little hope of a clear answer at this stage. One can only quote Christopher Brooke,

It has long been disputed whether the patricians who came to rule the cities of Europe in the central Middle Ages (to adapt Lady Bracknell's words), were born in the purple of commerce or had risen from the ranks of the aristocracy – or as the problem was more commonly phrased, were the sons of the feudal nobility or self-made merchants. For two reasons, the problem

thus stated is now seen to be quite unreal. First of all, we only know the origin of a tiny percentage of the patricians of the crucial period between 1050 and 1150, and these mainly from a few cities, possibly not typical . . . . Secondly, it takes too little account of the pattern of economic life in this age. (Brooke, 1975, 77–8)

That is, there was a complex mixing of the two groups, even if they were ever separate.

Langton's Newcastle study, pitched as it is so very much later in the late seventeenth century, seems to have little relevance to the central and insoluble problem of the urban patriciate as far as Britain is concerned. But his analysis of the location of the practitioners of trades and crafts is most pertinent to Vance's ideas. He concludes that an analysis of the 1665 Hearth Tax returns shows that occupational groups were concentrated and segregated and that finer distinctions existed within broad mercantile, victualling, shipping and manufacturing quarters. Newcastle, he maintains, was 'four sectored' and that there was no single centre about which all activities clustered. But he also arrives at a further point from his analysis: 'It seems, then, that the core areas of the wealthier trades contained the wealthier members of those trades and, in addition, "creamed off" the wealthiest practitioners of crafts whose members were generally poorer' (Langton, 1975, 21).

At this point what must be one of the most thorough and distinguished of analyses of pre-modern towns can introduced, that of Coventry by Phythian-Adams. His analysis of the city in the early sixteenth century is based on two unique 'censuses' of 1520 and 1523 and a rental of 1522. Collation enables the houses in each ward of the city to be classified into three groups based on their rental values. Reviewing the resultant histogram (Figure 9.4a) Phythian-Adams concludes:

The proportion of dwellings paying rents of over 12s tends to corroborate the usual image of the classic pre-industrial social pattern. The top four wards, with over 50 per cent of their houses in this category, were all clustered together towards the centre of the city [Figure 9.4b]. Bailey Lane ward contained the administrative and ritual centre (and nineteenth-century sketches show part of it dominated by three-storeyed medieval houses), Cross Cheaping, the major food market. Southford ward was restricted to the important east–west axial road, while Earl Street ward . . . although similarly biased, had a long tail of ever-more modest housing out towards the city wall. . . . None of the top four wards gave onto an important city gate: all the others did. (Phythian-Adams, 1979, 165)

He then goes on to stress that there was a considerable mixture of the lower classes in these wards and variation in the peripheral wards, a situation already considered in this chapter in relation to scale.

Phythian-Adams was particularly concerned to examine the disastrous decline in the fortunes of Coventry – 'the desolation of a city' – in the years about 1550. Two further pieces of evidence forming part of his argument can be abstracted for the purpose of this chapter. The first concerns institutions and social change. He argues that 'during the three decades following the short-term crisis there can be little doubt that most formal institutions in the city experienced a contraction of membership and a distortion of function, while some were abolished altogether' (Phythian-Adams, 1979, 269). Thus in 1534 the last banquet was held by the Corpus Christi Guild. 'It was certainly patronized to an unusual extent by practically all the aldermanic elite of the city. . . . It was a meeting that symbolized the end of an era' (Phythian-Adams, 1979, 269). A year later the Corpus Christi Guild was united into the Trinity Guild. 'At a single stroke, the social age-compartmentalization at the upper end of society and the traditional sequence of senior civic office-holding were swept away'

(Phythian-Adams, 1979, 270). The second piece of evidence relates to urban ceremony for with these changes went 'the complete collapse of the ceremonial system as an ideal mirror of [the] community. . . . As outdoor ceremonies vanished, and the cathedral was demolished, so too did the ritual centre of the city lose its significance' (Phythian-Adams, 1979, 275). As this occurred so the culture which emerged 'was no longer a public, visual affair concerning all those who participated or cared to watch; but a private matter for the individual citizen in the furnishing or decoration of his house, his reading matter and his worship' (Phythian-Adams, 1979, 278).

This analysis has been quoted at some length since if it is to be universally applied it portrays a period of urban change which has strong spatial implications. The abandonment of public ceremony – the medieval mirror shattered – together with the transformation of the higher echelons of society, suggest that there must have been a falling off in the significance of the centre, a feature which Phythian-Adams quite explicitly maintains. Moreover, as culture becomes private and of the home, rather than public and of the city streets, so the incentive for central residence falls away. The home might under these circumstances preferably be in country surroundings. Given the limited mobility this was impossible, but the changes which Phythian-Adams sets out might well mark a shift from a ritual centre dominated by

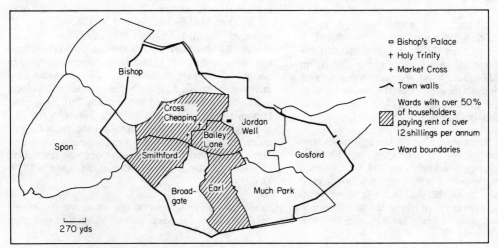

9.4.   (a) Coventry: ward-ranking by proportions of householders in each ward paying specific categories of rents in 1522–3.
Numbers of inhabited houses categorized according to three broad rental valuations in 1522 and expressed as percentages of all household in 1523.
(1) Houses valued at and under 6s rent *p.a.*
(2) Houses valued at 6s 8d to 12s rent *p.a.* inclusively
(3) Houses valued at *more* than 12s rent *p.a.*
Notes: Freeholds have been apportioned proportionately between (2) and (3) only.
    (b) The distribution of wards with over 50 per cent over 12s per annum.

an urban elite, a true patriciate, to a series of commercial sectors dominated by mercantile interests. They already existed in Coventry. 'In the old Earl's half which had thus been historically excluded from the traditional marketing area, the emphasis was more on the wool, textile and clothing industries. Not only did this area contain the site of the sheep fair . . . but it could boast the Wool Hall and the Drapery, that vast cloth market' (Phythian-Adams, 1979, 160). There were other specialized sectors.

All this evidence suggests that the model derived from consideration of the central area in chapter 8 is acceptable. Trade or craft sectors with their own markets and members' associations were characteristic. What is more difficult to identify is the role and nature of the centre. Possibly many medieval cities had been characterized by a patriciate, an elite which dominated a public life which was acted out at a ritual centre (Phythian-Adams, 1972). But late-medieval decline and economic change brought about a radical restructuring. The centre, therefore, lost its ritual function and became slowly translated into a commercial district. Residential prestige moved to the private houses of the merchant sectors and the situation identified by Langton in Newcastle develops.

At this point it is instructive to turn to the New World and a study of ante-bellum Charleston. John P. Radford (1979) abstracted a 10 per cent sample of occupational data from the 1860 census manuscripts and classified them into seven categories. Four of these are shown in Figure 9.5 by means of frequencies plotted for six concentric zones. The gradients, in general, conform to those predicted by the Sjoberg model, even though slaves

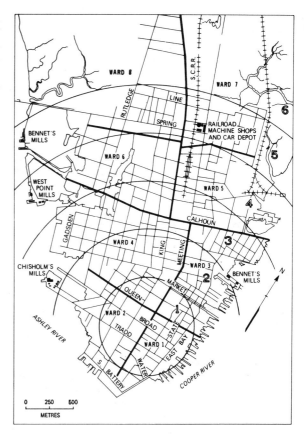

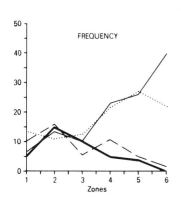
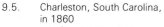
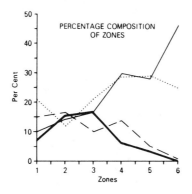

9.5. Charleston, South Carolina, in 1860
 (a) General plan and distance zones
 (b) Distribution of occupational status groups by concentric distance zones (see 9.5a)

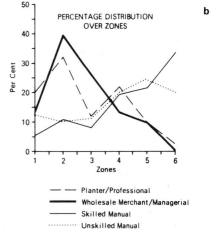

— — — Planter/Professional
——— Wholesale-Merchant/Managerial
——— Skilled Manual
·········· Unskilled Manual

are largely excluded since occupational data for them do not exist. The sole anomaly is the interruption of the downward trend for planters and professional occupations in zone 4. This is explained by an area chosen for summer residences, many of them permanently occupied. Radford concludes:

> occupational-status gradients from centre to periphery can thus be demonstrated in Charleston in 1860, but they are less sharply defined than in the Sjoberg model. Poor as well as rich lived in the centre of the city, especially in the area near the Cooper River wharves. Equally, some members of the upper class lived away from the central area, notably on carefully selected sites close to the Ashley River. As a result, the occupational gradient from west to east across the Lower Wards was almost as marked as that outwards from the city centre. (Radford, 1979, 400)

Further than this, however, Radford notes the significance of the symbolic centre where the Court House, City Hall, Guard House and Church were located at the intersection of Broad Street and Meeting Street. 'Here then was the nerve-centre of Charleston, quite distinct from the mercantile centre near Broad and East Bay Streets. It was the orientation point for Charleston's residents and the area which, during a period of intensifying sectional antagonisms and racial threats, became a symbol of order and continuity in the minds of the city rulers' (Radford, 1979, 401). The important feature which emerges is the continued dominance of the non-mercantile planter-professional elite over the merchant class which echoes some of the features discerned in the analysis of European cities.

4 Ethnicity in the pre-industrial city

The other element creating finer differences according to Sjoberg was ethnicity, but it is one which is difficult to analyse in any detail given the lack of data. That the pre-industrial city was characterized by distinctive ethnic enclaves is indisputable, for it was in such a condition that the ghetto itself came into being. The segregation of the Jews can in part be considered not a result of external pressure but due to needs arising from their own religious customs, particularly their own ways of preparing food, the demands of attendance at a synagogue and the need to take part in the various aspects of communal life. Their migrations after the diaspora can be compared to those of the Irish in nineteenth-century Britain or the blacks in twentieth-century America, and the formation of distinctive urban areas was as a result of much the same process. But the Jews became subject to harsher, legalized conditions which institutionalized the ghetto. The origin of the word itself is disputed although it seems there are now two possibilities. The first is derived from the relations between the Jews and the Venetian state at the beginning of the sixteenth century. Venice was prepared to tolerate the Jews in return for the financial advantages they brought through taxation, but constant

friction and periodical attacks followed and the solution seemed to be in a designated and protected area.

> The practice of establishing Jewish quarters separated from Christian dwellings by actual physical barriers was not without medieval precedents. . . . But it fell to the Venetians in 1516 to contribute the word ghetto to the vocabulary of persecution. . . . Zaccaria Dolfin, a member of the Collegie, referred on 26 March 1516 to Francisan warnings about the 'corruption of the state' . . . which would inevitably ensue if Jews were still entertained in the city. He suggested that they be enclosed in the area which was already – before Jewish occupation – known as the Ghetto Nuovo, the new 'foundry' in Venetian dialect. This was 'like a fortress', with a single entrance that could be guarded at night. . . . It could therefore perform the double function of protecting the Jews from violence and plunder, and of enabling an effective curfew to be imposed upon them. (Pullan, 1971, 486–7)

If this is the origin of the word ghetto then it appropriately stands for the distinctive nature of ethnic areas in pre-industrial cities. It is worth adding that the word could also possibly be derived from the Hebrew word 'get' meaning divorce or separation (Encyclopaedia Judaica, 1971 (7), 542).

The degree of segregation varied considerably and in many cities the Jewish presence was too limited to provide distinctive areas. In British cities the concentration is sometimes preserved in the word 'Jewry', as in Old Jewry in the City of London. In Europe, however, the areas were larger and more clearly marked. Perhaps the most well known of the ghettos was that at Frankfurt-on-Main. The Jews had early settled in that significant commercial centre initially under the protection of the emperor. They were subject, however, to periodic pogroms, the worst in 1349, when, blamed for the Black Death, the whole community was massacred. Eventually in 1462, partly as a result of demands from the emperor and even the pope, in order to ensure their security, they were transferred to a specially constructed street, the Judengasse (Figure 9.6). This was situated in a sparsely inhabited portion of the city, far removed from the rest of the inhabitants, on the border between the old and the new city, on a part of the dried-up moat which ran along the wall of the old city' (Wirth, 1928, 42). The Judengasse was enclosed with walls and entered by gates so that it formed a clearly defined and discrete area of the city. There were 110 registered inhabitants in 1463 and the number had increased to 900 by 1569 and 3000 by 1610. But since the ghetto was enclosed by walls there was no opportunity for expansion, with the result that as the population grew storeys and back premises were added to houses which were subdivided. The general location is shown on Figure 7.3, p. 133 from a map of Frankfurt of 1572. The map is derived from a woodcut by Hans Grave dated 1552. Figure 9.6 shows an enlargement of the Judengasse where the building on to the backs of the houses, the walls and the gates are clearly identifiable. At the peak of its prosperity this small area not only produced some of the most famous of financial families, the Rothschilds, for example, but became a centre of Jewish learning. It suffered attack and devastation in 1614–16 and was destroyed by fire in 1711, but it was not until 1798 that the prohibition which maintained the ghetto was lifted.

'The typical ghetto of the sixteenth century', wrote Wirth, 'is a densely populated, walled-in area usually found near the arteries of commerce or in the vicinity of a market' (Wirth, 1928, 51). The location characteristic is epitomized in the ghettos of Venice and Frankfurt. Away from the main core of settlement, they were symbolically set apart but still retained an adjacence to the centres of commercial activity.

5 Familism in the pre-industrial city

It will be recalled that Sjoberg noted that finer divisions of the city resulted not only from occupational grouping and ethnicity but also from 'family ties'. He does not, however, follow this up in an ecological context and his chapter VI, which deals with marriage and the family, is aspatial in its treatment. On the basis of social custom it would be difficult to envisage clear life-cycle contrasts. Pre-industrial societies were dominated by the extended family; a couple on marriage did not set up an independent home but most frequently resided with the husband's family. Moreover, marriages were arranged between families for dynastic purposes; love matches were a product of the social changes brought by industrialization (chapter 10, p. 186). The whole development of an elaborate social ritual in the nineteenth century marked the transformation (Davidoff, 1973) from one condition to another, but in the pre-modern city the old order was predominant. In consequence, the whole of the life-cycle was played out under the ancestral roof and not by means of a succession of moves to residences of a

different nature. If there were such moves they followed an *annual* pattern according to the seasons and took place between the many establishments which the elite families held. It would, therefore, be surprising to find an independent life-cycle component of spatial patterning; it would presumably be closely associated with social class and ethnic group.

This is generally confirmed by Phythian-Adams's evidence from Coventry, part of which is reproduced in Table 9.1.

There are considerable technical problems which must affect the conclusions which may be drawn from this table. One obvious conclusion is 'that certain broad factors were at work which varied markedly between the more affluent and the poorer wards (see Figure 9.4). From the marital statuses of the householders . . . it may be seen that proportionately far fewer households in the wealthier wards were headed by "single" people . . . and contained correspondingly less solitaries . . . than their poorer neighbours' (Phythian-Adams, 1979, 224). A scrutiny of the percentage of households with children, however suspect the figures, reveals the same general character. Again examination of households within rental groups bears out the same conclusion. The evidence is complex and tenuous, the interpretation necessarily tentative, but in general terms there is a clear confirmation that household size and family structure were closely related to social status. It is this close association of what in the factorial ecologies of present cities are regarded as independent dimensions which is the critical feature to stress.

Table 9.1: Coventry 1523. Children and factors influencing distributions and sizes of groups

Ward	Hhs. with 'children' %	Hhs. headed by single people %	One person Hhs. %	Couples without 'children' %	'Only' children as % of all children	Mean sizes of 'sibling' groups*
Bailey Lane	69.1	22.2	6.2	22.2	17.8	2.1
Cross Cheaping	63.0	24.9	11.0	25.4	19.1	2.1
Smithford	61.6	19.2	11.0	30.5	*29.3*	*1.8*
Earl	55.6	22.2	12.6	31.4	20.1	2.05
Gosford	*56.7*	15.9	8.3	*37.1*	*29.6*	*1.7*
Broad Gate	*42.5*	27.6	14.2	*52.2*	24.3	*1.9*
Much Park	*31.0*	26.5	14.8	*63.2*	19.4	*1.9*
Bishop	55.0	28.7	11.5	37.6	23.7	1.8
Spon	*42.9*	30.6	18.4	*50.0*	*36.4*	*1.6*
Jordan Well	*33.6*	25.9	19.6	*55.7*	*11.3*	*2.2*

(Suspect results are in italics)
*Relationships are not specified in the enumerations, and 'only' children have been included in the calculation of what are described, purely for convenience, as 'sibling' groups.

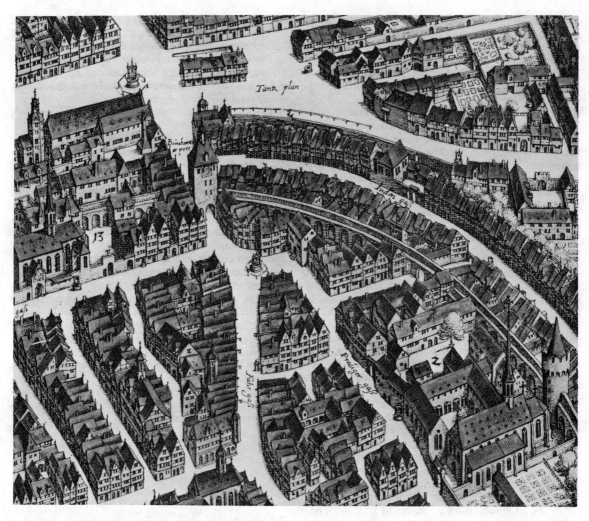

9.6.   Frankfurt-on-Main in 1628: The Judengasse can be
        clearly identified on this map. An earlier map (Fig. 7.3,
        p. 133) identifies the general location. The area
        enlarged here is from Matthaeus Marian's map in his
        Topografia of 1628.

6 Conclusion

This chapter began with Sjoberg's generalizations
concerning the ecological structure of what is called the
pre-industrial town. It has become evident that those
generalizations are only valid at the grossest level where
they are little more than self-evident. It has been a major
criticism of the concept of the pre-industrial city that it is
a rag-bag for all cities which are not manifestly
industrial. When the concept is extended across space
and time then such criticism is surely valid. The
difficulties which have arisen in attempting to reconcile
the earlier situation of cities under the control of an
aristocratic patriciate and the later dominance of a

mercantile oligarchy, indicates that there were a whole
series of situations which are but crudely compacted into
the notion of a pre-industrial city. Maybe it is possible to
envisage some sequence of change from the early
medieval city with its patrician elite and its ceremonies
and rituals, to a mercantile or pre-modern city with a
more spread pattern of wealth which was to constitute a
stage in the transformation to the modern city. During
this change the dimensions of modern social difference – class, family and ethnicity – became, in part,
divorced. What is evident is that that change itself was
gradual. Given the slow transformation and a whole
series of early situations with different socioeconomic
organization and internal structures then the simplicity
of a single model is of little value though the possibility of
an evolutionary sequence can be contemplated.

Further reading

Any consideration of the pre-industrial city must begin with Sjoberg, G. (1960): *The Pre-industrial City* (New York). A good deal of critical work has been devoted to the book. The most often quoted is that by Wheatley (1963) in the references, and:

THRUPP, S. 1961–2: The creativity of cities. *Comparative Studies in Society and History* IV, 61–2.

COX, O.C. 1964: The pre-industrial city reconsidered. *The Sociological Quarterly* 5, 133–44.

BURKE, P. 1975: Some reflections on the pre-industrial city. *Urban History Yearbook*, 13–21.

Two books which include relevant material are:

SCARGILL, D.I. 1979: *The Form of Cities* (London), Chap. 7, 182–203.

VANCE, J.E. 1977: *This Scene of Man. The Role and Structure of the City in the Geography of Western Civilization* (New York), especially Chap. 4, The expression of liberalism: the face of the medieval city and Chap. 6, The prince's capital and the merchant's town.

TIMMS, D.W.G. 1971: *The Urban Mosaic* (Cambridge) contains much interesting material but it is scattered throughout the book.

WEBER, M. 1958: *The City* trans. by MARTINDALE, D. and NEUWIRTH, G. (New York) should be read on the notion of an urban patriciate with the paper by Hibbert (1953) and the book by Reynolds (1977) providing basic material. A general study of English towns is:

CLARK, P. and SLACK, P. 1976: *English Towns in Transition 1500–1700*. London,

and a reader which includes a useful selection of essays is:

CLARK, P. 1976: *The Early Modern Town*. London.

ABRAMS, P. and WRIGLEY, E. A. (eds.) 1978: *Towns in Societies*. Cambridge,

has some useful essays including a version of the paper by Hibbert.

WIRTH, L. 1928: *The Ghetto*. Chicago,

was a classic study, reprinted in 1956, and still of value. It has Chapter 4 on 'Frankfurt: a typical ghetto' but the material in it was largely derived from:

PHILIPSON, D. 1894: *Old European Jewries*. Philadelphia.

There is an extensive literature on the Frankfurt ghetto and the best entrée is the article on Frankfurt in:

Encyclopaedia Judaica (1971), (Jerusalem), Vol. 7, 83.

The most impressive study of a single city is:

Phythian-Adams, C. 1978: *Desolation of a City. Coventry and the Urban Crisis of the Late Middle Ages*. Cambridge.

10

The Social Areas of the City: 2 The Industrial City

1 Introduction

In the previous chapter an attempt was made to outline the characteristics of what, rightly or wrongly, has become known as the pre-industrial city. If the stereotype of that category be accepted it can be argued that the widely agreed dimensions of modern factorial ecological studies were not then independent but, rather, closely associated. The two situations can be represented diagrammatically in Figure 10.1. The changes which have taken place are represented by the redirection of the dividing lines which have swung through 90 degrees so that what once were correlated aspects of city social structure have become uncorrelated dimensions, varying independently.

The spatial implications that follow from Figure 10.1 are complex. It is relatively straightforward to envisage the contemporary situation where each of the independent dimensions produces its own characterizing intra-urban pattern. It is less easy directly to relate the pre-industrial structure to city space as it was set out in the last chapter. The key, however, is immobility. Thus, the whole of the life cycle was played out under the same roof so that socioeconomic status and life cycle were part of the same household characteristic. Again, ethnicity was closely tied to socioeconomic status and to those cultural inheritances which determined the role and nature of the family. It was the substitution of a high level of mobility for a relatively static condition which was most characteristic of the industrial transformation and it follows that mobility is one of the features which must be considered. But mobility provides no complete explanation for it was but an aspect of a whole series of changes in technology which created the industrial city. Further, technological change is of itself of little significance unless it is socially desired and implemented, it is but an aspect of a broader economic transformation. It is proper, therefore, to review a series of contributory factors, all of which played a part in the major reorientation set out in Figure 10.1.

2 The causes of nineteenth-century intra-urban transformation

To claim, as the heading of this section implies, to be able to isolate the causes of nineteenth-century urban change is too bold. Even so, a series of contributors can be set out, in which although the individual elements vary in nature and significance and are seldom unrelated to each other, they make up an operational complex.

(i) Changes in technology

It has already been suggested that changes in technologies were secondary rather than primary in nature. But they were the immediate and recognizable impulses and with them consideration should start.

(a) Industrial technology. Traditionally this is the first and critical sector of change in what has been so widely identified as an industrial revolution. The older situation had been one of small-scale craft industries based on workshops scattered throughout the town and producing for a local market. Even where there was export the small scale, virtually domestic, operation still dominated. This was radically transformed in the late eighteenth and nineteenth centuries. Large-scale factory industry came into being demanding extensive areas of land. As a result the urban core location was made inadequate and hence obsolete and new segregated industrial regions developed, often where there was good access to water and rail transport.

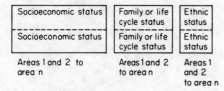

10.1.   Dimensions of contrast in pre-industrial and industrial cities.

The significance of these changes for residential patterning was twofold. First, these industrial regions, although in the early stages of formation possibly including the residences of entrepreneurs and managers, were active repellants of high-quality housing. Second, large labour forces were needed at a time when mobility for those lowest in the social scale was greatly restricted and the journey to work was universally on foot. All the evidence indicates that while there was considerable residential relocation movement amongst these populations, it was essentially short-distance (Pooley, 1979). Large working-class areas were in this way built up adjacent to industrial regions. However, due to their stability over time they developed considerable internal homogeneity and for this reason have been described as 'urban-villages'.

(b) Retail technology.   Changes here have already been discussed in chapter 8, but their importance for residential development lay in the coming of the lock-up shop and eventually the multiple store. Owner and manager no longer lived on the premises and hence a new demand for middle-class housing was generated.

(c) Transport technology.   Many interpretations would put this as paramount amongst all the changes. It was a lubricant to that friction of distances which held the pre-industrial city within confined circumstances. The pent-up pressures which had been built up even within the pre-industrial city were released and rapid physical extension followed. The railway, the street or tram-car, the motor bus and eventually the motor car ended the notion of the walking city, which was replaced by that of the metropolis. Certainly the effect cannot be exaggerated, but the immediacy can. For a large section of the population walking to work and to shop remained characteristic into the present century. In short the changes operated differentially according to the ability to pay and a segregating influence of considerable strength was introduced.

Perhaps the most convincing evidence for this has been presented by the Philadelphia Social History Project (Hershberg, ed. 1981). Table 10.1 extracts information gathered by that study on the journey to work for lawyers, carpenters, those employed in banks and sugar workers.

Hershberg writes of one of these groups. 'Almost all lawyers maintained their offices in the CBD and shifted their residences to areas considerably removed from the downtown area. In so doing lawyers were among a small vanguard of white-collar personnel who, in separating home and work, abandoned the city's core for more desirable residences in its surrounding rings' (Hershberg *et al.*, 1981, 136–7).

In contrast artisanal proprietors such as carpenters demonstrate the way in which craft industry fared, with an increase in those combining home and work as small operations proliferated during the great expansion of the construction industry between 1850 and 1880. The journey to work for industrial workers, as represented by the sugar industry increased over the 30-year period. In 1850 a journey of half a mile was the common experience of over 80 per cent but a similar proportion by 1880 travelled roughly one mile. But 'although the journey to work had nearly doubled over the period the absolute distances remained short and industrial workers continued to walk to work' (Hershberg *et al.*, 1981, 139). Finally, 'bank employees, as white-collar workers in the private sector, lived on the periphery of the CBD in 1850. They spread into newly developed residential areas to the north, west and south of the city centre during the next three decades. They had somewhat longer journey to work than most blue-collar workers, some of the riders on street railways by 1880 may well have been clerks and tellers travelling to and from their work in the CBD' (Hershberg *et al.*, 1981, 136–7).

Here is clear evidence of the increasing significance of

Table 10.1:   Philadelphia (a) The Journey to work 1850 and 1880 of lawyers and carpenters. Cumulative percentage at specified distances from worksite in miles.

	Work and home combined	0.1	0.5	1.0	Median distance in miles
Lawyers					
1850	52.6	63.2	89.5	100	0.18
1880	17.6	17.6	29.4	47.1	1.30
Carpenters					
1850	39.0	44.2	63.6	84.4	0.61
1880	53.0	58.3	76.5	87.0	0.51

(b) Dispersion of work force around potential worksites 1850 and 1880. Cumulative percentage at specified distances in miles.

	0.1	0.5	1.0
Sugar			
1850	25.8	81.6	–
1880	3.0	62.1	84.6
Banks			
1850	22.2	77.8	–
1880	1.9	44.3	–

the journey to work in the latter half of the nineteenth century. Even so, a study of the street railway system suggests that it was not a significant element in dispersal until after 1910. Pred (1966) in his study of Manhattan in the first four decades of the nineteenth century concluded that displacement was little more than a mile. In contrast, Warner (1962) in his analysis of Boston in the last decades of the century argued that the proportion commuting had increased from 20 per cent in the 1870s to 50 per cent in the 1890s and that the use of street-cars had produced residentially homogeneous suburbs.

The conclusion from these investigations is that without question 'advances in technology made it possible for white-collar workers to choose where they wished to live' (Hershberg *et al.*, 1981, 165) and hence there followed the development of class-based suburbs. The same is not true of those lower in the social scale and it would appear that the labour markets of different industries, attracting populations of different demographic, ethnic and occupational characteristics, predominated in creating the working-class residential areas of the inner ring.

(d) Housing technology. The study of nineteenth-century housing has to a considerable degree been dominated, even obsessed, by working-class accommodation. Certainly the provision of dwellings for the assembled labour force was critical and the condition of housing disastrously poor. But the leading edge of change was represented by innovation, by the provision of a range of new conveniences (in all senses of the word) which were to become widely demanded and eventually standard. It is not necessary to trace those developments which changed domestic living during the century (Burnett, 1978) but the installation of fixed baths and water-closets flushing into the town drains, of internal hot-water systems, of town gas for lighting and heating, all attracted the increasingly prosperous sections of society into new housing where all these were available. Again, however, this was not until late in the nineteenth century. The water-closet was not built in to houses until the 1870s, bathrooms were put into speculative housing only in the 1880s.

(e) Public utilities and technology. It might seem idiosyncratic to include these under technological changes but such, in fact, they were. The transformations in industry and in transport which have been noted led to noisy and dirty city sectors developing. But even further, the mass housing of the labour force without adequate provision of pure water and effective drainage, produced recurrent epidemics of cholera and typhus. Technology here developed all too slowly.

The results of these conditions have been set out in characteristic style by Lewis Mumford.

The early romantic suburb was a middle-class effort to find a private solution for the depression and disorder of the befouled metropolis: an effusion of romantic taste by an evasion of civic responsibility and municipal foresight. The instincts that prompted this exodus were valid: caught in the new urban wreckage, the old cry 'women and children first', was a sound one. Life was actually in danger in this new urban milieu of industrialism and commercialism, and the merest council of prudence was to flee with all one's goods as Lot and his household had fled from the sultry hell of Sodom and Gomorrah. (Mumford, 1961, 492)

(ii) Changes in society

The nineteenth century saw a great elaboration of the structure of society in the industrializing countries. This was in part a derivative of the industrialization process itself for it generated demand for an ever-widening variety of skills. At the same time there was a concomitant increase in the professions, in addition to the emergent class of entrepreneurs and businessmen, from which a middle class, itself with an elaborate structuring of prestige and wealth, was created. But it was a highly competitive society where status was not only ascribed but could be earned. Upward mobility was considerable. The result was that members of any stratum were critically concerned with distinguishing themselves from the stratum below and adopting the *mores* and style of the stratum above. Just as the nouveau rich (the term itself is significant) aped the landed gentry and the aristocracy, so too the semi-skilled looked to become part of the working-class elite (Crossick, 1978). Nor was the distinction solely of wealth. The office clerk at the base of the lower-middle-class probably regarded himself in status as superior to the more highly paid skilled manual worker and attempted to demonstrate that social superiority by the lifestyle he tried to adopt. It is worth observing that the Oxford Dictionary records the word 'snob' as used in 1852, in a context now obsolete, as referring to 'a person belonging to the lower classes of society; having no pretensions to rank or gentility'. But in 1848 it records the modern use, 'one whose ideas are prompted by a vulgar admiration for wealth or social position'. Here about mid-century is class consciousness fully alive. From it emerged stereotypes which have dominated social life in Britain even into the second half of the twentieth century.

In the end it was the middle class, with the help of a fundamentally bourgeois royal family, which determined the accepted *mores*.

The 'new' class was the most family-conscious and home-centred generation to have emerged in English history. Originating perhaps in the 1820s, a distinctively middle-class family pattern grew up which was in full development by the middle decades of the century . . . it was one which, in time, the middle classes were largely successful in imposing on the orders above and below themselves. It had certain well defined characteristics based upon a set of values and beliefs which were imbued almost with religious authority – the belief in male superiority . . . and wives and children owed only obedience to this God-like creature; the belief that a 'lady' did not work, that her vocation in life was a prudent marriage, and that the primary purpose of that marriage was the procreation of children . . . . The home, in this view, itself became almost a sacred institution, the pivot not only of domestic comfort but of moral rectitude, the Christian commonwealth in miniature . . . (Burnett, 1978, 95–6)

From these views it followed that strivings for status, as well as the central theme of the family, were best displayed, visibly and physically, in the house itself. To link back to housing technology already discussed, it was not only modern convenience that counted, but external appearance as a symbol of status. The middle classes sought to convert themselves into a landed aristocracy. The separate house gave the privacy on which family life rested, but the extensive grounds (another piece of estate-agent jargon) constituted a mini-estate, the shrubbery was the woodland, even the dogs were the livestock. The gothic exuberance of many houses expressed both the supreme confidence of the age, its individuality and its wealth. Likewise the lower middle class sought to imitate their 'superiors' and to distance themselves from the manual workers. 'An intense white-collar status consciousness was the main component of that separation, as salaried workers under pressure sought to mark themselves off from prosperous artisans as the only way to demonstrate their superiority . . . . As resources were mobilized for speculative suburban house-building, the final aspect of this changing relationship appears as a process of residential segregation that progressively demolished the mid-Victorian liberal community and isolated the manual working class' (Crossick, 1977, 49).

The consequences of the elaboration of the class structure and the growing perceptions of class identity were to stress the desirability of social distancing and hence residential segregation. At the same time the increase in mobility offered the opportunity, just as the onset of pollution and disease created the necessity, of outward movement. Only those who could afford it, however, could move and hence a class differential was written in to the emerging residential areas.

(iii) Changes in political control

In looking at the pre-industrial city two stages in the history of political control were suggested. The first was that where an urban patriciate dominated, largely concerned with an elaborate ritual of government. This gave way gradually and imperceptibly to the control of merchants more concerned with the city as an effective economic mechanism. To a considerable degree the latter was inherited by the nineteenth century, though in a condition where an elite still exercised an effective dominance. In Britain, municipal history during that century was dominated by the efforts of the population at large to gain control. Municipal reform in the 1830s was a stage towards that goal, although it was not until the reorganization of local government towards the end

of the century that anything like a local democracy appeared (Lipman, 1949). Control, therefore, through the century shifted away from those patrician elements which had once exercised it.

Moreover, after 1848 there seemed little likelihood of violent uprising by an alienated and disaffected working class.

The moral self-help wing of working-class movements shared the dominant and puritan values of Victorian society, its emphasis on thrift, sobriety and self-discipline; and as the economic depression lifted, which had done so much to brutalize the relations of the enfranchised and propertied with the excluded and exploited, so articulate working men were increasingly absorbed into popular politics, into the demands for a wider franchise . . . the quest for land reform . . . the diminution of taxes and monopolies and patronage . . . . The poor were to enter into moral and political adulthood – at the price of abandoning their stance of class hostility on the one hand and their claim to paternalistic protection on the other. (Hollis, 1973, xxvii)

The meaning of all this is that the privileged no longer had any reason to occupy the centre in order to assert their control, for that control was itself being reformulated through the democratic process. Political interest no longer necessitated a central location. This was closely associated with a change in the role of middle-class women. Davidoff (1973, 73) noted that 'when leading families lived in or very near the central city, their control over local politics meant that social life was ultimately tied to the governing of the city. As families moved out to prosperous suburbs, local social life centred more on charity, the arts and the marriage market'. A whole new ritual grew up to moderate the relationships which developed from such activities. The old rituals of city governance were replaced by those of suburban etiquette.

Meanwhile, back in town the husbands took on another role. The pollution and disease which had become so widespread were a threat in their eyes not so much to human life as to the effectiveness of the work force and the safety of those who had to spend the working day in city centres. Out of this there arose the whole complex legislation, vigorously opposed it is true, concerned with public health and the provision of minimum standards of housing, water supply and drainage. During the century residential development came more and more under public control. In Britain the century was marked by a series of Public Health Acts from 1848 onward reaching a climax in the Public Health Act of 1875, and of Housing Acts beginning with the Lodging Houses Act of 1851 and reaching its peak at the Artisans' and Labourers' Dwellings Improvement Act of 1875, but with Housing of the Working Classes Acts in 1885 and 1890 consolidating and amending previous legislation.

The contrast with these attempts at public control can best be seen in the less fettered development of American cities. In two books, one concerned with a particular city and called *The Private City*, one concerned with a general history of the American city and entitled *The Urban Wilderness*, Sam Bass Warner (1968, 1972) has stressed the way in which what he calls privatism is 'the most important element of our culture for understanding the development of cities' (Warner, 1968, 4). The essence of privatism he defines as meaning that the individual should seek happiness in personal independence and in the search for wealth, and that socially the first loyalty is to the immediate family, whilst politically the community's main role is to arbitrate between competing money makers in order to keep the peace and ensure an effective environment for competition and prosperity.

The results of privatism Warner traces in his books, especially that on Philadelphia. At each stage he reaches a similar conclusion.

> The Revolution left the city a tradition of democratic goals grafted upon a society of private economic aspirations. Later political conflict between popular equalitarian goals and the goals of business profit would give rise to the modern municipal corporation and encourage its active participation in transportation, public safety, education and health. These municipal functions would be the public dimensions of a city of private aspirations. Urban problems that required direct and substantial reallocation of scarce resources . . . brought failure to the future city. No urban, economic democracy emerged with time because the popular goal of Philadelphia was the individual race for wealth. This was to be the essence of the American, urban experience. (Warner, 1968, 45)

This would at first seem at odds with the view sketched above that suburban dispersal came after the institution of democratic urban government. But it can be maintained that it was the effectiveness of government that mattered. The seventh chapter in *The Private City* is called 'Riots and the restoration of public order'. There was a succession of riots in Philadelphia between 1834 and 1849 and it was the eventual control of these that provided conditions analogous to those in Britain after 1848. Warner concludes,

> Of course, the new ethnic style of politics could not restore strong democratic government to the city. For the moment it obscured the slow breakdown of city government which had commenced in the 1840s. But in the long run it contributed nothing to the vital issues of the maldistribution of personal income, physical growth, and the need for new high-quality municipal institutions which were the major problems of the city for the next century. The big city of 1860 had regained public order, but as a meaningful democratic society it was out of control. (Warner, 1968, 156–7)

This adds another dimension to the notion of political control both in Europe and America. Restricting legislation there might have been, of varying effectiveness, but the prevailing belief was that of privatism or of *laissez faire*. The powerful forces which were to blow apart the pre-industrial city and create in its place a city where segregation was the predominant characteristic, acted with only marginal constraints. The city, therefore, came to epitomize events in society at large. When Disraeli wrote of 'the two nations' it was not surprising that those 'two nations' were effectively segregated in the new form of the 'big city'. And that form was in part a consequence of political beliefs and attitudes.

(iv) Demographic change

Changes in mobility which have already been discussed were largely related to intra-urban movement. But extensive intra-national movements were generated (Lawton, 1978) and from these new metropoles were created. These patterns of urban growth have been partly considered in chapter 5 and have been the subject of significant works from Weber (1899) to Robson (1973). Two points only need to be emphasized here.

The first is the explosive nature of the population increase. Lawton records that between 1801 and 1831 the urban population doubled, as compared with a total population increase of only 48 per cent, with 3.14 million (62.8 per cent of the total increase) being added to it. 'Many textile towns achieved spectacular growth, up to tenfold in places like Bury, Bolton, Bradford and Huddersfield, while of the regional capitals Manchester grew from 27,246 in 1773 to some 182,000 in 1831 and Leeds from 17,121 in 1775 to 123,000' (Lawton, 1978, 334). Metallurgical centres, seaports, naval bases and resorts registered equivalent increases so that the description introduced above – explosive – is not only fully justified but is used quite deliberately, for growth was of such a nature as to blow the pre-industrial city apart so that the fragments became reconstituted as the segregated city (Carter, 1981). Population growth was itself a significant driving force.

The second point is that these populations were necessarily derived from widely divergent sources. In general one can accept Ravenstein's law of migration, derived from this period, that movements were short-distance and that large displacements of population were the result of a large number of smaller shifts. But superimposed on that pattern were significant long-distance movements which brought 'alien' populations into the cities. In Britain these were constituted by the Irish but in North America not only by the Irish but by blacks from the South and a whole series of nationalities from southern and eastern Europe. Ethnic areas, where immigrant populations adapted to a new culture and way of life, became therefore distinctive sections of the industrial city.

(v) The housing market

It is not easy to undertake a summary of the housing market in widely divergent countries, but whereas modern studies of social areas have turned to consider it, as yet there is no such emphasis in nineteenth-century studies. As far as Britain is concerned two features immediately stand out. First there was effectively no municipal housing. Second, the bulk of the population rented accommodation. Thus in 1914 some 95 per cent of accommodation in Leicester was rented and only 5 per cent owner-occupied (Pritchard, 1976). Given the predominance of renting and the control of the landlord the consequence of raised rents was either eviction or the taking-in of lodgers. Overcrowding and slum conditions were in essence an intensification of use by which greater profits accrued to the landlord. Burnett (1978, 196), however, suggests that 'few Victorians bought their houses, partly because of the underdeveloped state of the building societies [but see Robson, 1973, 143] and partly because rented accommodation suited a class which was economically and geographically mobile. Contemporary advice often suggested that one should not take a lease longer than three years since by then one would be ready to move into different accommodation better adjusted to changing income and family needs'.

The last words of the last sentence are of some significance for they imply a close relationship between socioeconomic status and life-cycle stage. Elsewhere Burnett suggests, the sort of house which the average nuclear family needed.

The husband, a young professional or businessman, has prudently delayed marriage until the required age of 30 and the income of £300 a year has been attained. He rents his first home at £25 a year, a six-roomed terraced house with small drawing and dining-rooms and three bedrooms, the smallest of which is occupied by the single maid. In five years' time they move to a semi-detached house in the suburbs, with four bedrooms so that the two children may normally have separate rooms, and with a somewhat larger dining-room which does not disgrace the monthly dinner party. In another five years, by which time the husband is 40 and his income has expanded to £750 a year, the important move is made to a newly-built detached villa, perhaps in another town, at a rent of £75 a year. It is a house of 'character' in the fashionable 'Gothic' style, with 10 rooms – not counting the spacious hall – a large dining-room and an elegant drawing-room opening to a conservatory, a study, a kitchen and adjoining domestic offices sufficient for the manservant, cook and two maids who are now kept, six bedrooms, the principal one having its own dressing room, and, for the first time, a bathroom with a fixed bath and a piped water supply .... This might well be the family house .... (Burnett, 1978, 100–1)

This passage brings together a number of features apart from the significance of the rented market. The influence of housing technology is apparent, and also mobility for in the last stage of the model the family is envisaged as possessing, 'a two-wheeled carriage, the manservant combining the functions of groom and footman and sleeping in the coach house' (Burnett, 1978, 101). But it also brings into play life-cycle stages, for movement is partly related to the demands set up by the children. However, at no point do these needs become independent of increasing business or professional esteem and income. In short, in this model life-cycle and socioeconomic status have not become separate dimensions operating independently of each other.

In this section a summary has been presented of the variety of changes which contributed to the eventual transformation of the pre-industrial city in the context of the articulation of residential areas.

3 The nature of segregation

There is little doubt that by the second decade of the present century the large western city presented a pattern of class-based segregated residential or social areas, and although the standard causes for this condition have been traced in the last section some doubts still remain.

(i) The definition of segregation

Any measure of segregation is intimately related to scale and any statement about it only has validity at a defined scale (Carter and Wheatley, 1980). It is also related to the nature of social structure. An upper-class household at mid nineteenth century would most certainly have included a range of servants, grooms, gardeners and others so that the number of lower-class households was probably greater. The implications for any notion of a single social-class area are considerable. If, therefore, by segregation one means the emergence of exclusive single-class areas then that was very late indeed.

(ii) When did segregated class areas appear?

This has been one of the main areas of contention in nineteenth-century geographical studies. Many factorial ecologies have tended to replicate the results of modern investigations and imply that certainly during the second half of the century class-based residential areas had appeared. Ward, however, has been a consistent proponent of a very late emergence of such segregated living (Ward, 1980). Indeed, his work on Leeds suggests that in the central decades of the century although a small, though growing, section of the middle class were becoming increasingly concentrated in the fashionable parts of the city (though perhaps such concentration was *making* them fashionable), the remainder of the population not only lived in mixed areas but differentiation by class decreased rather than increased. 'Diminishing levels of residential differentiation in the middle decades of the century also suggest that the increasingly differentiated residential patterns of late-Victorian cities did not emerge from a gradual increase in the complexity of early-Victorian arrangements' (Ward, 1980, 133).

(iii) What were the processes underlying class sorting?

These processes have been apparently outlined in the beginning of this section under the title of 'causes'. Ward seemingly rejects these causes for his view that class segregation came about at a later date must invoke other reasons. He suggests that 'the extension of residential differentiation to the upper strata of the less affluent involved broad changes in consumption patterns which have been associated with the transition to finance or corporate capitalism at the beginning of the present century' (Ward, 1980, 162). This implies that the industrial city was not a segregated city, and it was not industrialization which precipitated class-differentiated areas but rather the consequences of the later structural changes underlying the emergence of the so-called post-industrial period.

These three problems need to be considered in the context of empirical studies, but whatever the nature of the processes creating social class-based segregation, the large immigration of diverse populations had given rise to ethnically distinctive areas, although even in this case scale is again relevant for they were seldom as exclusive as the Jewish ghetto of the pre-industrial city or the black ghetto of the post-World War II American city. Again, intra-urban mobility, although generally limited to those higher in the social scale as far as longer-distance shifts were concerned (Pooley, 1979), had developed to a stage where life-cycle adaptations were apparent, although the class link meant they were not separated from socioeconomic status.

The summary above is redolent of those arguments which Shevky and Bell first used when they presented the bases on which social area analysis was developed (Shevky and Bell, 1955). Their contrasts, it is true, were of rural society with modern urbanism, rather than of pre-industrial with industrial cities, but even so their notions remain effective. Changes in the range and intensity of relations, they argued, would result in a changing distribution of skills. It was on such skills, both manual and professional, that the class structure of the industrial city had become based. Again, the concept of the differentiation of functions proposed by Shevky and Bell related to changes in the structure of productive activity. The household as a discrete economic unit of production would disappear. This applied as much to craftsmanship as it did to farming. The nature of the family changed, therefore, and no longer was life with all its changes lived out under one roof. Perhaps the original 'urbanization' construct of Shevky and Bell caught more clearly those changes taking place in the nineteenth century than the life-cycle dimension into which it has since been converted. 'Urbanization' was related more clearly to changes in the family role, with the criteria of definition related to family size, women in the workforce and single-family households. These were, indeed, the basic changes from pre-industrial to industrial context. Finally, Shevky and Bell identified complexity of organi-

zation as one of their postulates concerning industrial society, an aspect of increasing scale. From this arose the diversity of the populations brought together in the city and, in consequence, ethnic segregation.

Although it has become fashionable to disparage social area analysis, and especially the way in which the constructs were derived, reflection will show that with considerable prescience Shevky and Bell identified and presented those fundamental bases on which the industrial city contrasted with its predecessor. The nineteenth century was the period of change, of transformation but it is far from clear how that change and transformation took place, as has been noted. Consideration must now be directed to some detailed material on that issue.

4 Social areas in nineteenth-century cities

It is useful to demonstrate at the outset the clear segregation of those highest in the social scale which is accepted by all writers on nineteenth-century cities. A study by Shaw on Wolverhampton (Shaw, 1977 and 1979) had as

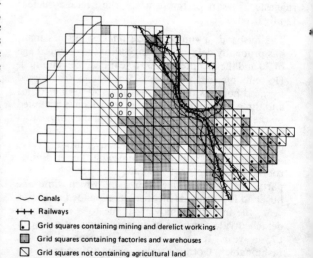

〜 Canals
+++ Railways
▫ Grid squares containing mining and derelict workings
▦ Grid squares containing factories and warehouses
◳ Grid squares not containing agricultural land
⊡ Grid squares containing the Park

10.2.   (a) Wolverhampton. Land-uses in 1871; (b) Wolverhampton. Percentage of household heads in social classes I and II in 1871 (after M. Shaw).

its basis an attempt to demonstrate the association of a whole range of factors controlling the town's growth and making an impact on this process of detachment of the high-status group. Even so, it is possible to extract just one, the nature of the physical environment. This is outlined on Figure 10.2a and in its elucidation Shaw quotes one Post Office Directory in 1860. 'The soil on the west

Table 10.2: Liverpool 1871. Loadings on the first three components (after Lawton and Pooley)

		Component 1		Component 2		Component 3
Percentage of variation accounted for		24.6		13.6		9.3
Cumulative percentage		24.6		38.2		47.5
Loadings of variables Positive	Population density	78	Socioecon. gp. 4 & 5	95	Age 15–64	89
	Housing density	75	Socioecon. gp. 5	74	Lodgers	51
	Residential land	70	Scoioecon. gp. 4	53	Servant index	38
	Resdient in courts	68	Resident in courts	43	Servants	33
	Multiple occupance	64	Irish	41	Women in work-force	33
	Irish	64	Houseful size	37	Widowed heads	31
	Houseful size	46				
	Socioecon. gp. 4	43				
	Socioecon. gp. 5	43				
	Lodgers	33				
Negative	Distance from centre	78	Socioecon. gp. 3	92	Age 0–14	92
	English migrants	74	Residential land	39	Age 0–14	76
	Socio-econ. gp. 1 & 2	49	Welsh migrants	37	Nuclear family	59
	Servants	49	Scots migrants	36		
	Servant index	47				
	Houseful size	33				

Note: Figures are percentages except for distance and densities. The servant index is servant/nuclear + extended family × 100. Decimal points have been omitted.

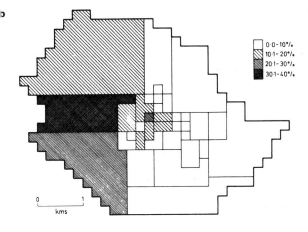

0 — 1 kms

0·0–10%
10·1–20%
20·1–30%
30·1–40%

and north of the town is rich and fertile; but on the south and east there is a continued extent of coal and iron mines, in some places the coal cropping out to the surface . . . and . . . the . . . whole of the district is worked for coal and ironstone' (Shaw, 1979, 204). The clear contrast between the 'Black Country' which had developed to the east and the rural fringes of the west was reflected in the residential patterns which had developed by 1871. Those in social classes 1 and 2 (the professional and managerial and associated occupations) are mapped in Figure 10.2b and it is evident that those who could escape the environmental deterioration of the eastern parts had moved westward to the rural suburbs, leaving a relict element still at the centre and consigning the east to the working class. Here is an absolutely classic picture of the

emergence of a high-quality residential sector repelled by industry and attracted towards a park and to open land.

Moving on from such an initial statement it is appropriate to consider what is the most detailed study of an English city, that of Liverpool by Lawton and Pooley (1976) for the section which deals with social ecology is developed about the question, which is central to this chapter, as to whether Liverpool by 1871 exhibited those social dimensions which are seen to be characteristic of the modern city. A set of 34 variables was derived from the 1871 census enumerators book for 394 revised enumeration districts, that is, districts with major irregularities eliminated. A 10 per cent sample was abstracted from the census data and certain other variables, such as distance from the city centre, added. These data, with appropriate transformations, were subject to a principal components analysis with varimax rotation. The results are shown on Table 10.2.

The interpretation of these components, as in all such exercises, becomes one of subjective judgement. Nevertheless, although they are complex in nature their major lineaments appear to be reasonably established. The first component contrasts a high-density characteristic and associated multiple occupance and court housing and high Irish in-migrant proportions low in social status, with high-status, servant-employing households largely English in origin. Lawton and Pooley maintain that 'while there is no occupational association with this factor, it has a strong ethnic element, in particular a positive association with Irish and a negative association with English migrants. This factor indicates the main line of differentiation within mid-Victorian Liverpool, a dichotomy between high-status servant-keeping areas and central areas of decaying overcrowded housing, occupied by the Irish and avoided by migrants from England' (Lawton and Pooley, 1976, 45).

The second component is much more clearly identifiable for it contrasts working-class areas lowest in status and with a considerable Irish in-migrant element, with those of the skilled working class with distinctive Welsh and Scots in-migrants. This can legitimately be called an ethnic factor. The third component is also manifestly a life-cycle or family-status dimension distinguishing between mature, economically active families where there are also lodgers with younger nuclear families in separate households.

As the authors admit, the production of these components is largely a reflection of the input variables but even so four conclusions, or avenues for investigation as they are called, can be noted.

1   Occupational status can be clearly identified as a major basis of differentiation. High-status, servant-employing families are separated from those lower in the hierarchy. As at Wolverhampton, therefore, a distinctive difference at the aggregate scale is engendered apparently regardless of ethnic, migrant or family status.
2   Within the working class there appear significant differences between the skilled and the unskilled. After mid century there apparently emerged a working-class elite regarding itself as very different from the unskilled labourer. This contrast gave rise to notions which were to be epitomized as that between 'the respectable' and 'the roughs'.
3   There is a strong association of working-class status and ethnicity. In particular the Irish were strongly related to the lowest socioeconomic status.
4   A life-cycle family-status dimension of difference appears, which presumably is independent of other associations and reflects the way in which family circumstances directed residential choice.

The next stage is to move from the identification of the components of variation and to examine the distribution patterns which are derived from mapping the scores of the derived enumeration districts on each of those components which can be meaningfully interpreted.

The first component suggests a centre–periphery, that is a zonal, pattern. A low-density dockside area where there were extensive non-residential tracts of land was succeeded by a high-density inner area where there were still high-status sections, but it gave way to a low density, emergent suburban fringe. The second component identified the lowest social category and Irish in-migrants and appeared as a series of inner sectors in the classic patterning. The third, life-cycle, component was again sectoral. The three can be combined to provide a schematic representation of Liverpool's structure in the early 1970s (Figure 10.3). The interpretation of Lawton and Pooley is best quoted verbatim.

> Though there is a complex mixture of sectors, zones and nuclei, a series of distinct elements emerge [sic]. First, the older central residential districts, approximately within the 1851 built-up area, had developed by 1871 into a series of distinctive sectors, largely constrained by the location of the docks, the principal routeways radiating from the centre and surviving islands of high-status property. Secondly, outside the 1851 built-up area broadly zonal characteristics are dominant: population from the central area moved out into the newer suburbs within which there were several areas of a transitional nature. Complementary to the mainly outward direction of internal population movement, the central zones were largely fed by in-migrants, some of whom were to stay permanently in low-status areas, others of whom soon moved out to the newer suburbs. There was also considerable movement between sectors of low-status housing, often caused by displacement due to urban redevelopment, though non-Irish families generally avoided the Irish areas. Thirdly, the high-status population moved sectorally into the third peripheral zone whilst, within the suburban ring, lateral movement took socially upwardmoving families into the high-status sector to the south. In addition to these distinctive movements, each area gained by in-migration at various levels of the social stratum. (Lawton and Pooley, 1976, 51)

It is at this point that the contrasts in interpretation which have already been referred to appear. Lawton and Pooley demonstrate that by the last quarter of the nineteenth century spatial segregation characterized the whole gamut of the social classes and that by 1871 Liverpool was taking on a distinctively 'modern' form. Figure 10.3 illustrates the nature of the changes taking place. In contrast Ward, as already indicated (p. 189), has consistently argued for a much later appearance of differentiation at the lower levels of the social scale and has suggested that such differentiation was not characteristic of the industrial city but rather derived from the transition to finance or corporate capitalism at the beginning of the present century (Ward, 1980, 162). Two further examples contrasted in size, function and location can be added in an attempt to resolve this apparent problem.

The first of these is the Welsh iron and steel town of Merthyr Tydfil (Carter and Wheatley, 1982). Thirty-six variables related to birth-place, occupation, socioeconomic status, demographic characteristics and a number of other features, such as the use of shared accommodation, were used. In order to maintain some degree of comparison with Liverpool a factor analysis of a correlation matrix of 36 variables with varimax rotation can be introduced (Table 10.3).

The first factor was a comprehensive one which contrasted the highest-status sections of the population with those lower in the social scale, particularly the skilled workers. But more than that, it associated with higher status the in-migrant non-Welsh elements (apart from the Irish) who were filling posts in public affairs and the professions. Also associated was single status, possibly reflecting the later marriage age of these higher-status categories. The second factor was clearly an ethnic one,

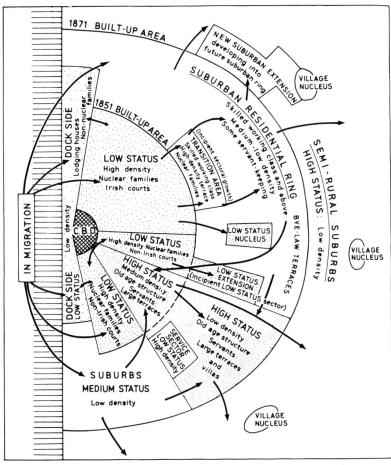

Within the diagram:

1871 BUILT-UP AREA

NEW SUBURBAN EXTENSION developing into future suburban ring

VILLAGE NUCLEUS

SUBURBAN RESIDENTIAL RING

Skilled working class and above
Medium - low density
Some servant - keeping

SEMI - RURAL SUBURBS
HIGH STATUS: Low density

1851 BUILT-UP AREA

DOCK SIDE
Lodging houses
Non-nuclear families

LOW STATUS
High density
Nuclear families
Irish courts

TRANSITION AREA
(Incipient sectoral growth)
Skilled working class
High density terrace
Nuclear families

BYE-LAW TERRACES

C.B.D.

Low density

IN MIGRATION

LOW STATUS
High density Nuclear families
Non-Irish courts

LOW STATUS
NUCLEUS

VILLAGE NUCLEUS

HIGH STATUS
Medium density
Old age structure
Servants
Large terraces

LOW STATUS
EXTENSION
(Incipient LOW STATUS sector)

DOCK SIDE
LOW STATUS

LOW STATUS
High density
Nuclear families
Non-Irish courts

SERVICE
SECTOR
LOW STATUS
High density

HIGH STATUS
Low density
Old age structure
Servants
Large terraces
and
villas

SUBURBS
MEDIUM STATUS
Low density

VILLAGE NUCLEUS

10.3. The structure of Liverpool in 1871 (after Lawton and Pooley). This schematic diagram, which is not to scale, attempts to summarize the main residential and social areas in Liverpool in 1871 and the associated processes of migration to the city and residential mobility within it. The high-status sector south east of the Central Business District should be noted and the contrasting working-class residential areas of the dock-side and the North End. Stages of growth may be seen in the sequence of suburban zones around the historic core.

Table 10.3: Merthyr Tydfil: Principal factors with varimax rotation. Thirty-six variables based on 1851 census

Positive loading variables		Negative loading variables	
Factor 1			
Employed in dealing	91	Employed in mining	59
Soc. econ. groups 1 and 2	91	Large family	46
Household servants	90	Locally born	40
Employment in professions	87	Soc. econ. group 3	34
Single heads of household	84		
Born in S.W. England	81		
Employed in other manufacturing	78		
Born in England and Scotland	69		
Employed in domestic service	55		
Foreign born	46		
Employed in building	57		
Independent means	37		
Factor 2			
Irish born	83	Local born	54
Shared accommodation	82	Agriculture	36
Employed in building	44	Elderly	35
Households with lodgers	42	Large family	33
Employed in labouring	39	Employed in mining	32
Density of households	31		

associating Irish in-migrants with multiple occupance and, therefore, high density and with unskilled labouring occupations. These were contrasted with mature large families of the local born engaged in agriculture and mining. Although there was a much more limited degree of independence of the three dimensions of social status, ethnicity and life cycle in Merthyr at mid century, there is, nevertheless, some similarity in these factors with those of the Liverpool study. When factor scores are plotted, however, contrasts immediately appear (Figures 10.4a and b). The ethnic dimension (Figure 10.4b) is comparable identifying two inner-city sectors north and south of the town centre, but the high-status areas (Figure 10.4a) were essentially central and coincided with the emerging central business district. Here, then, is a smaller town at an earlier stage of development. There were outlying high-status houses, those of the iron masters adjacent to the iron works, but they were too limited to register on aggregate maps. Merthyr would seem to show some features which throw forward to the modern period with the evolving working-class areas about its iron works and the lowest-quality ethnic areas near to the centre. But other features throw back to the pre-industrial city with those highest in the social hierarchy either resident adjacent to the works they owned, as the land-owning gentry were to their rural estates, or occupying the city centre itself.

Insofar as the Merthyr evidence casts any light on the nature of segregation it suggests that in part much of the controversy is based on semantics rather than reality. In 1851 there were certainly no residential areas that were the exclusive preserve of any one social class. Even the estates of the iron masters were locationally associated with the iron works, though they were large and in most cases isolated by a *cordon sanitaire* of parkland from the industrial areas proper. The central part of the town contained as many households low in the social scale as high, although they were tucked away in alleys and courts behind the façade of the High Street. But setting these mixtures aside, the degraded nature of the poorest areas, to which there is ample testimony, clearly led to the distinction of a 'rough' and a 'respectable' working class even at mid-century. The worst area in Merthyr, the district called 'China', itself creates an extensive literature of both official and private comment (Carter and Wheatley, 1982). It was, in modern terminology, a 'no-go' area. To imply, as Ward does, that there were no contrasts between this and the more respectable areas of the skilled working class, about which again there is much descriptive evidence, would appear to be denying the obvious.

Further evidence can be derived from a detailed study of Toronto by Goheen (1970), which covers the period 1850 to 1900. The population of Toronto in 1851 was 30,775 compared with Merthyr Tydfil's 46,378, so that it was slightly smaller, but in 1860, the date for which the first analysis is presented, it was 44,281 and can be taken as directly comparable. Goheen used 25 variables but of a much wider nature than the predominantly socially based

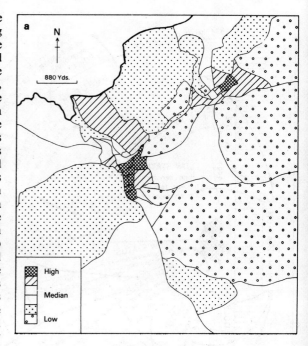

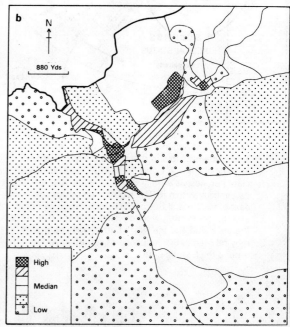

10.4.   Merthyr Tydfil (Mid Glamorgan) in 1851:
(a) Scores on Component
1. High Status/Non-Welsh
(b) Scores on Component
2. Irish/Low Status.

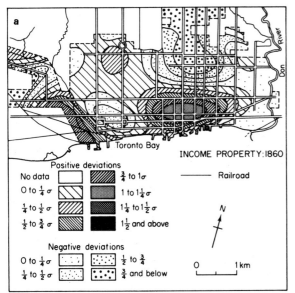

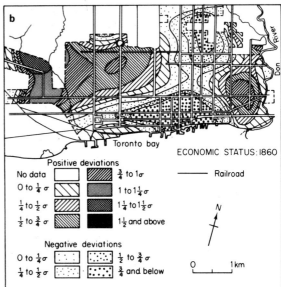

10.5. Toronto, 1860. Sixth degree polynomial trend surfaces:
(a) Income property; (b) Economic status (after Goheen).

character of those used in British studies. They include such items as the material in building construction, that is wood, stone or brick, and a valuation of personal property. Direct comparisons are, therefore, somewhat difficult to realize. The other difference is that while Goheen employs factor analysis he does not map factor scores for the eighth of a mile grid squares or cells which are the basis for his spatial analysis. Rather 'the distributional properties of these derived factors were investigated employing a method of mapping based on the calculation of polynomial trend expressions'. The use of trend surfaces is adopted in order to eliminate subjective bias from mapping.

For the 1860 analysis the first two factors are set out in Table 10.4. The first factor Goheen calls 'Income property' and the second 'Economic status'. Sixth-degree polynomial trend surface maps of these factors are shown in Figures 10.5a and 10.5b. The first of the maps (10.5a) demonstrates, 'patterning of economic utility as it was defined by the realized value of land' (Goheen, 1970, 119). This shows that 'the territory possessing high economic value appears to be highly centralized in the core of the city' and that the only variation is to the west where a newly built railway line had already resulted in some economic appreciation. 'The most extensive single area with consistently low scores for income derived

Table 10.4 Toronto, 1860. Variable loadings on the first two factors (after Goheen)

	Factor 1		Factor 2	
Per cent of variation	12.8		12	
Cumulative per cent	12.8		24.8	
Loadings of variables	Commercial land	93	Unskilled occupations	41
Positive	Taxable income	84		
	Ann. value of personal property or income	84		
	Skilled occupation	46		
Negative			Ann. value of real and personal property and income	−89
			Rental value of land	−88
			Value of personal property	−68
			Business occupations	−63
			Ann. value of personal property or income	−41

from property is the northerly district along Yonge Street. These low scores mean that only a few income-earning activities are found in the area. This district was the only large area of the city which appears to be developed exclusively for residential purposes, unaccompanied by a characteristic mix of industrial and commercial activities' (Goheen, 1970, 119).

The map of economic status (Figure 10.5b) shows that the area of high status, which is demarcated by negative values, as is apparent from Table 10.4, is 'anchored on the waterfront just west of the central commercial core' but 'extends northwestward in a sectoral pattern towards a second focus just south of Bloor Street along Jarvis. Areas of lower status are.consigned to corridors on either side of this high-prestige district' (Goheen, 1970, 121). Thus the city centre was still in 1860 the area of the highest prestige and Goheen suggests 'that the lowest economic class, the unskilled workers, were absent from it' (Goheen, 1970, 122). Indeed he goes on to argue that the business classes with the prestige devolving to a commercial elite in a trading city occupied the centre and that the unskilled, forming the lowest stratum, were found in the most inaccessible or undesirable peripheral locations. Here, then *mutatis mutandis*, is a comparison with Merthyr Tydfil, at least in the broadest outline of social area patterning.

If the last date for which Goheen presents an analysis,

1899, is now considered a very different picture emerges from a factor analysis of an enlarged (35) set of variables. The variable loadings on the first, third and fourth factors are given in Table 10.5.

The first point to be made is the obvious one that by 1889 a family-status dimension had appeared. It is mapped on Figure 10.6a where a distinctive zonal pattern can be identified. Related to the transport facilities of the 1890s city, a distinctive middle zone of mature families with a predominant renting tenure had emerged beyond the immediate city core. An outward wave stimulated by family demand for housing had brought into being a classic family-status zone of the modern city.

If one now moves to the fourth factor, then it can be suggested that it is a tenurial factor where districts where tenancy is lowest are identified by negative scores. These are the areas where house ownership predominates and are in consequence the prestige areas (Figure 10.6b).

Such areas stand out. First is the region persistently recognized as the one possessing the greatest residential prestige. We refer to the community adjacent to the university, including the "annex" north of Bloor Street as well as Jarvis Street . . . . South Rosedale had by this time developed into a substantial high-class community adjacent to the older high-status district. Secondly, the areas in the vicinity

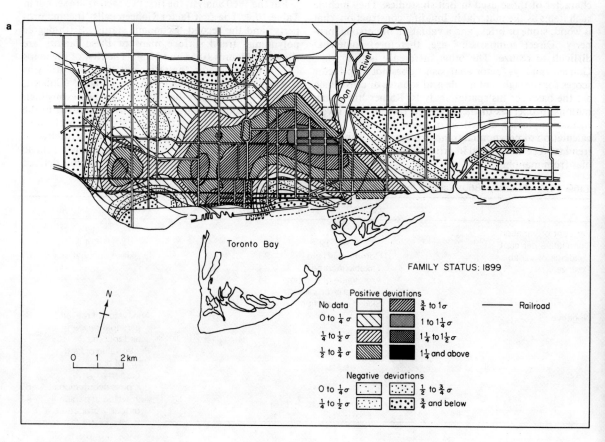

FAMILY STATUS: 1899

Positive deviations

No data		$\frac{3}{4}$ to 1σ	Railroad
0 to $\frac{1}{4}\sigma$		1 to $1\frac{1}{4}\sigma$	
$\frac{1}{4}$ to $\frac{1}{2}\sigma$		$1\frac{1}{4}$ to $1\frac{1}{2}\sigma$	
$\frac{1}{2}$ to $\frac{3}{4}\sigma$		$1\frac{1}{4}$ and above	

Negative deviations

| 0 to $\frac{1}{4}\sigma$ | | $\frac{1}{2}$ to $\frac{3}{4}\sigma$ |
| $\frac{1}{4}$ to $\frac{1}{2}\sigma$ | | $\frac{3}{4}$ and below |

Toronto Bay

N

0   1   2 km

Table 10.5:   Toronto 1899. Variable loadings on factors 1, 3 and 4 (after Goheen)

	Factor 1		Factor 3		Factor 4	
Per cent of variation	20.4		7.3		4.9	
Cumulative per cent	20.4		43.3		48.2	
Loadings of variables	Size of family	94	Roman Catholic	80	Number of contiguous	58
Positive	Male franchize	85	Separate school	95	units owned by one	
	Children 5–21	62	supporter		person	
	Age of head	32				
	Residential land	93				
	Vacant land	87				
	Value of building	84				
	Dwelling units in	70				
	building					
	Tenant	84				
Negative	Freehold	−59	Public school	−90		
			supporter			

Note: Factor 2 which is not shown in the table is a Value of Property factor which largely identifies commercial land. It explains 15.6 per cent of the variation.

10.6.   Toronto, 1899. Sixth degree polynomial trend
surfaces:
(a) Family status; (b) Tenure (after Goheen).

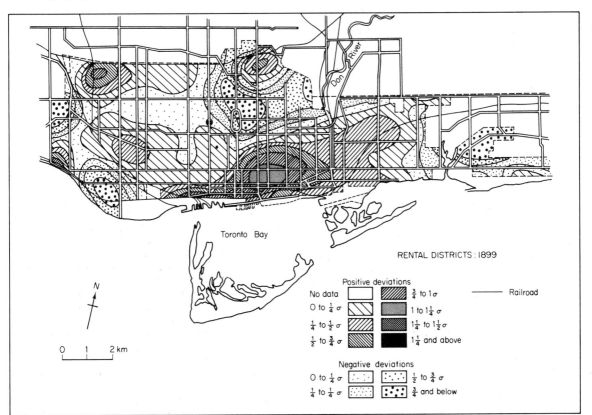

b

of High Park on the western borders of the city appear as a second district of residential prestige. This community was Parkdale. In 1899, for the first time, the two regions of highest economic status which have been recognized by recent studies of twentieth-century Toronto are identifiable (Goheen, 1970, 217-8).

The Roman Catholic factor can be taken as an equivalent of ethnicity since no birthplace or ethnic variables were included in the data set. 'What is important is . . . the lack of any substantial correlation between Catholicism and economic class in Toronto by the end of the century' (Goheen, 1970, 213). An independent ethnic surrogate had, therefore, emerged in the growth of the city.

The comparison of Toronto with Liverpool can be suggested with some confidence. Thus, the sectoral extension of those highest in the social scale was common and, again, the inner zones of the two cities beyond the commercial core are comparable, while Irish ethnicity (though one is never sure of its complete identity) in one can be set alongside Roman Catholicism in the other, although Irish ethnicity in Liverpool carried associations with lower social status.

The process which this section has presented has been one of a progressively complex social structure being associated with progressively increased segregation by social class. But it has been shown that this is not a view that has been without challenge. The apparent, if only part, contradiction has been put forward by Ward (1975 and 1980). Ward, referring to American evidence, has written of 'relatively weak levels of residential differentiation and a rather high degree of interspersal of both occupational and ethnic groups' (Ward, 1975, 137) and again, 'these considerations of social geographic changes in Victorian cities suggest that until late in the nineteenth century, "modern" levels and kinds of residential differentiation were quite weakly developed' (Ward, 1975, 151). By carefully associating levels with kinds, Ward offsets much of the criticism that can be made of an assumption of weak levels of segregation and of a 'jumble of confusion' within the city structure.

Two issues from this contradiction arise. The first is that discussion of some object called 'the nineteenth-century city' is without much purpose. There were large numbers of cities, of differing sizes, growing at different rates and reaching peaks of growth at different times so that single examples may well show different situations. Then there is the critical importance of scale. As has been stated, in the British city where there were domestic servants both living-in and occupying cottages adjacent in back streets, an ecological study would have revealed no segregation although it was firmly represented by upstairs–downstairs and the green baize door to the domestics' quarters. As more and more labour was needed to keep the growing industrial town going so the numbers at the bottom of the social scale increased. They were housed in courts and alleys so that a front street–back street scale of segregation emerged.

This is clearly shown in a study by Robb of the Gorbals

10.7.   The Gorbals, Glasgow, 1851: (a) Distribution of annuitants; (b) Distribution of paupers (after Robb).

area of Glasgow in the nineteenth century. Figures 10.7a and b indicate the distribution of annuitants, high in the social scale, and paupers, lowest in the social scale, in 1851. As Robb writes, 'the two groups were clearly segregated between different streets. Annuitants appear concentrated in fashionable S. Portland Street; paupers were relegated to the narrower back streets, particularly S. Coburg Street. This latter was built in speculative, small-house tenement style on the cheaper plots feued out . . . in the first two decades of the century' (Robb n.d., 25). This is a classic front street–back street dichotomy in an area which was to become Glasgow's most celebrated slum. That is, further changes, operating over a considerable period, were to see the abandonment of the area by the better-off and its conversion to a slum. What changes, therefore, is not segregation as such, for it was always there, but the scale on which it operated. Even by the end of the century, single-class homogeneous social areas were only beginning to appear as a consequence of the operation of the whole complex of forces

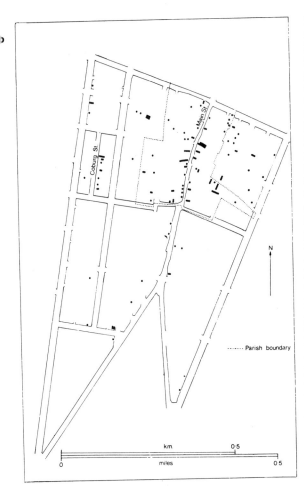

Coburg St

Main St

N

········· Parish boundary

km. 0·5

0 miles 0·5

which were set out at the beginning of the chapter. Ward is probably right in questioning the view that exclusive single-class social areas had emerged with any clarity before the end of the century (the highest-status areas excepted). But it was equally apparent that the processes which were to produce such a condition were already in operation.

5 Ethnicity and the formation of ghettos

It has already been noted that the ghetto was a characteristic feature of the pre-industrial city (chapter 9, p. 180). In western Europe limited mobility prior to industrial times meant that the one minority group which inhabited cities in any numbers was the Jews and hence, as has been demonstrated, the origin of the name by which such ethnic concentrations became known. Massively increased mobility in the nineteenth century saw much greater mixing of populations and the development of that heterogeneity of origin which Shevky and Bell saw as the basis of the construct they termed 'segregation'.

This has already been introduced in reference to the clear concentrations of Irish population which occurred in British cities, especially after the migrations following the famines of the 1840s (Lees, 1969). But the same problem that arose in considering social class, enters into consideration here for it is difficult to establish when a clustering can properly be called a concentration, and a concentration a ghetto. Lees in her study of the Irish in London concludes that there were concentrations of Irish but never in areas which were exclusively or even predominantly Irish. In short, there were no Irish ghettos. But her analysis is at a parish level and statements at such a scale must remain unconvincing. But elsewhere there were never exclusive 'areas'. As this chapter has already demonstrated, Irish concentrations have been identified in Merthyr Tydfil in 1851 but the proportion of Irishborn which was 6.29 per cent for the town reached a maximum of 28.4 per cent on an enumeration-district basis and in a 200-metre grid square 32.3 per cent (though ethnic identity by birthplace necessarily excludes British-born children). Exclusive concentrations were at the scale of court or alley. The Philadelphia project has produced rich evidence as to the location of ethnic groups in the nineteenth-century city. Between 1850 and 1880 the predominant groups were the Irish and the Germans. The former made up 17.6 per cent of the population in 1850 and 11.9 per cent in 1880, the latter 5.6 per cent and 6.6 per cent at the two dates. The distribution of German migrants in 1850 showed an identifiable clustering to the northeast of the city centre but Burstein notes, 'Initial inspection of the maps showing the residential patterns assumed by the German immigrants may indeed indicate a situation similar to the twentieth-century pattern of initial settlement in centralized ghettos and dispersion over time. However, the German concentration in the northeast was *not* an ethnic ghetto. Rather, as the more densely populated area of the city, it was shared by the German immigrants with a large number of individuals from other ethnic groups .... The northeast ... was not an area characterized by ethnicity as much as it was characterized by the presence of craftsmen and artisans, an occupation group to which the majority of German immigrants belonged' (Burstein, 1981, 182–3). Subsequently, by 1880, a characteristic process of dispersal was underway although the movement of building labourers employed in the construction of new housing for the affluent masked a simple pattern of high-status outmigration from the northeast.

The pattern of the Irish settlement was different. Again initially there was nothing like a ghetto, indeed without a large, cheap centralized housing supply there was considerable dispersal. There was, however, a clustering to the south and southwest of the central district in 1850 and by 1880 a greatly enlarged and more concentrated area had appeared. 'In terms of city-wide distribution, the Irish were more dispersed than the Germans, but those Irish who did reside in the major Irish residential concentration in the southwest lived in an area more similar to an ethnic ghetto than did the Germans' (Burstein, 1981, 186). But this cannot be compared to later immigrant ghettos since it was not created at the point of entry into the city but developed later from a process of intra-urban migration.

Burstein concludes that although ethnic spatial differentiation was not sharp in the nineteenth century it was nevertheless emergent. The ties of occupation, however, were significant and to a degree succeeded in overriding simple ethnicity as a conditioner of location. In the Philadelphia study there is certainly the implication that the Irish had skills to deploy whereas in Britain the predominant occupations were unskilled. It is possible to argue that the nineteenth-century city showed concentrations of the poorest and the unskilled rather than of the Irish as such. Such a contention has considerable relevance to contemporary views of the black ghetto in American cities and the beginnings of those ghettos need to be reviewed in the light of the discussion in this section.

The formative phase in the development of the black ghetto in American cities is usually ascribed to the present century as a response to the massive northward migration which took place during the decade 1910–1920. It is completely arbitrary to omit this from the present volume on the basis of a restriction to the nineteenth century but the modern ghetto has an ample literature and this section is devoted to a consideration of a preceding period and to the early phases of emergence.

The starting point of any such review must be the seminal book by Richard Wade on slavery in the cities, which deals with the urban south between 1820 and 1860 (Wade, 1964). The controlling factor at that earlier period was the nature of slavery which as an institution determined living patterns. By far the greatest proportion of urban slaves were domestics living in the master's house and there carrying out the vast range of chores which at that time were done by hand, for the operation of the house was a labour-intensive one. The result was that the blacks lived in close proximity, but at the same time separated and isolated. 'Overcrowded or not, the important thing about slave housing was the social view it embodied. Its basic object was to seal off the Negroes from outside contacts. Not only were the bondsmen's quarters placed close to the main building, but the plot itself was enclosed by high brick walls. The rooms had no windows to the outside and were accessible only by a narrow balcony that overlooked the yard and the master's residence. The sole route to the street lay through the house or a door at the side. Thus the physical design of the whole complex compelled slaves to centre their activity upon the owner and the owner's place' (Wade, 1964, 59).

This is the first stage in black urban residence. At the aggregate or ecological scale there was no segregation, but at the household scale it was absolute.

The next stage occurs with the loosening of the bonds of slavery. The cities of the south actively obstructed the cutting of alleys through the existing blocks not only because they broke across the domestic organization which has been outlined, but also because once alleys were opened they became centres of slave activity and of black residence, thus breaking the orientation of the slave to the master's house and providing an alternative system of contacts and directions. As the cities grew and the diversity of demands for labour increased the compound system gradually declined. 'Masters with too many blacks to keep on their premises, commercial and industrial owners whose bondsmen were not used as domestics, and, increasingly, slaveholders who found it profitable or convenient to let their slaves seek lodgings for themselves permitted a gradual loosening of the common arrangement. Negroes started to "live out", finding a room here, renting a house there, and in other cases, simply disappearing into remote sections of the town' (Wade, 1964, 62). However, employment opportunities in the walking city exerted a strong constraint and, although some black areas appear at city peripheries forming characteristic marginal, low-quality areas of the pre-industrial type, much black settlement was related to demand from the shipping wharfs and the town centre for labour. It, therefore, took over the alleys and back streets and eventually the run-down blocks of the inner city. Thus a front street–back street contrast between white and black represented an intermediate stage of development.

The process of black residential settlement in the late nineteenth century has been the subject of a study by Groves and Muller who have used Baltimore and Washington as exemplifying the cities at the southern borders where change came earlier than to the northern cities. Baltimore can be considered here. In 1880 blacks were apparently widely distributed comprising 10 per cent or more of the total population in three-quarters of the city's 20 wards and with no ward having over 33 per cent black. When Groves and Muller present evidence derived from the manuscript schedules of the 1890 census, however, a different picture emerges. Eight contiguous wards were selected (Figure 10.8) where the black proportions were over 20 per cent and the individual household figures were reaggregated into census-enumeration districts. 'The reconstruction of residential location in Baltimore revealed the existence of two areas of relatively intense black concentration. In general, a majority of the black population of eight wards (51 per cent) resided in numerous segregated alleys, courts and narrow secondary streets, reflecting ante-bellum patterns . . . . Nearly 20 per cent of the black population lived in the residences of white families for whom they were domestic servants, particularly in the wealthier districts to the north and northwest of downtown. The remaining blacks lived in houses on the blockfronts of major streets. Although the segregated enclaves of blacks were widely distributed throughout the eight wards, two separate areas of contiguous enumeration districts, in which blacks comprised more than 50 per cent of the residents, existed near the city harbour in the southwest and close to the wealthy neighbourhoods of the northwest' (Groves and Muller,

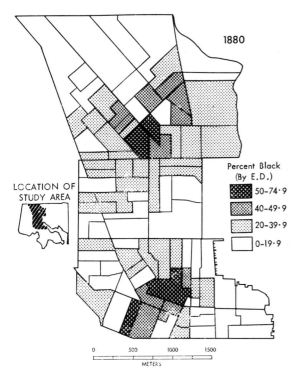

1880

LOCATION OF
STUDY AREA

Percent Black
(By E.D.)

▨ 50-74·9

▨ 40-49·9

▨ 20-39·9

☐ 0-19·9

0   500   1000   1500
METERS

10.8.   Baltimore in 1880. Blacks as a percentage of enumeration district population in the north central area
(after Groves and Muller).

1975, 182), (Figure 10.8). These high proportions were
derived not solely from back-alley populations but from
block-front residence by blacks. Groves and Muller
contend that 1890 saw an intensification of black
residence in precisely the 1880 areas of concentration so
that out of this process the black ghetto developed
expanding at its margin by a process of spatial diffusion.
Table 10.6 presents a suggested temporal framework for
this process.

It would be over-simple to make a comparison of the
way in which Irish population became concentrated in
Philadelphia by 1880 and the blacks in Washington by
1890, but there are elements in common, and indeed in
common with the process of social-class segregation
which had already been considered. In mid century

although certain elements, ethnic and class, are clustered
they are intermingled with a variety of other elements;
there is no exclusiveness. By the end of the century those
complex processes on which intra-city migration was
based had begun to diminish the admixture and produce
those distinctive sections which were ultimately to be
identified by the Chicago ecologists in the 1920s.

6 Conclusion

It is possible to represent the various changes which have
been outlined in the form of a diagram (Figure 10.9). The
sequence from domestic quarters to slum or, where
ethnic contrast is involved, ghetto, has been traced in
sections (3) and (4). The suburbanization process has also
been considered and the two stages are inserted in order
to indicate that often there was an inner suburban stage
before continued growth led to further extension.
Although there is room for class and ethnic segregation
in this interpretation, a family or life-cycle element is
difficult to integrate. There are two reasons. The first is
that during the nineteenth century it is impossible to
separate social class and family status for the ability
effectively to react to changing family conditions
depended so intimately on economic wealth. It is not easy
to maintain that the two dimensions were separated by
the end of the century, indeed it is not universally
accepted that in a country such as Britain they yet act
independently (Carter, 1981, 274, 312). The second is
that migration was such a predominant feature of the
nineteenth century that family status is closely associated
with a migrant status. At a minimum it is apparent that
the single and footloose were rarely suburban and at that
level a zoning according to life-cycle stage does appear as
the suburbs themselves extended.

It will be apparent that the diagram represents an on-
going process and that examination at any one time will
reveal contrasted city structurings, while analysis at different scales will also produce different conclusions.
Much of the controversy over nineteenth-century city
spatial organization can be resolved by relating empirical
results both to time and spatial scale; but again, not
absolute time, rather time related to the individual
example and its pace of growth.

The understanding of these aggregate changes would
seem to lie in the analysis of personal mobility for all the

Table 10.6:   Suggested temporal framework for black residential concentration (after Groves and Muller)

Growth patterns	South	Border Washington	Baltimore	North Primary	Secondary
1. Dispersed	early 19th century	early 19th century		early 19th century	
2. Enclaves/ dispersed	pre-1860	pre-1860	pre-1880	pre-1900	pre-1910
3. Emergent concentration	Post-Civil War?	1860-1800	1800-1900	1900-1910	1910-1920
4. Expanded concentration	Post-Civil War?	1880 +	1900 +	1910 +	1920 +

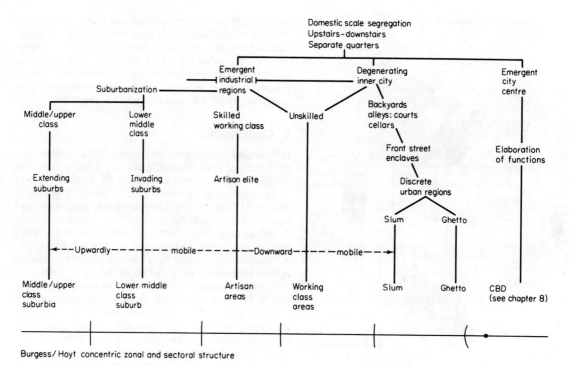

Burgess/Hoyt concentric zonal and sectoral structure

10.9.   The segregation of residence in the nineteenth
          century.

lines represented on Figure 10.9 are by implication lines of population movement. From his work on Liverpool, Pooley has constructed an interpretive diagram which is reproduced as Figure 10.10. Factors affecting individual residential mobility are divided into those relating to the person and those to the destination. These, in turn, produce mobility characteristics which relate to the three aspects of movement, its distance, its direction and its frequency. Finally these are viewed in terms of their effects on social areas and the formation of communities where long-term stability is seen as produced by high rates of short-distance mobility. With high rates of longer-distance mobility communities disintegrate, but with rapid in-flow followed by stability communities are formed. Long-term stability characterized the newly formed high-status areas where steady but low in-flows of population occurred. Short-term stability was associated with lower-status areas where there were frequent moves but over short distances. Disintegration could occur under the impact of central-area extension, especially into high-status areas. Finally, community formation was characteristic of the periphery as in-flows of population created new residential areas which also received flows from the centre.

In conclusion one can do no better than quote Pooley's words. 'Whatever the precise form of mobility patterns, it is clear that the Victorian city formed a dynamic system, where individual residential moves were frequent, but which collectively provided a sorting mechanism, reinforcing some communities and destroying others, and allowing a transition to take place from the essentially pre-industrial town of the early nineteenth century to the well structured industrial city of the mid- and late-Victorian period' (Pooley, 1979, 225). The only qualification one would make would be to remove the 'mid' from the last few words of the quotation for the well structured city was a characteristic of the latter part of the century and only reached its clear expression by the 1920s.

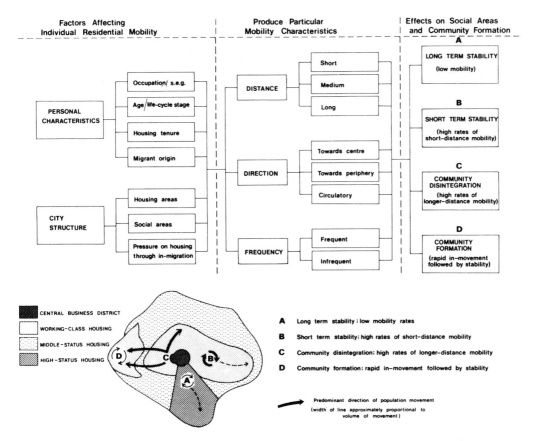

10.10. The residential mobility process and its effect on nineteenth-century urban structure (after Pooley).

Further reading

A number of historical works specifically concerned with the nineteenth century city provide admirable backgrounds. The most important are:

DYOS, H.J. and WOLFF, M. (eds.) 1973: *The Victorian City: Image and Realities*, 2 vols. London.

BRIGGS, A. 1963: *Victorian Cities*. London.

THERNSTROM, S. and SENNETT, R. (eds.) 1969: *Nineteenth Century Cities. Essays in the New Urban History*. New Haven.

Two general volumes on urban history have much of relevance, the first is American in orientation, the second British.

HANDLIN, O. and BURCHARD, J. (eds.) 1966: *The Historian and the City*. Cambridge, Mass.

DYOS, H.J. (ed.) 1968: *The Study of Urban History*. London.

The major American study is probably The Philadelphia Social History Project. It has been called 'the most ambitious effort at the systematic study of urban history yet undertaken'. The project has been described in: *Historical Methods Newsletter*, 9 (2 and 3), 1976 where listings of theses and publications are given. The most important book is:

HERSHBERG, T. (ed.) 1981: *Philadelphia. Work, Space, Family and Group Experience in the 19th Century*. New York.

A volume of the Transactions of the Institute of British Geographers was devoted to The Victorian City and this should be consulted. *Transactions of the Institute of British Geographers. New Series 1c*, 1979.

A series of essays on various aspects is

JOHNSTON, J.H. and POOLEY, C.G. (eds.) 1982: *The structure of nineteenth century cities*, London.

Undoubtedly the major technical matters relate to the interpretation of census data. The following are the most useful sources:

ARMSTRONG, W.A. 1966: Social structure from the early census returns. In WRIGLEY, E.A. (ed.) *An Introduction to English Historical Demography*. London.

ARMSTRONG, W.A. 1974: *Stability and Change in an English County Town: Social Study of York 1801–51*. Cambridge.

LAWTON, R. (ed.) 1978: *The Census and Social Structure: An Interpretive Guide to Nineteenth Century Censuses for England and Wales*. London.

KATZ, M. 1975: *The People of Hamilton, Canada West: Family and Class in a Mid-nineteenth Century City*. Cambridge, Mass.

WRIGLEY, E.A. (ed.) 1972: *Nineteenth Century Society: Essays in the Use of Quantitative Methods for the Study of Social Data*. Cambridge.

ROYLE, S.A. 1977: Social stratification from early census returns: a new approach. *Area* 9, 215–9.

Discussions of segregation can be found in:

CARTER, H. and WHEATLEY, S. 1980: Residential segregation in nineteenth century cities. *Area* 12, 57–62,

and

ZUNZ, O. 1980: Residential segregation in the American metropolis: concentration, dispersion and dominance. *Urban History Yearbook* (Leicester), 23–33,

as well as in the papers by Cannadine and Ward in the list of references, especially:

WARD, D. 1980: Environs and neighbours in the 'Two Nations'. Residential differentiation in midnine-teenth-century Leeds. *Journal of Historical Geography* 6(2), 133–62.

A classic study of the ghetto is:

SPEAR, A.H. 1967: *Black Chicago. The Making of a Negro Ghetto 1890–1920*. Chicago,

while ethnic variations in a British city are considered in:

POOLEY, C.G. 1977: The residential segregation of migrant communities in Mid-Victorian Liverpool. *Transactions of the Institute of British Geographers*, New Series 2, 364–82.

A study of mobility of value is:

DENNIS, R.J. 1977: Intercensal mobility in a Victorian City. *Transactions of the Institute of British Geographers*, New Series 2, 349–63.

This is an topic for which there is ample direct testimony. The two most well known in English are:

BOOTH, C. 1902–3: *Life and Labour of the People in London*, 17 volumes. London.

ENGELS, F. 1892: *The Condition of the Working Class in England in 1844*. London (first British edition).

A useful summary of Booth's work can be found in:

FRIED, A. and ELMAN, R.M. 1968: *Charles Booth's London*. New York.

Engels's work was first published in German in Leipzig in 1845 and subsequently in English in the USA. (1887). A modern edition with an introduction is:

HOBSBAWM, E. (ed.) (1969): *Frederick Engels' The Condition of the Working Class in England*. London.

Most nineteenth century novelists have material of relevance but the great interpreter of city conditions was Charles Dickens.

11
Afterword

The various topics which have been discussed in this book have been brought to a point where the proper successor is an analysis of the present urban scene. The present is a consequence of the past from which it has developed and it has been to the end of understanding that past that this book has been written. But it must not be assumed because this is an historical urban geography that the present is some final, fixed goal, for it, too, is in a process of change. Already it is being argued that the city as we know it is obsolete (Berry, 1975, 180); that an urban civilization without cities is emergent (Kristol, 1972). The standard urban geography which developed during the period 1950 to 1970, the subject of a plethora of text books, is essentially the urban geography of that period, the product of a particular time span and conditioned by the environment which it sought to interpret. There is, therefore, a continuing, on-going change and the comprehension of that process of change is central to urban geography, both in the sense that the present is derived from the past and that the future is evolving from the present.

It is not difficult to demonstrate in detail the need for historical geography. The buildings and street lines of towns are derived from the past. Lynch's question, 'What time is this place?' is an apposite one, for all townscapes are the product of earlier times and the whole movement for urban conservation is concerned with the preservation of that inheritance (Lynch, 1972).

In a less direct way the current critical problems of cities are not simply and directly related to the immediate operation of a socioeconomic and political system, but have antecedents which need to be comprehended. One of the dominant issues in urban studies at present is that of the inner city, but it is most certainly not a new one for its lineaments can be clearly discerned in the middle of the last century. As chapters 9 and 10 illustrated, a very crude interpretation of residential change over the last century is that of a turning inside out of the pre-industrial city. But the reference is usually limited to residential patterning when what has taken place is a progressive abandonment of the centres of cities by one-time major users of city space. It would be a neat situation if that progression showed up the users in the same periphery-to-centre order as the bid-rent curve, but unfortunately it does not quite follow that order. Certainly agricultural

uses were the first to do so, although they were pushed out rather than moved out, for it is worth recording that working farms could be identified within cities well into the last century. Residence was the next to shift towards the periphery but becoming segregated on a class basis as it did so. Industry should have been the next to move, then offices and finally the retailing of the core. Certainly there was an early inter-war shift of industry to the arterial roads of the periphery but the order in its critical effect becomes reversed. Retailing after the Second World War followed rapidly on the heels of housing. The out-of-town shopping centre and the suburban shopping mall severely damaged the viability of the central business district except where, as in Britain, planning restrictions applied constraints. Offices, too, began to become suburban. 'In 1970, St Louis lost 43 companies to the suburbs. In two recent years, Boston lost about 75. In Cleveland recent losses include the frozen foods division of Stouffer Foods; National Screw and Manufacturing; National Copper and Smelting; Fisher-FazioCosta (a major food chain); and the headquarters of B. F. Goodrich Chemical Co. Likewise in Detroit, S.S. Kresge, the retail chain, plans to move its corporate offices, as does the Michigan Automobile Club; Delta and Pan American Airlines, R.L. Polk, publishers; not to mention Circus World, the toy manufacturers. Things are so glum that former mayor Jerome Cavanaugh sometimes refers to "Detroit's sister cities – Nagasaki and Pompeii" ' (Berry and Kasarda, 1977, 255-6).

Finally and catastrophically industry and with it employment has moved out. The result has been the creation of a vacuum at the centre which has sucked in those lowest in the social scale, least equipped with the skills needed in an increasingly demanding market, and those newly arrived in the city without the resources to compete. All this at a time when the city centre was being denuded of jobs and services.

The purpose of this diversion is to show that the present condition of inner city areas is the consequence of a long-established process. It might well be that an understanding of that process and the length and strength of its operation might bring some realism into present planning proposals as if the investment of a few million pounds is likely to reverse the imperatives of counter-urbanization. Any proposals must be pitched in relation both to the way past changes have operated and to the sort of urban future that must be envisaged.

Another example of this need for a time perspective is the concept of the city system as an evolving set of relationships. An historical perspective which does no more than simply demonstrate the rise and decline of cities poses significant questions. The advantages of location (given no major disruption of the patterns of movement), together with the benefits that accrue to scale and agglomeration, are likely to maintain the outline of a national system of cities as it is. But consideration of growth and development has shown that city systems are complex and composite collections of members from different genetic phases. As the causes of origin change so members of the system become outmoded and redundant. In the past the consequences were decline and eventually disappearance. But neither can now be tolerated with equanimity. However, there is still no simple resolution to the problem either from socialist or capitalist countries. The dilemma remains as to whether resistance to change in the interest of social justice and the freezing of a system at a certain stage in the process of historical change should be pursued, or rather the acceptance of change with the consequent disruption and debasement of individual lives that is difficult to avoid. Again what an historical view offers is a perspective against which policies are derived.

The presentation of contemporary problems of the inner city and declining towns has not been made with the implication that somehow an historical awareness would make decision making in planning any easier. What it does emphasize is that each problem has an antecedent condition to be understood. In academic urban geography the appreciation of that condition is critical. It is also as vital that the urban geographer sees himself at his work as the product of an urban condition and the representative of a particular historical phase, as well as having values determined by more individual attitudes.

In reviewing, as this book has done, the contribution that historical studies can make to contemporary urban analysis perhaps the predominant reaction is the general paucity of material and how limited that contribution has been. In one field, at least, work is abundant for studies of urban morphology constitute the oldest tradition. But it seems that the establishment of any theoretical basis is no nearer than when Garrison so lamented its absence at the Lund conference in 1960 (Norborg, 1962, 463). It is true that some generalizing concepts have been introduced in the form of fringe belts and fixation lines but welcome as they are, they do not yet constitute part of a theoretical framework, and there is no surge of work to exploit any potential they might have. The predominant approach is still that of a chronological narrative of town-planning episodes with an increasingly standardized set of examples. Works of great detail have appeared but offering little in their contribution to generality.

As one moves away from urban morphology the contributions themselves become decidedly thinner. The next popular field has probably been the growth of the city system but in spite of a goodly number of studies on scales both local and national and short-term and long-term it would be difficult to identify significant conclusions, particularly generalizations which contribute towards the relation between city sizes and economic development. This is probably to undervalue the work of Pred and the recent symposium at Amsterdam, the proceedings of which have been edited by Schmal (1981), but even so the synthesizing of many divergent pieces of work has yet to be accomplished. Closely associated with this is the field of urban demography. As this book has revealed, even straight population totals for pre-census cities are difficult to estimate and suggestions vary greatly. In many ways real evaluation of city system growth is vitiated by the absence of the basic data in reliable form.

Given the comments on urban population in the last paragraph it is to be expected that the nature of work carried out on the internal structure of the city should show a close relation to data availability. The fact that the manuscript censuses reached a stage in the mid-nineteenth century where extensive data can be abstracted both in the UK and the USA has resulted in a great deal of analytical work. But to a large extent such work has been limited to what can be called the realm of social area analysis and particularly to the evolving character of segregation by socio-economic status and ethnic status. Even in this field the complex change of residential locations from the early modern period to the beginning of the twentieth century is only revealed at the crudest of scales with no account for variations in size, rapidity of growth and function of towns.

Again influences which were significant in change are only partly studied. Work on land ownership and the willingness of owners to release land, on the building industry and its impact, indeed on the complex of the housing market, has been sporadic and thin. Even more limited is direct work on land-uses in cities and the development of specialized land-use areas. As chapter 8 has shown, some attention is now being paid to the growth of retailing and the appearance of homogeneous shopping areas but it is still very limited. Scola began his 1975 paper on food markets and shops between 1770 and 1870 with the comment, 'It is one of the minor oddities of the recent boom in urban history that we know so little about so central an activity as how the people living in nineteenth-century towns bought their food' (Scola, 1975, 153). Perhaps it is not so much of an oddity when so little has been achieved in the analysis of the way in which specialized land-uses, including retailing, were grouped into discrete urban areas completely restructuring the city centre. Even more surprising is the paucity of studies of the replacement of the scattered crafts during the nineteenth century by large urban industrial regions. There are, it is true, classic studies such as Hall's book on the industries of London after 1861 (Hall, 1962) as there are of the impact of the railways in Kellett's well known book (1969). But these are single studies not part of a large corpus of work from which general principles have emerged and consensus been reached.

This afterword has sought very briefly to make two points. The first is the need for evolutionary studies so that the past is used to put the present into an appropriate and effective context. The second is the comparative lack of developed and effective work in historical urban geography. In many ways this book rather than an integration of studies, a synthesis of ideas, is an indicator of a field where a great deal of fundamental work remains to be done.

References

ABRAMS, P.A. and WRIGLEY, E.A. (eds.) 1978: *Towns in societies. Essays in economic history and historical sociology*. Cambridge.

ADAMS, E.B. and Fr. A. CHAVEZ trans. 1956: *The Missions of New Mexico, 1776* by Fr. Francisco Atanasio Dominguez. Albuquerque.

ADAMS, R.McC. 1966: *The evolution of urban society*. Chicago.

ADBURGHAM, A. 1964: *Shops and shopping, 1800–1914*. London.

ALEXANDER, A. 1970: *Retailing in England during the Industrial Revolution*. London.

APPLEBAUM, R. 1970: *Theories of social change*. Chicago.

ARMSTRONG, W.A. 1966: Social structure from the early census returns. In WRIGLEY, E.A. (ed.).

——1974: *Stability and change in the English county town: a social study of York, 1801–51*. Cambridge.

ASHWORTH, W. 1954: *The genesis of modern British town planning*. London.

BAKER, A.R.H. 1979: Historical geography: a new beginning. *Progress in Human Geography* 3(4), 560–70.

BARKER, D. 1978: A conceptual approach to the description and analysis of an historical urban system. *Regional Studies* 12, 1–10.

——1980: Structural change in hierarchical spatial systems in south west England between 1861 and 1911. *Geografiska Annaler 62B, 1–9*.

BARLEY, M.W. 1969: Nottingham, In LOBEL, M.D. (ed.).

——1976: *The plans and topography of medieval towns in England and Wales*. Council for British Archaeology, Research Report No. 14. London.

BARLEY, M.W. (ed.) 1977: *European towns: their archaeology and early history*. London.

BARLOW, F., BIDDLE, M.et al. 1976: *Winchester in the early Middle Ages. An edition and discussion of the Winton Domesday*. Oxford.

BARTH, G. 1975: *Instant cities: urbanization and the rise of San Francisco and Denver*. New York.

BATER, J.H. 1976: *St Petersburg: industrialization and change*. London.

BELL, C. and R. 1969: *City fathers: the early history of town planning in Britain*. London.

BENEVOLO, L. 1980: *The history of the city*. Trans. Culverwell, G., Cambridge, Mass.

BENTON, J.F. (ed.) 1968: *Town origins. The evidence from medieval England*. Boston.

BERESFORD, M.W. 1958: The poll taxes of 1377, 1379, and 1381. *The Amateur Historian* 3, 271–8.

——1967: *New towns of the Middle Ages. Town plantation in England, Wales and Gascony*. New York and Washington.

BERRY, B.J.L. 1975: The decline of the aging metropolis: cultural bases and social processes. In STERNLIEB, G. and HUGHES, J.W. (eds.), *Post-Industrial America: Metropolitan decline and inter-regional job shifts*. (New Brunswick, NJ), 175–85.

BERRY, B.J.L. and HORTON, F.W 1970: *Geographic perspectives on urban systems*. Englewood Cliffs, NJ.

BERRY, B.J.L. and KASARDA, J.D. 1977: *Contemporary urban ecology*. New York.

BIDDLE, M. 1971: Archaeology and the beginning of English society. In CLEMOES, P. and HUGHES, K. (eds.), (392–8).

BIDDLE, M. 1975: The evolution of towns: planned towns before 1066. In BARLEY, M.W. (ed.), 19–32.

BIDDLE, M. and HILL, D. 1971: Late Saxon planned towns. *Antiquaries Journal* 51(1), 70–85.

BIDDLE, M. and KEENE, D.J. 1976: The late Saxon burgh. In BARLOW, F., BIDDLE, M., *et al.*

BIRD, A.J. 1975–6: John Speed's view of the urban hierarchy of Wales in the early seventeenth century. *Studia Celtica* x–xi, 401–411.

BIRD, J. 1977: *Centrality and cities*. London.

BLAINEY, G. 1966: *The tyranny of distance. How distance shaped Australia's history*. Melbourne.

BLOCH, R. 1958: *The Etruscans*. London. This is a revised and expanded version of *Le mystère etrusque* Paris, 1956; trans. Hoad, S.

BLOCH, R. 1960: *The origins of Rome*. London. This is a revised and expanded version of *Les origines de Rome* Paris, 1959; trans. Shenfield, M.

BÖHNER, K. 1977: Urban and rural settlement in the Frankish kingdom. In BARLEY, M.W. (ed.), 185–202.

BOON, G.C. 1957, revised 1974: *Roman Silchester*. London.

BOOTH, C. 1902–3: *Life and labour of the people in London*. London, 17 vols.

——1968: *Charles Booth's London* ed. FRIED, A. and ELMAN, R.M. New York.

BORCHERT, J.R. 1967: American metropolitan evolution. *Geographical Review* 57, 301–32.

BRAIDWOOD, R.J. and WILLEY, G.R. 1962: *Courses towards urban life. Considerations of some cultural alternates.* Edinburgh.

BRAUDEL, F. 1967: *Capitalism and material life.* London. (Chap. 8 deals with towns, 363–440.)

BRETT-JAMES, N.G. 1935: *The growth of Stuart London.* London.

BRIDBURY, A.R. 1962: *Economic growth: England in the late Middle Ages.* London.

BRIDGES, W. 1811: *Map of the city of New York and Island of Manhattan.* New York.

BRIGGS, A. 1963: *Victorian cities.* London.

BRIGGS, L. 1951: *The ancient Khmer empire.* Philadelphia.

BROOK, A. 1975: Spatial systems in American history. Paper presented to *Institute of British Geographers, Annual Conference*, Oxford.

BROOKE, C.N.L. 1975: *London 800–1216; the shaping of a city.* London.

BROOKS, N.P. 1977: The ecclesiastical topography of early medieval Canterbury. In BARLEY, M.W. (ed.), 487–98.

BRUSH, J.E. 1962: The morphology of Indian cities. In TURNER, R. (ed.), *India's urban future* (Berkeley and Los Angeles).

BUCKINGHAM, J.S. 1849: *Natural evils and practical remedies.* London.

BUCKLIN, L.P. 1972: *Competition and evolution in the distributive trades.* New York.

BURGESS, L.A. 1964: *The origins of Southampton.* Univ. of Leicester, Dept. of Local History. Occasional Papers, 16.

BURGHARDT, A.F. 1971: A hypothesis about gateway cities. *Annals of the Association of American Geographers* 61, 269–85.

BURKE, G. 1971: *Towns in the making.* London.

BURKE, P. 1975: Some reflections on the pre-industrial city. *Urban History Yearbook* 13–21.

BURNETT, J. 1978: *A social history of housing, 1815–1870.* London.

BURSTEIN, A.N. 1981: Immigrants and residential mobility: the Irish and Germans in Philadelphia, 1850–1880. In HERSHBERG, T. (ed.), chapter 5, 174–203.

BUTLIN, R.A. 1978: The late Middle Ages c. 1350–1500. In DODGSHON, R.A. and BUTLIN, R.A. (eds.), *An historical geography of England and Wales.* (London), 119–50.

BUTZER, K.W. 1976: *Early hydraulic civilization in Egypt: a study in cultural ecology.* Chicago.

CALZA, G., BECATTI, G., GISMONDI, I., de ANGELIS d'OSSAT, G. and BLOCH, H. 1953: *Scavi di Ostia: topografia generale.* Rome.

CAMDEN, W. 1610: *Britannia.* London. First English translation by Philemon Holland. The first Latin edition was published in 1586.

CANNADINE, D. 1977: Victorian cities: how different? *Social History* 4, 457–82.

——1980: Lords and landlords: the aristocracy and the towns 1774–1967. Leicester.

CAROE, L. 1968: A multivariate grouping scheme: association analysis of East Anglian towns. In BOWEN, E.G., CARTER, H. and TAYLOR, J.A. (eds.), *Geography at Aberystwyth* (Cardiff), 253–369.

CARTER, H. 1955: Urban grades and spheres of influences in south-west Wales: an historical consideration. *Scottish Geographical Magazine* 71, 43–58.

——1956: The urban hierarchy and historical geography. *Geographical Studies* 3, 85–101.

——1958: Aberystwyth, the modern development of a medieval castle town in Wales. *Transactions of the Institute of British Geographers* 25, 239–53.

——1965: *The towns of Wales. A study of urban geography.* Cardiff.

——1969: *The growth of the Welsh city system.* Cardiff.

——1981: *The study of urban geography*, 3rd edn. London.

CARTER, H. and ROWLEY, G. 1966: The morphology of the Central Business District of Cardiff. *Transactions of the Institute of British Geographers* 38, 119–34.

CARTER, H. and WHEATLEY, S.E. 1979: Fixation lines and fringe belts, land-uses and social areas: nineteenth century change in the small town. *Transactions of the Institute of British Geographers* New Series, 4, 214–38.

——1980: Residential segregation in nineteenth-century cities. *Area* 12 (1), 57–62

——1982: *Merthyr Tydfil in 1851.* A study of the spatial structure of a Welsh industrial town. Board of Celtic Studies, Social Science Monograph No. 7 Cardiff.

CASTAGNOLI, F. 1971: Orthogonal town planning in antiquity, trans. Caliandro, V. Cambridge, Mass. 10–72.

CASTELLS, M. 1976: Theory and ideology in urban sociology. In PICKVANCE, C.G. (ed.), *Urban Sociology: Critical essays* (London), 60–84.

——(1977): *The urban question: a Marxist approach*, trans. Sheridan, A. London.

CHADWICK, E. 1842: Report of an inquiry into the sanitary condition of the labouring population of Great Britain. Lords Sessional Papers, XXVII, 240.

CHALKLIN, C.W. 1974: *The provincial towns of Georgian England. A study of the building process, 1740–1820.* London.

CHAMBERS, J.D. 1952: *A century of Nottingham history, 1851–1951.* Nottingham.

CHANDLER, T. and FOX, G. 1974: *3000 years of urban growth.* New York.

CHAPIN, E. 1937: *Les villes des foires de Champagne des origines au début du XIVᵉ siecle.* Paris.

CHAPMAN, S.D. (ed.) 1971: *The history of working-class housing, 1780–1918.* London.

CHERRY, G. 1972: *Urban change and planning. A history of urban development in Britain since 1750.* Henley-on-Thames.

CHILDE, V.G. 1950: The urban revolution. *Town Planning Review* 21, 3–17.

CLARK, P. (ed.) 1976: *The early modern town*. London.

CLARK, P. and SLACK, P. 1976: *English towns in transition, 1500–1700*. Oxford.

CLARKE, D.L. 1968: *Analytical archaeology*. London.

CLAY, G. 1973: *Close-up. How to read the American city*. New York.

CLEMOES, P. and HUGHES, K. (eds.) 1971: *England before the Conquest. Studies in primary sources presented to Dorothy Whitelock*. Cambridge.

CLIFFORD, E.M. 1961: *Bagendon: a Belgic oppidum*. Cambridge.

COEDES, G. 1963: *Angkor. An introduction*, Trans. Gardiner, E.F. Hong Kong.

COLLIS, J.R. 1971: Functional and theoretical interpretations of British coinage. *World Archaeology* 3, 71–84.

——1974: A functional approach to pre-Roman coinage. In CASEY, J. and REECE, R.M. (eds.), *Coins and the archaeologist* (Oxford), British Archaeological Reports 4, 1–11.

CONZEN, M.P. 1975: Capital flows and the developing urban hierarchy: state bank capital in Wisconsin, 1854–1895. *Economic Geography* 51, 321–38.

——1977: The maturing urban system in the United States, 1840–1910. *Annals of the Association of American Geographers* 67, 88–108.

CONZEN, M.R.G. 1960: Alnwick: a study in town plan analysis. *Transactions of the Institute of British Geographers* 27.

CORFIELD, P.J. 1982: *The impact of English Towns 1700–1800*. Oxford.

COX, O.C. 1964: The pre-industrial city reconsidered. *Sociological Quarterly* 5, 133–44.

CROSSICK, G. (ed.) 1977: *The lower middle class in Britain*. London.

——1978: *An artisan elite in Victorian society. Kentish London, 1840–1880*. London.

CUNLIFFE, B. 1971: Some aspects of hill forts and their cultural environment. In HILLAND, D. and JESSON, M. (eds.), *The Iron Age and its hillforts* (Southampton), 55.

——1974: The Iron Age. In RENFREW, C. (ed.), *British prehistory. A new outline* (London), 248.

——1976: The origins of urbanization in Britain. In CUNLIFFE, B. and ROWLEY, T. (eds.) 1976, 95–133.

CUNLIFFE, B. and ROWLEY, T. (eds.) 1976: *Oppida: the beginning of urbanization in Barbarian Europe*. British Archaeological Reports, Supplementary Series, No. 11. Oxford.

CURL, J. 1970: *European cities and society. A study of the influence of political climate on town design*. London.

DAUNTON, M. 1978: Towns and economic growth in eighteenth century England. In ABRAMS, P.A. and WRIGLEY, E.A. (eds.).

DAVIDOFF, L. 1973: *The best circles: society, etiquette and the season*. London.

DAVIES, W.K.D. 1967: Centrality and the central place hierarchy. *Urban Studies* 4, 61.

DEFFONTAINES, B. 1929: Montauban. Etude de geographie urbaine. *Annales de Geographie* 38.

DEFOE, D. 1726–32: *The complete English tradesman*, 2 vols. London.

DENNIS, R.J. 1977: Intercensal mobility in a Victorian city. *Transactions of the Institute of British Geographers* New Series 2, 349–63.

DEWHIRST, R.K. 1960: Saltaire. *Town Planning Review* 31(2), 140.

DICKINSON R.E. 1953: *Germany. A general and regional geography*. London.

DISRAELI, B. 1845: *Sybil, or the Two Nations*. London.

DOBB, M. 1946: *Studies in the development of capitalism*. London.

DODGSHON, R.A. 1977: The modern world-system. A spatial perspective. *Peasant Studies* 6, 8–19.

DONKIN, R.A. 1973: Changes in the early Middle Ages. In DARBY, H.C. (ed.), *A new historical geography of England* (Cambridge), 123–35.

DYER, A.D. 1973: *The city of Worcester in the sixteenth century*. Leicester.

DYOS, H.J. 1961: *Victorian suburb. A study of the growth of Camberwell*. Leicester.

——(ed.) 1968: *The study of urban history*. London.

——1973: *Urbanity and suburbanity*. Leicester.

——1977: Editorial, in *Urban History Yearbook 1977*, 2–5.

DYOS, H.J. and WOLFF, M. (eds.) 1973: *The Victorian city: image and realities* 2 vols. London.

EDWARDS, K.C. (ed.) 1966: *Nottingham and its region*. Nottingham.

ELIADE, M. 1949: *Le mythe de l'éternel retour*. Paris.

Encyclopaedia Judaica, 1971. Jerusalem.

ENGELS, F. 1887: *The condition of the working class in England in 1844*. First English translation of *Die Lage der arbeitenden Klasse in England* (Leipzig, 1845).

——1892: *The condition of the working-class in England*. This was the first British edition (see also under HOBSBAWM 1969). London.

ENNEN, E. 1968: The variety of urban development, in BENTON, J.F. (ed.) 12. This is a translation (with emendations) of ENNEN, E. 1956: Les différents types de formation de villes européennes. *Le Moyen Age* LXII, 397–411.

——1979: *The medieval town*, trans. Fryde, E. Amsterdam.

EVENSON, N. 1979: *Paris: a century of change, 1878–1978*. New Haven, Conn.

EVERITT, A. (ed.) 1973: *Perspectives in English urban history*. London.

——1974: The Banburys of England. *Urban History Year book*, 28–38.

FAIRSERVIS, W.A. 1961: The Harappan civilization – new evidence and more theory. *American Museum Novitates*, No. 2055. American Museum of Natural History (New York), 18.

FEBVRE, L. 1932: *A geographical introduction to history*, trans. Mounford, E.G. and Paxton, J.H. London.

FINLEY, M.I. 1963: *The Ancient Greeks*. London.

FLANAGAN, D. *et al.* (eds.) 1965: *Cities*. New York.

FLICHE, A. 1925: *Aigues-Mortes et Saint Gilles*. Petites monographies.

FOGG, W. 1939a: Tribal markets in Spanish Morocco. *Journal Royal African Society* 38, 322-6.

——1939b: The importance of tribal markets in the commercial life of the countryside of north-west Morocco. *Africa* 12(4), 445-9.

FRANCASTEL, P. (ed.) 1960: *Les origines des villes polonaises*. Ecole practique des hautes études – Sorbonne. Sixième section: sciences économique et sociale. Congrès et colloques 11 (Paris).

FRERE, S.S. 1966: The end of towns in Roman Britain. In WACHER, J.S. (ed), *The civitas capitals of Roman Britain* (Leicester).

——1971: *Verulamium excavations 1*. Oxford.

——1975: The 'origin' of 'small towns'. In RODWELL, W. and ROWLEY, T. (eds.), *Small towns of Roman Britain*. British Archaeological Reports 15, 115-24.

FRIED, A. 1960: On the evolution of social stratification and the state. In DIAMOND, A. (ed.), *Culture in History* (New York), 729.

FRIED, A. and ELMAN, R.M. 39 1968: *Charles Booth's London*. New York.

FUSTEL DE COULANGES, N.D. 1864: *La cité antique*. Paris.

GADD, C.J. 1962: The cities of Babylon. In EDWARDS, I.E.S. *et al.* (eds.), *The Cambridge ancient history* (Cambridge) vol. 1, Chapter XIII, 34.

GADOL, J. 1972: *Leon Battista Alberti: universal man of the early Renaissance*. London.

GANSHOF, F.L. 1943: *Etude sur le développement des villes entre Loire au moyen age*. Paris and Brussels.

——1959: Contribution to – 'La discussione sul tema Italia'. In *La città nell' alto medioevo*. Settlimane di studio del centro Italiano di studi sull 'alto medioevo, Spoleto, 202-3.

GAULDIE, E. 1974: *Cruel habitations. A history of working-class housing, 1780-1918*. London.

GEDDES, P. 1949: *Cities in evolution*. London. This is an edited version of the original 1915 edition.

GIEDION, S. 1954: *Space, time and architecture*, 3rd edition. Cambridge, Mass.

GIEYSZTOR, A. 1959: Les origines de la ville slave. In *La citta nell' alto medioevo*, 279-303.

GLASS, D.V. 1965: Two papers on Gregory King. In GLASS, D.V. and EVERSLEY, D.E.C. (eds.).

——1966: London's inhabitants within the walls. *London Records Society Publications* 2.

——1968: Notes on the demography of London at the end of the seventeenth century. *Daedalus* 97, 581-92.

GLASS, D.V. and EVERSLEY, D.E.C. 1965: *Population in history. Essays in historical demography*. London.

GLASS, D.V. and REVELLE, R. 1972: *Population and social change*. London.

GOHEEN, P.G. 1970: *Victorian Toronto, 1850-1900: Pattern and process of growth*. Dept. of Geography, Research Paper 127. (Chicago).

GOTTMANN, J. 1967: Why the skyscraper? In ELDREDGE, H.W. (ed.), *Taming megalopolis* (New York), vol. 1, chapter 10, 429-47. The paper was first published in *Geographical Review* 56, (1966).

GREATER LONDON COUNCIL 1900-1980 continuing: *Survey of London*. London. 39 volumes to date.

GREEN, C.M. 1965: *American cities in the growth of the nation*. New York.

GRODECKI, A.L. (ed.) 1965: *Plans en relief de villes Belges levés par des ingénieurs militaires français – XVIIᵉ – XIXᵉ siècle*. Brussels.

GROVES, P.A. and MULLER, E.K. 1975: The evolution of black residential areas in late nineteenth century cities. *Journal of Historical Geography* 1, 169-91.

GUTKIND, E.A. 1964 continuing: *International History of City Development*. 1: *Urban Development in Central Europe* (1964); 2: *Urban Development in the Alpine and Scandinavian Countries* (1965); 3: *Urban Development in Southern Europe, Spain and Portugal* (1967); 4: *Urban Development in Southern Europe, Italy and Greece* (1969); 5: *Urban Development in Western Europe, France and Belgium* (1970); 6: *Urban Development in Western Europe, Great Britain and the Netherlands* (1971); 7: *Urban Development in East Central Europe, Poland, Czechoslovakia, and Hungary* (1972); 8: *Urban Development in Eastern Europe, Bulgaria, Romania, and the USSR* (1972). New York and London.

HAGGETT, T., CLIFF, A.D. and FREY, A. 1977: *Locational models*. London.

HALL, P.G. 1962: *The industries of London since 1861*. London.

HANDLIN, O. and BURCHARD, J. (eds.) 1963: *The historian and the city*. Cambridge, Mass.

HANSEN, V. 1976: The pre-industrial city of Denmark. A study of two medieval founded market-towns. *Geografisk Tidsskrift* 75, 51-7.

HARDOY, J. 1967: *Urban planning in pre-Columbian America*. London.

HARRIS, M. 1968: *The rise of anthropological theory*. London.

HARVEY, D. 1973: *Social justice and the city*. London.

HARVEY, P.D.A. 1969: Banbury. In LOBEL, M.D. (ed.).

HASSAN, R. 1972: Islam and urbanization in the medieval Middle-East. *Ekistics* 33 (193), 108-9.

HATCHER, J. 1977: *Plague, population and the English economy, 1348-1530*. London.

HAUSER, P.M. and SCHNORE, L.R. (eds.) 1965: *The study of urbanization*. New York.

HEINE-GELDERN, R. 1963: *Conceptions of state and kingship in Southeast Asia*. Data Paper: No. 18. SE Asia program. Dept. of Asian Studies, Cornell University, Ithaca, NY.

HERSHBERG, T. (ed.) 1981: *Philadelphia. Work, space, family and group experience in the 19th century*. New York.

HIBBERT, A.B. 1953: The origins of the medieval town patriciate. *Past and Present* 3, 15-27.

HIORNS, F.R. 1956: *Town building in history*. London.

HOBSBAWM, E. (ed.) 1969: *Frederick Engel's The*

condition of the working-class in England. London.

HODGES, R. 1982: *Dark Age economics. The origins of Towns and trade AD 600–1000*. London.

HOLDEN, W. 1811: *Annual London and country directory of the United Kingdom and Wales*. London.

HOLLINGSWORTH, T.H. 1976: *Historical demography*. Cambridge.

HOLLIS, P. 1973: *Class and conflict in nineteenth century England, 1815–1850*. London.

HOLMES, R.S. 1977: *Continuity and change in a Mid-Victorian resort. Ramsgate, 1851–1871*. Unpub. PhD thesis, University of Kent.

HOSKINS, W.G. 1935: *Industry, trade and people in Exeter, 1688–1800*. Manchester.

HOWELL, R. 1972: Hearth tax returns. In MUNBY, L.M. (ed.), *Short guides to records*. Historical Association (London), No. 7.

HUBERT, J. 1959; Evolution de la topographie et de l'aspect des villes de Gaule du Vᵉ au Xᵉ siecle. In *La citta nell 'alto medioevo*, 529–58.

JACOBS, J. 1969: *The economy of cities*. New York.

JEFFERSON, M. 1939: The law of the primate city. *Geographical Review* 29, 227.

JOHNS, E. 1965: *British townscapes*. London.

JOHNSON, G.J. 1980: Rank size convexity and system integration: a view from archaeology. *Economic Geography* 56, 234–47.

JOHNSON, J.H. (ed.) 1974: *Suburban growth*. London.

JOHNSON, J.H. and POOLEY C.G. (eds.) 1982: *The structure of nineteenth century cities*. London.

JOHNSTON, R.J. 1979: *Geography and geographers. Anglo-American human geography since 1945*. London.

——1980: *City and society. An outline for urban geography*. London.

JONES, E.L. and FALKUS, M.E. 1979: Urban improvement and the English economy in the seventeenth and eighteenth centuries. *Research in Economic History* 4, 193–233.

KALINOWSKI, W. 1972: Polish urban settlement before the 13th century and evolution of cities in the High and Late Middle Ages, in GUTKIND, E.A. (1964–)7, 17–51.

KATZ, M 1975: *The people of Hamilton, Canada West: family and class in a mid-nineteenth century city*. Cambridge, Mass.

KEENE, D.J. 1976: Suburban growth. In BARLEY, M.W. (ed.) *The plans and topography of medieval towns in England and Wales*. Council for British Archaeological Research, Report 14.

KELLETT, J.R. 1969: *The impact of railways on Victorian cities*. London

KENYON, K. 1957: *Digging up Jericho*. London.

KING, A.D. 1976: *Colonial urban development. Cultural, social power and environment*. London, Henley-on-Thames and Boston.

KITTO, H.D.F. 1962: *The Greeks*. London, Pelican reprint, 71.

KRAELING, C.H. and ADAMS, R.M. 1960: *City invincible: urbanization and cultural development in the ancient Near East*. Chicago.

KRIESIS, A. 1965: *Greek town building*. Athens.

KRISTOL, I. 1972: An urban civilization without cities. *Washington Post Outlook*, 3 Dec., p. 31.

LAMPARD, E.E. 1955: The history of cities in economically-advanced areas. *Economic Development and Cultural Change* 3, 92.

——1965: Historical aspects of urbanization. In HAUSER, P.M. and SCHNORE, L.R. (eds.), 519–44.

LAMPL, P. (n.d.): *Cities and planning in the ancient Near East*. London.

LANGTON, J.1975: Residential patterns in pre-industrial cities: some case studies from seventeenth century Britain. *Transactions of the Institute of British Geographers* 65, 1–28.

——1977: Late medieval Gloucester: some data from a rental of 1455. *Transactions of the Institute of British Geographers*. New Series, 2, 259–77.

——1978: Industry and towns, 1500–1730, In DODGSHON, R.A. and BUTLIN, R.A., *An historical geography of England and Wales* (London), 173–98.

LATOUCHE, R. 1937: Un aspect de la vie rurale dans le Maine au XIᵉ et au XIIᵉ siecle: l'établissement des bourgs. *Le Moyen-Age* 1 and 2.

LAVEDAN, P. 1959: *Histoire de l'urbanisme. Renaissance et temps modernes*. (Paris).

——1960: *Histoire de Paris*. Paris.

LAVEDAN, P. and HUGUENEY, J. 1966: *Histoire de l'urbanisme. Antiquité* 2nd edn., Paris.

——1974: *L'urbanisme au moyen age*. Geneva and Paris.

LAW, C.M. 1967: The growth of urban population in England and Wales,1801–1911. *Transactions of the Institute of British Geographers* 41, 125–44.

LAWTON, R. (ed.) 1978: *The census and social structure: an interpretive guide to nineteenth century censuses for England and Wales*. London.

——1978: Population and society, 1730–1900. In DODGSHON, R.A. and BUTLIN, R.A. (eds.), *An historical geography of England and Wales* (London), 313–66.

LAWTON, R. and POOLEY, C.G. 1976: *The social geography of Merseyside in the nineteenth century*. Final Report to the Social Science Research Council (British Lending Library).

LAZZARONI, M. and MUNOZ, A. (eds.) 1908: *Filarete, scultore e architetto de Secolo XV*. Rome.

LEES, L.H. 1969: Patterns of lower-class life: Irish slum communities in nineteenth-century London. In Thernstrom, S. and Sennett, R. (eds.), 359–85.

LEWIS, C.R.1970: The central place pattern of Mid-Wales and the Welsh Borderland. In CARTER, H. and DAVIES, W.K.D. (eds.) *Urban essays: studies in the geography of Wales* (London) Chap. 10.

——1975a: Trade directories – a data source in urban analysis. *National Library of Wales Journal* 19, 181–93.

——1975b: The analysis of changes in urban status. A case study in Mid-Wales and the middle Welsh Borderland. *Transactions of the Institute of British Geographers* 64, 49–65.

LEWIS, E.A. 1912: *The medieval boroughs of Snowdonia.* London.

LIPMAN, V.D. 1949: *Local government areas, 1834–1945.* Oxford.

LOBEL, M.D. 1969: Hereford. In Lobel, M.D. (ed.).

——(ed.) 1969: *Historic towns. Maps and plans of towns and cities in the British Isles, with historical commentaries, from earliest times to 1800.* Oxford.

LONDON, B. and FLANAGAN, W.G. 1976: Comparative urban ecology: a summary of the field. In WALTON, J. and MASOTTI, L.H. (eds.), *The city in comparative prospect* (London).

LOPEZ, R.S. 1966: The crossroads within the wall. In HANDLIN, O. and BURCHARD, J. (eds.).

LOTCHIN, R.W. 1974: *San Francisco, 1846–1856: from hamlet to city.* New York.

LOYN, H. 1971: Towns in late Anglo-Saxon England: the evidence and some possible lines of enquiry. In CLEMOES, P. and HUGHES, K. (eds.), *England before the Conquest* (Cambridge).

LUXEMBOURG, R. 1913: *The accumulation of capital.* London.

LYNCH, K. 1972: *What time is this place?* Cambridge, Mass.

MacCAFFREY, W.T. 1958: *Exeter, 1540–1640. The growth of an English county town.* Cambridge, Mass.

McKELVEY, B. 1969: *The city in American history.* London.

McKENZIE, R.D. 1933: *The metropolitan community.* New York.

MADDEN, C.H. 1956: Some indications of stability in the growth of cities in the United States. *Economic Development and Cultural Change* 4, 236–52.

MAINE, H.S. 1894: *Ancient Law.* London.

MAITLAND, F.W. 1898: *Township and borough.* Cambridge.

MARTIN, R. 1956: *L'urbanisme dans la Grèce Antique.* Paris.

MARTINDALE, D. and NEUWIRTH, G. (trans. and eds.) 1958: *The city* by MAX WEBER. Prefatory remarks: the theory of the city. New York.

MARX, K. 1967: *Capital: a critique of political economy.* New York.

MASOTTI, L. H. and HADDEN J.K. (eds.) 1973: *The urbanization of the suburbs.* Urban Affairs Annual Reviews No. 7 (Beverly Hills).

MELLAART, J. 1967: *Catal Huyuk. A Neolithic town in Anatolia.* London.

MILLER, Z.L. 1968: *Boss Cox's Cincinnati.* New York.

MILLON, R.1972: Teotihuacan: completion of map of giant ancient city. *Ekistics* 33 (195), 137–41.

MILNES, D.C. 1972: Angkor: a theocratic system of urban development. *Ekistics* 33 (195), 130–6.

MOHOLY-NAGY, J. 1968: *Matrix of man. An illustrated history of urban environment.* London.

MOLS, R. 1954: *Introduction à la démographie historique des villes d'Europe du XIVe au XVIIIe siecle*, 3 vols. (Louvain).

MORELOWSKI, M. 1960: L'évolution de l'urbanisme de Wroclaw. In FRANCASTEL, P. (ed.).

MORGAN, M.H. (trans.) 1914: *Vitruvius. The ten books on architecture.* Cambridge, Mass., republished New York, 1960.

MORIZE, J. 1914: Aigues-Mortes au 13e siecle. *Annales du Midi.*

MORNING CHRONICLE 1850: *Labour and the poor.* The mining and manufacturing district of South Wales. Letters to the *Morning Chronicle.*

MORRILL, R.L. 1965: *Migration and the spread and growth of urban settlement.* Lund Studies in Geography, Ser. B. Human Geography, No. 26. Lund.

MORRIS, A.E.J. 1972: *History of urban form.* London.

MRUSEK, H.J. 1955–6: Zur städtebaulichen Entwicklung Magdeburgs im hohen Mittelalter. *Wissenschaftliche Zeitschrift der Martin-Luther-Universität* 5, 1219–1314.

MUMFORD, L. 1961: *The city in history.* London.

MUNDIGO, A.I. and CROUCH, D.P. 1977: The city planning ordinances or the Laws of the Indies revisited. *Town Planning Review* 48. Part I: Their philosophy and implications, 247–68; Part II: Three American cities, 397–418.

MYRDAL, G. 1957: *Economic theory and under-developed regions.* London.

NASH, D. (1976): The growth of urban society in France. In CUNLIFFE, B. and ROWLEY, T. (eds.).

NOBLE, F. and SHOESMITH, R. 1967: Hereford city excavations, 1967. *Transactions of the Woolhope Naturalists Field Club* 39(1), 44–70.

NORBORG, K. (ed.) 1962: *Proceedings of the Lund symposium in urban geography, Lund 1960.* Lund.

NORTON, J.E. 1950: *Guide to the national and provincial directories of England and Wales (excluding London) published before 1856.* London.

OLSEN, D.J. 1964: *Town planning in London. The eighteenth and nineteenth centuries.* New Haven, Conn.

OWEN, H. (ed.) 1902–36: *The description of Pembrokeshire, by George Owen of Henllys*, 4 vols, Cymmrodorion Record Series. London.

PATTEN, J. 1977; Urban occupations in pre-industrial England. *Transactions of the Institute of British Geographers*, New Series, 2, 296–313.

——1978: *English towns, 1500–1700.* Folkestone.

PEARSON, H.W. 1957: The economy has no surplus: critique of a theory of development. In POLANYI, K. *et al.* (eds.).

PELLIOT, P. 1951: *Mémoires sur les coutumes du Camboge de Tcheou Ta-Kouan.* Paris.

PENCE, M.L. 1968: *The Laramie Story.* Laramie.

PHYTHIAN-ADAMS, C. 1972: Ceremony and the citizen: the communal year at Coventry, 1450–1500. In CLARK, P. and SLACK, P. (eds.), *Crisis and order in English towns, 1500–1700* (London), 57–85.

——1979: *Desolation of a city. Coventry and the urban crisis of the late Middle Ages.* Cambridge.

PIRENNE, H. 1925: *Medieval cities*. Princeton, NJ.

——1937: *Economic and social history of medieval Europe*. London

POLANYI, K, 1957: Marketless trading in Hammurabi's time. In POLANYI, K. *et al.* (eds).

POLANYI, K. *et al.* (eds.) 1957: *Trade and market in the early empires*. New York.

POOLEY, C.G. 1977: The residential segregation of migrant communities in mid-Victorian Liverpool. *Transactions of the Institute of British Geographers*, New Series, 2, 364–82.

——1979: Residential mobility in the British city. *Transactions of the Institute of British Geographers*, New Series, 4, 258–77.

POUNDS, N.J.G. 1969: The urbanization of the classical world. *Annals of the Association of American Geographers* 59(1), 143.

PRED, A. 1966: *The spatial dynamics of US urban-industrial growth, 1800–1914: interpretive and theoretical essays*. Cambridge, Mass.

——1973: *Urban growth and the circulation of information: the United States system of cities, 1790–1840*. Cambridge, Mass.

——1977: *City-systems in advanced economies*. London.

PRITCHARD, R.M. 1976: *Housing and the spatial structure of the city*. Cambridge.

PULLAN, B. 1971: *Rich and poor in Renaissance Venice*. Oxford.

RADFORD, J.P. 1979: Testing the model of the pre-industrial city: the case of ante bellum Charleston, South Carolina. *Transactions of the Institute of British Geographers*, New Series, 4, 392–410.

RAHTZ, P. 1977: The archaeology of West Mercian towns. In DORNIER, A. (ed.), *Mercian Studies* (Leicester), 107–29.

REDDAWAY, T.E. 1951: *The rebuilding of London after the Great Fire*. London.

REDFIELD, R. and SINGER, M. 1954: The cultural role of cities. *Economic Development and Cultural Change* 3, 53.

REES, G. 1969: *St Michael: a history of Marks and Spencer*. London

REES, W. 1948: *The Union of England and Wales*. Cardiff.

REISSMAN, L. 1964: *The urban process. Cities in industrial society*. New York.

REPS, J.W. 1965: *The making of urban America. A history of city planning in the United States*. Princeton, NJ.

——1972: *Tidewater towns. City planning in colonial Virginia and Maryland*. Williamsburg, Va.

——1979: *Cities of the American West. A history of frontier urban planning*. Princeton, NJ.

REYNOLDS, J.M. 1966: Legal and constitutional problems. In WACHER, J.S. (ed.), 70.

REYNOLDS, S. 1977: *An introduction to the history of English medieval towns*. Oxford.

RICHARDSON, M.W. 1973: The theory of the distribution of city sizes: review and prospects. *Regional Studies* 7, 239–51.

RIVET, A.L.F. 1966: Summing up: some historical aspects of the civitates of Roman Britain. In WACHER, J.S. (ed.).

ROBB, J.G. (n.d.): Suburb and slum in nineteenth century Gorbals: problems of a small-scale study of social segregation. *Discussion Paper*, Dept. of Geography, University of Strathclyde.

ROBSON, B.T. 1973: *Urban growth: an approach*. London.

RODGERS, H.A. 1956: The market area of Preston in the sixteenth and seventeenth centuries. *Geographical Studies* 3, 46–55.

RODWELL, W. 1976: Coinage, oppida and the rise of Belgic power in south-eastern England. In CUNLIFFE, B. and ROWLEY, T. (eds.).

RODWELL, W. and ROWLEY, T. (eds.) (1974): *Small towns of Roman Britain*. British Archaeological Reports No. 15, Oxford.

ROWLEY, T. 1975: Alchester and Dorchester on Thames. In RODWELL, W. and ROWLEY, T. (eds.).

ROYLE, S.A. 1977: Social stratification from early census returns. *Area* 9, 215–9.

ROZMAN, G. 1976: *Urban networks in Russia, 1750–1800, and premodern periodization*. Princeton, NJ.

RUSSELL, J.C. 1948: *British medieval population*. Albuquerque.

RYKWERT, J. 1976: *The idea of the town: the anthropology of urban form in Rome, Italy and the Ancient World*. London.

SANDERS, W. 1965: The cultural ecology of the Teotihuacan valley. Unpub. Mss. cited in HARRIS, M. (1968).

SANDERS, W. and PRICE, B. 1968: *Mesoamerica: the evolution of a civilization*. New York.

SAWYER, P.H. 1977: Kings and merchants, in SAWYER, P.H. and WOOD, I.N. (eds.) *Early medieval kingship*. Leeds.

SCARGILL, D.I. 1979: *The form of cities*. London.

SCHAEDEL, P.P., HARDOY, J.E. and KINZER, N.S. (eds.) 1978: *Urbanization in the Americas from its beginnings to the present*. The Hague and Paris.

SCHMAL, H. (ed.) 1981. *Patterns of European urbanization since 1500*. London.

SCOLA, R. 1975: Food markets and shops in Manchester, 1770–1870. *Journal of Historical Geography* 1, 153–67.

SCOTT, M. 1959: *The San Francisco Bay area. A metropolis in perspective*. Los Angeles.

SHAW, G. 1978: *Patterns and processes in the geography of retail change with special reference to Kingston-upon-Hull*. (Univ. of Hull), Occasional Papers in Geography No. 4.

——1982: *British directories as sources in historical geography*. Institute of British Geographers. Historical Research Series, 8.

SHAW, G. and WILD, M.T. 1979: Retail patterns in the Victorian city. *Transactions of the Institute of British Geographers*, New Series, 4, 278–91.

SHAW, M. 1977: The ecology and social change: Wolverhampton 1851–71. *Transactions of the*

Institute of British Geographers, New Series 2, 332–48.

——1979: Reconciling social and physical space: Wolverhampton, 1871. *Transactions of the Institute of British Geographers*, New Series, 4, 192–213.

SHEAIL, J. 1972: The distribution of taxable population and wealth in England during the early sixteenth century. *Transactions of the Institute of British Geographers* 55, 111–26.

SHEVKY, E. and BELL, W. 1955: *Social area analysis.* Stanford, Calif.

SHOESMITH, R. 1974: The city of Hereford, archaeology and development. Birmingham. West Midlands Rescue Archaeology Committee.

SINCLAIR, A. 1962: *Prohibition: Era of excess.* London.

SJOBERG, G. 1960: *The preindustrial city.* New York.

——1965: The origin and evolution of cities. In FLANAGAN, D. *et al.* (eds.), 25–39.

SKELTON, R.A. 1966: *Braun and Hogenberg. Civitates Orbis Terrarum. 'The towns of the world', 1572–1618* Three volumes. Cleveland and New York.

SLATER, T. 1976: Estate ownership and nineteenth century suburban development. In MCWHIRR, A. (ed.), *Archaeology and history of Cirencester.* British Archaeology Reports 30 (Oxford).

SMAILES, A.E. 1953: *The geography of towns.* London.

SMITH, C.A. 1970: Exchange systems and the spatial distribution of elites: the organizational stratification in agrarian societies, in SMITH, C.A. (ed.) *Regional Analysis 2* London. 309–74.

SMITH, C.T. 1967: *An historical geography of Western Europe before 1800.* London.

SPATE, O.H.K. 1948: The growth of London, AD 1660–1800. In DARBY, H.C. (ed.) *An historical geography of England before 1800* (Cambridge), 529–48.

SPATE, O.H.K. and AHMAD, E. 1950: Five cities of the Gangetic Plain. *Geographical Review* 40, 260–78.

SPEAR, A.H. 1967: *Black Chicago. The making of a Negro ghetto, 1890–1920.* Chicago.

STANFIELD, R. 1973: *The economic surplus and neo-Marxism.* Lexington, Mass.

STANISLAWSKI, D. 1946: The origin and spread of the grid pattern town. *Geographical Review* 36, 105–20.

STEPHENSON, C. 1933: *Borough and town. A study of urban origins in England.* Cambridge, Mass.

STEWART, C. 1952: *A prospect of cities.* London.

STILL, B. 1974: *Urban America. A history with documents.* Boston.

SUMMERSON, J. 1945: *Georgian London.* London.

SUTCLIFFE, A. (ed.) 1974: *Multi-storey living. The British working-class experience.* London.

SWAUGER, J. 1978: Pittsburg's residential pattern in 1815. *Annals of the Association of American Geographers* 68, 265–77.

TAIT, J. 1936: *The medieval English borough.* Manchester.

TARN, J.N. 1971: Working class housing in 19th-century Britain. *Architectural Association Paper* 7.

——1973: *Five percent philanthropy. An account of housing between 1840 and 1914.* Cambridge.

TAYLOR, A.J. (ed.) 1975: *The standard of living in Britain in the industrial revolution.* London.

TESTUT, L. 1920: *La bastide de Beaumont.* Bordeaux.

The Urban History Yearbook (1974 *et seq.*).

THERNSTROM, S. and SENNETT, R. (eds.) (1969): *Nineteenth century cities. Essays in the new urban history.* New Haven, Conn.

THRUPP, S. 1961–2: The creativity of cities. *Comparative Studies in Society and History* IV, 61–2.

TIKHOMIROV, M. 1959: *The towns of ancient Rus.* Trans. Sdobnikou, Y. from second Russian edition. Moscow.

TIMMS, D.W.G. 1971: *The urban mosaic. Towards a theory of residential differentiation.* Cambridge.

TRABUT-CUSSAC, J-P. 1954: Bastides ou forteresses? *Le Moyen Age* 60, 81–135.

UCKO, P.J., TRINGHAM, R. and DIMBLEBY, G.W. (eds.) 1972: *Man, settlement and urbanism.* London.

VANCE, J.E. 1971: Land assignment in pre-capitalist, capitalist and post-capitalist cities. *Economic Geography*, 47, 101–20.

——1977: *This scene of man. The role and structure of the city in the geography of western civilization* (New York).

VAN WERVEKE, H. 1963: The rise of the towns. In POSTAN, M.M., RICH, E.E. and MILLER, E. (eds.) *The Cambridge Economic History of Europe. Vol. III. Economic organization and policies in the Middle Ages* (Cambridge), Chap. 1, 3.

VERCAUTEREN, F. 1934: *Etude sur les civitas de Belgique Seconde.* Académie Royale de Belgique Mémoires. Deuxième Series. vol. 33, 90–4.

VIDAL, G. 1953: *The judgement of Paris.* London.

VON GERKAN, A. 1924: *Griechische Städteanlagen.* Berlin and Leipzig.

de VRIES, J. 1981: Patterns of urbanization in pre-industrial Europe, 1500–1800. In SCHMAL, H. (ed.), *Patterns of European urbanization* (London).

WACHER, J.S. (ed.) 1966: *The civitas capitals of Roman Britain.* Leicester.

——1974: *The towns of Roman Britain.* London.

WADE, R.C. 1964: *Slavery in the cities. The South, 1820–1860.* New York.

——1965: *The urban frontier. Pioneer life in early Pittsburgh, Cincinnati, Lexington, Louisville and St Louis.* Chicago.

WALLERSTEIN, I. 1974: *The modern world-system.* New York.

WARD, D. 1964: A comparative historical geography of street car suburbs in Boston, Massachusetts and Leeds, England: 1850–1920. *Annals of the Association of American Geographers* 54, 477–89.

——1966: The industrial revolution and the emergence of Boston's Central Business District. *Economic Geography* 42, 152–71.

——1971: *Cities and immigrants. A geography of change in nineteenth century America.* New York.

——1975: Victorian cities: how modern? *Journal of Historical Geography* 1, 135–51.

——1980: Environs and neighbours in the 'Two Nations': residential differentiation in mid-nineteenth-century Leeds. *Journal of Historical Geography* 6(2), 133–62.

WARNER, S.B. Jr 1962: *Streetcar suburbs: the process of growth in Boston, 1870–1900*. Cambridge, Mass.

——1968: *The private city. Philadelphia in three periods of its growth*. Philadelphia.

——1972: *The urban wilderness. A history of the American city*. New York.

WEBER, A.F. 1899: *The growth of cities in the nineteenth century. A study in statistics*. New York.

WEBER, M. 1958: *The City*. Trans. and ed. by Martindale, D. and Neuwirth, G. New York.

WEBSTER, G. 1966: Fort and town in early Roman Britain. In WACHER, J.S. (ed.), 31.

WHEATLEY, P. 1963: 'What the greatness of a city is said to be'. Reflections on Sjoberg's 'Preindustrial city'. *Pacific Viewpoint* 4, 163–88.

——1971: *The pivot of the four quarters*. Edinburgh.

WHEELER, M. 1968: *The Indus civilization*, 3rd edn. Cambridge.

WHITE, D. 1971: Metroland. *New Society*, 1 July, 5.

WHITEHAND, J.W.R. 1966: Fringe belts: a neglected aspect of urban geography. *Transactions of the Institute of British Geographers* 41, 223–33.

——1972: Urban rent theory, time series and morphogenesis: an example of eclecticism in geographical research. *Area* 4, 215–22.

——1974: The changing nature of urban fringe: a time perspective. in JOHNSON, J.H. (ed.), 31–52.

——1978: Long-term changes in the form of the city centre: the case of redevelopment. *Geografiska Annaler*, Series B, 60, 79–96.

——(ed.) 1981: *The urban landscape: historical development and management. Papers by M.R.G. Conzen*, Institute of British Geographers. Special Publication No. 13 (London).

WHITEHILL, W.H. 1959: *Boston. A topographical history*. Cambridge, Mass.

WHITEHOUSE, R. 1977: *The first cities*. Oxford.

WILLEY, G.R. 1962: Mesoamerica. In BRAIDWOOD, R.J. and WILLEY, G.R. 101.

WILLIAMS, G.A. 1966; The Merthyr of Dic Penderyn. In WILLIAMS, G. (ed.), *Merthyr Politics: the making of a working class tradition* (Cardiff).

WIRTH, L. 1928: *The ghetto*. Chicago.

——1938: Urbanism as a way of life. *American Journal of Sociology* 44, 1–24.

——1964: Urbanism as a way of life. In *On Cities and Social Life*. Selected papers edited with an introduction by A.J. Reiss Jr (Chicago), chapter 4.

WITTFOGEL, K.A. 1957: *Oriental despotism. A comparative study of total power*. New Haven, Conn.

WOHL, A.S. 1977: *The eternal slum. Housing and social policy in Victorian London*. London.

WOLFE, A.B. 1932: Population censuses before 1790. *Journal of the American Statistical Associations* 27, 180.

WOOLLEY, L. 1942: *Ur of the Chaldees*. London.

——1963: The urbanization of society, In HAWKES, J. and WOOLLEY, L. (eds.) *History of Mankind*, vol. 1, Prehistory and the beginnings of civilization (UNESCO, Paris), Part 2, Chapter 3.

WRIGHT, R.B. (ed.) 1967: *California's Missions*. Los Angeles.

WRIGHT, T. 1872: *Viriconium: an account of the ancient Roman city of Wroxeter*.

WRIGLEY, E.A. 1966: *An introduction to English historical demography*. London.

——(ed.) (1972): *Nineteenth century society: essays in the use of quantitative methods for the study of social data*. Cambridge.

——1978: A simple model of London's importance in changing English society and economy, 1650–1760. In ADAMS, P.A. and WRIGLEY, E.A., Chap. 9.

WYCHERLEY, R.E. 1962: *How the Greeks built cities* 2nd edn. London.

ZIPF, G.W. 1941: *National unity and disunity*. Bloomington, Ill.

ZUNZ, O. 1980: Residential segregation in the American metropolis: concentration, dispersion and dominance. *Urban History Yearbook* (Leicester), 23–33.

Index

Figures in italics refer to captions to Figures or Tables. Dates in parentheses refer, as in text, to the source mentioned or quoted.